Aspen's Fundraising Series for the 21st Century

Capital Campaigns

Strategies That Work

Second Edition

Aspen's Fundraising Series for the 21st Century

Planned Giving Essentials: A Step-by-Step Guide to Success, Second Edition
Richard D. Barrett and Molly E. Ware, CFRE

Fundraising Basics: A Complete Guide, Second Edition
Barbara Kushner Ciconte, CFRE, and Jeanne G. Jacob, CFRE

Developing Major Gifts: Turning Small Donors into Big Contributors
Laura Fredricks, JD

Strategic Fund Development: Building Profitable Relationships That Last, Second Edition
Simone P. Joyaux, ACFRE

Capital Campaigns: Strategies That Work, Second Edition
Andrea Kihlstedt

Direct Marketing for Nonprofits: Essential Techniques for the New Era
Kay Partney Lautman, CFRE

Successful Special Events: Planning, Hosting, and Evaluating
Barbara R. Levy, ACFRE, and Barbara Marion, CFRE

Corporate and Foundation Fund Raising: A Complete Guide from the Inside
Eugene A. Scanlan, PhD, CFRE

Donor Focused Strategies for Annual Giving
Karla A. Williams, ACFRE

Aspen's Fundraising Series for the 21st Century

Capital Campaigns

Strategies That Work

Second Edition

Andrea Kihlstedt
Campaign Specialist
Lancaster, Pennsylvania
New York, New York

AN ASPEN PUBLICATION®
Aspen Publishers, Inc.
Gaithersburg, Maryland
2002

This publication is designed to provide accurate and authoritative information in regard to the Subject Matter covered. It is sold with the understanding that the publisher is not engaged in rendering legal, accounting, or other professional service. If legal advice or other expert assistance is required, the service of a competent professional person should be sought. (From a Declaration of Principles jointly adopted by a Committee of the American Bar Association and a Committee of Publishers and Associations.)

Library of Congress Cataloging-in-Publication Data

Kihlstedt, Andrea.
Capital campaigns: Strategies that work / Andrea Kihlstedt.
p. cm.—(Aspen's fund raising series for the 21st century)
Includes bibliographical references and index.
ISBN 0-8342-1902-6
1. Nonprofit organizations—Finance. 2. Fund raising. I. Title. II. Series.
HG4027.65.K55 2002
658.15'224—dc21
2002018536

Orders: (800) 638-8437
Customer Care: (800) 234-1660

About Aspen Publishers • For more than 40 years, Aspen has been a leading professional publisher in a variety of disciplines. Aspen's vast information resources are available in both print and electronic formats. We are committed to providing the highest quality information available in the most appropriate format for our customers. Visit Aspen's Internet site for more information resources, directories, articles, and a searchable version of Aspen's full catalog, including the most recent publications: **www.aspenpublishers.com**
Aspen Publishers, Inc. • The hallmark of quality in publishing
Members of the worldwide Wolters Kluwer groups

Editorial Services: Joan Sesma
Library of Congress Catalog Card Number: 2002018536
ISBN: 0-8342-1902-6
Printed in the United States of America
1 2 3 4 5

Table of Contents

Preface ix

Acknowledgments xi

Chapter 1—Capital Campaigns: More than Money 1
    What Is a Capital Campaign? 1
    The Transformative Power of Capital Campaign Fund Raising 1
    Building on a Culture of Philanthropy 2
    Organizational Cycles and the Campaign 4
    Types of Campaigns 4
    Special Characteristics of Capital Campaigns 6
    The Phases of a Capital Campaign 7
    Requirements for a Successful Campaign 9
    A Time for Heroes 12

Chapter 2—Get Ready, Get Set 13
    Planting in Fertile Soil 13
    Donor Readiness 13
    Organizational Readiness 15
    Development Office Readiness 17
    Preparing the Development Office 20

Chapter 3—Preparing for a Campaign 31
    The First Stage of Campaign Planning 31
    The Case for Support 32
    The Campaign Goal and the Gift Range Chart 40
    Developing the Gift Range Chart 40
    The Gift Range Chart and Prospect Planning 42
    The Feasibility Study 43
    Feasibility Study Consultants 49
    Enlisting a Feasibility Study Committee 52
    The Work of the Committee 52
    The Interview Process 54
    The Feasibility Study Report 55

Chapter 4—Building the Campaign Team 58
    Seeing the Big Picture 58
    Defining Key Campaign Positions 58
    Defining Staff Roles 60
    Volunteer Campaign Leadership 63
    Campaign Consultants 68
    Expanding the Campaign Team 81
    The Campaign and the Board of Directors 83
    Creating a Positive Atmosphere 85

Chapter 5—Planning the Campaign 86
    The Importance of Campaign Planning 86
    The Planning Process 86
    Refining the Case for Support 91
    Refining the Goal 92
    Developing Non-Monetary Goals 93
    The Gift Range Chart 93
    Donor Recognition 93
    Campaign Structure 96
    Projecting a Realistic Campaign Timetable 99
    Determining How Gifts Will Be Solicited 102
    Deciding What to Count and How Much It's Worth 103
    The Capital Campaign and Annual Giving 105
    Gift Accounting and Reporting 105
    Estimating Campaign Costs 106

Chapter 6—Who's Who? Prospect Research and Donor Cultivation 109
    Getting It Right 109
    Whither the Search? 109
    Where Not to Look . . . and Where to Look 111
    Building a Prospect List through the Research Process 111
    Setting Up a Prospect Information System 118
    Filling in the Details with Secondary Sources 123
    Knowing Right from Wrong 127
    Donor-Focused Development 127
    Patience and Practice 128

Chapter 7—The Nucleus Fund 129
    The Nucleus Fund 129
    Soliciting Lead Gifts 137
    Special Techniques for Soliciting Foundations and Corporations 149
    Using Gifts Strategically: Challenge Grants 151
    The Power of Lead-Gift Fund Raising 153

Chapter 8—The Public Campaign 154
    Going Public 154
    The Campaign Kickoff 154
    Media and the Campaign Message 157
    The Special-Events Committee 157
    Soliciting Major Gifts 160
    Soliciting the Broad Base 169
    Telephone Solicitation and the Capital Campaign 170
    Direct Mail and the Capital Campaign 176
    Welcome Relief after a Stressful Campaign 180

Chapter 9—Campaign Communications 181
    Campaign Communications 181
    Developing a Communications Plan 181
    Managing Campaign Announcements 183
    The Power of Materials in Positioning a Campaign 186
    Using Communications Professionals 186
    Campaign Theme and Logo 188
    Campaign Materials 190
    Miscellaneous Materials 198
    Spinning the Campaign 198

Chapter 10—Practicing the Discipline of Gratitude **199**
    The Discipline of Gratitude 199
    Saying Thank You 199
    Recognizing Donors and Volunteers Publicly 207
    Plaques 210
    Reaping the Rewards of Gratitude 213

Chapter 11—Beyond the Campaign **215**
    Finishing the Campaign 215
    Evaluation, Reporting, and Stewardship 218
    For the Record 221
    Institutionalizing the Power of the Campaign 222
    Looking Ahead 224
    Campaign Lessons 224

Appendix A—Troubleshooting Guide to Capital Campaigns **226**

Appendix B—Glossary of Common Campaign Terms **239**

Appendix C—Bibliography **242**

Index **245**

About the Author **253**

Preface

Since Cathe Schwartz and I wrote this book in 1996, I have received many calls and comments from people working on capital campaigns who have found it a valuable resource. Development directors, executive directors, and even campaign consultants have used this book to answer their campaign questions. Recently, I was on a train to New York and the woman sitting next to me saw my copy of the book and told me how helpful the book had been when she ran a successful campaign in Texas. Many people have thanked us for the extensive detail in the original version. Many others have expressed their pleasure at the underlying views of philanthropy that shape most of the content. And others have suggested topics to include in a second edition. Every call and comment has helped me realize the power and reach of a book like this. I am fortunate indeed to have the opportunity to provide a resource for the field that will help many people take their organizations to the next level.

In the years since Cathe and I completed the first edition, I have worked on numerous campaigns and have taught many classes on capital campaign fund raising. I've been faced with new questions, and I've come to understand aspects of campaigns I didn't understand when we wrote the first edition. This second edition has given me the opportunity to share the many new ideas about campaigns that I have had in the past few years. It has also given me the opportunity to clarify and reorganize much of the material, making it a better practical guide.

This second edition is a clearer, more complete manual than the first. I have reorganized the material in a way that more closely follows the progress of a campaign, thereby making it easier for practitioners in the field to work through the book chapter by chapter as their campaigns progress. I have also added new material in many sections, and updated and fine-tuned information in other sections.

This edition presents campaigns in a larger context, looking not only at capital campaigns but also endowment campaigns, combined campaigns, and comprehensive campaigns. It also takes a broader approach to campaign communications and provides a new model for conceptualizing a communications plan. The chapter on prospect research has been updated in keeping with the radical shift in this field from print resources to Web-based research that has taken place in the intervening years.

The new edition takes the issue of campaign readiness far more seriously than the earlier version and offers a series of questions designed to help every development director understand the many aspects of the fund development program that should be in order prior to a campaign. For this edition, I've added a glossary that defines the terms commonly used in campaign fund raising, and I've both added and deleted material to sharpen the focus of the book and to eliminate redundancies.

In revising this book, I've been reminded what a privilege it is to be in the capital campaign business. Through campaigns, we have opportunities to work with organizations and donors in ways that make a significant difference in the world around us. This mutual investment of resources by both donor and organization is a far cry from asking for alms. It is a partnership that calls on the best in all of us and reminds us of the pleasure that comes from working together for the greater good.

Acknowledgments

The spirit of generosity that shapes campaigns has also shaped the second edition of this book. When I sat down to the task, I made a list of all of the areas in campaign fund raising that I didn't know enough about, and I began calling people in the field for their assistance and advice. Everyone I spoke with shared information and ideas with me freely. They gave their time, their expertise, and their opinions. They were universally willing to use this as a vehicle to share what they had learned in the field with a wider audience.

First, my thanks to Jan Grieff of Jan Grieff Research Associates, Reading, Pennsylvania, and Chris Cannon at the St. Louis Zoo for their extensive work on the chapter about prospect research. Both professional prospect researchers, they gave me a new understanding of the field and its important role in lead-gift fund raising. They also provided a great deal of resource information.

My thanks again to John Synodinos, who has been my mentor in the fund-raising field since I first entered it in 1984. Without him, this book would not exist. For this edition, he was the person who pointed out the need for a section on challenge grants, and he helped me craft that section.

Cynthia Alperowicz, Director of Editorial Resources at WGBH in Boston, gave me an entirely new way to think about campaign communications by sharing the wonderful plan and materials they used for their very successful campaign. Thanks too to Paula Sidle of Carol O'Brian Associates for sending me to Cynthia.

Eric Serritella of Howell Liberatore & Associates, Inc. read the chapter on communications and clarified for me the distinct difference between a graphic designer and someone experienced in the broader field of marketing-communications. His insight has greatly improved that chapter.

Todd Lindsley of the Lindsley Consulting Group in Lancaster, Pennsylvania, a first-rate campaign consultant with an in-depth knowledge of development systems, generously shared with me the questions he uses in conducting internal development office assessments. Todd has also shared his experience with me during many time-consuming phone calls.

My day-to-day contact with client organizations teaches me more than anything, and to them I am in great debt. Thanks to Charlie Trautmann of the Sciencenter in Ithaca, New York, who has helped me come to respect the importance of sharing the work with campaign volunteers. Thanks to Jay Bucher and Becky Bumsted, whose work on a campaign for the Lancaster General Hospital taught me many new things about lead-gift cultivation and the power of a strong case. Thanks to Ann Berry for generously sharing information from the Lebanon Valley College Campaign and helping me begin to understand the power of a comprehensive campaign. Thanks to DeeDee Schwartz and Geoff Gratwick of the Maine Humanities Council, who have reminded me of the importance of having the courage to think big and of the power of process. The Reverend Louis Butcher Jr. of Brightside Baptist Church in Lancaster, Pennsylvania, has helped me understand that the world of major donors seems out of reach for many groups of people and that a capital campaign can be the means to bridge diverse cultures.

There wouldn't be a second edition of this book if it weren't for the long, hard labor of my associate Cabell Kladky. Cabell read and reread and read this manuscript again. She helped organize the new edition, providing comments and editing and proofreading draft after draft. The astonishing level of care and effort she has put into this manuscript exemplifies the attention to detail we should strive for in our campaigns. Her good humor, tart wit, and "old Quaker expressions" made this rewriting process bearable. She was aided in her work by the fluffy yellow cat, Hairy Potter, who liked nothing better than to lie on the pages of whatever chapter was in progress and turn his ample tummy up for a good scratch. I can only hope that the unquestioning affection of one feline friend and vast appreciation from me made it all worthwhile!

And finally, my husband, Tyko, has been sorely neglected during these months. My deep thanks to him for not complaining and for always being there. And now, it is time to cook a good meal!

Chapter 1
Capital Campaigns: More than Money

Chapter Outline

- What Is a Capital Campaign?
- The Transformative Power of Capital Campaign Fund Raising
- Building on a Culture of Philanthropy
- Organizational Cycles and the Campaign
- Types of Campaigns
- Special Characteristics of Capital Campaigns
- The Phases of a Capital Campaign
- Requirements for a Successful Campaign
- A Time for Heroes

WHAT IS A CAPITAL CAMPAIGN?

The most cost-effective, intense, and high-stakes form of fund raising, capital campaigns are taking their rightful place as a standard way of increasing revenue for many nonprofit organizations. A capital campaign is a particular method of building an organization's assets that raises a significant amount of money in a limited time for a special project designed to improve that organization's service to its community. Many people consider these campaigns to be the ultimate test of an organization's philanthropic potential.

Capital campaigns are major fund-raising episodes in the life of a nonprofit organization. While organizations rely on annual giving and special-event fund raising to nourish them as they evolve, organizations undertake capital campaigns when they are ready to take a major step forward—erecting a new building, renovating current facilities, adding equipment, or developing a major new program.

Compared to the staff time and expense of special events or direct-mail programs, the capital campaign is one of the most efficient, cost-effective ways to raise funds for a nonprofit organization. Although such a campaign demands extensive planning and preparation and requires the best skills and fullest commitment of everyone close to the organization, the returns on these investments far outstrip those from other types of fund raising. The following characteristics are typical of capital campaign fund raising:

- Capital campaigns have goals far in excess of annual giving goals.
- Capital campaigns enable an organization to accomplish specific project goals.
- Capital campaigns have clearly defined, often-tight timetables.
- Capital campaigns are occasional (or even unique) events in an organization's life.
- Capital campaigns are challenging—perhaps scary—but always exciting.
- Capital campaigns are volunteer intensive.
- Capital campaigns boost an organization to a higher level of effectiveness and significance in the life of the community.

> *Capital campaigns are among the most cost-effective ways to raise money.*

THE TRANSFORMATIVE POWER OF CAPITAL CAMPAIGN FUND RAISING

Capital campaigns provide opportunities to transform an organization. Because of their very scale and the high stakes they represent, campaigns serve as a catalyst for organizations to review their missions, to clarify long-term visions, and to reorganize for maximum results. (See article by Carol O'Brien, "Thinking beyond the dollar goal.") With a campaign on the horizon, organizations are often willing to invest in infrastructure and expertise that will help them increase the financial results of their campaign. They might invest in strengthening the development office, bringing in new staff members, or training current staff. They might invest in long-overdue communications and information systems.

Perhaps more important, organizations considering campaigns are often motivated to involve board members, key volunteers, major donors, and staff in shaping the future directions. This process, which often pushes an organization to evaluate and reexamine its mission, vision, and programs, is vital in clarifying and articulating institutional messages. For many organizations, the demands of day-to-day operations distract both staff and board from taking a longer view. Routine planning often evaluates what *is* rather than considering what *might be*. It often takes the prospect of large financial returns promised by a campaign to provide the necessary incentives to motivate serious and inclusive institutional planning. The prospects of a campaign stimulate more courageous thinking, and in doing so, an organization has the potential of actively involving people in shaping the future. While the dollars raised through a campaign are always significant, they often pale when compared with the positive transformation in attitudes, potential, and direction that result from the campaign process.

Capital campaigns are by nature volunteer intensive. They draw people closer to an organization, extending and strengthening the organizational family. A campaign provides many opportunities to involve volunteers in authentic and meaningful short-term tasks. Campaign volunteers help plan the campaign process, oversee the consultant's work, share information about prospective donors, cultivate prospects, and solicit gifts. At every step of a well-executed campaign, volunteers are actively involved and deeply engaged. Involved volunteers invest in their organization, and a well-managed campaign cultivates volunteers who will support the organization long after the campaign is over.

> *Involved volunteers are often a campaign's best donors. By creating opportunities for involvement throughout the campaign, the organization extends and strengthens its donor base.*

Capital campaigns focus on major-gift fund raising. Most smaller nonprofit organizations do little to organize a program of major-gift fund raising and rely instead on smaller gifts from a broad base of donors. In fact, many development staff members and executive directors have little confidence in their ability to solicit and raise major gifts. Capital campaigns force organizations to explore the *terra incognita* of major-gift fund raising.

Capital campaigns strengthen an organization's ongoing fund-raising program. Through the campaign process, both staff and board members gain experience and confidence in their ability to build strong relationships with donors and to solicit major gifts. These new skills and the confidence that comes with them help reshape the organization's ongoing development program.

Capital campaigns increase an organization's visibility and boost its stature in its community. Not only does a campaign provide many opportunities for media attention, but word of mouth among donors and volunteers also tends to build confidence in an organization and communicate its accomplishments.

A capital campaign is hard work—for staff, for board members, and for volunteers. Yet, when well-planned and conducted, it enables an organization to expand and strengthen its leadership, its volunteer base, its family of donors, and its visibility in the community, as well as its finances.

BUILDING ON A CULTURE OF PHILANTHROPY

The most successful campaigns are those that take place in organizations that have internalized an understanding of philanthropy into their culture. Rather than thinking of fund raising as a necessary evil, some organizations find a way to infuse their mission, vision, and values throughout every aspect of their operation, including resource development. In these organizations, every employee knows and believes the mission and understands the vision for the future.

In an organization with a culture of philanthropy, every donor is treated with respect and gratitude. The donors are recognized not because they ask to be recognized, but because the organization celebrates their generosity and wishes to hold it up as a model for all. In an organization with a true culture of philanthropy, fund raising is not akin to arm twisting but rather to an ongoing search for ways in which the organization and its donors can work together to make their world a better place.

In organizations that build a culture of philanthropy, one seldom hears language that demeans the fund-raising process. Donors aren't "hit up" for gifts. Rather, they are "invited to consider" making a gift. We don't go and "schmooze up someone"; we explore opportunities for mutually advantageous philanthropy.

Organizations that understand philanthropy treat every donor as an individual. They promptly acknowledge every gift in a personal way. In these organizations, a gift is considered just one step in a much longer relationship. As much time is invested in getting to know a donor's values, interests, and desires as in getting money. The development program is flexible, and solicitors are sensitive enough to respond to donors' needs and interests rather than just presenting the organization's needs. Once a gift is made to an organization that celebrates philanthropy, the development work is not over, it has simply moved to another level.

Testing for a Culture of Philanthropy

Below are simple ways to test the culture in your organization. The answers to these questions will give you a sense of how your organization feels about fund raising.

1. Does your organization feel welcoming to someone who walks in the door?
2. Does the receptionist know the mission of your organization? Can he or she summarize it in a way that makes you know that he or she believes in it?
3. Are the donor plaques your organization displays from prior fund-raising initiatives well displayed and well cared for? Or are they tarnished, hanging at odd angles, or tucked away in back corners?
4. How long does it take for a donor to receive a thank-you note after sending a contribution? Are the notes warm and personal or pro forma and impersonal?
5. How many times in the course of one day do you hear negative phrases about fund raising in your office?
6. How much non-meeting time do development staff members spend getting to know what's going on in the organization's programs?
7. How many donors do the development officers contact personally during an average week?
8. Does the board view development as an important part of their work?
9. Does your organization regularly invite major donors to come to see the results of their contributions?
10. Do the executive director and the board chair play an active and willing role in the development process?
11. Are key volunteers, staff, and donors meaningfully involved in strategic planning?
12. Is personal contact with donors seen as a way to build a mutually beneficial relationship or simply as a means of raising money?

Though it is possible to conduct a campaign in an organization that does not have a strong culture of philanthropy, the results are often far better when the culture supports the campaign. In preparing for a campaign, an organization will be well served to explore ways in which to establish practices that will reward generosity. Though the reality of reshaping an organizational culture requires strong leadership and broad participation, a shift in the practices of just one development officer can yield significant results.

Testing the Culture of Philanthropy

I decided to test the culture of philanthropy in my organization recently and asked my mother to call the main number and indicate that she was interested in making a contribution. I was shocked when she told me that she was put on hold and then passed to someone in the development office who took her name and address to send some basic information but didn't take the time to find out anything about her interests. It made me think about how I would like to be treated. I worked with the entire staff so that they came to understand the role of a donor and explored what having a culture of philanthropy would mean for our organization. I hope that the next time someone calls to inquire about making a gift he or she feels that ours is an organization that is truly interested in our donors.

—Executive Director

In a world marked by ever-increasing competition for both funds and effective volunteers, the organization that demonstrates real appreciation for all gifts will stand head and shoulders above the crowd. Those organizations that have embraced the concept of donor-centered philan-

I've Created a Culture of Philanthropy

I work for a health care alliance. Though it is not-for-profit, make no bones about it...it is also big business. I am the only development officer, the board functions like a corporate board, and organizationally we are about as far as you can get from having a "Culture of Philanthropy." Knowing we were going to have a campaign to raise money for a new hospital for women and babies, I set about doing what I could to create that culture. I spent as much time as possible every day getting to know the hospital's donors. I had breakfast, lunch, and dinner with people who had a reason to be interested in the hospital. I asked questions and I listened. I thanked donors personally and genuinely for their past gifts to the hospital. And I began exploring our donors' interests in the new hospital we were planning. In my own little corner of this big business, I created an office that really did love and appreciate donors. Now, 18 months and $7.5 million later, I know my efforts were worthwhile!

—VP for Development

thropy will be able to use a campaign not only to move their institution ahead but also to take their relationships with their donors to a new level of understanding and commitment. For donors, capital campaigns provide an opportunity to make a real difference both in the organization they support and in the world around them. And for the great majority of donors, this is the return on their investment they seek.

ORGANIZATIONAL CYCLES AND THE CAMPAIGN

Over the past two decades, capital campaigns have become a standard part of the fund-raising landscape. Organizations have begun to think about capital campaigns in the context of a long-range seven- to ten-year development cycle. Because capital campaigns provide an opportunity to raise the sights of both the organization and its wealthiest donors, these periodic events play an important role in helping an organization grow.

During each seven- to ten-year organizational cycle, an organization will undergo an intensive and far-reaching strategic planning process to chart out new visions and directions, plan and implement a capital campaign to move the organization ahead, and then stabilize at the new level of operation (Figure 1–1). The campaign process itself does so much to solidify relationships with donors and to identify and cultivate new donors that the campaign actually expands the annual giving program, thus lifting the organization's ability to raise funds for operations.

TYPES OF CAMPAIGNS

The phrase "capital campaign" is in some ways a misnomer. The phrase is used to refer to any major fund-raising initiative that will propel an organization ahead, enabling it to accomplish more for its constitu-

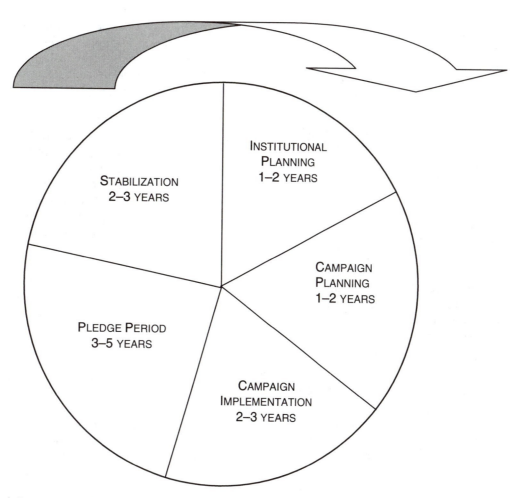

Figure 1–1 Institutional Campaign Cycle

ents. In fact, this phrase is an umbrella term that may refer to one or several different types of campaigns. See Exhibit 1-1 for a summary of campaign types.

Bricks and Mortar Campaigns: These campaigns are the simplest and truest use of the phrase "capital campaign." They are fund-raising programs that fund capital improvements. Their objectives are usually simple and straightforward, responding to an organization's capital needs.

Special Project Campaigns: Some organizations use the capital campaign model to raise funds for smaller, well-defined projects. A hospital might raise money this way for a special piece of equipment; a day-care center might raise funds for a new bus; a theater company might raise money for a new stage lighting system or renovations to the green room. These small projects lend themselves well to the strategies of capital campaign fund raising without imposing the organizational demands of a larger campaign.

Endowment Campaigns: Some organiz. campaigns to establish or develop endo These campaigns raise money that will be the institution rather than being spent on m ate projects. Strict endowment campaigns are challenging because they ask donors to turn on-trol of capital without any concrete, short-term result. Because the funds raised through endowment campaigns are not needed for short-term expenditures, they provide an opportunity for donors to make deferred gifts to the campaign through planned-giving instruments.

Combined Campaigns: More common are campaigns that combine bricks and mortar with endowment. An organization may conduct a campaign to build a new facility *and* to create an endowment fund, the income from which will pay for the long-term maintenance of the new building. Combined campaigns provide opportunities for both immediate and deferred gifts.

Comprehensive Campaigns: Many colleges and universities use their campaigns to raise money for bricks and mortar, endowment, *and* program. Campaigns of this

Exhibit 1-1 Types of Campaigns

Type	Purpose	Pros/Cons	Types of Gifts
Bricks and Mortar	Building projects	Clear Easy to articulate Immediate results Compelling results	Cash Appreciated securities Gifts-in-kind
Special Projects	Equipment Small construction projects One-time start-up funds	Clear Easy to articulate Immediate results	Cash Appreciated securities Gifts-in-kind
Endowment	Donor-restricted endowment Board-restricted endowment	Long-term results Small return on investment	Cash Securities Deferred gifts
Combined	Building Equipment Endowment	More complex Short- and long-term results	Cash Securities Gifts-in-kind Deferred gifts
Comprehensive	Building Equipment Endowment Program	Complex Harder to articulate Short- and long-term results Larger goals PR opportunities Economies of scale	Cash Securities Gifts-in-kind Deferred gifts Annual fund income

t often include all of the funds raised by the institution during the period of the campaign. Comprehensive campaigns include all money raised through the annual giving program projected through the campaign years. They often include program grants and, in some cases, even public funds as well as money raised for bricks and mortar and endowment. Comprehensive campaigns often have very large goals that reflect the total amount that will be raised by the organization over a period of five or even ten years. These large campaigns provide opportunities to increase the stature of an institution by making public its overall scope and reach.

SPECIAL CHARACTERISTICS OF CAPITAL CAMPAIGNS

Every type of capital campaign relies on practices used in all effective fund raising, but this type of fund raising is also different in many ways.

Campaign Goals Are Bigger

Those development directors who have been running annual fund programs and haven't yet done any major-gift fund raising will have to adjust the way they think about money. Whether a capital campaign's goal is $500,000 or $5 million, in general a campaign goal will be much larger than the goals set for any other fund-raising initiative. Campaign goals often shock both staff and board members who have little experience in major-gift fund raising.

The leap from modest annual fund-raising goals to large capital campaign goals often seems outrageous for an organization that is conducting its first capital campaign and that has little history of major-gift fund raising. However, for these organizations, donors' giving histories are often not accurate predictors of their giving capacities. If donors have never been invited to give major gifts to help fund large projects, there is no reason that they should ever have given at higher levels.

Campaigns Move an Organization to a Higher Level

Unlike annual giving, most capital campaigns do not fund operations. Campaigns for smaller organizations often raise funds for special, turning-point projects that take the organization to a new level of operation. A hospice might build a new administrative facility with an inpatient unit; a day-care center might build a new wing for an infant-care program; a private school might build a new gymnasium; a college might build three buildings and initiate a new academic center. Each of these projects represents a new, unique leap in the size and function of the organization. And while leaps can be frightening, they are also exciting opportunities that generate larger gifts.

> *Capital campaigns are strategic moments in the evolution of long-term fund-raising programs. The philosophy and values that support a capital campaign should be consistent with the goals and values of the organization.*

Campaigns Are Rare Occurrences

Campaigns have become regular occurrences for many large organizations such as hospitals or universities, with the next campaign in the planning stages even before the current one has been completed. It is uncommon, however, for organizations to conduct capital campaigns more than once in any 10-year period. And because many organizations have a high turnover of staff and board, it is unusual for development directors, executive directors, and board members to have extensive experience in this type of fund raising.

Capital campaigns are very special events indeed! The unique excitement that permeates organizations as they begin to contemplate a capital campaign helps motivate both staff and volunteer leadership to take the necessary preparatory steps. Once the plunge has been taken, it's hard to turn back, and the staff and volunteers are drawn almost inexorably into the vortex of the campaign, committing an extraordinary amount of time and energy to make it successful. Throughout the period of intense effort, the knowledge that when they declare victory there will not be another campaign right around the corner enables them to find the motivation and energy to continue to the end.

Campaigns Usually Result from Long-Range or Strategic Planning

Because most capital campaigns are organized to fund major new initiatives, they often emerge out of an extensive organizational planning process. In this process, the organization has paused to review its mission, evaluate its strengths and weaknesses, assess its current resources, and determine where it hopes to go during the next few years. If an organization is "working smart," it will bend over backward to involve key volunteers and those with the ability to give major gifts in the planning process, providing opportunities for these individuals to have a voice in determining the organization's future. Capital campaigns build on the sense of excitement and enthusiasm for the new directions that have been developed through the planning process.

Most Campaign Funds Are Raised Prior to the Announcement of the Campaign

Unlike the annual fund and special-event fund raising, the bulk of the money raised through a capital campaign is raised quietly, with little or no public announcement of the campaign. As with major business negotiations, the solicitation of major donors is conducted quietly, giving the donors ample opportunity to explore gifts that best suit their interests. Only when the majority of the funds have been raised and the specifics of the campaign and the project have been settled does the campaign become public knowledge.

THE PHASES OF A CAPITAL CAMPAIGN

Most community-based campaigns can be conducted in approximately 18 months from assembling the campaign-planning committee to celebrating the campaign's success. This estimate does not include the many months of planning and preparation, nor does it include the feasibility-study period. In fact, as discussed in chapter 3, one of the valuable elements of a feasibility study is a preliminary campaign timetable that will help establish calendar guidelines.

It is useful to think of the campaign's length in terms of its different parts. Most successful campaigns proceed in six distinct phases (see Exhibit 1–2):

1. preparation
2. planning
3. lead-gift phase
4. advance-gift phase
5. general phase
6. cleanup and celebration

Pre-Campaign Preparation

Before soliciting any gifts, an organization must spend ample time preparing for the campaign—building a strong and involved board, strengthening the development program, increasing the agency's visibility and reputation, conducting the strategic-planning process, and planning the project. The staff and board may spend one, two, or even three years preparing an organization for the work ahead.

Campaign Planning

Once the preparations have been completed, the campaign planning begins. During this period, many organizations engage a consultant to conduct a feasibility study and assemble the campaign-planning committee. With the guidance and support of an experienced consultant and the campaign-planning committee, the staff will prepare the case for support, outline a preliminary campaign timetable, establish campaign policies, determine a preliminary dollar goal, identify campaign leadership, prepare a table of gifts showing the size and number of gifts needed to succeed, and design the campaign structure. Campaign planning is likely to take three to six months, depending on the length of time it takes to recruit campaign leadership and the campaign-planning committee. This phase should result in a written document outlining the plan for the campaign. This document, though subject to revision as needed, will guide the staff and volunteers through the campaign.

Lead-Gift Solicitation

Once the campaign has been planned, the solicitation process begins. The first to be solicited are donors who have the potential to make the largest campaign gifts. These solicitations are usually planned individually to suit the situation, character, and timetable of each donor. Although there may be only 30 or 40 solicitations in this process, a campaign's fate rests on their success. Flexibility, patience, and persistence are the key words for this phase of a campaign. Every solicitation must bend to accommodate the timetables and realities of the lead donors. To ensure the needed flexibility, these solicitations are made prior to the public announcement of the campaign.

Exhibit 1–2 Phases of a Capital Campaign

Preparation	Planning	Lead-Gift Phase	Advance-Gift Phase	General Phase	Cleanup, Celebration
• Clarify mission and vision • Define need for campaign • Strengthen board • Cultivate donors and volunteers • Strengthen staff • Select consultant • Develop prospect lists	• Establish "kitchen cabinet" • Conduct feasibility study • Assemble campaign steering committee • Develop case for support • Outline campaign timetable • Establish campaign policies • Determine campaign goal • Identify campaign leadership • Review table of gifts • Write proposal copy • Establish campaign subcommittees • Identify and enlist volunteers for soliciting lead gifts	• Review prospect list for lead gifts • Evaluate prospects • Develop solicitation strategy for each gift • Prepare proposals • Train volunteers • Solicit gifts • Identify and enlist volunteers for soliciting family gifts	• Review prospect list for "family" gifts • Evaluate prospects • Develop solicitation strategy for each category of prospects • Train volunteers • Prepare proposals • Solicit gifts • Identify and enlist volunteers for general phase	• Review prospect list for general phase • Prepare proposals • Train volunteers • Campaign kickoff • Solicit gifts • Phonathon • Direct-mail campaign	• Solicitation follow-up • Reporting to campaign volunteers • Volunteers acknowledgment • Extra thanks to donors • Reinforce relationship with volunteers and donors

Optional Celebrations

Campaign kickoff
Goal-reaching party
Groundbreaking
Open house

Subcommittees

Building
Public Relations
Finance
Prospect Cultivation
Hospitality/Events

Advance-Gift Solicitation

The advance-gift phase of a campaign encompasses the period during which both lead gifts and "family gifts" are solicited. During this quiet period, those people with the greatest giving potential and those closest to the or-

ganization are solicited. These will include board members, campaign leaders, campaign committee members, and active volunteers.

Together, the advance solicitations must raise 50 to 60 percent of the campaign goal so that when the campaign is announced publicly, the commitment of lead donors, the board, and the other people who are close to the organization will provide a strong example of generosity and commitment to the rest of the community.

Although in the best of all worlds, the advance-gift phase may be completed in three to six months, the length of these critical early solicitation periods is actually determined by the dollar amount raised rather than by a calendar date. For example, an organization might solicit lead gifts for a campaign in June, hoping to be ready for a September kickoff, but then in August it may realize that several major gifts will not be confirmed until late October. Without these gifts, the campaign will have raised less than one quarter of its goal. A wise campaign director will postpone the kickoff until the campaign has raised more than half the goal.

General Solicitation

Once one-half to two-thirds of the goal has been raised, the campaign is ready to enter the general solicitation phase. In many community-based campaigns, the public part of the solicitation process might be as short as six weeks or as lengthy as twelve months. The length of this phase depends on the campaign's design, and the design will depend on the staff and volunteer resources. Organizations with staff members who work full time on the campaign and with a sufficient number of volunteers willing to solicit donors will be able to organize and manage a broad solicitation process in a short time period. Those who must rely on part-time campaign development staff and a limited number of deeply committed campaign volunteers must extend the solicitation period, spreading the solicitation of various constituencies over a period of months.

When the personal solicitation has been completed, most campaigns finish the solicitation process with a combination of telephone and direct-mail solicitations. These generally occur in the final months of the general solicitation phase.

Follow-Up

Most campaign veterans know that campaigns begin with a big bang and end with a dribble. They start in a flurry of well-organized energy and end in a mass of details that often takes several months of dedicated staff time to clean up. Often, long after the campaign has reached its goal, gifts still come in—sometimes in surprisingly large numbers.

A celebration during the cleanup period will bring the campaign to a public close. Long after the celebration, however, the staff is likely still to be tying up loose ends, thanking people, and making sure that the pledge payment system is functioning well. Indeed, since every pledge reminder is an excellent opportunity to communicate with donors, the campaign cleanup tasks will dovetail nicely with the ongoing development program.

Although campaign tasks fall into a very particular order that is critical to the campaign's success, there is great latitude as to the duration of each campaign phase. This permits a campaign design that fits the unique reality of a particular organization and its community of donors.

REQUIREMENTS FOR A SUCCESSFUL CAMPAIGN

Although capital campaigns vary in size, scope, and timing, there are some elements that characterize every successful campaign. Some of these elements should be in place prior to the start of the campaign, and some emerge through the campaign process. Fifteen elements are critical to the success of a capital campaign:

1. compelling needs and a credible plan
2. a strong case for support
3. a realistic goal
4. previous fund-raising success
5. a sufficient number of qualified prospects
6. strong staff support and resources
7. full and early commitment by the board
8. effective volunteer leadership
9. clear campaign organization
10. clear campaign policies
11. a realistic timetable
12. identification and early solicitation of major gift prospects
13. written proposals requesting specific gifts
14. personal solicitations by trained volunteers
15. a "top-down, inside-out" order of solicitation

Compelling Needs and a Credible Plan

Every successful campaign is driven by a compelling need in society or the community and an organization's plan to meet those needs. Those needs are identified through an organizational planning process that gives the leadership focus and direction. The needs must reflect those of the community, not those of the organization, although the project may also serve organizational needs. To convince donors to help meet those needs, this plan must be realistic for both the organization and the community.

> *The needs must reflect those of the community, not those of the organization, although the project may also serve organizational needs.*

A plan at its most basic level requires solid, realistic answers to the following questions:

- What is the community need that the organization is seeking to fill through this project?
- Why has the organization elected to undertake this project?
- How does the organization plan to carry out the project?
- Who is going to make it happen?
- When will it happen?

The answers to these questions will form the nucleus of the case for support.

A Strong Case for Support

The organization must be able to write a case for support that describes the compelling needs and the plan for the project in a way that is concise, clear, and easy to read. An effective case for support focuses on the needs of the community rather than on the needs of the organization. See chapter 3 for an in-depth discussion of the case for support.

A Realistic Goal

Successful campaigns have goals that make sense—both for the organization and for the community. There are dreamers in every organization who build castles in the air as they plan how to spend the vast sums of money that donors will give, but these hyper-optimists forget that both organizations and communities have tolerances and patterns of giving that shape reasonable goals. A pie-in-the-sky goal may sound impressive, but it will hurt the organization's credibility in the end if the goal is not reached. If an organization sets a goal that is too low, however, it artificially limits the amount of money that might be raised through a campaign. The right goal stretches an organization beyond what is easily accomplished, yet is achievable!

Previous Fund-Raising Success

Although in special circumstances it is possible for a new organization to run a successful startup campaign, most campaigns rely on prior donor relationships as the springboard for giving. Campaigns depend on well-developed annual giving programs to help identify campaign prospects and volunteers.

A Sufficient Number of Qualified Prospects

Because contributions to campaigns fit into predictable patterns, it is possible to estimate how many gifts it will take to reach a certain goal. Applying the generally accepted estimate that the campaign will get one gift for every four donor prospects, it is possible to estimate the number of prospects needed for a successful campaign. Not everyone who lives in the community is a qualified prospect. Qualified prospects are those who are already donors to the organization, have a reason to give to the organization (perhaps they have benefited from its services), or are part of the community leadership base that is known for giving to campaigns of similar organizations. For a campaign to be successful, an organization will need to identify enough such people so that it can see the potential of raising its funds from that constituency.

A generally accepted campaign rule states that the top 10 prospects will produce 80 to 90 percent of the gifts, with the remainder coming from a considerably larger group of donors of relatively small gifts. This rule illustrates the supreme importance of the top donors to the success of the campaign.

Strong Staff Support and Resources

Successful campaigns depend on strong staff leadership to organize and manage every aspect of the campaign. This role might be played by the executive director, the development director, or someone brought in specifically for the campaign, but it is a role that must be filled if a campaign is to flourish. A campaign director will need an adequate budget for promotional material, cultivation activities, and campaign events. Organizations new to the campaign scene must take to heart the advice "Spend money to make money."

Full and Early Commitment by the Board

A committed board is critical to a campaign's success. Although many small organizations do not have fund-raising boards, even these "working" boards must fully support the campaign financially to the extent of their abilities. For some boards, collective giving of $20,000 might be far more impressive than a $1 million commitment from another board. Beyond the dollar value, there is a symbolic value in board gifts as well. Other donors look to see whether the board wholeheartedly supports the campaign.

Effective Volunteer Leadership

Campaigns are made or broken by the quality of their volunteer leadership. The configuration of this leadership comes in many forms. Some campaigns have one chair and several division heads. Others have honorary co-chairs and managing co-chairs as well as a campaign steering committee. Whatever the design, at least some of the volunteers in leadership positions must have stature in the community, the ability to make a lead gift, and a willingness to follow through on their jobs.

Clear Campaign Organization

Because capital campaigns rely on a great many volunteers to solicit the most important gifts, clear and effective organization is of primary importance. Volunteers have only limited tolerance for ineptitude. They operate at their best when they know what they are supposed to do, how to do it, how their work fits into the larger project, when their work will begin, and when it will end. Good campaign planners take great pains to provide such organization and structure for their volunteers.

Clear Campaign Policies

Before venturing very far into planning a capital campaign, a great many policy questions for guiding key areas of the campaign must be answered. Questions such as what will count toward the campaign goal, what kinds of gifts will be accepted, how gifts that are not immediate cash or pledges will be valued, what sorts of naming opportunities will be available to donors, and a whole host of others must be answered before an organization begins soliciting gifts.

A Realistic Timetable

There are few things more calming than knowing that a big job has a beginning, a middle, and finally an end. Both staff and volunteers function more effectively if they know how long their efforts will be needed on the campaign. Realistic campaign timetables provide impetus for getting the job done. They help in planning for what's ahead, and they reassure staff and volunteers that the campaign will proceed according to schedule. It is a great comfort for all participants in the campaign to be able to envision a time for a jubilant celebration of the campaign's successful completion.

Identification and Early Solicitation of Major Gift Prospects

The success of most campaigns is determined by the top 10 gifts. And successful campaigns keep their focus on those gifts from the beginning. These top 10 donors are extremely important not only because of the gifts they can make but also because they are usually the people who have the clout, commitment, and ability to solicit the next 50 gifts. By identifying the top 10 donors early and involving them in the key decisions

that will shape the project and the campaign, one builds ownership in the campaign and sets the stage for success.

Written Proposals Requesting Specific Gifts

Campaigns rely on well-written proposals that invite people to consider making gifts of specific amounts. Because in capital campaigns people are always being invited to make gifts that are significantly larger than their usual donations, it is helpful to the donor when the solicitor suggests a specific amount or range. This must be accomplished in a non-pressuring way, but it must be done if the campaign is to succeed. Written proposals are the mechanisms by which organizations present a formal request for a gift. Lead-gift proposals are always followed up by one or more personal visits by trained volunteer solicitors.

Personal Solicitations by Trained Volunteers

Personal solicitations are the most effective way to raise money. In the best of all campaign worlds, every donor would be visited by precisely the right person asking for precisely the right amount of support for something the donor is vitally interested in. In the real world most of us live in, this can happen only some of the time. Often our knowledge of the donor is incomplete, or the right person is unavailable or cannot be identified. Nonetheless, in campaign times, an organization must do its very best to see every donor as an important individual and to ensure that committed volunteers take the time and energy to visit donors personally to ask for their gifts.

> *The power of personal relationships is an important concept in all areas of fund raising— it's just more important in the context of a capital campaign.*

A "Top-Down, Inside-Out" Order of Solicitation

Proceeding with the solicitation from the inside out and the top down—beginning with those closest to the organization and those who have the ability to make the largest gifts—allows the organization to engage the most important people in the early stages of the campaign. These insiders and leaders are the people who can move the campaign forward. Their early commitment and involvement is critical to the campaign's success. If they are unwilling to become involved, the unspoken message they send speaks louder than anything else.

A TIME FOR HEROES

Capital campaigns are exercises in courage, faith, planning, and hard work. They provide opportunities to unite the energies and talents of a large group of people around the possibility of moving an organization forward so that it can accomplish more for the community. When they are well designed and executed, capital campaigns create heroes. The many individuals who have helped create that success—staff members, board members, donors, volunteers—share a part in the campaign's success. These people are amply rewarded by the knowledge that they have helped a worthy organization reach a new level of service.

In an era when people spend an ever greater percentage of their time in passive activities, and when many neighborhoods are no longer unifying forces in our society, capital campaigns help us rekindle the excitement and rewards that come from individual responsibility, effective collaboration, service to others, and shared goals.

Throughout this book are strewn what may be an intimidating collection of rules, guidelines, and requirements. Underlying all of this information, however, is the author's strong belief that a relatively few people, if committed, astute, and hardworking, can make a major difference in the organizations that they serve and thereby create stronger communities.

Perceiving the world from a wonderfully broad perspective, the noted anthropologist Margaret Mead described this phenomenon in a way that the author believes might serve as guidance and inspiration for anyone who is beginning the process of planning a capital campaign.

> Never doubt that a small group of thoughtful, committed citizens can change the world. Indeed, it's the only thing that ever has. (Mead, 1992)

REFERENCES

Mead, Margaret. 1992. *The last word: A treasury of women's quotes.* Edited by Carolyn Warner. Englewood Cliffs, NJ: Prentice Hall.

O'Brien, Carol. 1998. Thinking beyond the dollar goal. *Capital Campaigns: Realizing Their Power and Potential. New Directions for Philanthropic Fundraising #21*, Andrea Kihlstedt and Robert Pierpont, editors. San Francisco: Jossey-Bass.

Chapter 2
Get Ready, Get Set . . .

Chapter Outline

- Planting in Fertile Soil
- Donor Readiness
- Organizational Readiness
- Development Office Readiness
- Preparing the Development Office

PLANTING IN FERTILE SOIL

Because capital campaigns are only occasional occurrences in the life of an organization, we sometimes lose sight of the fact that their success grew organically out of the culture and patterns of the organization and its community. A close look at the characteristics that lead to campaign success can help an organization target areas that need work in plenty of time to strengthen them before the campaign. These characteristics fall into three areas:

1. the readiness of an organization's donors to make large gifts
2. the readiness of the organization to grow
3. the readiness of the development office to conduct a campaign

An organization that is ready in all three areas is best positioned to undertake a capital campaign. However, in some cases, organizations that are not fully ready elect to use the campaign process itself to boost their operations to the next level. The high stakes and visibility force both staff and volunteers to make up lost ground, building relationships with donors, expanding the development operations, and strengthening the organization. There is no harm in this practice providing the organization has a realistic appraisal of its readiness and tempers its goals accordingly.

DONOR READINESS

Capital campaigns rely on a very few major gifts from individuals, foundations, or corporations that are ready to support the objectives of the campaign. In many if not most campaigns, a mere 10 to 15 gifts constitute approximately one-half of the campaign goal. Before moving into the topic of organizational readiness, therefore, it will be worth exploring the complexities of donor readiness.

Much has been written about donors and their motivations to give. People being what they are, it is not surprising that their reasons for giving are as varied as the backgrounds, value systems, and styles of the people themselves. There are, however, some aspects of the complex human drama that seem to assert themselves again and again. These aspects might well guide our understanding of donor readiness.

To become grounded in the subject of human motivation, it may be helpful to spend a few minutes writing down the reasons why one does anything. It is an enlightening exercise to write down a number of sentences beginning with the phrase "I do the things I do because . . ."

Different people may find different words to express the same concepts, or rank them differently in importance, but the author has found in asking friends and colleagues to perform this simple exercise that the reasons people give for doing what they do share common roots.

Some of the most common responses heard are as follows:

I do the things I do because...

- ... they make me happy.
- ... they make other people happy.
- ... I want what will result from doing them.
- ... I will suffer if I don't do them.

- ... someone asks me to do them.
- ... I want to impress other people.
- ... I will feel guilty if I don't do them.
- ... doing them will make me feel better.
- ... I want to make my community a better place.
- ... I want to fit in.
- ... they are the right things to do.
- ... I am compelled to do them.
- ... no one else is doing them.

This simple but provocative exercise provides useful clues as to what motivates people. These motivations appear generally to fall into three categories:

1. Pleasure. We do the things we do because we enjoy doing them.
2. Consequences. We do the things we do because of what will result from our actions.
3. Duty. We do the things we do because we feel that we ought to do them.

Of course, many things that people do are motivated by a complex of causes, and one dominant reason for doing things often masks other reasons. It appears, however, that people do most of what they do for some combination of the three reasons listed above. Capital campaigns are organized to build on all three of these primary motivating factors.

Campaigns often give people pleasure. People enjoy giving. They feel good about what their money will accomplish and about having done their duty.

Campaigns accomplish specific goals or results that will move an organization to a new level. Through a campaign, donors help an organization reach its goals for the benefit of the community. Often campaigns are able to help donors achieve personal goals such as a display or acquisition of influence or status.

Campaigns enable the people who feel a duty to the organization to give something back to the organization and the community. Campaigns often depend on this sense of duty to keep volunteers and donors engaged even during the inevitable frustrating campaign periods.

Why Does a Donor Give to a Specific Cause?

With the proliferation of nonprofit groups and the growing number of fund-raising appeals, every donor must choose among many organizations. Although some support a broad range of groups, even these donors must be selective. Here is how people weed the field.

First, people give to organizations whose mission appeals to them. While a savvy donor takes into account the organization's leadership, financial health, mission, and impact on the community it serves, that which tips the giving scale for many donors is their own interest in the organization's work. Their interest may stem from their background, hobbies, family circumstances, or moral and religious values. Even the wealthiest donors are not likely to be motivated to make a gift unless they are interested in the organization or at least sympathetic to its work.

Second, people give to organizations with which they have been involved. Volunteering for an organization gives donors a firsthand glimpse of how the organization is run. They learn about its strengths, its weaknesses, and its needs. Donors often have only a passing interest in an organization when they first become involved. Perhaps they are drawn in by a friend. But as they become more involved, their level of commitment grows.

Third, people give because they feel a kinship with others in an organization. When an individual has developed a relationship with individuals in an organization, that organization's standing tends to rise in his or her list of charities. Personal relationships help donors feel that they are "part of the family." Personal contact fosters a sense of trust between the prospect and the organization and enables staff and volunteers to get a clearer idea of the prospect's interests and personal history.

Fourth, people give because they have been touched by an organization's work. Many gifts are made by donors because the organization's work has moved them deeply. Organizations exist to meet community needs, and by doing so they affect the lives of many people.

Organizations that do good work benefit from a ripple effect in their communities. It is not uncommon for someone to become involved in an organization or make a contribution because he or she knows someone else whose life was touched by that organization's work.

Fifth, people give to support a project that they care about. People give to organizations through which they can make a difference in the world. Donors want to know that through their gifts an organization is going to address issues, solve problems, grasp opportunities, or create works of art that they could not create themselves. Such organizations provide the means through which many donors are able to make their dreams a reality.

Sixth, people give because they are asked to give. Many people are aware of causes to which they would like to give, but unless they are asked to give they are unlikely to do so. Whether from inertia, embarrassment, or the lack of knowledge and time, people must often be invited to participate in something, either financially or as a volunteer, before they become sufficiently motivated to do so.

Finally, people will give because they are asked to give by someone they know. It is harder to turn down someone you know and respect. The very fact that that person is willing to ask for money adds credibility and weight to the request and increases the psychological value of the gift.

Donor Readiness Evaluation

The following is a simple test to evaluate the readiness of an organization's donors. Begin by making a list of the organization's best 25 lead gift prospects. Use the checklist in Exhibit 2–1 to evaluate the readiness of each donor, placing check marks next to each area that is true for that donor. Count and record the number of check marks for each prospective donor. Prospects that have fewer than three check marks are unlikely to be ready to be solicited for a major campaign gift.

ORGANIZATIONAL READINESS

The Basics

Before launching into a capital campaign, several key organizational elements must be in place (Exhibit 2–2). At the most basic, any organization contemplating a campaign must have confirmation of its 501(C)(3) not-for-profit status. For any organization that has been raising money this will be obvious, but a start-up organization must not neglect this important step.

A campaign-ready organization should have an engaged and committed board. Though not all boards are "fund-raising" boards capable of giving a large percentage of the campaign goal, even a "working" board must be fully committed to the organization's direction and campaign plans. An organization that is having trouble filling board positions or with a board that does not show up for meetings might take a step back and evaluate their readiness. Volunteer leadership is critical to a successful campaign, and the board, wealthy or not, will set the standard by their example.

Exhibit 2–1 Donor Readiness Evaluation Checklist

1. Has active interest in the organization's mission	_____
2. Has history of involvement with organization	_____
3. Feels a kinship with others in organization	_____
4. Is or was served by organization	_____
5. Is knowledgeable about the proposed project	_____

Exhibit 2–2 Test for Organizational Readiness

____ Does your organization have its not-for-profit status?
____ Is your organization registered with the state bureau of charitable organizations (if required)?
____ Do you have a full, committed, and effective board?
____ Is your board involved in setting policy and working to implement it?
____ Do all of your board members make financial contributions to your organization?
____ Is your organization well respected in your community?
____ Is your organization widely recognized in the community?
____ Has your organization developed an effective strategic plan?
____ Has the strategic plan been accepted by the board?
____ Have the campaign projects grown from the plan?
____ Do you have a reasonable estimate of the project's budget and timetable?
____ Do you have a business plan that shows an operating budget for the new project?
____ If successful, will the campaign enable the organization to make a significant difference in your community?
____ Is the organization's leadership excited about the project?

A campaign-ready organization has a capable and committed director who has the credibility, zeal, and energy to take the organization from one level of operation to the next. Though it is not uncommon for an executive director to retire shortly after a completing a campaign, the director must have the energy left to provide effective staff leadership throughout the process. An organization with a new director will be well served to give that director enough time to build solid relationships with the staff, the board, and the community before moving ahead with a campaign. In fact, the executive director should have participated fully in the planning process that led to the campaign. If the executive director has been hired after the planning process is complete, he or she should take the time to test and fine-tune the plan while building relationships in the organization and the community.

The Organization and the Community

A capital campaign builds a bridge between the organization and the community it serves. All fund raising requires an organization to be accountable to its larger community. And, because many large gifts will be required for a successful campaign, the issues of accountability and reputation are even more important than in the everyday life of an organization.

An organization that has done an excellent job of building relationships in the community will be well rewarded in a campaign. An organization's reputation for doing good work, for being well organized, for having an important and powerful mission lays the groundwork for effective major-gift fund raising.

All too often in small social-service organizations, driven by the ongoing difficulties of small staffs and huge need, staff and board focus primarily on their own encapsulated worlds. They conduct their programs and struggle with the assorted challenges without involving the broader community in their efforts. They do little to make sure the leaders of their community grasp their mission and understand the results of their work. Larger organizations that have qualified professional development and communications staff have an easier time maintaining a focus on the external community, even during non-campaign periods.

Strategic Planning

Strategic planning is the process by which organizations renew and redefine their relevance in the community. This process is more than the program evaluation that should be part of an organization's regular planning process. Strategic planning is a powerful process that requires an organization to look at the big picture issues of its relevance, effectiveness, and direction. Through this process, board, staff, and community come together to redefine the organization, shaping its future directions and envisioning the mechanisms by which it can accomplish its goals. This is a process not only of looking at what is, but also of conceiving what could be. And it is often in answer to the latter query that the objectives of a capital campaign are born.

Effective strategic planning requires more than a one-day retreat. It requires careful design that will not only examine the organization and its community but will also give its staff and board the time and experience it needs to embrace a new or renewed vision of what the organization might be. (See Chapter 3 in *Strategic Fund Development* by Simone Joyaux.)

Capital campaign projects should result from a strategic planning process that has clarified the optimal future directions for the organization and identified the capital and program requirements to make these directions a reality. Just looking at pressing space needs without exploring the more far-reaching issues that are shaping the community and the organization is not enough. A major investment in an organization should grow from a comprehensive appraisal of programs; the needs of the community; and the strengths, weaknesses, opportunities, and threats facing the organization. When done thoroughly,

a strategic planning process not only helps clarify mission and vision, but also builds a strong sense of collaboration between the organization and the community it serves.

Project Planning

When complete, the strategic plan will outline a direction for the organization. Before an organization is campaign ready, these general plans must take firmer shape. For example, the goal might be the funding of a new building or an expansion of an existing facility. Ideally, the organization will control the land for the new facility and have architectural drawings. The drawings should be specific enough to convey to donors what the building will look like and to provide the basis for sound cost estimates.

In the real world, project designs are often in process during the campaign. In some cases, redesign continues even after construction has begun. One must beware, however, that changes in the building plans do not outstrip the organization's ability to make the project a reality. Unless an organization has a substantial financial cushion, the costs should be estimated quite carefully before moving into a campaign. The consequences of not being able to construct a building because the costs exceeded the funds raised are far greater than the consequences of waiting until the facts are in hand.

Business Planning

A strategic plan and project plans do not yet complete the planning process. To be credible, an organization

One Floor, Two Floors?

We were busily raising money even as the foundations were being poured. In fact, we continued to raise money for the Women's Pavilion after the Family Pavilion of our new hospital was open for business. We had been talking to several major donors about naming rooms in this part of the project. So it came as a shock that the plans we had been showing our donors were no longer accurate. The project had gone from one floor to two floors. Back we went to our donors, rolling out the new plans on their dining room tables. Fortunately for us, they were pleased that the project had grown. They gave generously even though we were designing as we went.

—VP for Advancement, Health Foundation

needs a business plan that outlines the costs of operating the new facility and lays out a reasonable strategy for generating those funds. A business plan should include estimates for start-up costs, staffing, utilities, building maintenance, and other ongoing operating expenses.

DEVELOPMENT OFFICE READINESS

A looming campaign should push an organization to assess its fund-raising program. This is the time to make sure the development arm of the organization is operating smoothly and is prepared to take on the significant added work of a campaign. Many organizations will hire a consultant to conduct a development assessment or audit. A consultant brings experience and a helpful objectivity to the task. During a development audit, a consultant will explore all of the areas of development that will affect the success of a campaign. Below is a series of questions that a consultant might ask in the process of assessing the strengths and weakness of a development program. Though the size and capacity of the development office will vary greatly depending on the size and maturity of the organization, the following questions will provide a structure for evaluating the program.

Administration

- Do the top administrators spend time and energy planning for the future?
- Do the top administrators have a good working relationship with the trustees?
- Are the top administrators highly visible in the community and among major donors?
- Are the top administrators actively involved in fund raising?
- Does the staff have confidence in the top administrators?

Development Program

- What is the structure of the development program?
- What are the ongoing fund-raising programs?
- Do these programs routinely meet or exceed their goals?
- Does the development program conduct periodic planning sessions?
- Does the development office have a budget in keeping with its need?
- What is the return on investment of the development office's budget?
- Is the development program innovative and creative?

Staffing Structure and Leadership

- What are the primary staff positions in the development program?
- Are the job descriptions for these positions in keeping with the actual work of the people in those jobs?
- Are job descriptions focused on those activities that will yield the most support for the organization?
- How are individual performances measured?
- Are staff members accountable for results?
- How do the members of the development staff coordinate and share information?
- Does the development program focus on major-gift fund raising?
- How does the development program involve volunteers?
- What are the strengths and weaknesses of the development program?
- Where is the greatest amount of fund-raising potential?
- How will the staff roles shift to accommodate a capital campaign?
- What additional staff will be needed? When?

Annual Giving

- What is the history of the annual giving program?
- How are goals for annual giving set?
- How are membership programs and special-event fund raising incorporated into the annual fund?
- Do you have annual-gift clubs? If so, how are they promoted?
- Has this program grown over the past five years?
- What are the key trends that emerge in examining the five-year pattern of giving?
- Does the annual giving program have a major-gift component?

Major-Gift Program

- Does the organization have a separately defined major-gift program?
- How many major-gift prospects are there?
- How is someone identified as a major-gift prospect?
- How are major-gift prospects cultivated?
- Who manages the major-donor cultivation process?

Corporate and Foundation Relations

- Who handles corporate and foundation relations?
- Is the organization doing proactive research to identify potential corporate and foundation donors?
- How does this aspect of the development program overlap with the annual giving program?

Endowment and Planned-Giving Program

- Does the organization have an endowment?
- If so, does it have written policies governing the use of the endowed funds? Does the organization have a planned-giving program?
- How is the program promoted?
- Are volunteers used in identifying and developing potential donors?
- Is there a planned-giving committee?
- Is there a planned-giving recognition society?
- Is the planned-giving program appropriate for the size and maturity of the organization?
- Does the organization maintain an up-to-date planned-giving inventory of bequest expectations?
- How well have endowment funds been managed? Are results communicated well to past endowment donors?

Prospect Research

- How does the organization get and manage information about donors and prospective donors?
- Does the organization have a list of qualified major-gift prospects?
- Does the staff member responsible for prospect research work closely with the major-gift team?
- How is information about donors and prospects captured, maintained, and stored?

Information Systems

- Does the information system capture all gift information and maintain it in a way that is flexible and easy to format for reports and other uses?
- Does the system accommodate multiple gifts and pledges per donor?
- Does the information system enable the staff to capture and maintain background information about prospects?
- Does the system support a pipeline process of prospect management?
- Do people in the organization know how to fully use the capacity of the information system?
- Is the system adequate for projected growth in size and sophistication of the development program?

Gift Accounting and Acknowledgment

- Is there an efficient and well-organized system of depositing and recording gifts?
- What is the system for acknowledging gifts? Does this system provide for different thank-you procedures for gifts of different amounts?

Donor Relations

- How does the organization develop relationships with its donors and donor prospects?
- In what ways does the organization reach out to past donors?
- Is there a system in place that guides these processes?

Volunteers

- In what ways does the development office make use of volunteers?
- Who are the volunteer leaders? Who are the potential leaders?
- How are the potential leaders identified and recruited?
- How are volunteers recognized for their service?
- Are volunteers adequately trained for the jobs they are asked to do?
- What roles do board members play in the development process?
- Is the board leadership active in the broader community?
- Does the organization engage an adequate number of volunteers to execute the development plan?
- How are volunteers structured?
- Is the staff able to effectively manage all of the volunteers?

Culture

- In what ways does the development office celebrate its successes?
- Do members of the development staff regularly interact with program staff?
- Do members of the development staff treat one another in the way they would like to treat their donors?
- Does the development staff feel ownership of the plan to move ahead?

Communications/Public Relations

- How does the development staff interface with the communications /marketing/PR staff?
- Are the messages from the development office in synch with those of the communications office?
- Do the publications for communications/PR support and coordinate with fund-raising initiatives?

An exploration of the questions outlined above will yield a clearer understanding of the strengths and weaknesses of the development program. Even in a small organization with one or two development staff members, these questions will serve as a guide. For even in the smallest shop, many of the elements touched on above should be thought through prior to a campaign.

Campaign Readiness

Though the comprehensive questions outlined above touch nearly every aspect of organizational life, there are twelve specific elements that are critical to have in place or at least in progress before launching a campaign (Exhibit 2–3):

1. **Organizational planning:** Every organization should have a written, strategic plan that charts the course for the next three to five years. The plan should begin with a statement of mission, goals, and objectives and then move into specific programs and budgets. The board and other segments of the constituency should have been involved in developing the plan and validating the program and the financial needs expressed in it.

2. **Written statement of case, needs, and goals:** Every organization will need a written case statement for fund-raising purposes. The board, staff, and other key leaders must be able to express the case in exciting terms that communicate their own commitment.

3. **Constituency:** The organization must have defined a constituency beyond those intimately involved with its program. It must have developed an outreach program to increase its constituency. It must analyze the makeup of this constituency for fund-raising purposes.

4. **Market involvement:** The board and staff must know the extent and makeup of the organization's market. They must determine the interests, needs, and inclinations of that market and strengthen communication, understanding, and participation by various segments of the market.

5. **Gift support history:** The organization should have experience in attracting gift support for current programs (annual fund), for capital purposes, and/or for endowment. It should have experience in raising major gifts and have fund-raising programs directed at all market sources available (individuals, foundations, and corporations).

6. **Prospect development plan:** The organization should know who its potential givers are. It should have research that has been conducted over years on prospects and major-gift donors. This information should be properly recorded and retrievable for use by volunteers and staff involved in fund raising.

7. **Efficient recordkeeping system:** A donor and prospect recordkeeping system should be in place that provides storage and retrieval of essential data on the constituency in a timely and effective fashion. This system should enable the organization to acknowledge all gifts within a 48-hour period.

8. **Communications:** The organization should have a constituency-wide communications plan that is soundly conceived and implemented to involve community members in a warm, supportive relationship with the organization. The plan should outline the way in which the organization communicates with donors and cultivates their involvement.

9. **Fund-raising staff:** The organization should have a competent, qualified staff available to plan fund-raising programs and to support volunteers. The

Exhibit 2–3 Test for Campaign Readiness

Point Range	Your Score	
0–10	_____	A sound plan for the future
0–5	_____	A written statement of case, needs, and goals
0–5	_____	An informed constituency
0–5	_____	A history of market involvement
0–5	_____	A history of gift support
0–5	_____	A prospect development plan and research system
0–5	_____	An efficient recordkeeping system
0–5	_____	A creative, effective communications plan
0–10	_____	Competent staff with adequate time and training
0–15	_____	An involved, contributing board of trustees
0–15	_____	Qualified potential lead-gift contributors
0–15	_____	Capable volunteer leadership
Total	_____	(Highest possible score is 100)

A score of below 75 might indicate that the organization is not ready to mount a major campaign and should work on each of the elements with a low score.

staff must be able to devote their full time and energy to fund raising.

10. **Involved governing board:** The board must play an active role in governing the organization—planning, developing, and approving policy; overseeing management; and generating resources through fund raising. Board members should be willing to make financial commitments and ask others to give.

11. **Potential lead/major gifts:** The organization should attend to the critical process of identifying, cultivating, and soliciting prospective major donors for current program support, endowment, and special projects. It should have a valid list of qualified potential major donors, primarily individuals and families.

12. **Fund-raising leadership:** The organization should have capable, creative volunteer leaders who are committed to raising the money required.

PREPARING THE DEVELOPMENT OFFICE

Although staff roles in the campaign are many and diverse, most of them require a well-organized internal system to manage information. Before the campaign, the development staff should analyze the information management systems that are in use in the development office to be sure that they will accomplish the tasks of the campaign, such as

- gift processing
- gift acknowledgment
- gift accounting
- donor information and tracking
- volunteer information
- computer and printer operations

Evaluating Development Systems

Some organizations conduct an internal review of their development systems. It is sometimes difficult to see the problems because one has learned to work around them, so it may be wise to hire an outside consultant to audit these systems and make recommendations as to how they might be strengthened in preparation for the campaign.

A traditional development audit conducted by a consultant usually evaluates the development programs, personnel, and internal communication as well as the information management systems. The following questions have been designed to guide a development director though an assessment of each system in the development office. These systems might function well enough

for the annual giving program, but it often takes the impetus of a capital campaign to motivate the development staff to make sure that each area works as well as it should. Well-conceived internal development practices and systems will benefit both a capital campaign and an organization's ongoing development program. The author recommends that the development director take the time to write a report that addresses these questions. Such an exercise will help clarify the structure and function of the development systems and will also serve as a useful tool to inform the campaign consultant and executive director, as well as the campaign chairs.

Through answering these questions the development director should become more aware of the capabilities and weaknesses in the development systems. The campaign consultant should be able to make specific suggestions about ways to strengthen the systems.

Gift Processing

Checks. Write a step-by-step description of what happens to a contribution check from the time it arrives in the mail until it is deposited in the bank.

- Who opens the envelope?
- What is done with the envelope and any note or other enclosures?
- Who records the gift amount?
- Is the pledge form or remittance enclosure saved with a copy of the check?
- Is the gift amount credited to the specific fund-raising program that generated it?
- What other information is recorded from the check?
- Are the address and spelling checked against the donor files and recorded if new?
- Is the phone number checked and recorded?
- In whose name is the gift acknowledged?
- Whose name is used if the check is in two names and the note in only one?
- What name is used if the check comes from a business or foundation?
- How are memorial gifts credited, to operating or endowment?
- Is there a policy that guides to what fund bequests are credited?
- Who records specific donor instructions, and where are they recorded?
- Do at least two people record the amount of the check?
- How are the receipt figures reconciled?
- How often are they reconciled?
- Is a copy of the check made before it is deposited?

- Are checks of every amount processed in the same way?
- Is the development director notified when a large gift is received?
- What qualifies as a large gift?
- How many days elapse between the receipt and deposit of a check?

Pledges. Prepare a written description of the procedures for handling pledges.

- Who records the pledge?
- Is the total amount of the pledge recorded?
- How are future payments recorded?
- Is there a system for sending payment-reminder notices?
- Are reminder notices used to convey other information about the organization?

Securities. Prepare a written description of the procedures for handling a gift of securities.

- Where is the organization's brokerage account?
- Who is the organization's broker?
- Who pays the broker's commission?
- Who is responsible for overseeing the transfer of securities?
- How do the finance department and the development department interact with regard to the transfer of securities?
- What is the mechanism for tracking securities that have been transferred to the organization's brokerage account without a donor name?
- Is the information that the donor needs to transfer securities (name of the organization's broker, federal ID number, and account number) easily accessible?

Gift Acknowledgment

Describe the procedures and policies for acknowledging gifts in your organization.

- Does every donor receive a gift receipt?
- If not, who receives a receipt and who does not?
- What information is included in the receipt?
- Is the receipt information incorporated into the thank-you letter format?
- How many thank-you notes does the donor receive?
- Who writes thank-you notes?
- Who signs thank-you notes?
- Are some thank-you notes individualized?
- Are some thank-you notes handwritten?

- Do some typed letters have handwritten personal notes added to them?
- Are there different thank-you note policies for gifts of different sizes?
- Are donors of gifts of certain sizes called on the telephone? If so, who calls them?
- What internal mechanisms trigger thank-you notes and/or phone calls?
- Is the family member notified of the receipt of a memorial gift?
- Are donors of memorial gifts thanked in a special way?
- If a gift was solicited in person, how is the solicitor informed of its receipt?
- How many days elapse between the receipt of a gift and mailing the first thank-you note?
- If a donor is to receive more than one thank-you note, how are the notes scheduled?
- How are donors of in-kind gifts recognized?
- Are donor names published in the annual report?
- Are donors listed alphabetically in the report or alphabetically within a giving category?
- Who keeps track of donor names for the annual report?
- Do donors have an opportunity to request that their names not be listed?
- How does the organization determine the way in which each name should be listed?
- Are records kept or copies made of thank-you letters sent to donors?
- What determines when a hard-copy file on a donor is opened?
- Are donors recognized for cumulative lifetime giving?
- Are donors specifically thanked at the end of the year for their cumulative contributions for the year?
- Is any sort of memento used for recognizing donors at different giving levels?

Gift Accounting

Describe the policies that guide how and when gifts are counted toward specific fund-raising goals.

- Who tallies the gifts that come in to the annual giving program?
- Are there specific starting and stopping dates for gifts that are counted for annual giving? for the capital campaign?
- Is the full amount of a pledge counted in the year it is received?
- What is the policy on writing off unfulfilled pledges?
- How are gifts of stock or other securities valued?

- How are gifts of life insurance counted? How are deferred gifts counted?
- Is there a mechanism for recording and counting in-kind gifts?

Donor Information

Describe in written form the system for gathering, updating, and tracking information about donors.

- Who is responsible for gathering information about donors?
- Who gathers information about donors from the newspapers and other media?
- How is donor information captured and stored?
- How is the mailing list updated?
- Is the mailing list periodically purged of nonresponders?
- How often is the mailing list purged?
- What guidelines are used to purge the mailing list?
- Where do new names come from?
- Whose job is it to assemble them?
- How are addresses updated?
- What percentage of the donor names have telephone numbers?
- What percentage of the donor records include information beyond the basic name, address, and phone number?
- Does the system have a place for both business and home addresses?
- Is there a way to store a wide range of donor information such as hobbies, alma mater, children's names, gifts to other organizations, and birthdays?
- Can total donor giving be easily retrieved?
- Can the system show the number and size of gifts made in any specified year?
- What are the mechanisms for obtaining information from the donors themselves?
- What types of information should be gathered?

Volunteer Information

Describe the ways in which information about volunteers is gathered and stored.

- Are accurate records of all volunteer involvement maintained and updated?
- What information about volunteer activity is systematically recorded?
- Are the dates on which people volunteered, the tasks they performed, and the number of hours they worked tracked?
- Can volunteers be sorted by specific activity?
- Can volunteers be sorted by date of involvement?

- Do staff members evaluate volunteers after each assignment?
- Are such staff evaluations summarized or indicated in any way in the volunteers' records?

Computer and Printer Capabilities

- Is the computer easy to use?
- Does the development office have at least one dedicated terminal for its use?
- Is the system powerful enough to handle the entire mailing list?
- Is someone in the development office fluent with the development software?
- Is it possible to design multiple reports without engaging a computer specialist?
- Is it possible to store appropriate salutations for letters to be signed by the board chair, executive director, and campaign chair?
- Is it possible to individualize letters using the mail-merge feature of the software?
- Is it possible to edit individual letters while performing a mail merge?
- Is it easy to mail-merge and print envelopes?
- Does the printer produce clean and professional-looking letters?
- Is it easy to feed letterhead and envelopes through the printer?
- Will the printer handle mailing labels and/or oversized envelopes?
- Does the software have the capability to flag special donors?
- Can donors be coded in special categories?
- Does the software enable donors to be given a primary affiliation?
- Can the donors be flagged for special acknowledgments?
- Can the software track pledges?

It is not necessary that an organization have systems in place that cover everything noted above. However, if after answering all these questions the development staff becomes aware that its systems fall far short of the ideal, the organization should consider investing the time and resources to develop systems for the areas found lacking and to acquire the hardware and software needed to support the systems.

At the very least, an organization must be able to sort donor names by the categories under which they will be solicited. The system must contain accurate and accessible information about donor names, addresses, and phone numbers, as well as records of giving and other information that document the donor's relationship with the organization. The system must be able to merge segmented donor lists into letters in which at least three pieces of information will vary from letter to letter. The system should include a printer that produces clean, clear copies, and that sheet-feeds both letterhead and envelopes quickly and easily.

Selecting Development Software

Although generations of development professionals based their campaigns on index cards, inexpensive and effective computing systems have rendered these rudimentary systems obsolete. Indeed, today even small nonprofits are able to afford computers and dedicated development software.

The vast array of products and vendors and the rapidity of change in the field make the process of selecting a development system almost overwhelming. Large institutions often engage computer-development consultants to help them assess their computer needs, select the right systems, and train the staff after the system is installed.

Although small organizations need not invest in an expert, they should do their homework by understanding the organization's needs, talking to colleagues, and gathering information from vendors.

First comes an assessment of the organization's needs. A determination must be made of how many names the software program must be able to handle. This estimate should project three to five years ahead. Information should be assembled about the software programs already in use within the organization so that the development software that is selected will at least have a compatible word-processing program. Although it is helpful to know what types of reports the development director will want to generate, in reality few who have not had experience with development software will be able to anticipate those needs.

Second comes talking to one's colleagues. The topic of computers invariably arises at professional meetings: "What kind of development software does your office use? Do you like it? Is it effective? Was it worth the investment?" Development professionals are seldom shy about voicing their praises or complaints about their computer software, and one can learn a great deal from other organizations' mistakes.

A campaign consultant is often a good source for software recommendations. Working in many different organizations, consultants have an opportunity to compare the strengths and weaknesses of different systems.

Third comes gathering vendor information. Information from four to six software vendors should be compiled. It is a good idea to find out whether a neighboring organization is using the software that is under consideration. If so, a visit to that organization allows the development officer to see the product in actual use in a development setting and to ask the users about their experience with the program and the vendor. Some vendors will send a salesperson to the organization to demonstrate their product.

In assessing hardware and software, the following questions will yield valuable information:

- What kinds of technical support are available? How is it billed? How long does it typically take the technical-support person to call back with an answer?
- What kinds of training are available?
- How often are upgrades issued? How are they priced?
- How long has the vendor been in business?
- Who are the vendor's clients?
- Will the vendor convert the organization's present data? What is the fee for conversion?
- Is it possible to see a copy of the software manual? (Look for a manual with an extensive index that is free of techno-jargon and easy to understand for a computer nonexpert.)

Forgetting a Crucial Question

One of my clients was planning to purchase new software prior to their campaign. They asked me to draft a list of questions for them to take along when they went to visit the vendors of the software that they were considering. I came up with a long list of items that I thought the program should be able to accomplish for the development office. My client then went to see the vendors and returned having made a purchase. They had been assured that the program could do everything I had specified plus many other, more sophisticated things. I was in high spirits.

It turned out that, although the system could do what we needed, getting even the simplest report or segmentation of the database required the assistance of an experienced computer programmer. The system could perform every task on my list, but at what cost in time, effort, and money? Their system had no flexibility, so the development director couldn't do anything that wasn't vanilla without engaging expert help. And often even with such help, it was difficult to get what we needed. Although my questions had been good ones, I neglected to ask a fundamental question: "Is the system user-friendly and flexible enough so that the development director will be able to design her own reports and get what she needs without the help of a programmer?"

—Campaign Consultant

- Is the software compatible with the organization's existing hardware?
- Is the software compatible with the organization's word-processing software, so that letters and other documents can be merged and produced easily?

Purchasing a software system should take place at least six to twelve months prior to the start of the quiet phase of the campaign. This will provide enough time to convert and enter data, train the development staff to use the program, and work out the bugs and be able to use the software fluently.

Staffing Requirements

Truly skilled development professionals are rare. They combine an ability to see the big picture with an enviable talent for the punctilious handling of details. They are able to work with the rich and powerful, and at the same time are willing to pitch in at any level to help get a job done. They think clearly and write well, and—perhaps their most important quality—they bring perspective and humor to even the most stressful situations.

> *A wise executive director will involve the development director early in the campaign planning process.*

Although it is often difficult to find this combination of characteristics in one person, most organizations are able to cover all these bases by combining the skills of a number of individuals into an effective development team. The most common configuration for a development team that is capable of conducting a capital campaign is an executive director who is able to free up approximately one-half of his or her time for the campaign, a full-time development director, and a full-time development assistant. With this level of staffing, it should be possible to maintain an annual giving program while planning and implementing a capital campaign.

Someone must be a stickler for details. Even well-organized campaigns flounder if the details are not right. At least one member of the development team must be detail oriented. Proposals must be letter-perfect. Donor records must be accurate; and every salutation, name spelling, and dollar amount must be absolutely correct. As the piles of paperwork mount during a campaign, such a high standard of quality becomes more and more difficult to adhere to. However, while from inside the development office a particular proposal letter may be just one among hundreds that are being prepared, to the donor that letter is often his or her first contact with the campaign. An incorrect salutation or a misspelled name reminds the donor that he or she is just one among many in a sloppy solicitation process—not the message any campaign would like to convey.

> *Errors that result from mail merging are common. Only the eagle eye of a dedicated error-catcher will pick up the small inconsistencies and inaccuracies.*

Someone must be creative, flexible, and visionary. Attention to detail is not enough to run a successful campaign. Someone on the development team must be able to see the broader campaign picture and be creative and flexible enough to design and redesign throughout the campaign process. Although campaigns begin with the development of a clear plan, inevitably the plan requires adjustment as pieces fall by the wayside here and there. Perhaps a lead gift falls through, or perhaps a campaign chair becomes ill, or perhaps the zoning for the building project is not approved. At every turn and with every

The Glass Half Empty

I'm an enthusiastic person. I guess I was born that way. So when the organization I worked for as development director decided to launch a campaign, I really got onboard. The idea of having larger and better facilities, which we really needed, excited me, and the thought of increasing the fund-raising ambitions of the organization—well, it made me anxious, but I was even excited about that.

Our executive director was not an enthusiast. I suppose he saw himself as a pragmatist. I saw him as a pessimist! Throughout the whole campaign, when it came to enthusiasm, we were polar opposites. A gift would come in, and I would jump up and down with glee while he worried that it should have been bigger. A donor would call and leave a message—I would be sure the call was about a gift, he was sure there was a problem. We would tally campaign progress—I would see how far we had come. He would see how far we had to go.

I guess we balanced each other, but I sure felt that at least half of my energies were wasted just by countering his "realism." In truth, if his views had been the realistic ones, we would never have reached our goal!

—Former Development Director

unanticipated change, the development team must respond with creativity, flexibility, and resilience. In these situations, the team must set a standard for creative problem solving that maintains the energy and enthusiasm of staff and volunteer leadership alike—even in the face of setbacks.

Someone must have excellent "people" skills. One or more individuals on the development team must be very good at dealing with people. They must be well spoken, friendly, and encouraging. Their style in dress and appearance must be appealing to all sorts of people. And they must have the courage and ability to persist in their efforts until they achieve their goals.

Staffing Alternatives

For some smaller organizations, it may not be possible to have the ideal campaign staffing that was discussed earlier in this chapter—one-half of the executive director's time, a full-time development director, and a full-time development assistant. Many successful campaigns have used other models. Sometimes the executive director runs a campaign with only clerical support; some campaigns are managed by teams of staff members each of whom oversees specific aspects of the campaign. In some cases, a committed volunteer might run the campaign instead of paid staff members, or volunteers might participate as part of an in-house campaign-management team.

Sometimes an executive director will take on the challenge of running the campaign. He or she will use a variety of clerical assistants to manage the paperwork and the flow of information, but the planning and implementation of the campaign will be tightly held by the person at the top. Given the right person, this strategy can be successful, but it takes its toll on the executive director, and more than a few directors have burned themselves out through the effort. Sometimes, however, if the director is able to delegate other pieces of the job to effective staff members and find a first-rate support person to work with, this arrangement can work well.

Often organizations have staff members who collectively possess all the talents and capabilities that are required for the campaign staff, but no one person has them all. Although the team approach to campaign staffing takes time and coordination, shared campaign leadership may yield a campaign team that will be able to accomplish more than any one or two staff members could on their own. Managing this effectively requires a strong commitment to conscious team building and communication.

In small organizations, it is sometimes possible to conduct a capital campaign using volunteers in lieu of paid staff. Although the heyday of the "professional volunteer" is long gone, sometimes an organization is fortu-

More for Less

When early in the campaign it became clear that the development director was on his way out, I wondered to myself just how the campaign was going to succeed. The library director wanted to use the campaign to learn more about fund raising and she decided that she and her assistant could pull it off. And they did! Kathy, the director's assistant, worked like mad to master the intricacies of the fund-raising software that had been developed by the departed development director. Mary, the director, delegated as much of the work of running the library as she could to her colleagues. Together Mary and Kathy dove into the campaign. They worked days and they worked nights. They set up meetings, cajoled volunteers and donors, and managed reams of campaign paper. When it was over, not only had the campaign succeeded, but the library functioned better than ever. Other staff members had learned new responsibilities. Mary had developed strong relationships with the funding leadership of the community. Kathy had become a first-rate development staff member who now handles the entire annual giving program. Although the two were more than happy to take their vacations after the campaign was completed, they both feel that they got back more than they gave, both for themselves and for their library.

—Campaign Consultant

nate to have a first-rate volunteer who is willing to take on the challenge of running a capital campaign. Such arrangements have inherent difficulties, but occasionally, if they are well structured in advance, they can work to the advantage of both the volunteer and the organization.

But beware of the well-meaning volunteer who offers his or her services to manage the campaign but who has little understanding of what the task will entail. In fact, the volunteer may have strong feelings about fund raising that are quite antithetical to sound campaign practice and may even be antithetical to the ethos and style of the organization. And, as anyone who has worked with volunteers knows, they can be difficult to guide and impossible to fire.

To ensure that a capital campaign being conducted by a well-meaning volunteer doesn't become a glorified bake sale and fall far short of its goal, the staff must spend considerable time educating the volunteer campaign director about capital campaigns prior to passing over the leadership torch. The director and the volunteer should discuss fund-raising approaches and determine whether they can agree on a sound campaign strategy. The director might assign the volunteer some small preliminary tasks to evaluate this person's competence and effectiveness.

Many retired people who volunteer for such a task begin with wonderful intentions but don't realize that the campaign effort is likely to extend for a year or longer—right through that planned trip to Florida and the skiing vacation in Aspen.

Nonetheless, the perfect volunteer does surface now and again. And as long as both the volunteer and the organization clearly understand the tasks and responsibilities, the likely timetable and duration, and the fund-raising strategies that are required for sound capital campaign fund raising, there is no reason not to take advantage of a mutually beneficial situation.

A more common model for campaign staffing is the organization that has a full-time development director who is able to find two or three part-time volunteers to assist with the campaign. Although the paid staff member is responsible for campaign direction and leadership, competent volunteers might well serve in well-defined support roles. Of course, in this situation as well, all roles must be spelled out with precision to avoid unmet expectations, and volunteers should be tested in other, less crucial roles before being given major campaign responsibilities.

Preparing the Entire Staff for the Long Haul

Once the larger questions focused on the readiness of the donors, the organization, and the development pro-gram have been addressed, it is wise to develop strategies to help all of the organization's staff through the inevitable stresses of the campaign. Time spent strategically preparing the staff before the campaign begins will be time well spent.

Upstairs/downstairs: Many organizations struggle with a division between the "upstairs" staff members, those who raise and process the money and handle the upper-level administrative tasks of the organization, and the "downstairs" staff members—the service providers. Downstairs people feel that they do all the work but that the management, or upstairs, folks get to wear the suits and earn more money. And the more the executive director's job takes him or her in the direction of money, the more the development staff has access to the director and the more the workers in the trenches feel left out.

> *Campaign consultants often interact only with the major players, understand the organization's program only superficially, and are insensitive to the stresses caused by the campaign in other areas of the organization.*

Petty jealousies, misunderstandings, and especially a general lack of communication between these two groups tend to plague organizations, especially when they are growing rapidly. When an organization is small and intimate, everyone has access to the director and information tends to flow easily. As the organization grows, easy access and open communication among the staff are often among the first casualties. Since many campaigns follow periods of rapid growth, it is not uncommon for the campaign to be an added burden upon an organization that is already coping with internal stresses. If not treated carefully, the campaign is likely to exacerbate the stresses and widen the breach between the upstairs and the downstairs staff.

As the executive director becomes more and more consumed with the tasks and responsibilities of the campaign, he or she usually has less time for internal issues, yet is often unable or unwilling to delegate such responsibility to others. Downstairs staff members can no longer get the attention and resources they need to maintain their programs. Upstairs staff members realize that the campaign will afford them an opportunity to move themselves and their organization into a much more powerful sphere in the community. The power and potential of new contacts and opportunities are usually so compelling (and anxiety producing) that the executive staff tend to lose touch with what's really going on downstairs. To compound the problem, the director is usually spending money on what might be thought of as upstairs priorities (the campaign and the plans for the new project) while holding a tight rein on downstairs spending (staff and equipment for direct services). It's no wonder, then, that friction grows and tempers flare!

Informing the staff about the campaign: Although some upstairs-downstairs stress is inevitable, keeping the downstairs staff informed about the campaign does help. They should understand what the campaign is, how and when it will be conducted, how it will affect them, and what its outcome is likely to be. Staff members appreciate the opportunity to meet in small groups with the campaign consultant to hear about the process and ask questions. This process also helps the consultant learn more about the actual function of the organization and explore with the downstairs staff ways in which they might help and support the fund-raising process.

In some cases, the problem goes deeper. Development priorities are set, money is raised, and projects are funded, often without direct (or even indirect) consultation with those who will have to live with those decisions and who are the real experts to boot. The head of information systems may not know about a grant for a new computing system; the head nurse may not be consulted on the design for the renovated nursing stations; and so forth. If the direct-service staff has not had opportunities to provide input into the planning of the project, it should come as no surprise if the downstairs staff resents and does not support the capital campaign.

As the campaign progresses through the quiet phase, there are several ways to keep staff members informed. Many organizations have small, weekly newsletters designed just for staff. Stories or campaign updates help build support for the campaign among the staff and help keep the downstairs staff from feeling out of the information loop.

Getting the Work Done

Organize the paper: Campaigns generate paper—lots of paper. Managing all this paper is a challenge to even

Friends or Strangers?
We were concerned that the development office wasn't able to gather enough information about patients who might be prospective donors. So we decided to conduct a series of small-group meetings with the service providers to explore how we might improve the information flow. Those meetings turned out to be important and rewarding in ways we had never expected. At the most basic level, staff members had a chance to find out who we were. They had seen us around two or three days a month huddling with their leaders but didn't know who we were or what we were doing. It had made them a bit anxious. The meetings also gave them a chance to learn more about fund raising and to begin to understand it as an opportunity for donors rather than as a repugnant form of arm twisting. Finally, it gave us a chance to ask them how we should approach the design of a staff campaign within the larger campaign. After every meeting we got feedback from the staff about how pleased they were to have been included in the process.
—Campaign Consultants

the most organized. Through years of watching executive directors, development directors, development assistants, and campaign volunteers struggle with campaign paper, the author has come to believe that every campaign should maintain two filing systems—one in file folders and the other in a three-ring notebook. In the file folders can be kept the inevitable duplicate copies of material that might be needed later in the campaign. Papers can be put in and taken out as necessary throughout the campaign. In the three-ring notebooks should be filed one copy of every piece of paper generated for the campaign. Once something has been filed in a notebook, it should not be taken out. These notebooks then become the permanent record of the campaign. The file headings might be organized as follows:

- Co-conspirators Planning Meeting
- Campaign Planning Committee
- Campaign Plan
- Plaques and Donor Recognition
- Campaign Steering Committee
- Public Relations Committee
  - Campaign Materials
  - Press Releases
- Lead Gift Division
- Family Division
  - Board
  - Former Board
  - Staff
  - Former Staff
  - Volunteers
  - Former Volunteers
- Special-Events Committee
  - Cultivation Events
  - Campaign Kickoff
- Major-Gifts Division
- Phonathon
- Direct-Mail Campaign
- Campaign Cleanup
- Campaign Evaluation

In a typical campaign, one might fill two or three large three-ring binders with paper, but if the dual system is maintained with discipline, it will minimize the amount of time that campaign workers spend looking for the papers they need.

More paper management tips: Every document that is produced for the campaign should bear a date. Campaigns often go through many drafts of every document. Plans change, cases for support are edited and updated, timetables are revised; and unless every piece of paper is dated, it is difficult to know which paper represents the most recent version.

The computer file name for each document should be added to the document itself. Few things are more frus-

---

Dog-Eared but Effective

At the beginning of our campaign, I bought a huge three-ring notebook and a bunch of tabbed dividers. I divided up each phase of the campaign, made a list of what needed to be done by whom and by what date for each phase, and inserted the list at the front of each section. After that page, I put all the supplemental material, like who the prospects were, the committee structures, a copy of the campaign plan, notes about campaign leadership—just about everything but the kitchen sink! Rather than the notebook being overloaded with paper, I knew exactly where everything was and was able to refer to it quickly. I prepared all the information on my word-processing system so it could be updated easily. Needless to say, by the end of the campaign my notebook was full and looked pretty dog-eared, but it had served me well.

—Development Director

---

trating than not remembering how a particular document was filed in the computer and having to open dozens of files to find it.

Several inexpensive three-hole punches should be purchased and left in strategic places. The three-hole binder system fails most often because the three-hole punch is hidden under paper or has been borrowed by another department. Once a large three-hole binder has been littered with unpunched pages sticking out in all directions, the motivation and discipline to maintain it quickly evaporate.

One Step at a Time

A campaign is a monumental undertaking and an immense challenge to all but the most imperturbable. While one always wants to know what lies ahead, it can often be enough to restrict one's gaze merely to the next step . . . and the next . . . and the next—until finally one does get to the end. Anyone who is a runner knows the power of just putting one foot in front of the other as a way of combating fatigue and loss of heart. The success of completing each small step inspires the next one. Particularly in the early phases of a campaign, when the job seems so monumental and uncertain, there is comfort and encouragement in focusing on the next task and being sure that one does it thoroughly and well.

Look Ahead

At the same time, quick glances a longer distance ahead are necessary to make sure that the campaign stays on course. Often the campaign consultant will take the role of looking ahead, designing and redesigning the best path to bring the campaign to a successful conclusion. Throughout the campaign, looking ahead becomes more and more effective. In the early phases, with too much uncertainty, one might focus on tomorrow's task, but as the campaign gets close to its goal, its very proximity draws one ahead and motivates staff members and volunteers alike.

> *As the campaign gets close to its goal, its very proximity draws one ahead.*

Set Realistic Deadlines

Realistic and reasonable deadlines motivate both staff and volunteers, so:

- Get input from other people when setting deadlines. Deadlines that are set with input from the people who will be responsible for meeting them tend to be more successful than deadlines that are imposed from above.
- Use deadlines to take advantage of different people's working patterns. For example, if a person works better under pressure, his or her schedule should plan to put him or her to work on the task just shortly before the deadline. Or if the campaign chair is always late in fulfilling his commitments, the staff might set up a meeting with him to review his progress several days before the actual deadline.
- Schedule meetings to create interim deadlines. Meetings spur people to complete their assigned tasks. Schedule short meetings frequently to move a project along.
- Be flexible. Occasionally deadlines must be changed. People don't always run according to plan. Stick to deadlines when they make sense and set new ones when they don't.

Tips for Working Smart

Take time to reorganize your office. As a campaign heats up, working smart becomes critical. Take time to look around your office. Is it set up for efficiency? Is there a computer terminal at your desk? Are file drawers within easy reach? Can you close the door and have a quiet place to concentrate? Have the names and numbers of the people who are involved in the campaign been entered in your Rolodex? Is it possible to clear a desk or table just for the campaign? Just one day spent reorganizing and rearranging to make your life easier and help

you become more efficient will pay off in many hours saved during the campaign.

Practice immediacy: Most people procrastinate, and in doing so they spend more time delaying than doing. Campaigns require staff members to carry out many small tasks every day—making telephone calls, writing notes, following up with staff members, drafting agendas, preparing proposals, and then making more telephone calls. If one uses the campaign to practice the art of doing things immediately, it is possible to increase one's efficiency, reduce anxiety, and create a clear sense of forward momentum. Campaigns in which the staff acts and responds quickly tend also to be campaigns with effective volunteers.

Practicing immediacy is particularly important because the anxiety that is inherent in making many campaign calls tends to foster procrastination at all levels. If one can get in an "action" frame of mind for the duration of the campaign, that attitude will inspire and fuel the entire campaign.

Do what's important: As campaign pressures mount, the staff must learn to work strategically, doing what is needed to get the job done well and not spending time where it is not needed. For example, some volunteers and donors require extra time and attention, others are perfectly happy with an occasional phone call. Be sure to differentiate between them so that you will be able to use your time wisely.

Although in some respects every aspect of a capital campaign is important, lead gifts and their donors are the most important! If you are not able to accomplish everything, be sure to manage the lead-gift cultivation and solicitation process well. Indeed, success in this aspect of the campaign will bring success in every other.

Ask others to help: Don't forget the double value of asking others to help. When you ask someone to help, not only does it help get the work done, but it broadens the ownership of the campaign.

The Rewards of Hard Work

Many development directors in small- to medium-sized organizations have never participated in a campaign before and feel apprehensive about their own abilities in this new and overwhelming enterprise. Perhaps for the first time in their careers they are expected to interact with board members and community leaders and are expected to help solicit large gifts. Both the risks and the expectations are high.

Take comfort in the opportunities for learning that accompany all capital campaigns. A consultant can serve as a teacher or mentor. An experienced campaign chair is often happy to share ideas and experiences to help a young or inexperienced staff member. The lessons are many and immediate; and in capital campaigns, occasional mistakes are allowed and hard work is rewarded.

The chances to learn and experience the real power of fund raising through a capital campaign are unmatched in any other type of fund raising. The wise development director or assistant will jump at the chance to work on a campaign. In doing so, they expand their contacts in the community, learn and practice important skills in fund raising, and prepare themselves for moving up the development career ladder.

Ten Tips for Survival

1. **Find a confidant.** Every person who works on a capital campaign needs someone to confide in. No matter how successful the campaign, frustrations and discouragement are part of the process. A confidant outside of the organization will provide an outlet for fears, frustrations, and anxieties that will not negatively affect the campaign.

2. **Pamper yourself.** Capital campaigns are high-stress times. Counter the stress by treating yourself often to the special things you like. Take a yoga class, find a masseuse, get a facial, take a hot-air balloon ride. Do good things for yourself in the midst of the campaign.

3. **Celebrate every success.** Campaigns are full of small successes that all too often go by without remark. Do something to celebrate every success, whether the celebration is simply a trip to the lunchroom for a fresh cup of coffee, a round of applause by the development staff, or a nice lunch at a downtown restaurant. Notice success more than you notice failure.

4. **Build team spirit.** Team spirit doesn't just happen, it is built. Think of ways to listen to every member of the team. Remember their birthdays, celebrate their successes, share the leadership with them, encourage them to be creative risk takers by rewarding their successes. By working at building team spirit, the entire campaign will be more fun and effective.

5. **Lighten up.** Campaigns are serious business, but even campaigns must have their lighter moments. Find the part of your mind that sees the humor in things and use it well throughout the campaign.

6. **Juggle your schedule.** Sometimes it pays to take days off during the week and work on weekends. If it works for you, do it.

7. **Share stories.** Find opportunities for people in the office to share their most recent campaign experience or story. Telling stories creates bonds among people, helps them see the humor in their situations, and makes the campaign human and interesting.

8. **Laugh a lot.** Silliness has its place in a campaign—even sometimes with the most powerful of leaders, for they too are people and may enjoy a good laugh.

9. **Listen to your inner voices.** Most of us have inner voices. Sometimes they tell us things that are right, and sometimes they are wrong. In a campaign, when they nag about something again and again, chances are they are right!

10. **Don't look back.** An allowance for a good deal of failure is built into every campaign. If one begins to look back and second-guess why one thing or another didn't happen just the way you wanted it to, one begins casting blame. Far healthier is the process of involving people in figuring out how to make the next day successful.

Although the most successful campaigns are those in which the organization is truly ready at every level, the campaign process itself often drives an organization to recognize the areas in which it is weak and to make Herculean efforts to shore up those aspects of its operation. Prior to a campaign, many smaller organizations never even ask themselves the questions outlined in this chapter. Though playing catch-up during the campaign planning and implementation makes the campaign harder and more stressful, many if not most organizations do just that. For them, the long-term effects of the campaign on the development program are at least as important as the money it raises.

REFERENCE

Joyaux, Simone. 2001. *Strategic fund development: Building profitable relationships that last,* 2nd edition. Gaithersburg, MD: Aspen Publishers, Inc.

Chapter 3
Preparing for a Campaign

Chapter Outline

- The First Stage of Campaign Planning
- The Case for Support
- The Campaign Goal and the Gift Range Chart
- Developing the Gift Range Chart
- The Gift Range Chart and Prospect Planning
- The Feasibility Study
- Feasibility Study Consultants
- Enlisting a Feasibility Study Committee
- The Work of the Committee
- The Interview Process
- The Feasibility Study Report

THE FIRST STAGE OF CAMPAIGN PLANNING

As with much planning, campaign planning occurs in fits and starts. It begins with the sure knowledge that an organization needs money to bring its vision for the future to fruition. The project is planned, the programs are projected, and the budget is beginning to solidify. It's time for a capital campaign. Many organizations turn at this point to a consultant for guidance. And most consultants suggest that the organization conduct a feasibility or pre-campaign planning study to help evaluate the project's potential in the fund-raising market.

With or without a consultant, every organization should test its fund-raising potential before launching a campaign. This testing process requires the organization to develop four fundamental campaign elements: campaign objectives, the case for support, a preliminary campaign goal, and a table of gifts or gift range chart. These four elements of a campaign plan provide the information necessary to get feedback from the community. Together, they enable a prospective donor to get a good sense of the project and to consider whether and at what level he or she might consider supporting the campaign.

Determining Campaign Objectives and Preliminary Dollar Goal

During this early campaign-planning period, an organization must determine the objectives of the campaign. Will it raise money only for bricks and mortar? Will it raise money for the endowment fund? Will the campaign also raise money to support the organization's ongoing operating expenses for a specified period of time? All of these decisions will determine the size and shape of the campaign.

In general, the smaller and less mature the organization, the simpler and more straightforward the campaign. These organizations are more likely to be driven by real and pressing financial needs. They may not have a mature donor base; they may not have an endowment fund or any sort of planned-giving program. For these organizations, the debates are likely to center on issues of project financing rather than endowment funding. For these organizations, a successful campaign will be critical to their ability to grow. If they are not able to raise the requisite $2 million, for example, they will not be able to build the new building.

For larger, more mature organizations, a campaign plays a very different role. With a strong financial base, the organization could probably build the building with or without a campaign. A successful campaign will enable them to build a better building. It will enable them to coalesce their fund-raising efforts, raising the sights of their donors and the organization's visibility in the larger community.

The preliminary dollar goal must reflect the objectives of the campaign. The more comprehensive the objectives, the larger the goal. The dollar goal that is determined at this early stage of campaign planning is the number that will be tested in a pre-campaign study. This number must reflect both the cost of what the organization needs to accomplish its objectives and a reasonable estimate of what the organization might be able to raise.

In the example in Exhibit 3–1, an organization with a strong history of gift support in a community with a his-

Exhibit 3–1 Sample Statement of Campaign Objectives and Estimated Costs

Building Project		$2,700,000
Land	$250,000	
Site costs and landscaping (10%)	160,000	
Construction (15,000 sf @ $100/sf)	1,500,000	
Furnishings (20%)	300,000	
Architects and other fees (10–15%)	260,000	
Contingency (10%)	200,000	
Endowment		1,000,000
Scholarship funds	500,000	
Building maintenance fund	500,000	
Administrative and fund-raising costs		300,000
Total Project Costs		$4,000,000

tory of successful campaigns in that dollar range might well use the $4 million figure as its preliminary campaign goal. But if the organization has had little history with major donors and/or if it is located in a small community in which the largest successful campaign has raised only $2 million, there will be little point in testing a goal of that size. Rather, the organization will need to explore the possibility of funding a portion of the project in other ways—perhaps through a bond or other types of long-term financing. Or, if that proves impossible, the organization may elect to build the project in phases, thereby giving time to develop a stronger relationship with its prospective donors.

THE CASE FOR SUPPORT

What Is a Case for Support?

When an organization decides to conduct a capital campaign, there is much work to be done before the first gift is solicited. One of the first tasks in preparing for a campaign is developing a document that explains the project and its importance in the community. Such a statement is called the case for support.

The case for support lies at the heart of the campaign. Its words help persuade board members, volunteers, and donors to climb aboard the campaign train. It stirs them to action, moving them to support the campaign with their time and their dollars. And it reminds them why the organization is so important to their community. The case for support describes in simple and compelling terms those community needs that the organization hopes to address with the money it raises, and it presents a credible plan for satisfying those needs.

> *The case for support explains the campaign's rationale and answers basic questions that would convince a reader that the project is important and feasible.*

A preliminary draft of the case is presented to the organization's insiders and community leaders during the feasibility study, and their comments about it and about the organization will shape the direction of the campaign. The case for support is used to help recruit the campaign planning committee and steering committee as well as other volunteers, persuading them that they are signing on to a worthwhile venture that has an excellent chance for success. Volunteers use the case for support to devise talking points for face-to-face solicitations. The case for support serves as a starting point for grant proposals, direct mail letters, and press releases and is the most important resource for drafting the text of the campaign brochure.

> *The case for support is not just one document. It is an evolving and emerging story about an organization and the project it is about to undertake.*

How can one document possibly serve so many purposes? The case for support is not just one document. It is an evolving and emerging story about an organization and the new steps forward it is about to take. As a campaign progresses, the case for support grows and develops, becoming stronger and more compelling as details of the project become available for inclusion.

The case begins as a draft document and progresses through many iterations, each becoming more polished and refined. The case might begin as a three- to five-page statement for use during the feasibility study. Later, when the feasibility study has validated or adjusted the preliminary goal, when the steering committee has been formed, and as the organization begins to raise money toward its campaign goal, the case for support will be expanded to include the new information. Every time new information is added, the enhanced case for support will be all the more compelling in showing others that the campaign is likely to succeed.

The case is likely to take other forms as well. During the solicitation process it will become a spoken set of persuasive "arguments" to convince donors that they should support the organization. It will become a brochure. It may even become a video, a skit, or a direct-mail piece.

The Content of the Case

Even though some information in the case will change as it evolves, certain pieces of information remain the same. The case simply and succinctly explains to its readers how their gifts will make a difference, not only to the organization but to the community as a whole. More specifically, the case presents the following information:

- community or societal need that the organization addresses
- organization's goals and programs
- organization's past and present accomplishments
- summary of the organization's products and services
- organization's future opportunities in light of the community's needs
- projects or programs that will be made possible by the campaign
- realistic plan of action
- campaign dollar goal
- key people involved in raising the money

Wise authors understand that their words will continue to evolve and improve as the case for support is shared with others and as new information becomes available. Therefore, every organization should invest in a rubber stamp with the word DRAFT in large letters and a red inkpad to go with it. A document that is stamped as a draft encourages input from others, enabling them to contribute to the case.

The Power of Process

Just as important as the finished case is the process used to develop it. Since the case is written in a series of drafts, every draft gives people the opportunity to contribute their thoughts about the case and about the organization. A good case incorporates the ideas of many people into a coherent statement of values and possibilities for the organization; the case condenses and clarifies many ideas into a consistent and compelling story that underpins and strengthens the campaign. Paying attention to the ideas of others who care about the organization also builds ownership and encourages constituents to think about the organization perhaps more deeply than they have ever done before.

Developing a Credible Plan for Compelling Needs

The Declaration of Independence is a wonderful example of a case for support. Those who haven't read or

heard it in a while should track down a copy and see for themselves. Granted, Thomas Jefferson wasn't trying to raise $1 million to refurbish and expand the assembly room in Independence Hall, but in writing the Declaration of Independence he incorporated many of the same elements one finds in an effective case for support.

The Declaration presented a problem that affected American society as a whole. Jefferson did not hesitate to list reasons for declaring independence. Indeed, the injuries committed against the colonies by King George III and the British Parliament clearly resonated with many of the colonists who read or heard the Declaration. The list of grievances describes the compelling need, and a compelling need is precisely what must be outlined in a case for support.

Blown Away by the Draft

I'll never forget my meeting with our campaign consultant as we began work on the preliminary case for support. We needed to send it out to the committee that was overseeing the feasibility study, and it was a rush job. I was full of anxiety, trying to get every word perfect. At one point the consultant turned to me and said, "Where's your draft stamp?"

"My what?" I replied.

"Your draft stamp," she insisted, "so we can stamp the copies of the case document we're preparing. If we don't leave opportunities for the members of the committee to add their ideas, they'll feel they've been presented with a *fait accompli*, and we will have lost a great chance to build ownership in this project."

"Oh, right, draft stamp," I said, taken aback. It then took me a few minutes to accept the fact that my words didn't have to be perfect. In fact, the more I tried to create the perfect document, the more likely it was that I would become defensive about any proposed changes during our committee meeting.

Well, the idea of presenting a document that was deliberately less than perfect was tremendously liberating. The very next day I went out and bought a big red draft stamp. And now, knowing that when I use it I'm indicating that I'd like others' opinions has freed me up. I still like to present fine prose, but I plan from now on to leave the door open for other people's suggestions.

—Public Relations Director, Hospice

The Small Amish Structure

Recently I worked on a campaign to computerize a public library in the heart of Amish country. At the campaign kickoff the case for support was presented as a skit by a businessman who was serving on the campaign's steering committee. Wally was the head of a major business in the community, but he also just happened to be expert at speaking with an Amish accent.

As the skit opened, Amos (Wally dressed in black pants, oversized boots, and a black Amish hat) and his wife, who also dressed for the part, walked hesitantly into the public library. They were looking for reference material, and they clearly didn't know their way around very well. But they were embarrassed about informing the librarian just what it was exactly that they were researching. They indicated that they were looking for designs and specifications of—and here it became vague—a small structure. They didn't seem able to explain any better than that. The librarian thought she understood and tried to help them by consulting the microfiche catalog for information on sheds, barns, and garages. But none of those was quite what Amos and his wife were looking for. Finally Amos said, "No, no, we want to build a small building with a moon cut out of the door." Aha! At last the librarian understood, and she directed them to the library's reference material on the design, construction, and ventilation of outhouses. The audience understood how much easier a time the Amish couple would have had if the library had been automated and our friend Amos could simply have typed "outhouse" into the computer!

Without a doubt, Wally's presentation of the library's case for support was one of the most effective and memorable cases I have ever seen. People still chuckle about Wally's skit, but more importantly, they understood viscerally what library computerization was all about.

—Campaign Consultant

In the last paragraph of the Declaration of Independence Jefferson presents a plan of action—to break away from the mother country. It was a risky plan, yet those who pledged their allegiance to one another and to their new country believed that the goal was worth the risk. The plan conveys a sense of urgency while presenting a well-thought-out set of arguments designed to convince France to join with the colonists in their fight against England. Jefferson's style and tone urge the reader to action.

In terms of process, Jefferson himself was keenly aware of the problems that the colonies faced, and he was convinced of their need for independence. He wrote the first draft of the Declaration based on his own convictions. Then he submitted it to the committee of the whole for revisions. Through that process, every man in the Continental Congress who signed his name to the final document became a full owner of the Declaration and the ideas it represented. If an organization can produce a document as compelling as the Declaration of Independence, its campaign will certainly be off to a good start.

The first draft of a case for support should include four distinct segments that inform the reader why the organization must embark on the campaign.

1. **What needs will the campaign address?** This question is a good starting place. An organization's needs are often clarified and amplified as it develops a plan for the future. An organization might need a new building or a sophisticated computer system or improvements to its child-care center. Most needs addressed by a capital campaign are concrete and specific and will enable an organization to improve or increase its services.

2. **Why would the organization's needs inspire someone to give?** The needs of an organization are compelling only as they relate to the community it serves. For example, a donor is not likely to be excited by the fact that an organization needs a new office building. The new building becomes exciting to donors because of the good it will enable the organization to accomplish in the community. The case might describe the new adult literacy center inside the building, the increased numbers of patients who can be treated in the new hospital wing, the greater efficiency of the staff, or any of the other consequences that the new building will have in improving life in the community. People give in order to make a difference to others, not to finance an organizational wish list.

3. **Why is the proposed project important now?** Projects are usually fueled by changing circumstances in the community. To continue to provide good service, the organization must keep up with such changes. Perhaps its clientele is growing rapidly and the organization is running out of space, or perhaps it is responding to new needs that have surfaced in the community. Whatever the specifics, the case for support must convey a sense of urgency.

   Sometimes the answer to the "Why now?" question is simple: "Our building is being torn down." "We have long waiting lists of people we can no longer serve in our current space." "Our patient census has declined sharply because we can't perform the full range of services people require." All of these reasons contain the seeds of urgency. The strongest reasons for urgency are external—those based on community need.

4. **How will the organization meet the need?** It's fine to talk about meeting the needs of the community in a general fashion, but to convince anyone of the real need for funds, the case will have to tell the story of how the organization plans to address those needs. The plan must have its own logic, it must make financial sense, and it must resonate with the perceptions of both the organization and the community. The plan must describe the project crisply and clearly—size, shape, location, cost, timetable—so that, in a short time, the reader can grasp the gist of the project and understand that the organization has done its homework. Usually, the better the homework the clearer and more convincing is this part of the case.

The best cases for support are more than stuffy documents; they are lively, interesting, fun to read, unpretentious, and moving. In the end, such seemingly peripheral characteristics count for as much as the actual content.

> *The best cases for support are more than stuffy documents; they are lively, interesting, fun to read, unpretentious, and moving.*

In drafting the case for support, the following nine points should be kept in mind (see Exhibit 3–2):

1. **The case is an investment prospectus.** Prior to investing in a company, a smart investor finds out as much as possible about the company. What are its mission and corporate vision? Where does it see itself going in the next few years? Who runs the company? What is its financial position? The case for support must also present a sound investment opportunity. The "investor" should be able to tell what an investment in the organization will accomplish for the community. And those proposed accomplishments must be framed in a way that is interesting and compelling to the investor.

2. **The case answers basic questions about the organization.** After reading the case, a prospect should understand what the organization does; when and why it was created; and, in the final version, the names of the key people involved in the campaign. The case reflects the organization's mission and describes its priorities for the future.

Exhibit 3–2 Case Requirements

The case for support should . . .

. . . be an investment prospectus.
. . . answer basic questions about the organization.
. . . have broad implications for the community.
. . . be supportable and defensible.
. . . be both rational and emotional.
. . . be optimistic.
. . . be brief.
. . . be easy to remember.
. . . call people to action.

3. **The case must have broad implications for the community.** The case must have broad and current appeal. It must stress societal opportunities, not merely discuss the organization's needs. It should state the value that will accrue to the community if the proposed program is carried out and how the community's quality of life will be enhanced.

4. **The case must contain statements that are supportable and defensible.** The case is not the place to exaggerate the organization's accomplishments or capabilities. Simple, straightforward language that presents the organization's strengths in a realistic and distinctive way will be more effective than overstated claims.

5. **Successful cases are both rational and emotional.** People give with their hearts as well as their heads. The case must appeal to both. While donors are touched by stories of people who have been impacted by problems in society, recent, highly publicized scandals in the nonprofit world have served to make donors much more aware of the issues of an organization's fiscal responsibilities, board governance, and accountability.

6. **The case must be optimistic.** Care should be taken not to overwhelm the reader with the magnitude of the problem, to the extent that the reader becomes sure that it cannot be fixed. The case should evoke a feeling of hope and promise.

7. **The case should be brief.** If one wants one's prospects to read the case for support, then it must be brief and well written. It should be just long enough to cover the necessary information and inspire the reader, yet not so long that a casual reader will be put off by its length. If a reading of a draft of the case leads to eyes glazing over, then one may be sure that the case is too long and probably not well written.

8. **The case should be easy to remember.** The content of a good case is often translated into "talking

points" for board members, campaign volunteers, and solicitors. The written document gives them confidence and information, but its real power is in solidifying the arguments for the project in a form that is easily broken down into three or four major points that solicitors can recall and use in conversation.

9. **The case should move people to action.** Just like the project discussed in the Declaration of Independence, the organization's project must happen now. The case is one of the many ways of inspiring action, and action is what will be needed if the campaign is to succeed.

Who Should Write the Case?

Who should write the first draft of the case for support? Like many issues in campaign planning, there is no single correct answer. The case can be written by the development director, the executive director, the public-relations director (if the organization has one), the campaign consultant, or a freelance writer who specializes in development writing.

The case writer should have a good understanding of the institution's history. If the author is a staff person, much of the historical information will be readily available, either in memory or in the organization's files. However, staff members may be subject to political sensitivities within the organization, have a lack of objectivity about events in the organization's history, or be unable to step back and look at the organization with a fresh eye, thus limiting their effectiveness as writers of the case. If, on the other hand, a consultant writes the case for support, he or she will likely not be subject to such organizational pressures but will understandably need more time and assistance to learn about the organization.

A case is not written in a vacuum. The writer must be able to gather and process information from a wide variety of sources. These sources may include board minutes; annual reports; interviews with staff, key constituents, volunteers, and board members; and feature articles about the organization. The writer must be able to find the significant nuggets of information in these diverse sources and put them together to create a meaningful and persuasive document that engages the reader's heart and mind.

This may seem like a lot of work for what starts out as a short document. But even if the writer uses only a fraction of the accumulated material, the learning process will provide a feel for the case's audience, the style of language commonly used in the organization's materials, and the historical context in which the campaign is being planned. All of this background material will in-

form and improve decisions made throughout the campaign.

Finally, the writer must understand the purpose of a case for support. Writing such a document is different from writing a grant proposal, a press release, or an annual report. Whoever writes the case must understand these differences. The writer must know how the case will be used and have a thorough grasp of the elements that go into it.

It may be tempting to ask a board member or volunteer to draft the case for support, but here a word to the wise is in order. Writing a case for support can be a bruising task, and it is not wise to bruise an important volunteer. The willing volunteer may be happy to take on the task, but what if, as may well happen, the first draft is submitted and it's just plain bad? Then one is stuck either with an ineffective and poorly written case or with a bruised volunteer.

Board members and volunteers are wonderful sources for quotations, factual information, and general impressions about the organization, but unless one of them has particular expertise in this area, he or she should not be expected to take on the challenging responsibility of preparing the case for support. Furthermore, it is much easier for a board or group of volunteers to critique a document candidly and honestly if they know that one of their own was not involved in its creation.

Involving Insiders

Drafting the case for support is an opportunity to engage key insiders in thinking through the reasons for the campaign. The discussions, the give and take, and the compilation of everyone's hopes and dreams for the organization can be exhilarating and can help build the necessary understanding and support for a successful campaign.

Who are these special insiders? They are the individuals who are most closely involved with an organization. Typically, they include representatives from the following categories:

- founders
- board members
- former board members
- volunteers
- donors
- professional staff
- constituents
- key community leaders

There are many ways to involve these insiders. Some organizations, stretched for time and energy, assemble an ad hoc committee to work with the case writer. Other organizations conduct a series of interviews with their insiders.

Using a Committee to Develop the Case

A committee can spend one or more sessions discussing key elements of the case for support. They are then the first to review and comment on the initial draft. The committee should comprise from six to eight people representing a variety of the organization's constituencies.

Using Interviews to Develop the Case

In some organizations, instead of conducting meetings, the writer conducts a set of individual interviews with six to eight individuals familiar with different aspects of the organization and the community. During the interviews (see Exhibit 3–3), the writer builds a set of impressions and opinions about the organization and how it has made a difference in people's lives. These stories can then be used to breathe life into the case.

> *Good interviewing requires good listening. A good listener checks his or her ego at the door before starting the interview.*

Sitting Down to Write the Case

Once the interviews or committee meetings have been completed, the material gathered, and all relevant information amassed, it is time to begin sifting through the reams of notes and information for those invaluable bits and pieces that are going to build an outstanding case.

The pages and pages of notes can seem overwhelming. How does one begin to impose order on chaos, rather than the other way around? Some writers take multitudinous notes and then condense the material into a well organized and tight outline. Others review all the material in one sitting, then put it all aside and begin to write. Whatever process turns out to be the most satisfactory, it is important to remember that this document will be rewritten many times before the end of the campaign. And anyone who has ever written anything knows that the person who has the courage to do battle with a blank piece of paper deserves a medal.

Exhibit 3–3 Case Statement Interview Questions

1. How did you first become involved with the organization?
2. In your own words, describe the mission of the organization.
3. How has the organization's work affected you personally?
4. What contributions to the community does the organization make that are important to you?
5. What three words best describe the organization to you?
6. Why do you think this project is important to the community?
7. What is most compelling to you about the project?
8. What are your greatest concerns about the project?
9. What details would you like to see included about the project in the case for support?
10. What is the single most important reason that you believe someone would support the project?

For those who write best from an outline, a sample outline for the case has been included below. This outline may help in organizing one's thoughts into the four sections that generally work well in cases for support. It may be, however, that the muse will suggest a different organization for the case. As long as it covers all the necessary areas, has its own compelling logic, and reads well, any order is fine. Generally, however, the case document emerges more or less as follows:

1. The introduction to the project—a preliminary description of the project set in a context that describes community needs
2. The background for the project—information about the organization, including date of founding, mission, accomplishments, importance in the community, and growth
3. The project—a deeper look at the project: what, why, where, when, how, and how much
4. The project's benefits to the community—a summary of what the project will accomplish

Simple Guidelines for Effective Layout

Good graphics are just as important in a case for support as is good writing. With good word-processing and desktop-publishing software, it is possible to create a very satisfactory layout for the initial version of the case for support. It would be worthwhile to become familiar with the following six simple layout basics before preparing the first draft:

1. Use ample white space to show off text.
2. Use one easy-to-read serif typeface
3. Use bullets and headings to organize the flow of the argument.
4. Use drawings and charts to convey information and add variety.
5. Use quotations to add the human touch.
6. A graphic designer can help present your case in the most effective way.

Gathering Opinions, Building Ownership

Throughout this chapter, mention has been made of the importance of involving many of the organization's insiders in shaping the case. Not only will this help clarify the most compelling arguments for the project, but every time another individual contributes to the process that person learns more about the project and increases his or her stake in the project's success.

> *People should be involved strategically in developing and reviewing the case for support.*

People should be involved strategically in an order and with a protocol that builds support. Because the draft of the case for support may well be the first document that sets forth in writing the specifics of a new project, the process of sharing it must be handled with care. In the early stages, the case is simply a working document that will help the committee and the board grasp and clarify a project that they may have been talking about for some time. The very first draft should, therefore, be shared only with the board.

After the executive director, the writer, and perhaps the case committee are satisfied with the first draft, it should be shown to the board chair and the development committee chair for their comments. Then, after their suggestions have been incorporated, it can be sent to the entire board. It should be sent with a cover memo from the executive director and/or board chair reminding everyone about the case's purpose and setting some guidelines for the board's critique. Establishing a framework for comments will simplify the job of gathering and incorporating suggestions. A sample of such guidelines is in Exhibit 3–4.

The first draft of the case often makes for lively discussion, and meeting time should be set aside for the board to ask questions and provide input. However, the meeting should not deteriorate into an occasion for writing by committee, and so care should be taken to focus the discussion on ideas and content rather than the specific choice of words and phrases. When a board member has a comment about word choice, it should be graciously noted but not discussed.

Sometimes it is hard to know whose opinions to incorporate and whose to leave out. Such decisions are influenced by politics and power as well as by the quality of the suggestions. When unsure whose suggestions to use and whose to leave out, it is helpful to remember that if the draft document captures the spirit and essence of the project, then each contributor will be happy to believe that he or she was among those who helped develop it. It is important to acknowledge and to thank everyone who provided input, whether or not his or her particular suggestions were actually incorporated into the text. Even the suggestions that were not used help determine the essence of the case.

Once the suggestions of the board have been incorporated, the case will be ready to use in the feasibility study. The feasibility study consultant will use this brief document of perhaps three or four pages during the study. The draft will inform those interviewed about the project

MEMORANDUM

TO: Board of Trustees
FROM: Jennifer Schaeffer
RE: Review of Case for Support
DATE: July 20, 2001

Please review and critique the enclosed draft of the case for support and return it to me with your comments by August 15. I plan to use your comments to help fine-tune and polish our case. We will then send it to each of the people being interviewed in the feasibility study.

Please keep the following questions in mind as you read the case and let me know your suggestions about how we might make it more effective.

- Does it answer the basic questions about our organization?
- Does it clearly and completely describe the project we have embarked on?
- Does it frame the reason for this project in terms of our community rather than our immediate need?
- Does it appeal both rationally and emotionally?
- Does it inspire a sense of urgency?

Thanks in advance for your help! I look forward to receiving your suggestions.
Enclosed is a stamped return envelope.

4. Gather information.
5. Determine the best strategy for involving insiders.
6. Select the insiders to involve.
7. Enlist the insiders (either for the committee or for interviews).
8. Conduct the committee meetings or interviews.
9. Prepare the first draft of the case.
10. Review the text with the executive director.
11. Review the text with the case committee.
12. Revise according to committee input.
13. Meet with the graphic designer (optional).
14. Review with and get input from the board.
15. Revise according to board input.
16. Distribute the new version to those who helped develop it.

Checklist for an Effective Case

An effective case grows out of a process that involves many people. It crystallizes the essence and spirit of the project that the organization is about to undertake. If the case for support is effective and the process used to develop it was successful, an organization should be able to respond affirmatively to each of the following four questions:

1. Do board members and other insiders "own" the case?
2. Is the case exciting?
3. Does the case respond to community needs rather than organizational needs?
4. Does the case outline a clear and credible plan?

and campaign plans and will also provide an opportunity for the consultant to gather input for later versions of the case for support.

The Many Faces of the Case

Though every case begins as a simple written document, as the campaign evolves the case will take on many other forms. It will be translated into talking points for solicitors and into grant proposals, direct-mail letters, and press releases. When the campaign enters its public phase, the case will be presented graphically as a campaign brochure and, in certain cases, a video.

To develop the case step by step, follow these 16 guidelines:

1. Review the purpose of the case for support.
2. Review the answers to the five Ws: who, what, when, where, why.
3. Decide who will write the case.

Using Humor to Engage the Reader

The Sciencenter in Ithaca, New York, used humor to spice up one of the later versions of its case for support, seeding it with funny but relevant phony quotations like "The Sciencenter concept is relatively simple" (Albert Einstein), or "Combining science and fun is an illuminating idea" (Thomas Edison), or "You can't build a Sciencenter with peanuts" (George Washington Carver). Their tongue-in-cheek method made one want to read every word of the case.

THE CAMPAIGN GOAL AND THE GIFT RANGE CHART

The gift range chart or table of gifts is the final campaign planning tool to be developed during this early phase of campaign planning. This table indicates the pattern in which gifts will be needed if the campaign is to succeed. Often a campaign consultant will help design the gift range chart. However, the process of exploring different combinations is an excellent exercise to focus the attention of the leadership of an organization. An early informal meeting to devise a suitable gift range chart will force those involved in the planning process to begin thinking in specific terms about which particular donors are likely to give at the various levels.

The Geometry of Giving

Because people have different financial capacities and giving patterns, the gifts that make up a campaign range from large to small. Although it is tempting to think about raising $500,000, for example, from 500 donors who give $1,000 apiece, it is also unrealistic. That's not how actual campaign gifts come in.

The pattern of giving in virtually all capital campaigns looks like a triangle. At the very top are the few leadership donors whose major gifts secure the success of the campaign. In the middle is a larger number of donors, many of whom are individuals, businesses, or foundations, who have given at relatively low levels over the years but who have stretched their giving budgets for the campaign. Many people in this middle category, even though they are not lead-gift donors, are opinion setters in the community, and their generous giving is extremely important. At the base of the triangle is the largest number of donors. This group of donors is the bread and butter of the organization—the many people who believe in the organization but do not have the resources or inclination to make a large gift. For a person in this category, his or her gift of $300 may be every bit as meaningful as the lead gift of $50,000 is to its donor.

The width and height of the giving pyramid varies from organization to organization in patterns that are somewhat predictable. A young institution with a small number of donors must rely more heavily on leadership gifts—a tall pyramid with a narrow base. Mature institutions with many donors and constituents are likely to have a broader-based pyramid.

Giving patterns are also determined by the organization's culture, history, and constituency. Some institutions are afraid to solicit leadership gifts, either because they are afraid of the power that large donors wield or because they lack the self-confidence, vision, and training needed to think big. Other organizations have relied on a small number of leadership gifts to support many aspects of their programs. Some organizations, like private schools, have clearly defined constituencies, resulting in a narrow base, while others, like community libraries, have a broad-based constituency.

DEVELOPING THE GIFT RANGE CHART

Patterns of Giving

Campaign after campaign reveals patterns of giving that are remarkably consistent and from which we can learn important principles of capital campaign fund raising. Each organization has its own giving pyramid (see Figure 3–1). Clear thinking about the culture, donor base, and giving histories of an organization will help predict the pattern that a campaign's gifts are likely to form. These patterns of giving, projected early in the campaign, are tools that help clarify and plan the campaign.

Two rules guide the development of most gift range charts:

The 90/10 Rule: Of the total raised in the campaign, 90 percent will come from 10 percent of the campaign's donors. It seems hard to believe that so few people could contribute so much, but time and again this rule has been proven true. Most campaigns, no matter what their size, raise most of their money from only a few donors.

The Just 10 Rule: The just 10 rule is closely tied to the 90/10 rule. The campaign's success will depend on its top 10 donors, no matter how large or small the campaign goal. The lead gift should constitute at least 10 to 15 percent of the campaign goal—although in some cases the lead gift may be much higher. These top 10 gifts are often referred to as "strategic" or "leadership" gifts. They set the pace for the campaign and act as magnets for other donors. Together, the top 10 leadership gifts, given early in the campaign, create a sense of optimism and a belief that the campaign will be successful. And of course, people are much more likely to become part of a campaign when they believe that it will succeed.

A Campaign Road Map

The gift range chart—or table of gifts, as it is sometimes called—is the road map for a campaign. Based on standardized giving patterns and tempered by the realities of the specific organization, a sample table of gifts for a specific campaign appears in Exhibit 3–5.

In this table, the lead gift constitutes 15 percent of the campaign goal, and just under one-half of the campaign total will come from the 10 largest gifts. Tables of gifts vary depending on the organization and campaign for which they are developed. A small, young organization with a limited but wealthy donor base might, for example, use a gift range chart for a million-dollar cam-

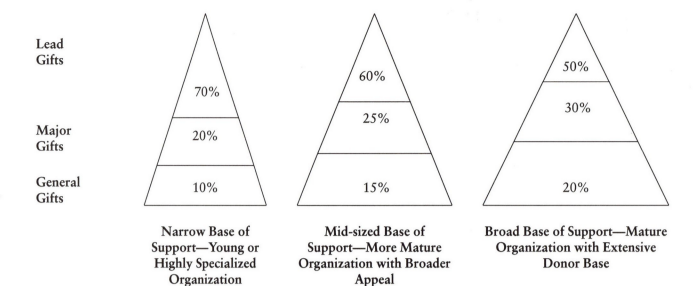

Lead Gifts			
	70%	60%	50%
Major Gifts			
	20%	25%	30%
General Gifts			
	10%	15%	20%
	Narrow Base of Support—Young or Highly Specialized Organization	Mid-sized Base of Support—More Mature Organization with Broader Appeal	Broad Base of Support—Mature Organization with Extensive Donor Base

Figure 3–1 Patterns of Giving

paign such as the one in Exhibit 3–6. In this gift range chart, half of the goal comes from just five gifts, and the total goal will be reached with 100-plus gifts.

For a broad-based, mature organization with thousands of annual donors and no history of major-gift fund raising, the pattern of giving might be more accurately projected with the table in Exhibit 3–7. Approximately one-half of the campaign goal for this organization will come from 41 donors.

Although the patterns of these three campaigns vary somewhat, they all require lead gifts of between 10 and 25 percent of the campaign goal and call for more donors as the size of the average gift declines.

In all of this, remember: Don't lower the lead gift! Although tables of gifts should be designed to fit the realities of each organization, it is difficult if not impossible to conduct a successful campaign with a lead gift that comprises less than 10 percent of the campaign goal. If a lead gift of at least that amount is not in the offing, the organization should either put off the campaign while it develops a major-gifts program to cultivate the lead gift, or lower the goal to a more appropriate level. Try-

Exhibit 3–5 Gifts Needed to Raise $1,000,000

Number	$ Amount	$ In Range	Cumulative $	% of Goal
1	$150,000	$150,000	$150,000	15%
1	75,000	175,000	225,000	22%
2	50,000	100,000	325,000	32%
6	25,000	150,000	475,000	47%
10	10,000	100,000	575,000	57%
20	5,000	100,000	675,000	67%
40	2,500	100,000	775,000	77%
80	1,000	80,000	855,000	87%
160	500	80,000	935,000	93%
300+/-	<$500	65,000	1,000,000	100%

Number of Gifts: 620+/-

Exhibit 3–6 Gifts Needed to Raise $1,000,000 (For a small, young organization with a wealthy donor base)

Number	$ Amount	$ In Range	Cumulative $	% of Goal
1	$250,000	$250,000	$250,000	25%
1	100,000	100,000	350,000	35%
3	50,000	150,000	500,000	50%
8	25,000	200,000	700,000	70%
12	10,000	120,000	820,000	82%
24	2,500	60,000	880,000	88%
40	1,000	40,000	920,000	93%
60	500	30,000	950,000	95%
100	<$500	$50,000	$1,000,000	100%

Number of Gifts: 250+/-

ing to run a capital campaign without a lead gift is not likely to broaden the bottom—it is more likely just to lop off the top.

Once an appropriate gift range chart for a campaign has been created, it can then be used as a tool to help design the campaign itself. It is a straightforward matter to estimate from the gift range chart how many prospects the campaign will have to solicit. Knowing how many solicitations will be needed will then make it possible to determine the number of solicitors and solicitation teams. Developing a gift range chart that fits the organization is critical to the design of a successful campaign.

THE GIFT RANGE CHART AND PROSPECT PLANNING

Estimating the Number of Prospects Required for Each Gift

Using the gift range chart as a guide, an organization can explore the number of prospects it has for each gift and compare that number to the number of prospects that are needed. Opinions vary on how many prospects are needed for each gift. Some people estimate more conservatively that it will take five prospects to get one gift. Others use a three-to-one ratio. Generally, however, an

Exhibit 3–7 Gifts Needed to Raise $1,000,000 (For a mature organization with a broad donor base)

Number	$ Amount	$ In Range	Cumulative $	% of Goal
1	$100,000	$100,000	$100,000	10%
1	50,000	50,000	150,000	15%
4	25,000	100,000	250,000	25%
10	10,000	100,000	350,000	35%
25	5,000	125,000	475,000	47%
60	2,500	150,000	625,000	62%
150	1,000	150,000	775,000	77%
300	500	150,000	925,000	92%
600+/-	<$500	$75,000	$1,000,000	100%

Number of Gifts: 1,150+/-

estimate of three to five prospects for every gift will be in the right ballpark.

By looking more carefully at the prospect-to-gift ratio, it is possible to fine-tune the numbers somewhat more precisely. One can divide the broad field of prospects into three categories of prospects who have different types of relationships with the organization, making them more or less ready to make a generous campaign gift. The prospect-to-gift ratio varies according to the relationship of the prospects to the organization.

- Highly qualified prospects are individuals and foundations or business decision makers
  - who have a strong and committed relationship with the institution
  - about whom there is substantial information regarding their area of interest, ability to give, and inclination to give

  Gift ratio: Two–three prospects per gift
- Somewhat qualified prospects are individuals and foundations or business decision makers
  - who have been identified as potential donors
  - who have some relationship with the institution
  - about whom there is limited information regarding their ability and/or inclination to give

  Gift ratio: Three–four prospects per gift
- Unqualified prospects are individuals and foundations or business decision makers
  - who have been identified as prospective donors
  - who have no relationship with the institution
  - about whom there is little information regarding their ability or inclination to give

  Gift ratio: Five–six prospects per gift

Although it may be cumbersome to use these categories when calculating the necessary number of prospects, it is nonetheless instructive, particularly when determining how many prospects will be required at the top of the giving pyramid.

With the help of the gift range chart, one can estimate approximately how many individuals must be solicited to make a campaign successful by evaluating how many prospects an organization has and estimating the appropriate multiplier for each giving category. Because the chances of getting a gift from an unqualified prospect are relatively low, it is wise to focus attention on more qualified prospects and consider any gifts from those less qualified to be unexpected windfalls.

An informal rating of an organization's donor lists by someone familiar with the organization and the community might lead to a reasonably accurate estimate of the number of solicitations that will be needed in the campaign. The goal is to review the donor lists, looking for prospects at each giving level. The prospect whose gift one is reasonably sure of should be given a multi-

plier of 2. Those who are likely to give to the campaign but whose giving level is less well defined might have a multiplier of 3 or 4.

In practice, the further down on the gift pyramid, the more difficult it is to accurately estimate the number of prospects needed. For the sake of planning, however, it is helpful to assume that for the lead gifts, a category in which one should only be soliciting well-qualified prospects, one will need two to three prospects per gift. For the mid-level or "major" gift categories, one will need three to four prospects per gift. And for the "general" or low-level gifts, one will need four to six prospects per gift.

A gift range chart used to estimate the number of solicitations might look like the one found in Exhibit 3–8.

THE FEASIBILITY STUDY

Dreams vs. Reality

Although fund-raising professionals tend to think of the feasibility study as belonging solely to the world of fund raising and development, professionals in many other fields also conduct such studies. An organization that is contemplating a feasibility study for a capital campaign may already have commissioned a feasibility study for the campaign's proposed project by a financial planner, land planner, architect, or land developer, thus there is often considerable confusion around the subject of such studies. The development officer and the campaign consultant may be bombarded with questions and comments from board members, and even staff, such as "I thought we had already done a feasibility study!" or "We need another feasibility study? What did all that money we paid to the developer go toward?"

What Is a Feasibility Study?

The purpose of all feasibility studies is to assist those who are planning a large project in evaluating the chances of the project's success before the project begins. Such studies provide an organized analysis of a project during its planning stages. This analysis allows the organization to determine what can realistically be accomplished in a campaign and indicates the most effective means of reaching those goals.

Feasibility studies are conducted by professionals, who gather data and examine and weigh the many factors that affect the outcome of the project. In particular, financial feasibility studies are likely to analyze market potential, population growth, demographic patterns, interest rates, income, expenses, and other elements that determine the financial feasibility of a project. Planning feasibility studies explore issues of zoning, land use, en-

Exhibit 3–8 Gift Range Chart and Prospects Required

LEAD GIFTS: 2–3 prospects/gift

	Gifts Needed	Amount of Gifts	Prospects Needed	Gift Range
	1	$150,000	2	$150,000
	1	$75,000	2	$75,000
	2	$50,000	6	$100,000
	6	$25,000	18	$150,000

Lead Gift Totals: 10 gifts   28 prospects needed

MAJOR GIFTS: 3–4 prospects/gift

	10	$10,000	30	$100,000
	20	$5,000	80	$100,000
	40	$2,500	160	$100,000

Major Gift Totals: 70 gifts   270 prospects needed

GENERAL GIFTS: 5–6 prospects/gift

	80	$1,000	400	$80,000
	160	$500	800	$80,000
	300+/-	<$500	1,500	$65,000

General Gift Totals: 700 gifts   2,700 prospects needed

Total: 780 gifts   2,998 prospects needed

vironmental restrictions, access roads, and other requirements and prohibitions that determine the development potential of a land parcel.

The Fund-Raising Feasibility Study Is Different

A fund-raising feasibility study, often referred to as a pre-campaign planning study, will consider in detail an organization's potential to raise funds for a particular project through a capital campaign. A well-done study will help the organization make the right decisions about conducting a campaign before the planning for a project has progressed very far. Specifically, a feasibility study

- assesses how much money can probably be raised for a project
- outlines the most effective fund-raising strategy
- assesses the organization's readiness for a campaign
- makes recommendations for a realistic and appropriate campaign goal
- presents a preliminary campaign timetable
- identifies potential campaign leaders and donors
- provides other insights about how the organization is viewed

As the name "pre-campaign planning study" implies, these studies do not directly answer the question "Can the organization raise money?" Rather, they indicate what amount of money can most likely be raised, and they outline how the organization should prepare itself for carrying out the capital campaign. But a pre-campaign planning study does much more than answer those questions. Such a study moves an organization forward by addressing more general issues. A study might highlight aspects of the organization that need to be strengthened and suggest concrete ways to address those issues. In other instances, a study may suggest alterations to the case for support that would be necessary to inspire contributors. A good study always provides important information to guide an organization to success, not only in its capital campaign but into its future as well.

> *A well-done feasibility study will help the organization make the right decisions about conducting a capital campaign before the planning for a project has progressed very far.*

The Feasibility Study Helps Build Relationships

In addition to providing crucial information about a campaign's chances of success, feasibility studies are excellent ways to involve and cultivate donors and leaders for the campaign. The primary data that inform a feasibility study are gathered through a series of interviews conducted by the consultant. Through one-on-one personal interviews, major donors, primary staff members, and key volunteers have a very real and important opportunity to participate in the project's decision-making process. Indeed, to be singled out to be interviewed for a feasibility study is to be singled out as a leader—someone whose opinion is valued.

> *A feasibility study is an excellent opportunity to involve people in the life of an organization.*

In many organizations, it is the feasibility study that constitutes the very first opportunity for individuals outside the immediate circle of the board to learn about and contribute to plans for advancing the cause of the organization.

Do We Really Need a Feasibility Study?

"All that unnecessary expense!" "Why don't we just start asking people for money and see what happens?" "We already know how much we need." "Let's just do it!" Such comments are often heard from board members or from the executive director.

Below are listed three of the most common objections and fears that arise when it is suggested that a feasibility study ought to be commissioned.

1. "It is too much of a risk to solicit candid opinions about our organization." While this fear probably won't be directly articulated, it may very well be an unspoken one among board and staff. It is not pleasant to imagine an outside consultant poking about, talking to the organization's major donors and key volunteers, who might say things that certain individuals would rather were left unsaid. The organization might learn some unpleasant things about itself that it would prefer not to know!

2. "If the study isn't positive, we may have to postpone our plan. And we have crucial needs, needs that can't wait." While it is not pleasant to contemplate the necessity of putting off attending to critical needs, it is much better to wait than to commit the organization to a campaign that is unlikely to succeed. As exemplified in the following story, a feasibility study can help an organization pinpoint

The Feasibility Study That Saved Us from Ourselves

Before I joined my organization, the decision had already been made to start a new program and afterward raise money through a capital campaign to pay off the debt. This decision ended up a financial and philosophical disaster. In an attempt to salvage what we could, we sought advice from a campaign consultant. She told us very clearly that it is difficult to find funding after the fact. Donors often prefer to create something new, and so are not particularly interested in paying off debt.

Eventually we decided to raise money for a new building to bring all of our services to one location. It sounded like a great idea, especially as we were about to begin celebrating our twenty-fifth anniversary in the community. Our consultant conducted a feasibility study, and told us that we were not yet ready to undertake a capital campaign. He recommended that we devote a year to involving our major donor prospects more deeply in the life of the organization. That was not news we were pleased to hear.

Internally he also felt we weren't ready, citing problems between our board and our executive director, who was new in her job and who did not yet possess the full confidence of the board.

We accepted the results of the feasibility study. We did not go ahead with a campaign. During the following year we began our major donor work, and following a traumatic wrangle with the staff and board, the executive director resigned.

As it turned out, the feasibility study saved us from blundering into something for which we were not prepared and which surely would have failed. Our entire agency would have been in trouble had we plunged ahead.

—Development Director

its weaknesses before committing itself to a campaign. Taking the time to prepare the organization thoroughly for the campaign is what spells the difference between failure and success.

3. "We were counting on the campaign to strengthen our development program. If the feasibility study says we can't move forward now, how can we generate the excitement that we need to advance our annual fund-raising program?" While it is true that one of the benefits of a successful campaign is a

strengthened and renewed development program, this cannot be the primary purpose of a campaign. Moreover, a lackluster campaign will undermine, not strengthen, the development program. If the organization's fund-raising programs are weak, then before even considering a capital campaign it will be necessary to concentrate on building and strengthening relationships with donors, fine-tuning recordkeeping systems, and working with the board on basic fund-raising techniques.

We Need $250,000. Please Give.

A small private school was forced out of the building it had occupied for many years. A college in the area offered land to the school and assistance if they could raise $250,000 to fund the project. The college was even able to locate an architect who was willing to donate a preliminary design. To raise the money, the school's board decided to hold their very first auction. The auction was held in the school's auditorium. Prominently displayed on the stage were drawings of the new building together with a list of rooms and the gifts needed to pay for them. The chairman of the board made an appeal from the stage, and then they waited for donations to come in. They have been waiting ever since.

The school's board learned several lessons from this auction, and they learned them, unfortunately, the hard way. They learned that it is impossible for a small organization to raise a quarter of a million dollars by bringing in 2,500 gifts averaging $100 each. They learned that their great need was not sufficient in and of itself to motivate people to make major gifts. They learned that if they wanted to raise major gifts they would have to make personal, targeted requests to individuals who already had an interest in the school. Finally, they learned that trying to raise money by the seat of their trousers without a credible plan simply would not work.

Although well intentioned, the board hadn't done its homework. (Not a good example for the students!) They understood their own needs—most of us are very familiar with our own needs—but they had no information about what their constituency might give to a campaign or what, for that matter, their constituency really thought about the planned relocation. There was no experienced fund raiser in the organization, and so, without background information and someone to guide them, they blundered ahead, souring their chances for a successful campaign.

Only when the fund-raising house is in order and fund-raising programs are stronger will the organization be ready to risk a campaign. Although campaigns require risks and an optimistic viewpoint, foolhardy risks and naïve optimism are no help at all. And undertaking a capital campaign without a feasibility study is a giant step down the path of foolhardiness.

A good feasibility study will repay its expense. It will cultivate major donors; it will provide a way of assessing the probability of a successful campaign; it will give a sense of whether there is a strong group of supporters who are eager to help or whether the development staff is so far out in front that volunteer support will quickly evaporate. The study may or may not provide the answers hoped for, but whether the study recommends "full steam ahead," a lower goal or longer timetable, or even "Do not pass Go, do not collect even two hundred dollars—yet," it will ultimately help the organization manage a successful campaign.

> *Not to have evaluated the probability of success for a capital campaign is to risk the future of the organization.*

Not to have evaluated the probability of success for a capital campaign is to risk the future of the organization. Because a capital campaign is highly visible and involves a great many individuals who are important to the organization, it is vital that it succeed. A pre-campaign-planning study provides the information and the plan that are necessary to minimize the risk of a failure.

When Should a Feasibility Study Be Undertaken?

The timing of a study is critical. Studies are conducted after a major project has been conceived and a general project plan developed but before the plan is finalized. A feasibility study explores the primary constituency's reactions to a specific project and invites selected individuals to provide constructive input. All parties whose advice is desired should be consulted at this point, because once a project plan has been finalized, there is a very limited opportunity to alter it to reflect further suggestions.

> *Studies are conducted after a major project has been conceived and a general plan developed but before the plan is finalized.*

Before a study is undertaken, therefore, the following aspects of the project should be known, at least in general terms:

- What project does the organization wish to accomplish with the money raised?
- How will this project be realized?
- When will it be completed?
- How much is it likely to cost?
- How will it be paid for?
- How much money does the organization anticipate raising through a campaign?
- Who are the key individuals on whom the success of the project depends (staff, architect, contractor, or other primary players if known)?

These questions are similar to those addressed in the case for support. Because people rarely give major gifts to organizations without knowing in some detail how their money will be spent, a clear idea of the project must be articulated before someone is hired to probe the reactions of the donor base. A donor might well evince small interest in making a large gift to fund an infant-care wing of a day-care center if that individual believes that a mother's place is at home with her preschoolers. That very same person, however, might give generously to fund a new wing to house an after-school program for elementary-school children. Therefore, a feasibility study cannot be successfully undertaken before a clear outline of the project has been developed.

It is also important to conduct the feasibility study fairly early in the planning process because it may be discovered that the organization's needs fail to match the donors' interests. It is far preferable to make such a discovery early than to launch a full-scale campaign for an enterprise that no one wants to support.

What Will the Study Evaluate?

A thorough study will evaluate both the readiness of an organization to undertake a campaign and the readiness of a community of donors to support it. It should evaluate the following elements of the program and donor base:

- the organization's reputation with community leadership
- the effectiveness and reputation of the organization's chief executive
- the strength and giving potential of the board
- the willingness of the board to work on a campaign
- the size and giving record of the donor base
- the availability of volunteers to work on a campaign
- the potential for lead gifts
- the likelihood of recruiting an effective campaign chair

A study will also test the reaction of leaders and major donor prospects to the proposed project and cam-

---

They Told Us They Wanted a Nicer-Looking Library

The goal of our campaign was to automate sixteen libraries in the countywide public library system. One of the things we learned from the feasibility study undertaken by our consultant was that many of our donors were quite eager to support the libraries, and, moreover, they thought that the automation project was very important. However, they didn't think it was quite so important as improving the appearance of the main library. We knew that the library needed repairs, but we had thought that a renovation campaign was a campaign better left for another day.

As a result of the feasibility study we decided to fashion a case for support that combined the automation project with building improvements. We came up with a price tag of $2.1 million, which deflated our enthusiasm somewhat, since the feasibility study had concluded that we could probably raise no more than $1.5 million. The core committee met and discussed the money issue at length. We considered and considered again just what it would actually mean to try to raise such a large amount. The group finally decided that we could do it—that we should "go for it." And so we did.

Ultimately, we did raise the entire $2.1 million by our deadline—with four days to spare—but we really worked hard to make that happen.

—Executive Director

---

paign. It will help answer some of the following questions regarding the project:

- Is the proposed project perceived as important to the community?
- Does the project make sense?
- Are the plans appropriate for both the organization and the community?
- Does the project have a strong chance of succeeding?
- Are donors who have the ability to make major gifts likely to be major contributors to this particular project?
- How much money is the organization likely to be able to raise for this project?
- Who are the individuals whose participation and assistance will be most likely to make this project succeed?
- What are the best strategies and approaches for the campaign?

- Are there enough people willing to help with the campaign, and will they be dedicated enough to see the campaign through to completion?
- Is there sufficient staff to conduct a campaign properly?
- How much is the campaign likely to cost?
- What is a reasonable timetable for the campaign?
- What must the organization do to get ready for a campaign?

The Feasibility Study Process

Who Conducts the Study?

A feasibility study gives the organization a chance to take an objective look at itself and the project it has planned. To obtain truly objective information will require the assistance of an outside consultant. Although the organization's staff will be able to plan the project, an objective study cannot be accomplished with internal personnel, who are by definition simply too close to the organization.

Because of the close, ongoing ties with individuals in the community, it will be awkward for a staff member to ask certain questions that must, however, be posed, and it will also sometimes be difficult to hear what people are really trying to say.

Conducting a Feasibility Study

The feasibility study process falls into four categories: (1) preparing a preliminary case for support; (2) developing a gift range chart; (3) gathering information through interviews and surveys; and (4) preparing and presenting the report.

1. **Preliminary case for support.** Because feasibility studies solicit information, testing the potential of a specific project, an organization must prepare a brief statement that clearly and convincingly describes the project that is to be evaluated. For the purposes of the feasibility study, the case for support is presented in draft or preliminary form. The case is usually three to five pages long, computer generated, simply presented, and copied. The preliminary case for support is sent to the people whose opinions are being sought through the interview process, giving them an opportunity to read and digest the information prior to the interview.
2. **The gift range chart.** During the feasibility study interviews, the consultant gathers information about size and number of potential lead gifts. Many consultants do this by showing the gift range chart to the people they interview and asking for their thoughts on where the lead gifts might come from.

We've Done Our Own Feasibility Study!

When I met with a prospective client recently, I was soon informed that they had already conducted their own feasibility study. They were ready to go, and just needed some consulting help with the campaign itself. As we talked about how their campaign might proceed, I asked them if they had identified any major donors through their feasibility study. They reported that they had asked key community leaders their opinions about the organization and the project, as well as questions about the "fund-raising climate" in the community, in the hope of gleaning information about their chances of success. They learned a lot from their interviews, but they didn't learn whether and how much their lead donors would be likely to give to them. These folks were flying blind. In essence, they had done a community-needs assessment through their interviews and not a fund-raising feasibility study. They still had to find a way to figure out how much money they would be likely to raise, but they had just not been able to bring themselves to pose to their major-donor prospects the necessary blunt and straightforward questions about potential gifts.

The director of this organization felt awkward asking these individuals how much they might consider giving to a capital campaign for his agency because it seemed almost as if he were asking for the money for himself, and he was afraid of being turned down. This organization may to some extent have done its own feasibility study, but the study had failed to give them the information they needed to make the necessary decisions.

—Campaign Consultant

Most consultants also ask the interviewees to indicate whether they will consider a gift and, if so, where on the chart they might place themselves.

3. **Gathering information.** The primary method of gathering information for a feasibility study is through personal interviews. A typical feasibility study for a community-based organization should include personal interviews with community leaders, leaders of the organization, the organization's major donors, and other key constituents. Some feasibility studies also gather information from a broader cross-section of people in a community by sending surveys in the mail.

Interview questions are designed to solicit information about the reputation of the organization and its programs, chief executive, and board; the project being proposed; and the potential for gifts and volunteer assistance to the capital campaign.

4. **Preparing and presenting the report.** After the material is assembled, a written report must be prepared. The feasibility study report should summarize the process by which the material was gathered, synthesize and summarize the information gathered, and present clear recommendations about whether and how to proceed with a capital campaign.

It is a common (and wise) practice for consultants to share a draft of the report with the executive director and board chair before distributing it to the full board. This practice will help the consultant catch any errors that might have been made prior to a wider distribution of the report. It will also give the director and board chair the opportunity to reflect on the information contained in the report and to determine how and when the report should be presented to the committee and the rest of the board.

With a lengthy and complex report—which most feasibility study reports are—the committee members and the board should receive a copy of the report at least five days prior to the meeting at which the recommendations will be presented.

Because the material in the report is insider information, each copy of the report should be stamped CONFIDENTIAL before being distributed.

FEASIBILITY STUDY CONSULTANTS

Although chapter 4 describes in detail the process of selecting a campaign consultant, when it comes time to conduct a feasibility study, one develops a clearer idea of whom one does or does not want as a consultant. In many ways, the feasibility study consultant will serve as the organization's representative to the leadership of the community, lead donors, key volunteers, and any other individuals who are likely to be important to the organization.

The consultant is likely to hear all sorts of things—both good and bad—about the organization and its leadership. And the consultant will leave a distinct impression on the people interviewed—people important to the organization. The selection of the consultant is not to be taken lightly.

What Can Be Expected?

What can be expected from the feasibility study consultant? Lots! The organization has engaged an expert to guide it through a complex and sensitive process, and

---

The Misinformed Director and the Misguided Feasibility Study

I had never worked for a nonprofit organization before, but I had considerable practical experience doing similar development work for other types of organizations. When this nonprofit advertised for a director, I thought, "This is something I'd like to do." They hired me, and, when I arrived on the scene, I was immediately handed a $2.6 million campaign goal, a goal that was based solely on the organization's needs.

In retrospect, I can't believe how naïve I was, but when I came in I was told by the board, "Don't worry, you won't have to do any fund raising yourself because we have a committee who will raise all the money. All you have to do is run the organization." Now, the board really believed this. They had engaged someone to head the campaign who was quite well known and well loved and who had raised a lot of money before. I thought we had it in the bag, and that all I would have to do was manage the building project. Well, that was mistake number one.

It also turned out that the "feasibility study" I had been shown was not a feasibility study at all, but rather something that one of the board members had written up about the project. It was really more of a modest first pass at a case statement than a feasibility study, but to the uninitiated it sounded pretty good.

When I finally realized that I couldn't just sit back and watch disaster strike, I brought someone on board to help us put together a business plan and to perform a real feasibility study. This feasibility study told us that we had a problem with name recognition in the community. The individuals interviewed could not conceive of a $2.6 million campaign for an organization that they had never donated to before. Facing a potential flop, we reconnoitered, reevaluated, and regrouped. We broke our campaign into phases, and now, having recovered from the first successful phase, we are gathering energy for the second.

—Executive Director

---

that is precisely what the consultant should do. In fact, by the time a contract has been signed, the consultant should have outlined the process and timetable of the study quite specifically. Answers should be obtained to the questions discussed below. To help put these questions and answers in perspective, each of the questions that might be put to the consultant will be discussed in some detail, for there is a wide range of styles and issues that determine whether the feasibility study, as proposed, is right for a particular organization.

Who Will Work with the Consultant?

Every consultant has his or her own way of organizing a feasibility study, but many experienced consultants encourage the involvement of key volunteers to oversee their work, thereby building internal ownership of the study. Experienced consultants understand that the purpose of the campaign is not only to raise money, but to build and strengthen relationships with the organization's donors. For these consultants, the process of organizing the feasibility study provides an excellent opportunity to involve key volunteers on an ad hoc feasibility study committee, thereby actively engaging key volunteers and donor prospects in the early phases of planning the campaign.

Who Will Draft the Preliminary Case for Support?

Will the development staff be completely responsible for the preliminary case for support, or will the consultant be involved in its development? The consultant's broad experience in capital campaigns can be employed to advantage in drafting an effective and compelling case for support. However, because the development staff knows and can articulate the organization's needs better than an outsider, the preliminary gathering of information and writing should be performed by staff.

How Will the Consultant Gather Information?

Most feasibility studies for community-based campaigns rely extensively on personal interviews. Occasionally, a consultant will suggest that only a very few interviews be conducted in person and that additional information be gathered by means of a telephone or mail survey. However, because people will often say things in person that they would not put on paper, the primary power of a feasibility study comes from personal interviews. The consultant who is selected should be willing to conduct enough interviews to cover all of the individuals who are most important to the organization as well as a good cross section of community leadership.

The number of interviews will vary, depending on the size of the organization and the size of the community. For an established agency in a community with a population of 100,000 to 250,000, one might expect a consultant to conduct 30 to 40 interviews.

If a consultant from the area has been engaged, it is likely that the consultant will want to schedule the interviews to make the most effective use of available time and to be as flexible as possible in fitting the schedules of the interview subjects. But if the consultant will be coming in from out of town on specified days, then it will probably make more sense for the staff to be in charge of scheduling. Scheduling is always a complex and time-consuming task, but for someone not familiar with the area it can be particularly difficult.

It is important for the development staff to know who, from the consultant's agency, will actually conduct the interviews and to have the opportunity to meet that person. Because it is difficult for one person to conduct several dozen interviews and remain open and fresh, the interviews might be divided among two or three interviewers who can then compare impressions with one another to form a more accurate picture than that which is obtainable by a single interviewer.

When Will the Consultant Report?

Although consultants vary in their practices, some consultants give a verbal report to the oversight committee after completing approximately one-half of the interviews. In that way, the committee has a chance to learn firsthand about the interview process and how it is proceeding. Moreover, at this midway meeting, both the committee members and the consultant will be able to ask questions that may have arisen. In some cases this is also a good time to reconsider the interview list. If, for example, the consultant has had a high percentage of individuals who are unable or unwilling to be interviewed, or if the interview subjects have themselves suggested additional interview prospects, the committee may choose to add some names to the list.

What Sorts of Questions Will Be Asked?

The consultants can be expected to develop a series of interview questions to help guide the interviews. Consultants vary widely in their manner of conducting interviews. Some use detailed forms that can later be collated and scored numerically, thereby providing the basis for a statistical analysis of the interviews. Others use a simple outline to guide more general conversations and rely on extensive note taking to capture information.

Most consultants gather information in four areas—opinions about the organization, the project, the funding, and the leadership. Interviews often begin with the most general questions and move to the specifics of the subject's ability and willingness to help. Initial questions often establish the interviewee's relationship with the organization and determine his or her views of that organization, its board, its programs, and its staff. Then interviews elicit opinions about the proposed project—its importance in the community, its feasibility, and any reservations or concerns that the person might have. The interviews then explore the potential for raising funds and attracting volunteer leadership, including where major gifts might be sought and who in the community might be considered as a campaign leader. And finally, the interviews should probe the giving potential of the subject and his or her willingness to help with the campaign.

In general, one is well advised to beware of statistical analyses with a small interview sample. Among those interviewed are certain to be a few individuals whose responses are absolutely crucial in determining the goals, timetable, and probability of success for the campaign. In a sample of 25 or 30 interviews, the importance of those few opinions that carry significantly more weight than the others will be lost in an analysis that accords equal weight to all responses. Therefore, although it may be interesting to see an objective statistical report on the response to each interview question, this type of reporting does not provide the judgments that are really needed.

What Will Be in the Report?

Feasibility study reports vary as widely as styles of consulting. Some consultants produce lavish, lengthy reports printed on elegant paper. Others prefer a simpler, more straightforward approach. Although there is no single acceptable format for the report, its style should reflect the requirements of the organization. It would not do, for example, for the consultant to submit a 70-page, triple-spaced report copied on only one side of a page to an organization whose primary mission was to save trees. On the other hand, an exclusive private school with a wealthy, high-powered board might not take seriously a report without a cover and an elegant format.

More important than the style is that the report be well written with no errors in spelling, grammar, or punctuation. (It is amazing how many reports are littered with such lapses.) The information should be clearly and simply presented. It should be prefaced with an executive summary for those who don't have the time or patience to read a long report. It should contain a summary of the interview findings, conclusions reached, recommendations as to how the organization should proceed, and a list of people interviewed.

The report of the feasibility study should include conclusions and recommendations on the following topics:

- the reputation of the organization
- the effectiveness and validity of the case for support
- the readiness of the volunteer and staff leadership to accept major roles in the campaign
- the willingness of key volunteers and prospects to make leadership campaign pledges
- the readiness of other major donors to support a campaign

- the conditions external to the organization that are likely to affect the campaign
- an outline of how to proceed, along with a preliminary timetable

Although not all consultants are willing to offer an estimate of how much money they believe can be raised if their advice is followed, such a recommendation (often in the form of a dollar range) should be part of every feasibility study report. This issue should be discussed with the consultant before a contract is signed.

How Will the Report Be Distributed?

Organizational leaders should discuss with a consultant how they plan to present the report to the organization at large. Will the executive director have the opportunity to review a draft prior to its broader distribution? Who will be responsible for duplicating and distributing the report? Will the consultant be available to present the findings at a board meeting in person? Once again, consultants vary in their practices. The organization should discuss the consultant's process beforehand.

How Long Will the Feasibility Study Take?

The feasibility study should take anywhere from six weeks to four months, depending on the size and scope of the study. From the consultant's point of view, the key issues in scheduling a feasibility study are the client's ability to enlist a committee to oversee the process and the difficulty in scheduling interviews. If the interviews require considerable travel (which is unusual for a community-based organization), the interviews will be more difficult to schedule. If the study takes place during the summer or over the holiday season, interviews may take longer to schedule because people are harder to reach and have less free time. A good consultant should be able to predict with reasonable accuracy the length of time the study will take. The consultant, however, has no control over the scheduling of committee and board meetings. These should be planned well in advance so that the organization itself is not responsible for delaying the process.

How Much Will the Study Cost?

The author has polled colleagues regarding feasibility study costs and has found a wide range of costs. For a community-based organization conducting a feasibility study with 25–35 interviews, the fee can range anywhere from $15,000 to $30,000, with most falling in the $15,000 to $20,000 range. The cost increases with the number of interviews. A study for an organization with far-flung donor base will also cost more.

ENLISTING A FEASIBILITY STUDY COMMITTEE

After the consultant has been hired and the organization's leadership has become familiar with the scope and purpose of the study, it is time for the organization to ready itself for the feasibility study to begin.

All fund raising is based on involving people in meaningful ways in the life of the organization. The organization's staff and leadership should seize every opportunity to make such meaningful experiences happen, and a feasibility study is just such an opportunity. To this end, a meeting of the executive director, the development director, the consultant, and the board chair should be called to determine who should be invited to serve on an ad hoc committee to oversee the progress of the feasibility study. The individuals who take part in this way will have a bird's-eye view of the emerging project. They will become familiar with the goals of the organization. They will come to understand the importance and excitement of the new project. They will actually have the chance to put in their two cents' worth (or perhaps even more) about the case for support. In essence, those involved in this process are very likely to become thoroughly engaged in planning for the organization's growth.

Because this will be a working committee, it should consist of approximately six to eight volunteers. Allowing for attrition and the inclusion of the development director or executive director and the consultant, this will result in a good size group for serious discussion. The group might include two or three of the strongest board members, a few of the most generous donor prospects, and also a few individuals who are emotionally committed to the organization and capable of clear and effective thinking. Ideally, the committee should be a mix of those already passionate about the organization and those who have financial or leadership potential and whose greater involvement would be especially beneficial.

The committee will probably wish to meet about four times over a period of two or three months. It will be charged with assisting and overseeing the work of the consultant on the feasibility study. When the study is completed, the work of the committee is completed.

The development director must be very clear with the volunteers as to what is expected of them, including what their time commitment will be and when their job will be finished. Clarity about expectations from the beginning offers the best chance of ending the process with happy and satisfied volunteers.

Thoughts about Volunteer Management

Volunteers will be far more likely to agree to do five well-defined, time-limited tasks, sequentially, than to sign on for one long, amorphous job. Volunteer involvement might be thought of as a series of links in a chain. Each link can be opened and closed, much like a loose-leaf binder ring. The task of involving volunteers is to define each link so that it is not too big and can be accomplished successfully. People are invited to help link by link, their success highlighted and recognized after each link. Those volunteers who worked well and were excited by their work in a particular link may be invited back to assist with the next link, but they are neither expected nor required to do so.

Having signed on for the short haul, volunteers are likely to be more willing to help. And since they have been offered only a limited engagement, the director can pick and choose whom to invite to help with the next stage of the project. During the transitions from one committee to another it is possible to let some volunteers go and bring new ones into the process without offending anyone. Committees become better and better as the collection of tried-and-true volunteers grows.

From a volunteer's perspective, it is much more attractive to sign on for a small task and then to sign on again if things went well. The volunteer is employed effectively and is amply recognized but doesn't feel saddled with a heavy burden. By the way, according to this theory, boards without term limits are not good for an organization. They are frozen links that tend to create organizations that stagnate and spoil.

This pattern of volunteer involvement can be used throughout a capital campaign. The first link may have been the committee to help choose the consultant. Perhaps the second link will be the feasibility study committee.

THE WORK OF THE COMMITTEE

The feasibility study committee has multiple tasks and these must be carefully explained to potential committee members before they are asked to serve.

1. **Review the case for support.** The committee members can be an excellent sounding board for the case for support, primarily because they will bring a variety of viewpoints to the task. If the case is unclear, or the explanation of the needs seems not to make sense, they will articulate these concerns. The input from these individuals will provide another opportunity to refine the case so that it is clear and precise before it is presented to campaign prospects.
2. **Develop the list of people to be interviewed.** Since the members of the committee are peers of those who will be interviewed for the feasibility study, they will be able to help determine whose opinions are really going to matter and which people are likely to be the most helpful during the course of the campaign.

3. **Review the questions** that the consultant intends to ask during the interviews. While the consultant is primarily responsible for developing the interview questions, the committee members may offer others or perhaps suggest different ways of phrasing a particular question. Because they know both the organization and many of the individuals who will be interviewed, they may have some interesting and useful insights into the effectiveness of particular questions in eliciting information.

4. **Help draft a letter** to be sent to all interview prospects prior to scheduling the interviews. It is customary and appropriate to send a letter requesting an interview to each individual on the interview list. This letter is usually sent by the organization and is signed by either the executive director or the chairman of the board. The letter explains that the organization has hired a consulting firm to conduct a feasibility study to evaluate the potential of raising funds for a specific project. It lets them know that they are among a small group of community and organization leaders who have been selected to be interviewed and requests that they make time to meet with the consultants. A copy of the preliminary case for support is sent along with the letter so that the person may choose to read about the project prior to the interview. A sample letter is included in Exhibit 3–9.

5. **Meet with the consultant for an update** sometime around the midpoint of the interview process to assess progress and make course corrections if needed. Staying in contact with the consultant during the study is very important. The feasibility study's course should be flexible, and certain adjustments may be needed. Making adjustments is not a sign of bad planning; rather, it implies that the oversight committee is paying proper attention to what is going on.

6. **Review a draft of the report.** Once the feasibility study is complete, the committee will receive a draft

---

Exhibit 3–9 Sample Letter for Interview Prospects

Date
x
x
x

Dear _____:

The Hamson Center is facing an important crossroads, and we need your help in making decisions that will determine the Center's future in Eastham.   As you may well be aware, the Center's main facility at 50 Central Avenue has become antiquated and, frankly, inhospitable to the people we serve. Bringing that facility into the 21st century is a major undertaking and expense, and we are now exploring the possibility of raising $5 million to renovate our headquarters site. This renovation is a critical ingredient in our ability to improve many of our programs, and to continue to play a central role in the well-being of the Eastham community that we serve.

To help us in our planning, we have engaged Jim Jamison to conduct a series of confidential interviews with people whose opinions we believe would be invaluable in assessing our plans. Jim is an experienced capital campaign consultant who specializes in community-based organizations like ours.

Within the next week Sandy Taylor of our External Relations Office will contact you to schedule an interview with Jim. I hope you will be willing to share your thoughts about our proposed plans with him. As background for the discussion, we are enclosing a draft description of the project and its rationale for you to review prior to the meeting. The interview should take no more than 45 minutes. Your comments during this discussion will be held in confidence, and you will not be asked for a gift in this meeting.

Thank you in advance for your guidance in helping us make plans and decisions that will reflect the needs and ideas of our community. I know you will find Jim engaging and your discussion interesting.

Sincerely,

Louis Banker   Jane McIntyre
President   Executive Director

of the report before it is sent on to the board. This gives both the committee members and the consultant the opportunity to review and discuss the report's recommendations while they are still in draft form. If the oversight committee has had a chance to review the report, and then accepts it and recommends its findings to the board, there is a good chance that the board, too, will accept it.

THE INTERVIEW PROCESS

During the interview process, the consultants will be spending considerable time in the community, speaking face-to-face with board members, major donor prospects, and key volunteers. If the consultants are good interviewers, they will do more listening than talking. But they will also find opportunities during the interviews to speak about the strength and effectiveness of the organization. They will try to engage each individual they interview in a discussion that brings out that person's specific interests, hopes, and concerns about the organization and the project.

In some cases, the consultants may have to rely on telephone interviews. Occasionally, someone on the interview list is not available in person or is residing in another state or even another country for a few months, and it is too costly or time consuming for the consultant to travel to that location. When necessary, telephone interviews are better than no interviews. Over the telephone, however, the interviewer can rarely build the kind of personal rapport that leads to the deeper understanding one hopes for from these interviews.

Most consultants prepare a preliminary gift range chart to take to each interview that shows how many gifts of specific sizes will be needed to make up the campaign goal. For a campaign of $1 million, for example, the table might show the requirement of one gift of $150,000, two gifts of $100,000, four gifts of $50,000, and so on. The interviewer will probably ask for an indication of the level on the table at which the individual might envision making a gift. Through this process, combined with other information gathered from the interviews, the consultant will be able to develop a reasonably accurate sense of the potential for leadership gifts for the project.

The Interview Process Can Be Stressful

The interview process often raises the level of anxiety within the organization. In fact, the entire feasibility study process makes some executive directors and development directors very nervous. After all, their major donors and volunteer leaders are being asked to give their candid opinions about them, and those opinions will be reported back to the full board!

To help alleviate some of this anxiety, the staff should stay in close touch with the consultants. The consultants may not be able to report everything they are hearing in the course of their interviews, but they will be able to dispel most of the horror stories that an overactive imagination may be concocting.

During this period, the community grapevine begins to become active as well. Soon after the consultants begin receiving information about the organization, the organization will begin to receive information about the consultants. The chairman of the board may call to report about his interview. A long-time volunteer who had recently been inactive may call the development director to schedule lunch in order to find out the latest and to gossip about the interview process. It won't take long before the grapevine begins to present a fairly clear picture about the interview process. Now it is time for the consultants to be nervous! All comments thus received should be listened to carefully. If for any reason there are a number of comments that ring alarm bells about the consultant, the feasibility study committee and the consultant should be summoned to discuss the problem and suggest remedies. There will be further discussion on how to handle this type of problem in the trouble-shooting guide in Appendix A.

> *During a feasibility study interview period, the community grapevine will probably become active as the community leaders who have been interviewed begin talking about the project.*

Thanking the Interview Participants

Immediately after completing an interview, the consultants should send a personal thank-you note to the individual they have interviewed. The official thank you from the organization is usually sent after the report has been written, so that the thank-you letter can include information about the outcome of the study. The consultant should assist in reviewing the list of interview subjects to decide to whom to send a full copy of the report and to whom just a summary.

At the conclusion of the interview process, there will usually be a few individuals who could not be reached. Perhaps they were out of town, or perhaps they simply were unwilling to be interviewed. Together with the consultant, the organization should decide how to reach closure with each of these individuals. In some cases, a letter of regret will be the appropriate response. In others, it may be desirable for a member of the organization to meet with that person in place of the consultant. In all cases, however, once the initial letter has been sent, the contact must be closed appropriately.

THE FEASIBILITY STUDY REPORT

Although many who have been through feasibility studies a number of times have come to understand that the process is at least as important as the product, it is quite natural for a first-timer to see the written report as the centerpiece of the study. As mentioned before, studies vary greatly in both style and content. Some consultants belong to the "heavier is better" school—a leftover attitude from high school and college. They figure that the client is paying a large sum for a report, and so the client may feel cheated if the report does not, through sheer heft, provide a sense that it is worth the money spent on it. It is not uncommon to see studies that run one hundred pages or more, with fancy dividers, charts, and graphs, and printed on heavy stock that further increases the weight of the report. Other consultants prefer reports that have distilled the essence of what they have learned.

But whether one prefers the heavy or light variety, every responsible report should include the following elements:

- Appearance. The report should feature an attractive, professional-looking title page and cover.
- Executive summary. An executive summary of one to two pages encapsulates the primary findings and recommendations of the report.
- Table of contents. There should be a table of contents with page numbers to facilitate locating information.
- Content. There should be sections in the body of the report that briefly describe the process used to conduct the study, a description and analysis of findings from the interviews, conclusions drawn from the findings, and specific recommendations about how the organization should proceed.
- Appendices. There should be an appendix of names of all those interviewed, as well as appendices that collect all the relevant information and material used to conduct the study. This will include a list of committee members, the case for support, the interview questions, the gift range chart, and any other relevant documentation.
- Quotations. Some consultants include a section of selected quotations from the interviews. These are often organized by topic and are presented without attribution. Although not necessary, a selection of well-chosen quotations gives those who read the study an understanding of the range of opinions heard during a set of interviews.
- Other report elements. Consultants sometimes employ charts to illustrate graphically the distribution of the interview subjects' responses to the various

questions. Although, as has been discussed earlier, these illustrations can be an effective way to present information, in the world of capital campaigns, not all men and women are created equal, not all opinions are equally important, and a neutral statistical analysis might actually be misleading.

The report should be written in prose that is clear, concise, and effective. Some consultants attempt to inflate their style through the use of passive verbs, but this only serves to make their writing turgid and dense. One can get an idea of the consultant's writing style by looking at one's accumulated correspondence. Many consultants do not have editorial assistance, so the style in their letters is likely to be what will appear in the report.

The consultant should be encouraged to submit a draft of the report to the development director, executive director, and board chair to read before it is shown to anyone else. This will provide a chance for these individuals to digest the material, to discuss any problematic areas with the consultant, and to catch any inconsistencies or errors that may have occurred. Once the report has been distributed to a larger group, it will be more difficult for the consultant to make changes without jeopardizing the credibility of individuals within the organization.

Once these three have had a look at the report, the next draft should be distributed to the feasibility study committee for their consideration before being presented to the board. A meeting of the committee should be called, and the report should be sent to the committee members several days before that meeting to give them sufficient time to read it. And as always, it should be stamped DRAFT in large letters on the front cover. The consultant should be encouraged to present the report as a draft at this meeting and to solicit advice and suggestions for its improvement. It should not have a fancy cover or any other "bells and whistles" at this stage, so that in its provisional appearance it will encourage the committee members to be free with their suggestions. Such an exchange will lead to a better report and will solidify the committee's support for the final version.

Once the report has been accepted by the committee, copies should be sent to every board member. Each copy should be attractively bound and be professional in appearance. These reports should be sent with a cover letter requesting the members to read the report and to be prepared to discuss it at the next meeting when the consultant presents his or her findings. Sometimes these reports are presented to the board as part of a longer meeting that covers other issues. Sometimes, if the report includes controversial or difficult material, the report is presented at a special meeting of the board. The consultant should make a verbal presentation of the report and then ask the board to accept the report.

What Next?

The recommendations made in the feasibility study provide a plan to move the organization into a campaign. In some cases, the study suggests that the organization take some time prior to a campaign to get ready. These readiness areas might include strengthening the volunteer leadership, identifying campaign chairs, increasing the capacity of the development office, improving the organization's visibility, or sharpening the case for support. In some cases, the study recommends that the organization move directly into a campaign and outlines the next steps. In either case, once it has been accepted by the committee, the report must be presented to the board as a recommendation of the feasibility study committee. This committee's recommendation constitutes an endorsement of the contents of the study. The board's approval generally leads to a motion to act on the recommendations made by the study.

Confidentiality

Most consultants begin each interview with a statement that the content of the interview will be held in confidence and that the material that has been gathered will not be attributed to any particular individual. This promise of anonymity frees the individuals who are being interviewed to express opinions that they might otherwise withhold if they knew that their thoughts would be reported back directly. People often use the interview process as an opportunity to pass constructive suggestions to the organization anonymously and sometimes even to vent their frustrations about the organization's direction or operation.

Because many people feel uncomfortable expressing criticism openly, opinions are often left unstated if they go against what is perceived as the consensus. There are more hidden opinions around a board table than there are those that are openly expressed. A feasibility study provides a voice to some of these undercurrents in a fashion that can lead to constructive debate.

Unless specific approval from an individual has been obtained, the consultant will be very careful not to attribute to a specific individual the ideas and opinions that have been gathered in the study. Members of the organization, on the other hand, will be very curious about who said what. When the process works well, and sensitive issues are put on the table, some individuals may have more courage to express their thoughts and ideas directly, closing a communications gap that had been hidden prior to the study.

When the feasibility study process works well, it encourages individuals to express their thoughts and ideas freely, sometimes closing a communications gap that may have been hidden before the study.

The consultant should not be asked to reveal specific information that cannot be shared. The interview forms will remain with the consultant, not with the organization, and the consultant's reputation rests on his or her ability to respect each interview subject's right to confidentiality.

Getting the Most out of the Feasibility Study

Once the study is complete (see Exhibit 3–10), there will be an excellent opportunity to build on the relation-

---

Exhibit 3–10 Feasibility Study Checklist

1. Are the function and purpose of a fund-raising feasibility study understood?
2. Can that understanding be articulated to board members, staff, and volunteers?
3. Has a consultant been hired who can conduct the feasibility study?
4. Has a preliminary case for support been drafted?
5. Is the consultant's role in conducting the feasibility study well understood?
6. Has a list of prospects for the feasibility study committee been drawn up?
7. Have materials for the feasibility study committee been prepared?
8. Is it clear what the committee's function will be?
9. Has the committee drafted the letter requesting a feasibility study interview?
10. Has it been made clear to the consultant that the organization's leadership expects to see the first draft of the report?
11. Is the confidentiality aspect of the feasibility study well understood?
12. Does the report make clear, timely, and specific recommendations?
13. Is the report being distributed so as to build understanding and ownership in the project?
14. Have interview participants been thanked and informed of the results of the study?
15. Have committee members been thanked?

ships that were strengthened during the study. This chance should not be allowed to slip away. Key board members and donor prospects should be telephoned. They should be invited to lunch; their opinions should be sought. They should be involved in the next steps outlined in the study. Feasibility studies usually raise a host of far-reaching issues around which people can rally. Using such opportunities to draw people closer to the organization is the wellspring of effective fund raising.

REFERENCES

The text of the Declaration of Independence is available on the World Wide Web at http://www.nara.gov/exhall/charters/declaration/decmain.html.

Chapter 4
Building the Campaign Team

Chapter Outline

- Seeing the Big Picture
- Defining Key Campaign Positions
- Defining Staff Roles
- Volunteer Campaign Leadership
- Campaign Consultants
- Expanding the Campaign Team
- The Campaign and the Board of Directors
- Creating a Positive Atmosphere

SEEING THE BIG PICTURE

Even those who have previous campaign experience are often unaware of all it takes to plan and implement a successful campaign. They often remember only their own specific tasks and are oblivious to the monumental edifice of staff and volunteer hours; the mountains of paperwork that flow through the development office; the thousands of telephone hours spent following up with volunteers and donors; or the myriad meetings to develop strategy for solicitations, encourage volunteers, and track results. Most see only the concrete manifestations of the campaign—the campaign brochure, the kickoff party, and the index cards that tell them whom they are to solicit—and seldom reflect on the underlying structure that guides the campaign process.

This chapter is a guide to building an effective campaign team. It defines key campaign positions, outlines the roles of the primary campaign volunteers and staff, explores the use of campaign consultants, and discusses the relationship of the board of directors to a campaign. In sum, this chapter reviews the building blocks of which campaigns are constructed.

DEFINING KEY CAMPAIGN POSITIONS

The Campaign Team

Literally hundreds of volunteers and staff are involved throughout the period of a campaign, but even in the largest campaigns, the core team is quite small. Key campaign positions vary somewhat from organization to organization depending on size, culture, budget, and individual personalities. However, in most campaigns the following people are members of the core campaign team: the CEO, the head development officer, the board chair, the development chair, the campaign chair(s), and the campaign consultant.

These people work together as a close group that guides the campaign from beginning to end. They meet frequently to plan, strategize, fret, and celebrate. As needed, they bring others into their team. The level of respect, trust, and engagement that develops in this group establishes the spirit and effectiveness of the entire campaign. This informal group, sometimes referred to as the core committee, might invite others to join some of their meetings. For example, the communications director, the major-gift officer, another board member, or other person whose work will affect the outcome of the campaign may participate in meetings when their work or interests dovetail with that of the campaign.

The Executive Director or CEO

Executive directors play complicated and demanding roles during a campaign period. Internally, they lead from in front, bearing aloft the campaign standard for the entire staff. Externally, they lead from behind, keeping themselves in the background, supporting the efforts of the key volunteers and ensuring their success while making sure that the actual work of the campaign is accomplished effectively. These tasks, of course, are added to the executive director's full-time responsibilities of running the organization.

Leading from the Front: Whether or not the executive director has been through a campaign before, the staff looks to the executive director to establish the tenor of the campaign. Optimism and enthusiasm combined with an insistence on high quality, hard work, and a healthy dose of good humor set the internal tone for a campaign. Both the development director and the development assistant take their cues from the standard of behavior set by the executive director. Although it is natural for even the most steadfast and experienced of executive directors to experience moments of anxiety, during campaigns—invariably times of change and stress—wise directors will use their will, courage, and determination to create the pattern for success.

Internally, when beginning a capital campaign, executive directors are usually managing organizations that are in transition, they must lead these already stressed agencies into new and demanding fund-raising territory as well. For example, an organization that is contemplating a major building project usually finds its staff in overcrowded and poor working conditions. In a cramped environment, rising noise levels, and work overloads, the prospect of adding a capital campaign to the mix is often greeted with something less than ardent enthusiasm.

Internally then, the executive director must support and motivate staff members to stretch themselves to navigate a successful campaign. This takes patience, open-mindedness, and a willingness to lead by setting examples for hard work, steadfastness, and commitment.

Leading from Behind: Externally, the executive director leads from behind. The visible positions in the campaign are occupied by the volunteer leaders, but without the effective behind-the-scenes leadership of the executive director, campaign volunteers are likely to lose momentum. The executive director, along with the development director, provides the structure and support that are necessary for the campaign leadership to do its best. The staff finds just the right way to accommodate the needs of each of the volunteer leaders. Some may need specific and detailed written instructions to guide their every move. Others may want to play a larger role in designing the campaign.

The most effective executive directors are willing to accept the blame for problems and give credit to their campaign volunteers when there is success. Because many people struggle with their own insecurities and vulnerabilities, this practice proves challenging for even the most seasoned of leaders.

The Development Director

Campaigns require the concentrated attention of staff members who are not only willing and able to carry out each and every organizational detail but who also have the will and fortitude to follow up on every loose end. Although big visions and careful design are extremely important, all of the planning in the world will come to naught without someone who can implement every aspect of the plan.

The development director often works with a development assistant to carry out the campaign plan. They think through every detail of every meeting, develop the materials needed to support the work of the group, and make sure that the people who could not attend are brought up to date after the meetings. After meetings, they follow up on every detail and begin to plan for the next step in the campaign.

Rather than using a development assistant who has many other responsibilities to the ongoing development program, some organizations hire campaign managers to handle this level of detail. This person may be part-time or full-time, depending on the phase of the campaign and the size of the organization.

Managing the Campaign from the Middle: The development staff members often find themselves playing challenging roles in managing the campaign from the inside. They often must support their executive directors, making sure that they are well informed and using their time where it is best spent. They also have considerable contact with campaign volunteers, calling to set up meetings, answering questions, and checking to make sure volunteers have completed their assignments. The development director, campaign manager, and/or development assistant are the people who develop firsthand knowledge of the donor data base. They know who has given and who has not; they keep track of obscure tidbits of information about one person or another that will be important to a solicitor. They are able to manipulate the software so it will churn out mailing labels, proposal letters, thank-you notes, and myriad other pieces of campaign material. Finally, they are the people who are responsible for making sure that all of the internal systems that support the campaign work smoothly.

The specific campaign staff responsibilities vary from one organization to another. Although the division of responsibilities must be clear and understood by all, there is no "right" way to assign responsibilities. Critical to the decision process, however, is that the key staff members must be fully committed and relish the opportunity to organize a successful campaign. Campaigns are too demanding for a staff member to undertake without genuine enjoyment and zeal!

DEFINING STAFF ROLES

Typically, the campaign work of the executive director, development director, and development assistant falls into six general areas.

Preparation. Prior to the campaign, the staff makes sure that requisite development systems are in place to facilitate the campaign. They also gather and organize information on prospective donors and volunteers.

Planning. The staff works with the campaign consultant to develop a clear and workable structure for the campaign. They help design a campaign architecture that enables volunteers to work effectively toward shared ends, and they develop ways to communicate that structure to all those working on the campaign.

Implementation. The executive director is often responsible for helping to enlist key volunteers and to solicit leadership gifts. Though these tasks are primarily assigned to leadership volunteers, the staff often participates in the process.

Coordination. Staff members pull together and manage all the pieces of the campaign; they keep track of every aspect of the campaign effort from beginning to end. They facilitate the hiring of outside professionals (graphic designer, printer, consultant, and sometimes even the architect) and make sure that these people have what they need to work effectively.

Information and Communication. Staff members manage both internal and external communication. They assemble information about the campaign—who is doing what, what gifts have come in, what gifts are pending, what is happening next, and so on; and they communicate with other staff members, volunteers, and donors to maintain a sense of clarity and forward momentum throughout the campaign. They also work with the public-relations staff and volunteers on communicating information about the project and the campaign to the community.

Support. Staff members support the efforts of everyone who is working on the campaign, simplifying and facilitating their jobs. They assemble and manage the paperwork that accompanies every solicitation. They establish internal systems to handle timely and effective donor and volunteer recognition. They call meetings, send follow-up notes, make reminder calls, encourage, nag, and, when necessary, browbeat.

Shifting Staff Roles

The period just before a capital campaign is an excellent time for an organization to reevaluate and shift staff roles in fund raising. Organizations that are short on staff in their development programs might consider adding a new staff member to take over some of the responsibilities for annual giving, thereby freeing some of the development director's time for the campaign. Or they might use the prospect of a campaign to replace a lower level development professional with someone more experienced.

It is not uncommon for capital campaigns in smaller nonprofits to inspire staff changes. As executive directors and development directors begin to experience the pressures, they realize that the demands of their jobs will soar during the campaign period. Those who are weak of heart or lacking in commitment may jump ship, but those who feel excited by challenge grasp a campaign as an opportunity for learning and promotion. Some executive directors who have never been interested in fund raising suddenly begin to play a more active role. Development directors who have confined their activities to direct mail, phonathons, and special-event fund raising find the courage to shift their sights to major-gift fund raising. Usually such transitions take place early in the campaign planning process, but sometimes they occur in midstream, causing significant interruptions in the work of the campaign.

Although these turnovers and shifts are often painful, most organizations become stronger because of them. If a campaign is viewed as an opportunity to raise an organization's level of fund-raising sophistication and ambition, it is reasonable to assume that it will be a time either to develop and promote fund-raising staff or to institute changes in this area.

Tasks Handled by Staff

Because many smaller nonprofits have never before conducted a campaign and because staff members take on campaigns in addition to their ongoing work, it is often difficult to predict accurately just how staff functions should best be handled. Even with careful and effective planning, staff members generally need to feel their way into this process, guided by the needs of the campaign, the ongoing demands of the organization, and their own abilities and zeal for the work.

For many smaller nonprofits, a team approach to staffing works well. A campaign team might include the executive director, the development director, and the campaign consultant. It might also include a development assistant or public-relations staff member. Together they learn, discuss, brainstorm, and explore every aspect of campaign planning and implementation. As it becomes clear that specific tasks are necessary, these are allocated to particular staff members or volunteers whose expertise best suits the need. Such a team approach, though time consuming, supports learning, lowers the pressure on any one staff person, and creates a group of individuals who are informed and excited about the campaign.

Although it is difficult to assign staff roles that will fit every organization, it is possible to develop an organized list of the tasks and responsibilities that are part of every campaign and to indicate the staff person who most often handles each task. One possible division of labor is shown in Exhibit 4–1. Sometimes these tasks are taken on by one primary staff member and sometimes they are shared by a group of people, but for every campaign these are the tasks that generally fall to staff members to accomplish. Even though many of them are behind the scenes and seemingly insignificant, collectively they are critical to the success of a campaign.

Anticipating Campaign Workloads

The intensity of staff work for a campaign varies from one phase of a campaign to another. During some phases, the executive director finds that it is necessary to work almost full time on the campaign. During other phases, the bulk of the responsibility shifts to the development director and development assistant. Figure 4–1 shows patterns of work flow that are typical to a campaign for a small nonprofit organization. It assumes that the organization has a full-time executive director, development director, and development assistant.

The executive director should anticipate spending considerable time working on the campaign during both the planning and the quiet phases. Most executive directors play an active role in soliciting major gifts and gifts from former board members and founders. They often work with the campaign chair and board chair or other volunteers during the quiet phase of the campaign. Directors are also often involved in the planning of the campaign kickoff. After the campaign kickoff, the director may continue to work on lead-gift or major-gift solicitations—following up on pending solicitations and initiating new solicitations if needed. During the latter half of the campaign, the total time that the director spends on the campaign often decreases. By this time in the campaign, the key volunteers are usually in place and functioning well, and the development staff understands the campaign process. Now the building project clamors for the director's attention.

During the early phases of the campaign, the development director and development assistant spend time assessing and strengthening the development department. During this early campaign period, a development director might also review the plans for annual giving to make certain that those plans can be carried out efficiently and with a minimum of extra effort during the campaign period.

In many small nonprofits, the executive works with the board chair and the consultant to carry out the early campaign planning. A development director who is excluded from this early campaign planning may feel left out and uninformed. It is easy for an executive director who is spending hour after hour outlining campaign strategies with the consultant and meeting with key volunteers to neglect to inform the development director about the content and progress being made in those meetings. For the development director and development assistant, who know that the campaign will place great but unspecified burdens on them, a sense that they have not been included in the planning process can give rise to anxiety and resentment. A wise executive director will bring these individuals into the planning process early in the campaign.

As the campaign progresses, the burden of work gradually shifts onto the shoulders of the development director and development assistant. The number of volunteer solicitors increases, the volume of solicitations mushrooms, and the development director and assistant often spend nearly all their time managing and communicating with volunteers and preparing and organizing the proposals and other paperwork that are needed to support the solicitation process.

Campaigns seldom go exactly as planned, so during this post-kickoff phase, the executive director works with the campaign chairs to make sure that the campaign is progressing as it should and to institute changes as necessary. This requires frequent progress updates, review of solicitations in progress, and regular analysis of projections.

While the ongoing burden of campaign work falls to the staff members to implement and oversee, campaigns gain power through their effective use of volunteers. While their management requires a great deal of staff time, capable volunteers add breadth and reach that staff cannot duplicate. And the campaign process, with its well-defined beginning, middle, and end, is an excellent time to involve them.

Exhibit 4–1 Campaign Responsibilities

Campaign Tasks	Executive Director	Development Director	Development Assistant	Campaign Consultant
Planning				
Recruit volunteers	✓	✓		
Solicit gifts	✓			
Design campaign strategies	✓	✓		✓
Plan project	✓			
Develop internal case for project	✓	✓		✓
Plan work of campaign steering committee	✓	✓		✓
Preparation				
Gather information about prospects	✓	✓	✓	
Identify and cultivate donors and volunteers	✓	✓		
Organize prospect rating sessions		✓	✓	
Assess development office systems		✓	✓	
Engage consultant, designer, etc.	✓	✓		
Implementation				
Recruit campaign leadership	✓			
Recruit campaign volunteers	✓			
Train solicitors		✓		✓
Solicit gifts	✓	✓		
Coordination				
Coordinate work of outside professionals		✓	✓	
Coordinate campaign materials		✓	✓	
Coordinate public relations		✓	✓	
Coordinate campaign events		✓		
Coordinate campaign newsletters		✓	✓	
Coordinate internal flow of information		✓	✓	
Coordinate direct-mail campaign		✓	✓	
Coordinate phonathon		✓	✓	
Coordinate staff campaign		✓	✓	
Coordinate donor recognition		✓	✓	
Coordinate plaque preparation		✓	✓	
Information and Communication				
Manage data and computer systems		✓	✓	
Keep donor records		✓	✓	
Thank donors	✓	✓	✓	
Track and report solicitation progress		✓	✓	
Track and report campaign progress	✓	✓		✓
Disseminate campaign information	✓	✓		
Schedule and present speeches	✓	✓		
Communicate with solicitors	✓	✓		
Communicate with volunteers	✓	✓	✓	
Communicate with campaign leadership	✓	✓	✓	
Communicate with staff about the campaign	✓	✓		
Prepare and distribute meeting notes			✓	
Support				
Schedule appointments	✓	✓	✓	
Schedule meetings		✓	✓	
Attend to details of meeting setup		✓	✓	
Follow up after meetings		✓	✓	
Send reminder notices			✓	
Make follow-up phone calls			✓	
Draft proposals	✓	✓		
Prepare proposals			✓	
Handle and coordinate all campaign paperwork		✓	✓	
Encourage and motivate	✓	✓		

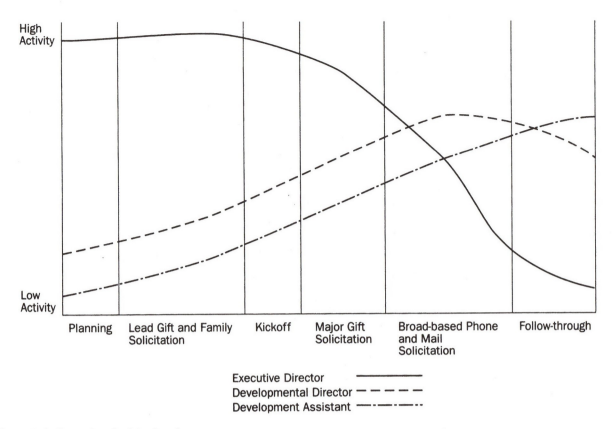

High
Activity

Low
Activity

Planning | Lead Gift and Family Solicitation | Kickoff | Major Gift Solicitation | Broad-based Phone and Mail Solicitation | Follow-through

Executive Director ————————
Developmental Director – – – – – –
Development Assistant —·—·—·—·

Figure 4–1 Campaign Activity Levels

VOLUNTEER CAMPAIGN LEADERSHIP

Characteristics of a Campaign Chairperson

Whoever assumes the position of a campaign leader guides by both word and deed. Campaign chairs are often the primary motivators and solicitors for the campaign (see Exhibit 4–2). The campaign chair is often the individual to whom the other committee members will look for acknowledgment and approval.

> *Whoever assumes the role or roles of a campaign leader guides by both word and deed.*

In most books on fund raising and capital campaigns, one reads about the salient characteristics of campaign chairs, and indeed these considerations are of great importance. Good campaign leaders really are responsible, trustworthy, generous, wealthy, and committed. These characteristics arise from an expansive definition of leadership that will be useful to examine here briefly.

"Leadership," states Max DePree in his book *Leadership Jazz* (1992, 7), "is not a position but a job. It's hard and exciting and good work. It's also a serious meddling in other people's lives." And so it is with the leaders of capital campaigns. They undertake a job that is challenging, inspiring, and demanding. They extend themselves and reach out to others. They sail on the highs and anguish through the lows. They push and pull, coerce and cajole to help everyone do their best to achieve the desired results.

The most effective campaign leaders have many of the following qualifications.

Campaign Leaders Lend Credibility to the Campaign

In every community there are individuals whose involvement carries with it the understanding that the project will succeed. These individuals have earned reputations as winners. They work hard to ensure that any project in which they are involved will succeed. They motivate others to extend themselves. They commit their own resources to the projects that they undertake, and they ask others to join them. They go above and beyond their job descriptions to make certain that they and the campaign succeed.

Exhibit 4–2 What We Need from Campaign Leadership

1. The leaders of a campaign must be willing to:
   - Make a generous and early financial commitment.
   - Be the public persona for the campaign in person, print, and the media.
   - Help enlist volunteers to serve in key campaign positions.
   - Solicit other campaign volunteers and major donor prospects.
   - Attend and chair regular steering committee meetings throughout the campaign.
   - Attend campaign kickoff, cultivation, and celebration events.
2. Campaign leaders might also:
   - Participate in frequent strategy sessions to guide the campaign and solicitation process.
   - Attend solicitor training meetings to help encourage and motivate volunteers.
   - Help rate prospects.
   - Review and edit proposals, letters, and other campaign material.
   - Make behind-the-scenes contacts to help motivate donors.
   - Speak about the organization and campaign in various public forums.

Campaign Leaders Are Capable of Making Leadership Gifts

Campaign leaders lead best by example. Sometimes the campaign chair will be able to make the largest gift to the campaign. In other cases, this may not be possible. However, every effective campaign leader must make a gift that is generous within the context of his or her resources. Although a true leader will understand this without being told, the importance of the chair's gift should be discussed before a particular individual is asked to serve in a leadership capacity. A wealthy chair who gives a small gift or a chair of modest means who doesn't give at all is probably worse than no chair at all.

Campaign Leaders Devote Time and Energy to the Campaign

The ideal campaign chair should have enough time to work on the campaign. The chair's jobs are varied and demanding. The chair cultivates and solicits lead donors, attends and conducts campaign meetings, and is an advocate for the campaign at public events and in the media. When recruiting campaign leadership, the organization should be specific and candid about the amount of time required of the chair so that there are no unpleasant surprises for the chair or for the organization once the campaign is in full swing. One should beware of the

The Chair Who Thought His Work Was His Gift

Because we knew that our board member Bill Jeffreys had been involved in several campaigns in our community, when we asked him to serve as our campaign chair we did not discuss explicitly his gift to the campaign. We assumed that when he said yes he was making a tacit agreement to give one of the leadership gifts to the campaign even though he had not given to our organization at a high level in the past. We were astonished to learn that he had no intention of doing so. Even more distressing was his unwillingness to ask anyone else for leadership gifts. We would have done our organization a great service if we had addressed this with him before inviting him to be chair—even if that meant he declined. In reality we now wish he had declined.

—Executive Director,
Social Service Organization

prospective chair who offers to contribute a name and a major gift but who has no time to work. That person might be better placed as honorary chair of the campaign, or as co-chair together with someone who may have a lesser name but more time.

The Chairwoman Who Was Too Busy

The nonprofit that I was working for during the campaign had asked a busy public figure to serve as its campaign chair. She was wealthy and had a well-known and respected name among most of our constituents—in fact, many of our prospects were honored to know that they might have the opportunity to meet this woman. Unfortunately, because of her busy schedule she simply didn't have enough time to meet with people. She believed in the organization's work one hundred and ten percent—she made one of the largest gifts to the campaign and was willing to solicit and cultivate prospects when she had the time. But all too often she just didn't have the time. In retrospect, we would have been better off using her as an honorary chair and bringing her in for the really big solicitations—and finding somebody else who might have had less stature but who had the time to do more of the day-to-day work.

—Development Director

Campaign Chairs Motivate Other Volunteers

As a volunteer, a campaign chair can relate to other volunteers and motivate them in a way that staff members cannot. He or she motivates others by example, by praise, or by a candid observation about what the volunteer is—or is not—doing.

The Team Approach to Campaign Leadership

Because of many structural changes in our culture, it is more and more difficult to find that one person who embodies everything one would wish for in a campaign chair. Many organizations, therefore, have been forced to explore other leadership configurations that spread the burdens and opportunities of leadership among two, three, or even four people. With the right combination of people and effective organization and communication, this team approach to campaign leadership can work very well. In some cases, the combined skills, gifts, and influence of a leadership team can be far greater than that of a single individual.

The simplest configuration for campaign leadership is that of one campaign chair who has all the characteristics and conditions needed to make him or her an ideal chair—money, time, commitment, energy, knowledge of the cause, leadership characteristics, name, reputation, integrity, and an established history with the organization. If there is one person who is an obvious choice, this clear-cut leadership model is ideal in that it avoids the pitfalls of more complicated structures.

Sometimes a person who has only some of the qualities required for the job may nonetheless be a good candidate for campaign chair. In many communities, "older generation" leaders seem to be tiring of chairing campaigns and are concerned that the next generation is not stepping forward or being trained effectively to take their places. Occasionally, one has a chance to capitalize on this concern by recruiting a younger campaign chair with the explicit help of an older powerful figure in the community. Although the older person need not take on the visible aspects of campaign leadership, that individual might be willing to help ensure the success of the campaign by working behind the scenes, reaping the satisfaction of passing the leadership torch to someone of the new generation with strong prospects as a community leader.

Sometimes, however, no one person surfaces as the clear and obvious choice. Many individuals have some but not all of the characteristics required of a campaign chair. Creating two chairs, or co-chairs, enables an organization to combine the skills and characteristics of two people into a workable leadership partnership. The key to successful co-chairing is enlisting two individuals

---

The Power Behind the Throne

When we were looking for someone to chair our campaign, I asked a gentleman who represents the old guard in our community for advice. I knew that he had chaired other successful campaigns in the community. Although I also knew that he was only passingly interested in our organization and was not a candidate for our campaign, I thought he might help me figure out what to do. Not only did he help me, he was pleased that I had thought to ask him for advice. I learned from him that he was concerned that our community had not done a good job of preparing the younger generation of business leaders to assume the mantle of volunteer leadership. We talked about who he thought was in the rising class and about how to structure a leadership team that would provide good training to someone younger and also be good for the campaign.

In the end, this gentleman became a behind-the-scenes coach to our campaign chair, who was a young man just rising in the ranks of a major insurance company. The younger man had the opportunity to learn from an old pro and to build a relationship with the real seats of power in our community. The older man was able to pass on his extensive campaign wisdom without having to put in long hours of work or being constantly in the public eye. Finally, as a nice addition to the package, the older man's foundation gave a generous gift to the campaign to help ensure his protégé's success!

—Executive Director of a Community Library

---

who respect and approve of each other and then carefully defining the role and responsibilities for each. In particular, it is important to establish clear lines of responsibility and communication so that everyone involved (board chair, executive director, and each co-chair) understands who will be expected to do what and how information will be communicated.

> *The key to successful co-chairing is enlisting two individuals who respect and approve of each other and then carefully defining the role and responsibilities for each.*

It may be advisable to assemble an even bigger leadership team. In some cases, a team of three co-chairs can be effective. This might be the case when the leaders of a community decide to lock arms on behalf of a high-risk but important community organization. When several well-known community leaders come together publicly to share the leadership of a campaign, their visibility makes a powerful impression.

It should be kept in mind, however, that too many cooks can turn soup into swill. In general, the larger and more complex the leadership team, the stronger the role the staff must play in guiding, communicating, and managing the process. There are many ways to configure the responsibilities of campaign leadership, and the best configuration is the result of clear, thorough discussion among the board chair, the director, and those being recruited for leadership positions.

Responsibilities of the Campaign Leaders

Make an exemplary campaign gift. The first responsibility of a campaign chair is his or her gift to the campaign. Expectations should be discussed before the fact, not after. The table of gifts and campaign goals should be reviewed with the candidate. If the candidate is a person of wealth, his or her gift should be among the top 10. If, however, the candidate does not have financial resources but brings other important qualities to the task,

then the gift should be a gift that is impressive but realistic for someone of that person's means.

Be publicly visible. The second responsibility of a campaign chair is his or her public visibility. The campaign chairs are the most visible people in the campaign, and they should fully understand the opportunities and responsibilities associated with this public image. Their names will appear on campaign materials. Their signatures will be used for all proposals and requests for funds. Their names and statements about the organization and the campaign will appear in press releases. They will be expected to give speeches at campaign events. And in their workplace and the community, they will be expected to represent the organization and the campaign in a responsible and constructive way.

People often recognize the potential for status and visibility that comes with a position of leadership, but they are less likely to understand the burdens and high risk that also come with the job. Clear and thoughtful discussion of the responsibilities of being a public figure prior to an individual's agreement to become chair will create an understanding of just what is being taken on, so that the person who eventually does become chair will walk into the task with open eyes. Although such a frank discussion may discourage the candidate from accepting, if the candidate accepts the position with a full understanding of the expectations, risks, and rewards, that individual is likely to give a better performance in this demanding role.

Set aside adequate time. The third responsibility of a campaign chair is his or her time. Just how much time will be required of the campaign leader? This, too, is an important consideration for a campaign chair, and figuring out the correct answer results from a blending of the campaign's needs and the volunteer's availability. Some campaign chairs turn the campaign into a full-time job. They attend every volunteer meeting; they work on the campaign at home at night; they are on the telephone at all hours recruiting people, following up on solicitations, and driving the staff. Others focus on the specific tasks that they know they alone can accomplish. Both of these models can work well. Trouble arises, however, when an organization thinks it is getting the first model and what the volunteer has in mind is the second! Once again, a thorough conversation about expectations before the fact will lay the foundation for a good relationship.

Solicit gifts. The fourth responsibility of a campaign chair is soliciting gifts. At a minimum, campaign chairs are responsible for soliciting the other volunteers who assume key positions in the campaign. Because all volunteers must make their own gifts before soliciting others, the structure and timing of these solicitations is important to the success of the campaign. The campaign leaders should understand that they will be expected to

---

A Great Team

In our campaign, we had no clear idea of who should be the chair. We badly needed someone with a well-known name because our organization did not have high visibility in the community, but we also needed someone who was really committed to our organization and who was a good speaker. We were fortunate to identify a great pair. We teamed up our former board chair, who was a young, attractive attorney committed to our organization and a great speaker but with limited means and visibility, with one of the *grandes dames* of our community who had resources and reputation but little time and no interest in being an active leader. It worked out really well. She gave a leadership gift, let us use her name, came to occasional steering committee meetings when she was in town, and made some backroom phone calls on behalf of the campaign. He chaired the meetings, presided over all the events and press conferences, and solicited gifts. They both had a good time getting to know each other and felt that they had each given what they were best at.

—Development Director, Hospice

Tailoring the Position to Fit the Individual

A small day-care center was planning its very first capital campaign. They had a working board and few connections in the world of money and power. One of the board members, however, was a longtime family friend of the wife of a retired industrial CEO in the community. This older woman had had only occasional contact with the center, but she was willing to learn more from her younger friend. She visited the center, where she found out about the needs the center was serving in the community and about its plans to expand. Although this woman spent five months each year in another state, she agreed to become the honorary chair of the campaign. Her photo with some of the children from the center appeared in the campaign materials, she gave a leadership gift, she hosted a cultivation gathering in her lovely apartment, and she solicited several of her friends for the campaign. Although her time commitment was limited, her role in the campaign was designed to fit what she was able and willing to do. The other leadership roles were taken over by younger, less well known people in the community. This team approach worked well, and the campaign went over its goal.

make their own contributions to the campaign early and that they will be responsible for soliciting those volunteers who assume committee and division leadership. If the campaign leaders understand and carry out their roles in this task early in the campaign, the entire campaign is likely to flow more smoothly.

Campaign leaders usually also solicit other major donors. Some campaign leaders solicit only a few key gifts for a campaign, others take on single-handedly the task of soliciting most of the major-donor prospects. Either of these patterns will work as long as expectations are clear. The early solicitation process also provides the added benefit of enabling campaign leaders to hone their solicitation skills on individuals already committed to the campaign, thus preparing them to solicit other major donors. Solicitation skills get better with practice, and people who are already committed are often helpful in finding the right words and building confidence in the process.

Attend meetings. The final responsibility of a campaign chair is attending meetings. Campaign leaders chair campaign steering committee meetings and preside over public events. The right level of involvement for a specific campaign will depend on the character, desires, and abili-

ties of both the staff and the leaders. Many campaigns are largely staff driven. Staff members prepare the agenda, schedule the meetings, and instruct the campaign leaders on their roles. In others, however, the campaign leaders will want to participate more fully in the design and planning. To work well, the leadership and staff must complement one another. Advanced discussion of roles and expectations will help all parties determine whether they can create an effective team.

Job Descriptions for Campaign Leaders

Written job descriptions help clarify the expectations of campaign leaders. A job description for a volunteer campaign leader, however, might serve better as an agenda for in-depth discussion than as a prescription for the role. The most effective approach to recruiting campaign leadership demands flexibility, comfort with collaborative exploration, a thorough understanding of the fundamental responsibilities of campaign leadership, and a healthy dose of creativity.

> *You honor a person with an invitation to serve as the chair of a campaign. A recruitment meeting should be thought of as a discussion about opportunities for mutual gain.*

Conversations with prospective campaign leaders should be more like collaborative discussions about how to build a successful campaign than like job interviews. That said, the job description may look something like Exhibit 4–3.

Questions to Guide the Recruitment Discussion

A set of questions, prepared in advance, will help guide the discussion into and through areas that might be uncomfortable for both parties. The questions might include the following:

- How much input into the campaign process will the chair want to have?
- How much time does the chair anticipate being able to devote to the campaign?
- What is the chair's leadership style?
- With what roles is the chair comfortable and what roles would be better avoided?
- What would the chair like to take away from his or her leadership experience?
- In what range does the chair anticipate making a gift to the campaign?

Exhibit 4–3 Sample Committee Chair Job Description

Job Description
Special Events Committee Chairperson

Committee Goals: To assemble a committee of capable and knowledgeable individuals to assist the museum in planning special events for the campaign. These will include the campaign kickoff event, two cultivation gatherings prior to the public phase of the campaign, and a campaign celebration at the conclusion of the campaign.

Tentative Timetable:

Cultivation events:	December 1997 and March 1998
Campaign kickoff:	June 1998
Campaign celebration:	March 1999

Responsibilities of the Chairperson:

- Help identify and enlist six to eight individuals to serve on the special events committee.
- Conduct committee meetings to plan each event.
- Assist with the work of the committee.
- Serve on the campaign steering committee, which will meet monthly throughout the campaign.
- Serve as advocate for the campaign.

Staff Support: The staff will work with the chair of this committee to maintain effective communication and follow-through for all aspects of the committee's work. The committee will also meet with the campaign consultant as needed.

When to Enlist the Campaign Leadership

In some campaigns it is obvious from the very beginning who will chair the campaign. Sometimes one person has driven a project, is capable, and is willing to lead the campaign. Even in such cases, however, a structured discussion about the role of the campaign chair will help clarify expectations, provide an official opportunity for that person to be invited to serve as the chair, and allow for consideration of others who might serve on a leadership team. The board chair and/or executive director are responsible for setting up the recruitment meeting, and if possible, this meeting should occur before the campaign planning meetings.

In many campaigns, the choice of campaign leadership is less obvious. Often, by the time an organization is prepared to proceed with a campaign, many people have agreed to help and several people may be seen as leadership candidates, but no one person is a clear choice or clearly willing to take on the task. In such cases, the recruitment of the campaign planning committee pro-

vides an excellent opportunity to prepare someone for the job of campaign chair. The small co-conspiratorial group convened to determine the membership of the campaign planning committee might well be used to identify and engage the campaign leadership. Although these co-conspirators have no official role, by taking responsibility for selecting and enlisting the campaign planners they are in fact acting as campaign leaders. Astute observation of each of these individuals will often provide clues that will lead to wise decisions about campaign leadership. If so, the leadership recruitment might occur between the co-conspirators' meetings and the planning committee meetings.

In more difficult cases, the optimal configuration of campaign leadership may not reveal itself until later in the process. If the leadership is in place prior to the planning meetings, that person will chair those meetings. If not, someone else, often the board chair, must be recruited for that task.

The longer one waits to decide who will chair a campaign, the more unspoken anxiety will permeate the campaign organization. An organization is ill served, however, if it hurries to nail down the campaign leadership without striving for the very best and strongest leaders it can get.

CAMPAIGN CONSULTANTS

What Is a Campaign Consultant?

As an organization considers embarking on a capital campaign, it must evaluate whether to hire a consultant. A campaign consultant can bring the knowledge and expertise that can benefit and strengthen the organization's entire development program, yet the consultant's services can be a "big ticket" item in the campaign budget. Thus, to decide whether hiring a consultant is a wise investment, it is necessary to consider carefully the development department's current capabilities and how they can be enhanced by a consultant's services, as well as the size and complexity of the campaign. Whether or not a consultant is eventually engaged, it is worthwhile to interview a few. The interview process itself will help staff and board members understand what is to come. The consultants who are interviewed will provide useful information about running a capital campaign, the organization's readiness to undertake a campaign, and whether or not a consultant is necessary for the campaign to succeed.

Consultants Bring Experience to the Campaign

A campaign consultant has experience designing and overseeing campaigns in a variety of organizational settings. A good consultant offers a depth and breadth of experience gained from many campaigns, an outside perspective from which to view problems, technical know-how, and the ability to impose a discipline from without that will help shape the campaign and keep it from wandering from its goals.

The best consultants are good teachers. They instruct the organization's fund-raising director and staff in how to apply their prior development knowledge to the campaign process. They help break down the campaign into manageable tasks.

> *Good consultants are excellent teachers who leave their clients with powerful knowledge to guide them into the future.*

When the relationship works well, the consultant acts as a teammate who helps structure and design a campaign that makes sense for the organization. The consultant remains flexible throughout the campaign, helping the staff adjust the campaign's design as circumstances change, thus maximizing the chances for success. The consultant can impart confidence, stand firm in the face of conflicting opinions, and articulate credible reasons for designing and running a campaign in a particular way.

Capital campaign fund raising involves a very significant investment of time and energy. Therefore, it is im-

Practicing the Art of Diplomacy

We have a long-standing, well-respected board member—I'll call her Mary—who carries a lot of weight on the board. She was convinced that the bulk of the campaign money should be raised through special events—auctions, charity balls, and so forth. I knew that wasn't the way to go. It would be fine to incorporate a special event into the campaign, but to succeed, we would have to rely on gifts from individuals. Thank goodness for our consultant. She helped put Mary's ideas in a larger context, getting her to focus on the campaign kickoff while designing a larger campaign around it. In the end, Mary felt great about her role, but she might have caused some big problems had she gotten other board members to support her original idea. Fortunately, we had the consultant, who was able to redirect her energy. No one on our staff could have done that.
—Development Director

portant to involve someone on the team who has campaign experience and who knows how to apply that experience to the organization's particular situation. For example, an experienced consultant is keenly aware of the long-term consequences of decisions made early in the campaign. The campaign's direction is shaped by such early decisions—whom to involve and how to involve them, or when to act and when to hold back. Astute campaign decisions that are made early have far-reaching consequences and are more effective than massive last-minute corrective actions.

Experience also makes a difference when one of those niggling little questions comes up about campaign procedure, or protocol, or policy that just hasn't been considered before and that is seldom addressed in books or workshops. A consultant is likely to know the solution to a problem that might otherwise take hours for the staff to solve.

Consultants Put Problems in Perspective

"Our campaign is stalled," wails the development director in frustration to the campaign consultant. "Contributions have fallen off, the volunteers are burned out, and I'm just about ready to quit and move to Antarctica. We should never have gotten ourselves into this mess!"

"Relax," replies the consultant. "I've seen this happen in many campaigns. It's the nature of the beast. The middle is always tough, so let's take a deep breath, review what's really happening, and figure out how to pull the campaign out of the slump."

Now that the consultant has put the situation into a perspective that has been gained from other capital campaigns, the consultant and the development director can sit down together in relative calm and develop some workable strategies to get the campaign back on track. Together with the volunteers, they work to implement these strategies, and usually the campaign regains its momentum. The development director is soon celebrating the campaign's success, and the longing for Antarctica melts away like the snows of yesteryear.

A skilled consultant will listen to problems, sympathize with frustrations, and then assist with finding solutions to those problems and focusing on specific tasks to get the campaign back on track.

Consultants Provide an Outsider's Viewpoint

Good consultants are likely to have useful information about gift accounting, naming opportunities, and the solicitation process; more important, as outsiders, they can help the organization take a fresh look at its operation, thus breathing new life into stagnant systems. Consultants often leave an organization with a wealth of new insights and instincts, a stronger program, and enhanced skills.

Consultants Are Skilled Writers and Editors

In small organizations, key staff members commonly have a background in the agency's program area. Day-care directors, for example, often began as preschool teachers; hospice directors were often nurses; many library directors were formerly reference librarians. Writing may not be a strong suit for many agency directors, but good writing is important throughout a capital campaign, and a skilled consultant is able to provide help in this area. While the staff will provide the ideas, the organizational "language" and style, and the content, a consultant can help provide the shape for the many written pieces—the case for support, brochures, proposals, and appeal letters—that the organization will need in order to convey the campaign vision to others. The consultant can also help with ideas, language, style, and content.

Consultants Provide Gentle (and Not So Gentle) Nudges

Since consultants are only as good as their last campaigns, they have a strong interest in making every campaign that they undertake a success. So when the staff and volunteers begin to slip into complacency, feeling secure about progress to date and certain that the next $50,000 is just an ask away, the consultant will be relentless in asking whether Mrs. Smith-Jones has been contacted again, or whether Mr. Torquemada has been invited to the executive director's luncheon. The consultant will help focus and refocus attention on the campaign. In small organizations, the staff often continues to work on other projects during a campaign. A lack of single-minded focus can push the campaign onto the back burner, but there is nothing like an impending meeting with the consultant to generate time for campaign work. By something as simple as a meeting schedule, the consultant can drive the campaign's progress.

> Since consultants are only as good as their last campaigns, they have a strong interest in making every campaign that they undertake a success.

Consultants Take Tough Stands

Consultants are able to take tough stands without flinching. Informed and empowered by their status as experts, they have both the experience and the understanding to shore up their opinions. So when, for example, a board member says, as he has so many times in

> **The Specific Amount Battle**
> We knew full well that our proposal letters to businesses should request specific amounts of money, but when we held the solicitors' meeting, one businessman was quite vocal about how that practice irritated him. Unfortunately, our consultant was not present at that meeting, and I simply couldn't get the gentleman to see otherwise. He was just not going to listen to me, and that was that. Deciding finally on a tactical retreat, I abandoned the argument until the next meeting, when our consultant could face the issue head on. At the next meeting the consultant explained her reasoning, and this time the businessman listened. The group eventually came around, and the day was saved.
> —Campaign Director, Library Campaign

the past, "I just don't think we should ask people for specific dollar amounts," the consultant can hold firm, with the knowledge gained from experience that asking for specific amounts, though annoying to some, raises more money than making nonspecific requests. Sometimes the director or board members are able to accept ideas suggested by the consultant that the development director has been suggesting for years. A wise development officer can use a consultant to help push through some of the development practices that the organization has resisted in the past.

> As outsiders, consultants can sometimes broach subjects that are taboo within the organization.

Consultants Address the Issue of Board Giving

In many community-based organizations, any discussion of the subject of board giving is taboo. The executive director is uncomfortable talking to the board about their contributions; the board chair may not have the courage to deal with the issue directly; and the development director doesn't feel it is his or her role.

As a board moves an organization into a capital campaign, a consultant is able to address the issue of board giving directly. Consultants often help design and even execute a process that encourages the board to determine its own collective goal. By clarifying the board's key role in the campaign, the consultant helps refocus the board's attention on their responsibilities as donors and as leaders of the campaign.

Consultants Provide Emotional Support

The importance of hand-holding should not be discounted. During a capital campaign the stakes are high, and anxiety runs rampant. So it can be an invaluable asset to have someone knowledgeable at hand—someone the staff likes and feels comfortable with, someone who can reassure when reassurance is needed.

What Can't a Consultant Do?

In spite of all of the positive qualities and skills that the consultant brings to a campaign, the consultant is not, alas, superhuman. Many consultants complain of organizations that have impossible expectations of them. In reality, there are some things that consultants usually cannot accomplish.

Consultants Cannot Change a Leopard's Spots: If certain members of the board aren't willing to solicit gifts, a campaign consultant may not be able to change their minds. They may seem to gear themselves up a bit after a pep talk, but they will be back to their old ways before long. A campaign consultant, however, may be able to help the board understand the importance of personal solicitation and the board's role, which may in turn inspire the board to nominate "fund-raising types" when they next nominate new board members.

Consultants Will Not Lessen the Workload: A campaign consultant is not a campaign manager. A consultant will offer suggestions on how to organize the work of the campaign, but the development director, the executive director, and the volunteers are the ones who must carry out the work. To perform effectively, the consultant must have a basic understanding of how the development office functions and who the organization's key players are. The consultant will need to know quite a bit of fundamental information about the organization. Consequently, to bring the consultant up to speed on the organization will require pulling together development records, donor files, and fund-raising analyses. One may be sure that the workload will not be lighter! And having come to understand the organization, the consultant may well make a number of suggestions that will result in even more work. The consultant may help find ways to learn more about potential donors, to cultivate key community leaders, and to involve ad hoc committees, all of which may be great preparation for a campaign but are also enormously time consuming.

Consultants Will Not Raise the Money: Fund-raising consultants are often mistakenly referred to as fund raisers. The truth is that the best fund raisers for an organization are the board members, volunteers, and the executive director. Prospective donors want to hear about the organization's future plans from the people who will be responsible for implementing that future. No one wants to talk to the consultant, who will be gone and forgotten when the campaign is over. Donors want to speak with those who are committed to the organization for the long term—those who themselves have made contributions and who are willing to put themselves on the line for the organization's cause.

An exception to this hands-off practice is a consultant who specializes in raising funds for churches. These are individuals of a particular faith who are trained to serve as solicitors for churches around the country. Although such a strategy may work in a congregation that is unified by a common faith and parlance, as a general practice it is not advisable to hire outsiders to solicit funds on the organization's behalf.

In some states it is actually illegal for registered consultants to solicit gifts on behalf of a client. In these states, the registration for fund raisers is more stringent than that for consultants and often requires that the fund raiser be bonded.

Finding a Consultant

Unlike attorneys, doctors, or accountants, who are subject to stringent professional standards, fund-raising consultants have no real accreditation process. While some consultants have moved into the field from development offices, where they may have earned Certified Fund-Raising Executive (CFRE) status, the CFRE designation does not provide an organization with a guarantee that the person in question is a qualified consultant. Similarly, while membership in a professional organization such as the American Association of Fund-Raising Counsel (AAFRC) may indicate a certain professional commitment to consulting, it says nothing about the abilities of a consultant, nor does it ensure that a particular consultant is going to be suitable for a particular organization.

Fortunately, there are many fine campaign consultants across the country, and it should be possible to find a suitable one. However, those who have never worked with a fund-raising consultant may have no idea where to begin hunting for one.

What Kind of Consultant? Consultants have different working styles and personalities, and they have many different approaches to fund raising. It is important, therefore, to find a consultant who will be a good "fit" for the organization. The consultant will need to mesh well with the board, volunteers, and development director. Will the members of the organization respond well to someone who is highly aggressive and forceful, or will they work better with someone who takes a gentler approach? Are the board members and volunteers high-powered sophisticates or down-to-earth, no-nonsense folks? The consultant should match, or be able to adapt well to, the personality of the organization.

And what about the development director? Would he or she be better off working with someone who can act as a mentor, someone who will be patient in explaining the whys and wherefores of campaign planning and execution? Will the consultant tell the development director what to do, or will the two of them work collaboratively to explore alternatives? Will the development director be more comfortable with an informal style, or with tighter structures? These are all valid consulting styles, but not all of them work equally well in a given organization. Only through an understanding of the dynamics of the organization and how the different personalities in it function can one determine what type of consultant is to be sought.

> *The consultant should match, or be able to adapt well to, the personality of the organization.*

Where Does One Look for a Consultant? Most successful consultants obtain their clients through word-of-mouth marketing. Some advertise in places like *The Chronicle of Philanthropy*, but many excellent consultants do not advertise at all. They rely on their former satisfied clients to spread the word. The best informational sources about consultants, therefore, are peers and colleagues in similar organizations. One should explore organizations that do the same type of work as one's own elsewhere in the country as well as organizations in the community that may not do similar work but are of similar size.

Although many consultants travel extensively and serve clients in a broad geographical area, there may be ad-

---

A Board Member's Pet Consultant

One of our board members suggested that we interview a consultant with whom he had worked on a major campaign in New York. This board member thought the consultant was truly God's gift to capital campaigns. The consultant had a long client list, having made his reputation back in the 1960s. My instincts told me that he was not the right consultant for our organization, but I didn't want to offend the board member. So I included him in the interview process. I also invited the board member to serve on the committee. I was anxious about the outcome, but surprisingly, the consultant helped me out.

It was clear already in the first few minutes of his presentation that this consultant wasn't going to spend much time listening to what we wanted from him and what some of the special characteristics of our organization were. Indeed, he spent most of his time telling us how other clients have appreciated and benefited from his wisdom and about his unbreakable rules of campaign management. He was unbelievably pompous. I didn't see him as the kind of person who would be a good mentor for me, which is really what I felt I needed. I wanted to learn from this campaign, not just take orders from some highfalutin consultant, particularly one so full of himself. After the consultant left, the reaction among the committee was a big thumbs down. Even the board member who had suggested him agreed that while he had an impressive record of success this particular consultant wasn't quite right for our organization.

—Development Director

---

vantages to working with a consultant who knows the organization's community and is near at hand. A state's bureau on charitable organizations is another source of information. If the state requires fund-raising consultants to complete an annual registration, the bureau will probably be able to provide a list of consultants. State registration does not imply endorsement, but it will give a preliminary source of names.

Generally, organizations that have experience with capital campaigns will be more than happy to share that experience. They will tell you whom they employed as a consultant and will offer an evaluation of their experience—they will undoubtedly have some good experiences to relate and some bad. It will be worthwhile to obtain the following information:

- What is the consultant's name, address, and telephone number?
- What was the organization's campaign goal and purpose?
- Was their campaign successful?
- Who recommended the consultant?
- What is the consultant's working style?
- Were there any problems? If so, how were they resolved?
- How did board members and volunteers react to the consultant?
- Did the consultant do what was expected?
- What were the consultant's strengths and weaknesses?
- Would they hire the consultant again?

It may also be useful to ask for recommendations from the more experienced fund raisers on the board or from local foundation executives who may have worked with consultants on other projects. Names of consultants can also be obtained from the local chapter of the Association of Fundraising Professionals (AFP), the American Association of Fund-Raising Counsel (AAFRC), and the National Center for Non-Profit Boards. (See the reference list at the end of this chapter for address information.)

Selecting the Consultant

The organization's needs have been considered, some names have been pulled together, and possibilities have been discussed with key people in the organization. Now it is time to call the consultants who have been selected through the scouting process.

These conversations will provide a sense of the consultants' personalities and styles. The consultants will get a sense of the key person with whom they may be working, the organization's mission, the preliminary goal, and the organization's fund-raising history. They may offer to send some information about their services, a client list, and a brief summary of their background and qualifications. If they do not offer to send this information, it can certainly be requested.

Here are some points that should be kept in mind for this first conversation with prospective consultants:

The devil is in the details. The small details of the very first conversation are likely to reveal as much about the consultant as any other part of the selection process. Who answered the phone? Was the consultant difficult to reach? Did the consultant return the call promptly? How tuned in was the consultant when first addressed? Did the consultant ask relevant questions? Did the consultant sound like someone worth meeting, someone with whom it would be worthwhile to work?

Careful attention to the details of how a consultant presents his or her firm will provide valuable clues about how the consultant will perform.

What organizations has the consultant worked for? When an organization hires a consultant, it is counting on obtaining the benefit of that consultant's range of experience. Therefore, it is important to take a good look at his or her campaign experience. Although it is not particularly important that the consultant has worked on campaigns for organizations exactly like one's own, the consultant should be experienced in designing campaigns for organizations of similar size and geographical range. Because most consultants do not want to impose on their former clients more than necessary, they usually prefer that only those listed specifically as references be contacted. One should not hesitate, however, to contact an acquaintance who has worked with a particular consultant.

Who will actually work with the client? In some large consulting firms, the principals seldom do the major work on small campaigns. Junior staff may, of course, be perfectly capable of providing the required assistance, but it is important to interview the individual who will serve as consultant should that firm be engaged. This isn't usually a problem in small shops, but when consultants work with associates, it is necessary to clarify just who will be assigned to the project.

Does the consultant *feel* right? If something feels troubling about a consultant in the course of preliminary telephone conversations, that feeling should be taken into consideration, even if it is something that can't be clearly articulated. This individual is, after all, someone who

The Persistent Executive Director

We entered into the consultant-search process with the feeling that we had to do this right. We did our homework and interviewed five consultants. Of the five, one firm seemed right, but their fee structure seemed high. I was on the verge of contracting with that firm, but I kept hearing that old nagging internal voice that just wouldn't be stilled. So I decided to hold off. I then called a colleague whose organization was just finishing a campaign. She recommended someone she knew, and after just one phone call, I knew I had found the right person. I'm really glad I listened to that "inner voice."

—Executive Director

might be a working partner for as long as two years, and those nagging warning signals have a way of growing into major irritations.

Preparing Material to Send to Consultants

Before calling consultants, an organization should assemble packets of material to send to each of the consultants being considered for an interview. The material might include annual reports, program descriptions, a copy of the organization's mission statement, and a brief description of the project for which the organization is considering a campaign. A complete information packet will provide consultants with the material necessary to understand the organization's needs and will help them be more productive and specific by the time they arrive for the interview.

Reviewing Printed Material from Consultants

Material received from each of the consultants who is contacted should be dated. Although it is a minor consideration, and may have no bearing on how the consultant operates, in the selection process everything should be seen as an indicator. Material that arrives late might be a sign that the consultant is very busy or disorganized. Of course, material that arrives the next day may indicate a prompt and efficient work pattern, or it may signal that the consultant doesn't have enough work. In any case, it is worth noting every detail, because details may eventually fit into a pattern that develops as the selection process proceeds.

Printed material is also very telling in more obvious ways. The style and content of the cover letter can reveal much about the consultant. Did the consultant respond to what was actually said in the telephone conversation? Is the letter clearly and grammatically written? Is the text placed on the page so that it is visually appealing and easy to read? If the answer to any of these questions is "no," the proceed-with-caution light should be illuminated. If the consultant is sloppy and inattentive during the courtship, imagine what things will be like after the vows have been taken.

As the consultant's background information is reviewed, it is important to look closely at its style as well as its content. What is the consultant's apparent market? Is it smaller organizations or large universities? Did the consultant send an expensive, glossy, four-color brochure, or only a few poorly copied typewritten sheets? It may not be glossy, but is it classy? Is it pragmatic? Is it clear? Is it appealing? Does it speak to what the organization needs? If not, hiring that consultant may lead to a *liaison dangereux*.

As the development director, the executive director, and campaign chair begin to narrow down the list to three or four of the strongest candidates, Exhibit 4–4 might prove useful in deciding whom to interview.

Assembling a Selection Committee

After the field has been narrowed to three or four consultants, it is time to assemble a committee to help select the right consultant. The selection process is an excellent opportunity to educate key board members about capital campaigns. By taking part in the interview process, they will not only learn from the various consultants' approaches, but they will also begin to acquire a sense of ownership in the campaign process even before it starts. And, even more important, when key board members have a voice in choosing the consultant, their endorsement gives the consultant considerable internal credibility right from the start.

Three or four key board members should join the executive director and development director for the interview process. Ideally, all of the interviews should be scheduled for a single day. Approximately 45 minutes per consultant interview should suffice, with another 15 minutes between interviews for discussion and breaks. The committee should be sure to arrive at least one-half hour prior to the arrival of the first consultant and plan on remaining at least one hour after the final interview has been completed. Thus, the team can work together to plan the flow of the interview process when it first gathers and, if possible, make its decision before the committee disbands.

Well in advance of the interview day, each committee member should be provided with a copy of the material about the consultants to be interviewed and encouraged to review it carefully. Committee members might also receive a consultant evaluation form to fill out during

---

Exhibit 4–4 Consultant Evaluation Form

The consultant:	YES	NO
☐ has worked primarily with community-based organizations	___	___
☐ has worked with organizations our size	___	___
☐ has worked on campaigns with similar dollar goals	___	___
☐ possesses a style that seems to fit the organization	___	___
☐ responded promptly	___	___
☐ sent clear and effective materials	___	___
☐ has several years experience working with similar campaigns	___	___

the interview process. Exhibit 4–5 is a sample of such a form.

Interviewing the Consultant

Before the consultants are contacted to arrange the interviews, some time would be well spent reviewing the organization's needs, its expectations of the consultant, and how those needs and expectations might best be framed into questions. A list of questions might then be developed to guide the interviews. The questions should be varied enough to give a clear sense of how the consultant responds to different types of issues, though some questions might be quite specific while others are more open-ended. The following questions are just a few among the many worth considering:

- What strengths do you bring to a campaign?
- What do you like best about campaigns?
- What led you to specialize in campaign consulting?
- What is your philosophy of capital campaign fund raising?
- How many campaigns have you counseled?
- What have been their goals?
- How would you describe your consulting style?
- What has been the most valuable lesson you have learned in your work?

Exhibit 4–5 Consultant Rating Form

Name of Consulting Firm: _____

Name of Representative: _____

Name of Committee Member: _____

	Negative	Neutral	Positive
First Impression			
Appearance			
Style			
Presentation			
Clarity			
Appeal			
Knowledge			
Experience			
Material			
Appearance			
Organization			
Writing Style			

	High	Moderate	Low
Cost			
Feasibility Study			
Campaigns			

General Comments:

Personal Ranking: _____

- What is your usual fee for a campaign of this size?
- On what basis do you determine your fee and how do you handle billing?
- What other clients are you working with at this time, and how would you fit our project into your schedule?
- What was your worst campaign experience and how did you cope with it?
- What is your least favorite part of the campaign process?
- How would you deal with a campaign in which the leadership gifts did not come in as planned?

(See the Troubleshooting Guide in Appendix A for other difficulties that might be addressed.)

The committee should meet prior to the interviews, at which time question areas might be assigned to each committee member. In this way, every member of the interview committee will have an opportunity to interact directly with each consultant. Once again, close attention should be paid to the details of the consultants' behavior, for they are telltale signs about how the consultant would function while at work on the campaign. Are the consultants on time? Are they dressed in a style that fits your organization? Do they take the time to learn about each member of the committee? Do they seem well informed about the project? Do they speak in a manner that engages the attention of the committee? Do they mumble or speak too fast? Do they seem authentic to you? Do they treat each committee member, including staff, with respect?

It is crucial that the consultant be someone who can present him- or herself clearly and authoritatively before a formal group (the board, for example) and also be a friend, teacher, advisor, and collaborator for the campaign staff.

Following the interviews, but before any discussion, it might be a good idea for each committee member to write down the name of the consultant that he or she would most prefer. This encourages each person to do some independent thinking before being drawn into the vortex of committee politics. It often happens that the decision is clear, and everyone leans toward one person. Sometimes two or more candidates may seem equally appropriate. But occasionally the group is not sold on anyone or is sharply divided.

Soliciting Consultants' Proposals

Once the field of consultants has been narrowed to two or three consultants, they should be invited to submit proposals for the work that has been outlined. To facilitate comparing proposals, it may be helpful to provide each consultant with a written description of the scope of the work to be addressed in the proposals. Consultants operate differently both in terms of fee structure and how they divide the work that is specified in their proposals. If more than one consultant is still in the running, these proposals should provide a simple way of helping to make the final decision. Each committee member should be sent copies of each proposal, and a committee meeting to make a final decision should be scheduled.

If, even after discussion, there is no clear consensus among the committee members to support one of the candidates, the committee would be well advised to take a step backward and reopen the consultant search. It is extremely important that the entire committee feel that they have selected the right consultant, and whatever is needed to make that happen should be done. There really is a suitable consultant out there somewhere.

Finding the Perfect Match

I was feeling a little bit uncomfortable with the way our campaign had started. We had received a challenge grant from the National Endowment from the Humanities and had to raise $1 million from private sources. This was lots more than we had ever raised. Our board was composed largely of professors and other academic types, and we really didn't know what we were doing. Through a string of events, I ended up talking to a neighbor at a Christmas party who had a son who worked for a big consulting firm. I drove up to meet the son. We had a three-hour breakfast meeting. He took a look at our plan and basically agreed that, yes indeed, we had some problems and probably needed a consultant. At that point, we didn't even know that there were such things as fund-raising consultants.

The consultant felt we were an emergency case. Some people from his firm came up to meet us the next week, all dressed up in their business suits and white shirts. They convinced us that we needed some help, but somehow we didn't feel very comfortable with their Madison Avenue approach to fund raising. At that point we started asking around for a second opinion. We learned that a former university development director was out on her own doing consulting, and we spoke with her. She seemed to fit our organization, and we eventually hired her.

—Executive Director

Checking References

When the committee has developed a prioritized list of its top two or three candidates, it's time for a reference check. The consultants-elect should be able to provide a list of clients to call, and it is well worth calling all of them. Occasionally, during the reference checks red flags surface and should be heeded. Conversations with references can cover the standard due-diligence questions and also focus on suggestions about how to get the most out of the consultant who is selected. Other clients' experiences can be a great help in starting out on the right foot with the new consultant.

Hiring the Consultant

Once the decision has been made about hiring a consultant, the relationship will have to be clarified and solidified. This will require a written document that outlines the specifics of the working relationship between the consultant and the organization. Sometimes this is done by drafting a contract, but often a letter of agreement attached to the proposal more simply provides what is needed. No matter what kind of document is agreed on, it should answer the following seven questions:

1. How much will the agency pay the consultant?
2. What services will the consultant provide?
3. What will be the timetable for the consultant's work?
4. To whom will the consultant report?
5. How will the consultant report progress to the client? In what form and on what timetable?
6. In addition to the consulting fees, what expenses will the organization have to pay? Travel? Phone? Copying? What are these likely to amount to? Will the consultant add administrative overhead to the expenses or rebill them at cost?
7. Can either party cancel the contract? If so, what are the terms of cancellation?

The consultants will usually be able to prepare a contract or letter of agreement. Whether or not it is then sent to the organization's attorney for review, it most certainly should be carefully perused. In fact, it may be worth the time and effort to review it point by point with the consultant to make sure that both parties interpret the document in the same way. The contract or letter of agreement should be signed in duplicate by the consultant, the executive director of the agency, and the board chair.

Registration: Today, many states require that fundraising consultants be registered with a bureau of charitable organizations. This agency's name varies from state to state. The consultant should be able to vouch for an up-to-date registration and should provide a registration number for the organization's files. In many states, a consultant must pay a fee and submit documentation annually on the firm's activity and staffing. Consultants are generally required to register in every state in which they have clients. This process can become costly and time consuming, and sometimes consultants who work in several states disregard the registration requirements.

Although state registration says absolutely nothing about the effectiveness or abilities of a consultant, it is a sound idea to work only with registered consultants. Problems in this area have an uncanny way of causing trouble when least expected. In some states, an organization that hires an unregistered consultant may be fined or otherwise reprimanded, and tangling with government bureaucracies can be costly and frustrating, even if an unregistered consultant has been hired unwittingly.

Information Flow and the Consultant: Consultants are outsiders. Their offices are remote from the organization, and they usually visit the clients only periodically. So it is very important that consultants receive a steady flow of information from the organization. Shortly after hiring a consultant, an organization should add the consultant to the mailing list to receive all mail that routinely goes to external constituents as well as add the consultant to relevant internal distribution lists. These internal lists are likely to include board mailings and materials and development committee mailings.

Consulting is a lonely job. Consultants appreciate getting feedback; being kept in the information loop; and being treated with warmth, openness, and honesty.

Consultants and Fees

Ways of paying consultants fall roughly into three categories:

1. billing according to time
2. billing by the task
3. combination billing

Most consultants bill according to time, basing their fees on a daily rate. As of 2001, this rate can vary from $1,000 per day all the way up to $4,000 per day. The daily rate is generally determined by the market in which the consultant usually works. Larger institutions and larger cities generally support higher fees, and consultants who work in those areas tend to be at the upper end of the scale. These consultants also sometimes add a significant percentage of markup to their expense billings to cover the office expense of rebilling. Consultants who specialize in small clients and operate outside of the major metropolitan areas generally have lower fees.

A consultant might suggest a schedule of a certain number of days per month over a specified number of months, or perhaps a base number of days with an additional fee for any time spent in excess of the agreed-upon time. In negotiating with the consultant, it is necessary to understand how the number of days that are worked on a project is calculated. If the consultant must travel any distance, is the standard day rate to be paid for travel time?

Because it is difficult to predict the exact amount of time any long task will take, it may be advisable to encourage the consultant to agree to a maximum fee for the job. If the job takes longer than is covered in that fee, it would then require official approval for additional payment. The effect of this arrangement is to put pressure on the consultant to complete the task in a timely way and to protect the organization against unanticipated expenses. There is no one correct type of relationship, but it is necessary to understand exactly what type of relationship is being entered into, how much it will cost, and the scope of services to be received.

Some consultants prefer to bill by the task, determining in advance a flat fee for a specified amount of work. Usually consultants who use this arrangement determine the number of days that they think the work should take and then base their fee on that estimate. With a flat fee, it is known from the outset what the project will cost, and the consultant can focus on the work at hand rather than the number of hours or days. However, when the task is long and complex, like providing counsel for a capital campaign, it is often difficult to determine the correct fee up front, and few consultants are willing to take that risk. If a consultant is engaged to work this way, it will probably be necessary to make it clear that if, as the project progresses, the consultant has vastly miscalculated, then the fee can be renegotiated.

Some consultants prefer to combine various methods of determining their fees: flat fees with add-ons for extensions; a daily rate with an agreed-upon number of days that the consultant will not exceed; a flat fee plus additional fees per interview (in the case of feasibility studies); and so on. Clearly there is much room for creativity and exploration in the negotiation process.

Negotiations will proceed well if the needs of the organization and of the consultant are clearly understood. From the perspective of the organization, it is important to know ahead of time what the consultant is going to charge for his or her services so that there will be no financial surprises. On the other hand, because the timeliness of the consultant's work will depend in large part

---

The Woes of a Real-Life Consultant

I used to charge by the day until I realized how unpredictable my working effectiveness was. On the days when I could only stare at my computer and couldn't write a word of a client's report, I felt so guilty that I wouldn't charge them for that day. And then there would be times when I could write an entire report in one day. Unfortunately, my contracts with my clients didn't distinguish between the days when I was a dolt and those when I was a wizard! I never knew how many days to bill for, since I suspected that I needed the doltish days to get to the wizard state.

—Campaign Consultant

---

on the organization's ability to assemble committees, respond to draft documents, and gather information, the consultant would like to be protected from unnecessary project delays. In some sense the only product that consultants have to sell is their time, and no consultant is able to bill for all time worked. Thus, any consultant

---

The Procrastinating Client

Last year I accepted a contract to conduct a feasibility study for a small social service organization. They decided to engage my services and sent the signed contract and first payment check the following month. But from then on my work with this client has been disheartening. After a delay of three months, they called to get dates for a preliminary meeting, saying that they were anxious to get going as soon as possible. I gave them several dates for the meeting, but then I didn't hear from them for another two months—not a peep. In response to my calls they told me that they were still assembling the background material they needed for the meeting. Two more months passed before they called to say they had scheduled a meeting with some of their board members on a specific date two weeks later. I had another appointment for that date, but ever anxious to oblige, I juggled my schedule so that I could attend. The day before the meeting, they canceled, telling me that several board members could not attend. As of this writing, I am still waiting. Their material is buried in my files, and I am no longer eager to work for them.

—Campaign Consultant

---

who has been in business for any length of time will want to be sure that he or she is paid appropriately for the actual time spent on a project.

The Scope of Consulting Services: Capital campaign consulting generally fits into two broad areas: pre-campaign studies and campaign counsel. Consultants vary on whether they prefer to contract for both at once or to cover the services in two separate contracts. The issues are colored by the importance of using the same consultant for both the feasibility study and the campaign itself. The consultant who conducts the feasibility study interviews obtains a great deal of confidential information through that process. Some of this information cannot be shared directly with the client, yet it will help shape a consultant's judgment about how the campaign should be designed. It is unwise, therefore, to change consultants in midstream.

On the other hand, because the information obtained during the feasibility study will help shape the campaign, it is very difficult to predict the scope and timetable for the campaign prior to the completion of the feasibility study. In general, therefore, it is recommended that the consultant be invited to submit two separate proposals, the first prior to the feasibility study and covering just those services, and the second outlining the campaign

---

Success in Spite of Themselves

A couple of years ago, I was called by an agency to see about providing campaign counsel. They had already had a feasibility study completed by a local consultant and had not found him to be a good fit. And indeed, when I reviewed his report, I understood why. This agency, often viewed as a left-wing organization, was very ecologically minded. And not only had the consultant relied excessively on the use of statistical analysis and multicolored photocopied charts to illustrate the results of a mere thirty interviews, but the entire report was triple spaced and printed only on one side. It was a job that could only be described as expensive, wasteful, and not particularly insightful. In a weak moment of exaggerated confidence, I agreed to become their campaign consultant. I spent the next two years trying to avoid the land mines I would have known about had I done the feasibility study myself. Now, I take a perverse pleasure in knowing that the campaign succeeded in spite of the inadequate feasibility study. But I rather suspect that I would have designed the campaign differently had I been the one to conduct the feasibility study.

—Campaign Consultant

---

counseling services at the conclusion of the feasibility study.

Resident Consultants: Not many years ago, it was common practice for the large consulting firms to place a consultant in an organization for the campaign planning and solicitation period. The consultant would set up a full-time office (often with a secretary), conduct the feasibility study, and then proceed to serve not only as consultant, but also as campaign manager. Specifically, the consultant was responsible for spending a constant number of days per month at the organization, carrying out the campaign tasks directly by implementing and managing the campaign. This practice was widely used by large social-service agencies and one still occasionally encounters it today.

Traditionally, resident consultants were used because it was believed that an organization in the midst of a capital campaign needed the complete and undivided attention of one consultant. No one likes to think their needs are taking a back seat to someone else's, which is just the feeling that can arise if the on-demand consultant's time is divided among several clients. Organizations that engaged resident counsel did so as an alternative to hiring permanent staff. However, before a contract is signed with a resident consultant, it is important to consider carefully certain factors.

There are certain advantages to using an on-site consultant. The consultant will be focused on meeting short-term campaign goals, so things will necessarily happen at a fast pace. There will be full-time access to the consultant. The organization will receive a standard approach to the campaign, since most resident consultants are employed by firms that have their own established campaign plan that has worked with many organizations.

However, these advantages are often undermined by the relatively high cost of a resident counsel. Generally, substantial expenses for travel, housing, and office space increase the project fees. Because most organizations are concerned with keeping costs down, the consultant may no longer be on-site at the campaign's end, when the majority of large gifts have already been raised. The organization is forced, therefore, to implement the final stages of the campaign on its own. And while staff may have had the opportunity to acquire some knowledge from the consultant, the consultant was probably not focused on sharing campaign strategy and skills with the staff while on-site. As a result, the staff may have little idea about how to bring the campaign to a satisfactory conclusion. Typically, the resident consultant is a junior member of the consulting firm, and, while equipped with the firm's campaign plan and other resources, he or she may lack the experience necessary to make sound judgment calls in situations that fall outside the scope of the plan.

Finally, and perhaps most critically, the resident consultant often focuses on an organization's ability to raise money to meet the campaign goal as quickly as possible rather than balancing immediacy with the organization's potential to build long-term and lasting relationships among donors and community leaders. Short-term resident counsel sometimes undermines this important long-term campaign outcome, and organizations may be better served by investing in permanent staff who can balance broader campaign objectives such as identifying new donors, building an organization's constituency, and raising its sights with the immediate needs of a capital campaign.

Consulting Help for Small Campaigns

Although there are many advantages to working with a campaign consultant, it usually doesn't make financial sense to use the full range of consulting services for campaigns with goals of under $1,000,000. Because it takes as much or more of a consultant's time to help raise $1,000,000 for a very small inexperienced organization as it does to help raise $5,000,000, consultants' fees become a disproportionate amount of the total campaign goal for small campaigns. No one likes to see a capital campaign in which the expenses exceed 15 percent of the funds raised, and consultants are wise not to encourage that practice.

> *Small, young organizations can seldom afford consultants but are often in the greatest need of them.*

What should be done, then, to get help for a campaign to raise $250,000? That's a great deal of money for a small organization to raise, even though most consultants will turn up their noses at it. And the process of raising $250,000 for a small organization may well be every bit as complex as it is for a larger organization to raise 10 times that amount. Although there are no perfect solutions to these problems, there are some alternatives.

Self-Education: Although capital campaigns are complex processes, they aren't rocket science or brain surgery. They aren't even trigonometry. With a fair amount of common sense and a willingness to learn, it is possible for the development director to lead the organization through a successful campaign.

This book is certainly a good starting place, and it should be read carefully. There are several excellent seminars offered on capital campaign fund raising. (See the list of resources at the end of the chapter.)

The Generous Consultant

People often call me asking for help with small campaigns. I always tell them the same thing. "I won't be able to serve as a consultant to so small a campaign, but I'd be most happy to meet with you or some of your committee members once at my expense to help get you going in the right direction." They invariably take me up on the offer, and we spend a couple of hours discussing campaign basics and first steps. Sometimes they are so unnerved by the idea of asking people for large gifts that the project simply dies right there. Sometimes there is someone on the committee who is passionate enough about the project to be able to drive it ahead successfully. And sometimes they don't believe a word I've said and they try to raise the money through a direct-mail campaign. I consider it a success if I achieve either of the first two outcomes.

—Campaign Consultant

Using Consultants Strategically

Even if a consultant can't be retained for the entire range of services, there are several times during the campaign planning process that a consultant's expertise and credibility will be invaluable.

The Feasibility Study. A feasibility study consists of personal interviews with members of the organization's constituency. It will give the organization an idea of where it stands with its donors. The information received either will provide encouragement to begin the campaign with the confidence that it can be successfully completed or will reveal that the campaign should be postponed until weak areas can be strengthened.

Since the results of the feasibility study will determine whether the campaign will proceed or be postponed, it is most important that the study be done properly. It must be done by someone whose opinion and advice will be respected and accepted by both the board and the community leaders. A consultant—as an objective observer—can provide that sort of credibility. Although engaging a consultant for the feasibility study will be costly, this will be money well spent.

Because the consultant will not be retained for ongoing campaign counsel, negotiations with the feasibility study consultant should seek to include as much of a campaign plan as possible in the consultant's report. Although most consultants do include some campaign planning in the report, one might request that this section of the report be expanded.

Campaign Planning. It may even be desirable to extend the feasibility study contract through the campaign design and planning phase. Since part of that process is forming a powerful campaign planning committee, it can be an important confidence-building measure to have someone who can help guide the process of enlisting that committee and conducting the planning meetings. The best campaigns begin with a well-thought-out planning process, and the hands-on, seasoned experience of a campaign consultant can help guide the campaign planning committee through the decision-making process.

Case for Support. The consultant might assist in providing advice in developing the case for support. A consultant's opinion and experience could help shape a document that will provide much of the language used in proposal letters, brochures, press releases, and speeches for the duration of the campaign. A local consultant may be willing to share his or her resource collection of good and bad examples without charging a fee. The case for support and the process that produces it are central to the success of the campaign, and money spent on a consultant at this stage may be money well spent.

Occasional Guidance. Finally, it may be possible to hire a consultant who will be available to the campaign for occasional guidance, advice, and encouragement on an as-needed basis. Perhaps an arrangement could be made between the development director and the consultant for a monthly meeting to bring the consultant up to date and discuss any questions and issues that have arisen. Perhaps the consultant could be placed on a small retainer that would make it possible to call for advice as the need arises.

Learning from Mistakes

When all is said and done, one hires consultants to avoid making their past mistakes. There is nothing like experience to inform and educate. Because capital campaigns are such occasional events and so organizationally complex, very few people other than consultants have amassed enough mistakes to know what they are doing. And those directors and volunteers who have indeed made mistakes on one campaign or another may not have had enough opportunities to learn from their mistakes.

It is certainly possible to conduct a capital campaign without the benefit of a campaign consultant. In some cases, the sans-consultant route is the right route. For many organizations, however, the right consultant will strengthen the organization's ability to conduct a successful campaign. Whatever the decision, there is much to be learned through the process of exploring the options.

EXPANDING THE CAMPAIGN TEAM

Although the small group of campaign insiders will meet throughout the campaign to make critical decisions and keep the campaign on course, the campaign will need

---

We Just Didn't Know Enough

Before I was hired as development director, my organization went through a strategic planning process. The decision was made to do a capital campaign to raise money for endowment and program initiatives. The organization hired an experienced "old-school" consultant to do a feasibility study. He told us that we might run into trouble raising money but that we needed to think big. So, the board decided to move forward.

I was hired after the decision to go into a campaign had been made. I had several years of development experience and had been on the periphery of a campaign in my last organization. I did some research on my own about campaigns and felt pretty comfortable handling the nuts and bolts of things that were bound to come up—gift tracking, prospecting, researching, training volunteers—but in retrospect, I realize that my organization and I were pretty naïve about what else a campaign entailed.

We talked about hiring a consultant and interviewed a few, but none seemed quite right for our organization. After discussing it, we decided that there wasn't anything scientific about capital campaigning and that we could do it ourselves.

To make a long story short, the campaign eventually ran out of steam. We ended the campaign far short of our goal. In retrospect, I can attribute the problems we had to two things. First, we didn't have enough information from our feasibility study to know how high to set our goal. Second, no one in our organization really understood capital campaign fund raising, and we hadn't hired a good consultant.

If we had hired an experienced consultant, perhaps we would have decided to delay the campaign, or perhaps we would have lowered our goal. Perhaps we would have changed the timetable or campaign structure. Capital campaigns can be very lonely, and I would have liked to have a consultant's expertise and support.

—Development Director

---

many more powerful volunteers to give the campaign the reach and impact required to succeed.

Many campaigns develop a committee structure in stages, moving from the core group described above to a larger campaign planning committee to a campaign steering committee or cabinet. (See Figure 4–2.)

Core committee. The core committee or kitchen cabinet comprises perhaps six to eight people and does the preliminary campaign planning. This group determines who to enlist in a larger campaign planning committee.

Campaign planning committee. The campaign planning committee may consist of 12 to 18 people who come together for three or four meetings to work with a consultant to develop a written plan that will guide the campaign. The next chapter describes the role of the campaign planning committee and the elements of a campaign plan in detail.

Campaign steering committee. Finally, a campaign steering committee or cabinet is made up of the chairs of each division and committee along with the campaign chairs and other key volunteers who wish to stay actively involved in the campaign. This committee oversees the campaign and may meet quarterly or more often as needed throughout the campaign process.

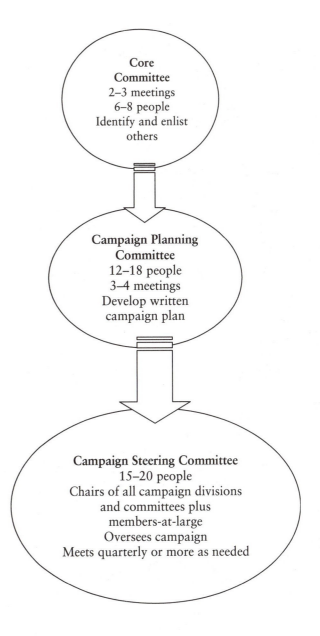

Figure 4–2 Campaign Planning Committee Structure

Some organizations and consultants elect to establish only a core committee and a campaign steering committee, leaving out the planning committee. In this case, the campaign steering committee begins its work by developing the campaign plan. This method works well if the organization is able to recruit powerful volunteers to this committee who are willing to stay involved throughout the entire campaign.

Many organizations, however, find it easier to involve the powerful people in their community for shorter, more limited roles. They may be willing to lend their names to the campaign and attend three or four meetings and key campaign events but are not interested in coming to campaign meetings for two or three years (see Exhibit 4–6). Rather than recruiting them for the steering committee and not having them show up, it may be wiser to invite them to serve on a planning committee of a shorter duration.

THE CAMPAIGN AND THE BOARD OF DIRECTORS

Where does the board of directors fit into this process? Stories abound about organizations whose board members raised more than half of the campaign goal from their own pockets. This pattern is the norm for "power" institutions in large cities. In these organizations, the board members literally pave the way for success with their own commitment, wealth, and generosity. For organizations like this, there will be extensive overlap between the planning committee, the steering committee, and the board.

But for smaller, less powerful organizations a "working" board is more the norm. In these organizations, the campaign planning committee will be spiked with wealthier people and the board members will play a less central role. But even in these organizations, the board plays an important role in the campaign. These more modest organizations often recruit the wealthier and more powerful members of their community to serve on an ad hoc campaign steering committee rather than on the board. This temporary service works well for the organization, the individuals, and the community.

Exhibit 4–6 Ten Suggestions for Enlisting Volunteers the Right Way

1. Always invite people to do things that they are likely to be able to do successfully.
2. Enlist the most powerful and important people first.
3. Provide long horizons between asking someone to do something and the actual task.
4. Assign a person of similar class, wealth, and position to help enlist a particular candidate.
5. Prepare a list of clearly written expectations before asking anyone to do anything.
6. Define the end or exit of every volunteer project before recruiting people for the beginning of it.
7. Break all volunteer activities into small, manageable links that join together to create a longer chain. Then ask volunteers to help link by link.
8. Let "no" be an acceptable answer.
9. Celebrate all successes, no matter how small.
10. Don't forget to tell them that it's likely to be fun.

The Potential for Conflict

Because campaigns have their own committee structures that overlap with but do not encompass the entire board and because campaign committees often have more resources and community power than the board, the relationship between the board and the campaign steering committee sometimes becomes strained. Social-service agencies in particular have difficulties in this area. Their boards are usually explicitly structured as non-fund-raising boards, some of whose members do not have the ability to make significant financial contributions or are not among the powerful players in the community. However, even though the campaign committee may be more visible and better heeled, the board of directors continues to be responsible for the organization's health and well-being.

Most board members of smaller organizations have never been involved in a capital campaign. Because they are legally responsible for the health of the organization, they are often wary, curious, and excited as their organization plans a capital campaign. The better the board understands the campaign process and the more each member is involved, the more effective it will be in guiding the organization through the campaign period.

Particularly if a board is not a fund-raising board, it is likely to have many misconceptions about the campaign, the campaign committees, and the campaign chair. It is not uncommon, for example, for a board to believe that hiring a campaign consultant absolves it from doing any of the work. Conversely, if the campaign leadership and committees are more powerful and wealthier than the board, then board members may feel powerless to carry out their legitimate responsibilities.

Usually, boards of smaller organizations represent a broad mixture of various strengths and capabilities. The task of involving a board in the design and execution of a campaign is that of determining what each board member is capable of doing well and finding a campaign assignment that fits that person's skills and position. All too often, executive directors feel stymied by a board that seems unwilling to participate in the campaign. Yet in most cases, board inaction is not due to a lack of commitment on the part of the board, but is rather the result of a failure to match the skills of board members to the appropriate campaign tasks and not adequately engaging these important individuals in the campaign process.

In most cases, board inaction is not due to a lack of commitment on the part of the board, but is rather the result of a failure to match the skills of board members to the appropriate campaign tasks.

Getting the Board Involved

From the perspective of a board member who has neither extensive financial resources nor moneyed contacts, it is both perplexing and demeaning to be expected to raise leadership gifts. Even the most willing board members are likely to become disenchanted if they are assigned tasks that they have little hope of completing successfully. Campaigns require work of many kinds, from soliciting leadership gifts to stuffing envelopes, from delivering public addresses about the organization to speaking about it at dinner parties or with friends, from hosting a cultivation dinner at the country club to preparing refreshments for a more intimate cultivation meeting. In this panoply of tasks, there can most certainly be found an appropriate job for every board member, a task that will make each of them feel that they have an important part to play in the success of the campaign.

There are four principal techniques of keeping the board engaged and informed throughout the campaign.

1. **Educate the board.** Every available opportunity should be taken to educate the board about campaigns. The consultant can be invited to a special meeting with the board to describe the process, philosophy, and practice of capital campaigns. Individuals from the community who have just finished comparable campaigns can be invited to share their experiences with the board. Opportunities can be provided at every board meeting for discussing the campaign. The campaign chair, if he or she is not a board member, can be invited to speak with the board. The chairs of the various campaign committees can be invited to educate the board about their particular segments of the campaign.

   Educating the board is not a one-time affair. Campaigns extend over a long period of time. They go through many phases. They evolve as they proceed. The board should be privy to the growth and progress of the campaign and not only through monthly reports of how much money has been raised. The executive director and the board chair should design an ongoing campaign curriculum for the board, to explain to them what is going on at every stage in the campaign and to maintain their interest and involvement.

2. **Know the board.** In order to involve every board member, an executive director should become familiar with each member's interests, capabilities, and skills. Many organizations already know their board members well and have only to set about developing the best strategy for involving each board member. Some directors, however, know little about their board members' interests and abilities. While preparing for a campaign, therefore, the director or board chair should gather as much information as possible about each of these individuals in order to determine how that person might most effectively assist the campaign.

3. **Identify appropriate campaign roles for board members.** Board members should be involved in every aspect of the campaign. Not only does this provide a role for every type of person on the board, but it provides an initial group of committed and informed volunteers to begin filling some of the many volunteer positions in the campaign.

   The board chair, development chair, and other key board members should serve on the most important campaign committees. One of these board members should be responsible for communicating with the rest of the board about the campaign, and should do so at regular board meetings.

   One should beware of the temptation to generalize about board responsibilities. All too often one hears statements such as "It's up to the board to raise the money," or "The board is not contributing enough to the campaign," or "The board is not lifting a finger to help the campaign." Although there may be some merit in generalizing about a board's culture or behavior, such sweeping generalizations are not going to be helpful in motivating individual board members to action. The key to involving a board in a capital campaign is to develop a plan for engaging each member in the way most appropriate to that individual's abilities and temperament, and then to provide sufficient opportunity for each board member to learn, to share information with others, and to celebrate successes.

4. **Remember the chain of command.** The board of directors shoulders the responsibility for the organization. The board, then, has the responsibility of approving or denying the campaign plan that is outlined by the campaign planning committee. The plan developed by this committee should be drafted as a set of recommendations to be presented to the board of directors for their approval. The board should not be seen by the campaign planning committee as an obstacle to the success of the campaign but as the commanders-in-chief to whom the planning committee presents proposals for the campaign ahead.

CREATING A POSITIVE ATMOSPHERE

> *People who work on campaigns must constantly remember to recognize, acknowledge, and applaud every accomplishment and every little step forward.*

As the campaign team expands, an understanding of some simple principles of group dynamics will help maintain a positive and constructive atmosphere for volunteers and staff alike. Campaigns in which volunteers experience unpleasant meetings, ill-defined tasks, or illogical processes are marked by a rapid attrition of capable volunteers. To build and maintain a team of fully committed staff members and volunteers, keep in mind the following:

1. Make sure every meeting has clear, well-defined, achievable goals.
2. Every meeting should have a clear agenda and be followed up with a clear, brief, and cogent summary indicating the task assignments that were made in the meeting.
3. Be sure that all staff and volunteers are in the communications loop for every piece of good news.
4. Find creative ways to keep meetings fresh and compelling.
5. Be sure meetings start and stop on schedule.
6. Acknowledge work well done at meetings.
7. Be sure everyone who attends meetings has a real chance to play an active role.
8. Celebrate early and often and in many ways.
9. Treat campaign volunteers like insiders. They are!
10. Model the behavior you wish others would adopt.

An effective campaign team of staff and volunteers who work well together are critical to a successful campaign. Careful attention to building that team early in the planning process prevents or minimizes debilitating personnel or personality problems from emerging at critical junctions of the campaign. And a team that works well together, with respect, enthusiasm and trust, can imbue the entire campaign with a special creative energy that yields astonishing results.

REFERENCES

American Association of Fund-Raising Counsel, 25 West 43rd Street, Suite 820, New York, NY 10036; 212-354-5799.

Association of Fundraising Professionals, 1101 King Street, Suite 700, Alexandria, VA 22314; 703-684-0410.

DePree, Max. 1992. *Leadership jazz.* New York: Currency Doubleday.

National Center for Non-Profit Boards, 200 L Street NW, Suite 510, Washington, DC 20036; 202-452-6262.

The Fund Raising School, The Center on Philanthropy at Indiana University, 550 W. North St., #30, Indianapolis, IN 46202–3272; 317-684-8933.

Chapter 5
Planning the Campaign

Chapter Outline

- The Importance of Campaign Planning
- The Planning Process
- Refining the Case for Support
- Refining the Goal
- Developing Non-Monetary Goals
- The Gift Range Chart
- Donor Recognition
- Campaign Structure
- Projecting a Realistic Campaign Timetable
- Determining How Gifts Will Be Solicited
- Deciding What to Count and How Much It's Worth
- The Capital Campaign and Annual Giving
- Gift Accounting and Reporting
- Estimating Campaign Costs

THE IMPORTANCE OF CAMPAIGN PLANNING

Successful campaigns are carefully planned. They have clear goals, structure, policies, timetables, and practices that have been determined and agreed upon in advance. The process of developing a campaign plan educates and engages the volunteers. A carefully developed, realistic campaign plan enables volunteers to understand their particular roles and to see how their efforts fit into the larger campaign. The planning process gives the campaign leadership an opportunity to explore various options for campaign design and to shape the campaign so that it is appropriate for their organization and their community. A thorough campaign plan provides information and material that will answer questions that are likely to arise during the campaign itself. Through the planning process, staff and volunteers acquire an understanding of how the campaign will unfold, a sense of commitment to its goals, and confidence that the campaign will succeed. This chapter reviews all aspects of campaign planning, beginning with a discussion of the planning process and then reviewing each component of a campaign plan.

THE PLANNING PROCESS

After many months or even years of preparing for a campaign, an organization finally begins the campaign by assembling a team of influential individuals to explore, develop, and embrace a campaign plan. The campaign planning committee members serve as the architects of the campaign. The committee draws together people who have the power, influence, and resources to make a campaign successful, and it engages them in shaping the campaign. If well executed, the planning process is an opportunity to educate staff and volunteers in capital campaign fund raising, to demystify the campaign process, and to present a clear and comprehensible picture of the campaign.

The Campaign Planning Committee

Assembling the committee that will plan the campaign is the first concrete step in the campaign process. This campaign planning committee is charged with the weighty task of developing a specific, reasonable, clear, and sound plan for the campaign. The plan will include decisions on many of the critical issues that affect a campaign's success, such as the campaign goal, timetable, volunteer structure, and policies on gift accounting and donor recognition.

> *Assembling the committee that will plan the campaign is the first concrete step in the campaign process.*

In planning a campaign, an organization must begin by assembling a group of the most powerful, most wealthy, most wise, and most influential volunteers it has the ability to recruit. These people will set the tone and standard for the entire campaign. Their involvement lends credibility to the campaign from the start, making it easier to attract both donors and volunteers throughout the campaign process.

Optimum Planning Committee Size

The size and membership of the campaign planning committee will vary from organization to organization. Large, well-established organizations with big, powerful boards of directors might enlist a subcommittee of the board to plan the campaign. Smaller institutions with working boards often begin by enlisting their key board members and then add powerful individuals from the broader community.

Planning committees vary in size roughly from 12 to 20. The smaller size is easier to work with and encourages greater individual participation. A larger group allows for broader representation and enables an organization to expand its power base in the community. The best strategy is often to assemble a planning committee that combines board members and community leaders.

Defining Committee Tasks

Because the planning committee often involves individuals with varying levels of commitment to the organization, the planning committee's tasks are tightly defined and of limited duration. Those invited to serve on a campaign planning committee are asked to attend three or four meetings, bring their experience and wisdom to the task of designing the campaign, and lend their names to the campaign.

Over the course of its meetings, the committee will develop recommendations for the campaign that will be submitted to the board of directors for approval. After the campaign planning process is complete, most, if not all, of the committee members will be invited to help implement the campaign. The relationship of the committee members to the organization will determine the design of the planning process. Those with a deep commitment to an organization will probably be willing to give more time and energy than those with only a passing connection. The duration and responsibilities of the campaign planning committee must therefore be designed to reflect what the majority of its members are likely to be willing to do. Those with a great commitment and long familiarity with the organization—current board members, former board members, and founders—may be willing to assume ongoing responsibilities for the campaign. If, however, to strengthen its power base, an organization must reach beyond those individuals with a strong vested interest in its mission and operation, the planning committee should be designed to require a shorter commitment. For example, small organizations without "power" boards may decide to break the commitment into smaller, more time-limited pieces rather than invite the participants at the outset to help with the entire campaign. Someone with less commitment to an organization is more likely to agree to attend three meetings and help plan a campaign than to agree to serve on a campaign committee that will meet for two years and be responsible for the success of the entire campaign

Choosing the Planning Committee

Choosing and enlisting the members of the planning committee is one of the most important steps in a campaign. One wants to be able to identify and enlist the very best people for the job. On this committee, then, should be people who themselves have the potential to be major donors, people whose names would bring credibility to the campaign, people who are knowledgeable about the organization and committed to it, and people who represent various aspects of the organization's constituencies.

A Limited Involvement Yielded Big Returns

My father-in-law is the CEO of a major company in our town. When I was involved in helping our local Planned Parenthood move into a capital campaign, I asked him to serve on the campaign planning committee. I knew he was very busy and was sure that he wouldn't be able to give us much time, but I also knew that his name and clout in the community would really help our campaign. He had never met the organization's director, had never been to the Planned Parenthood offices, and had little more than a passing acquaintance with what we did. I suppose he agreed to come to the three planning meetings only because I asked him. He actually only showed up for two of the three meetings. He participated in the discussion and really helped plan the campaign. He allowed us to use his name on the letterhead. And when it came time to solicit lead gifts not only did his foundation make a really generous gift, but he helped me leverage another big gift from a foundation we had never thought would contribute at all!

—Former Development Director, Planned Parenthood

It is easier and less time-consuming for the executive director and board chair to select and recruit the people to serve on the campaign planning committee, but it is more effective to assemble a small group of powerful people for the task. Although this process takes time, for many small and medium-sized organizations, an effective recruitment process is the key to successful campaigns. The very first committee, therefore, should be a small ad hoc group of the influential people who will help determine the membership of the campaign planning committee.

This crucial group of decision-makers—let's call them the "invited co-conspirators"—will attend one meeting to review names and discuss the composition of the campaign planning committee. Their knowledge of the community, their judgments about people, and their willingness to help enlist others often determine the actual outcome of the campaign.

The size of this ad hoc group should be no larger than six. Larger groups seldom muster the requisite conspiratorial zest, and that zest adds energy and enthusiasm to the campaign process. Each committee member should have significant power and influence in his or her own right and should bring specific knowledge about a segment of the organization or the community. The group might, for example, include an industry leader, a major donor, the head of a large foundation, a well-respected board member, someone who has played a leadership role in other campaigns, and the executive director. The spheres of influence of the members should, in aggregate, cover all the relevant power bases in the community.

Recruiting the Invited Co-conspirators

Because one begins capital campaigns by enlisting the most powerful individuals, the enlisting process should be conceived just as carefully and strategically as that of soliciting major gifts. Depending on the organization and the specific personalities, the board chair and/or the executive director are probably the best choices to help recruit the campaign planning committee.

Most people would be pleased to be asked to join the very inner circle if they believed that those who would be sitting with them are worthy of their company. So to increase the chances of positive response, it is a good idea to begin by enlisting the most powerful individual possible and then use that person's acceptance as an inducement to others.

> *Most people would be pleased to be asked to join the very inner circle if they believed that those who would be sitting with them are worthy of their company.*

Although all of the people invited to attend the first meeting will probably join the campaign planning committee, one begins by inviting them to only one meeting. For powerful people who have not had deep involvement with the organization, this first meeting may help induce them to serve on the larger committee when asked at a later time. At that meeting, the group should develop a prioritized list of planning-committee prospects and determine the strategy for enlisting each of them. If the ideal planning committee has as many as 20 members, this list will need to have up to 25 or 30 names to allow for the few people who decline.

The campaign planning committee should constitute the most powerful and influential group that the organization is able to assemble. The committee should include key members of the board of directors, community leaders, major-gift prospects, and a representative sampling of the relevant subgroups of the organization's constituencies. Organizations that serve more than one geographic area should be sure that the committee includes at least one person from each of the most important regions. The sample form in Exhibit 5–1 has been designed to help evaluate the composition of the planning committee.

Organizations whose services or alumni are geographically dispersed may have to organize mini-campaigns in several different regions. In those cases, the campaign planning committee will include representatives from each constituency (alumni, parents, etc.) and from each major region.

Recruiting the Campaign Planning Committee

The process of recruiting the members of the campaign planning committee will emerge from the co-conspirators' meeting. If that meeting is successful, it will determine not only who should be invited to serve on the planning committee, but also who is best suited to proffer each invitation. One begins by enlisting the most powerful and respected members and then moving down through the power hierarchy. If the most important individuals are unavailable, perhaps on vacation or out of the country, it is usually worth delaying the process in order to involve them first.

Before enlisting the members of the planning committee, the dates and times of its meetings should be determined. The meetings should be planned to begin four to six weeks after all invitations have been extended. The longer the intervening period, the better the response rate will be.

Because there will likely be several individuals enlisting people to serve on the planning committee, all of the relevant information about the purpose of the meetings, the dates and times, and the specific responsibilities of each committee member should be written in a clear,

Exhibit 5–1 Campaign Planning Committee

	Recruitment Worksheet				

Date _____

	Primary Name	Alternate	Code*	Enlister	Yes/No
1.					
2.					
3.					
4.					
5.					
6.					
7.					
8.					

*These codes should indicate the position this person would fill on the committee. They might include indicators such as **B** (board member), **LD** (lead donor), **BS** (business), **PF** (patient family), etc.

easy-to-read document to be distributed to each of those helping to assemble the committee.

Responsibilities of the Campaign Planning Committee

The planning committee is responsible for developing a set of recommendations that will form the basis of a planning document to guide the campaign. The resulting planning document will be presented to the board of directors for discussion and approval.

That document should include the following:

- a statement of campaign objectives and a case for supporting those objectives
- a recommended preliminary dollar goal for the campaign and a table of gifts showing the number and size of gifts needed to reach the goal
- policies covering questions of campaign accounting, duration, goals, methods of solicitation, naming opportunities, giving levels, and constituencies to be solicited
- a campaign organization chart with committee structures, responsibilities, and reporting relationships
- a procedure for identifying and evaluating prospective donors
- a campaign timetable

Together, these elements constitute a campaign plan. Although some elements of the plan might be altered as the campaign proceeds, the shape, structure, and policies set forth at the start will guide the campaign from beginning to end.

Number of Meetings and Topics

It usually takes the campaign planning committee three to four meetings to accomplish its tasks. Ideally, these meetings are conducted weekly over three to four weeks. This timetable should be tight enough to create a sense of urgency and accomplishment but provide enough time between meetings for research and reflection. When the members of the committee all come from the same community, they will often have many conversations among themselves between meetings, a practice that can increase their sense of ownership and heighten the excitement.

When planning-committee members are scattered across the country and must travel long distances to get together, the planning process will have to be scheduled so as to minimize travel and increase the chances that everyone will attend. In this case, the meetings might be scheduled as a two- or even three-day retreat. The retreat format may create a sense of momentum and camaraderie, though it is expensive and requires extensive planning.

When scheduled as three meetings, the planning process might be covered as discussed below.

At the first planning meeting, there should be

- a charge to the committee
- a presentation of the organization: past, present, and future
- a capital campaign overview

The first meeting of any new group sets the stage for the tasks ahead. People want to see who else is there. They begin to feel out their position in the group and explore the limits of safety. This meeting not only establishes the collection of individuals as a group, but also helps create and strengthen the connections between the individuals and the organization.

Because the best planning meetings are participatory work sessions, the meeting should begin with an icebreaker to reveal existing connections between the individuals and the organization. Inviting each person to give a brief personal introduction to the group and share a story about his or her connection with the organization often proves revealing. For example, at the first meeting to plan a campaign for a hospice, several group members discussed worries about their aging parents. One woman spoke about the death of her husband, and one man discussed the hospice care his daughter had received. These personal stories bonded the group around the mission of hospice and created an early sense of intimacy and familiarity that got the group off to an excellent start.

> *People remember more of what they say during a meeting than of what anyone else says. When someone has participated actively in a meeting, he or she leaves that meeting with a stronger sense of ownership.*

At a first meeting of a new group, everyone in the group wonders why he or she was chosen and what he or she will be expected to do. Anxieties are often lingering just under the surface, and these anxieties extend to even the most experienced participant. When these lurking questions are addressed and put to rest, one can quite palpably feel the group begin to relax. At this meeting, the chair should candidly address the process that has led up to the selection of the committee, highlighting its importance and indicating the care with which each member was chosen.

The first meeting must also give everyone enough information about the organization to allow for effective participation in the planning process. Because each member comes to the process with varying degrees of involve-

ment with the organization, the first meeting must level the playing field by synthesizing relevant background information. Simple reports about the organization's mission, history, programs, and staffing might be combined with an operating budget, annual report, and other printed material to paint a clear and lively portrait of the institution. Those already knowledgeable about the organization will get a refresher course, and newcomers will begin to make the organization their own.

The description of the organization and its past, present, and future should include a description of the needs that will be addressed by the campaign. Although a full presentation of the project will start off the next meeting, a basic understanding of the needs of the campaign will provide the proper focus as the committee begins the planning process.

Opportunities for questions are extremely important during the first meeting. Sometimes a few planted questions can pave the way for relaxed discussion and participation.

Finally, the first meeting should set the stage for the discussions that will begin during the second meeting. Although most people are familiar with the expression "capital campaign," very few outside of the fund-raising world have more than a vague notion of what those words really mean. To provide a context for campaign

---

Engaging the Planning Committee

We had had a somewhat lackluster first planning committee meeting. We covered the necessary material but no one seemed to get really engaged. There seemed to be no passion. We had set the second meeting aside for the discussion of the case for support, and I was worried that we would have a whole hour and a half for discussion and no one would participate. Wow! Was I wrong. We began the meeting by asking each person there to tell us their personal reasons for supporting the home, and before we got through three people, I knew we had a winner. Perhaps we were fortunate or perhaps it was in the meeting design, but from the very first person on, everyone spoke from their hearts. They spoke of their religious beliefs and convictions. They spoke of their parents who lived in the home. They spoke of their own fears of growing old. By the end of that meeting not only were we all clear about the case for supporting the home, but the group had bonded around the project.

—Development Director, Home for the Aged

planning, the consultant or development director should describe the principles of capital campaigns and the relationship of the campaign to the organization.

At the second planning meeting, discussion will center around

- refining the case for support
- determining a working goal for the campaign

The second planning meeting intensifies committee participation through a discussion of the case for support and a determination of the campaign working goal. A discussion of the case for supporting the project provides opportunities for participants to articulate the reasons why they would support the project and to confront their own reservations. The determination of the working goal quantifies what it will take to make the project a reality. The initial formulation of these two items will have occurred in the first planning phase in preparation for the feasibility study (see chapter 3). During this later phase of the planning, they are revised in light of the information gathered during the study. Through the process of discussing and agreeing on them, the committee increases its commitment to the project.

The third and fourth planning meetings focus on

- the table of gifts
- the campaign structure
- the campaign timetable
- the campaign policy

By the third meeting, the committee should have embraced the project and be ready to review and explore the nuts and bolts of the campaign. These more technical aspects of campaign planning elaborate a picture of how the money will be raised, where it will come from, and how much time will be needed to raise it. They also establish principles of accounting and donor recognition that will inform the entire campaign. Determining in advance the guiding principles of the campaign keeps an organization from making ad hoc decisions later that can be detrimental to the campaign.

Written Materials

Materials that will inform the work of each meeting should be prepared for all committee members and presented to them during or before the meetings. In addition, a summary of the decisions reached at each meeting should be distributed at the next meeting, thus providing a written record of the planning process. These should be clearly and attractively presented. Three-ring notebooks with tabbed sections work well, since material can be added at each meeting. Committee members will appreciate dividers that separate the material into

sections, making the different pieces easy to find. At the conclusion of the final meeting, a summary of the committee's final decisions should be sent to each committee member. These decisions, once they are presented to and approved by the board, constitute the campaign plan.

Role of the Consultant

If an organization has hired a consultant to help with the campaign, that person will be very important during the planning process. The consultant brings experience and knowledge from many other campaigns to the planning process. He or she not only helps plan and prepare for the meetings but also serves as a source of expert information during committee discussions.

REFINING THE CASE FOR SUPPORT

The pre-campaign planning study is usually the first application of the case for support. Often, however, time elapses between the study and the campaign planning process. Projects grow and evolve. The case developed for the study is likely to contain some information that is still pertinent but that requires updating, revision, and even some rethinking. The campaign planning process is an excellent opportunity to present, review, and revise the case for support. During the second planning committee meeting, the director or some other appropriate staff member should make an oral presentation of the case for support. The information that is presented should cover the following five questions:

1. How will the project serve the community?
2. Where will it be located?
3. What will it look like?
4. How much will it cost?
5. When will it be built or developed?

It is relatively easy to present large quantities of information about an organization and a project. It is far more challenging to distill that information down to its essentials and to present it in a clear and compelling manner. A good presentation enables the listeners to absorb just what they need to know without requiring them to wade through extraneous information. Charts, slides, models, or drawings (which need not be fancy) can be effectively combined with a brief spoken presentation.

A presentation of the case for support opens the way for active discussion. Every project has positive and negative aspects, and the planning committee should explore both sides of the issue—honing the case for supporting the project and understanding and responding to potential barriers to wholehearted support. Exploring both the positives and the negatives will enable committee members to resolve their own objections, thereby aligning themselves more securely with the project and preparing themselves and the organization to address such issues as they arise.

Because people are often uneasy about expressing their ideas (and particularly their concerns) in a group, the planning process should be designed in such a way that it gives every participant explicit license to contribute.

A constructive discussion of the case will yield perhaps four or five pros and two or three concerns. The responses common to most of the committee help clarify the most compelling arguments in support of a project and the most troublesome of its negative aspects. The committee can then summarize the positives and develop responses to the negatives, not only to satisfy itself of the project's ultimate worth but also so that it can be prepared to allay the anxieties of other potential supporters.

The material that is gathered from the discussion of the case for support will form an excellent basis for reshaping and refining the written case for support, which can then be distributed at the next meeting.

Index Cards and the Case Discussion

The index-card technique is a good way to give permission to share one's views: Two index cards are distributed to each member of the committee, who are then asked to take five minutes to write down the three things that they find most compelling about the project on one card and their three biggest concerns on the other. Then each person is invited to share what they've written while a staff person records the pros on one flip chart and the cons on another.

REFINING THE GOAL

Every campaign should succeed. Unlike a military campaign, whose goals, strategy, and timetable are usually set by exigencies beyond the power of the campaign generals, by the time a capital campaign is set in motion, the goals, strategy, and timetable should have been arranged so as to ensure success. The single biggest factor in ensuring success is determining the right campaign goal.

The single biggest factor in ensuring success is determining the right campaign goal.

Considering the Campaign Goal

Embedded in the campaign goal are the answers to the following five questions:

1. What does the organization need to enhance its effectiveness in the community?
2. How much money is it feasible to raise from the constituency or community?
3. What will count toward the campaign goal?
4. How committed and courageous is the campaign committee?
5. How long can the campaign wait before publicly announcing an official goal?

The answer to each of these questions affects the campaign goal.

What is needed? Most capital campaigns are based on specific and well-defined organizational needs. The organization has defined a particular need and has presented a convincing rationale for meeting that need in its case for support. Whether the need is a complex of projects and programs or something as concrete as a new building, the scope of the project, and consequently the dollar figure attached to it, must be commensurate with the needs of the organization and the community it serves. The goal might include, for example, the need for start-up funds for new programs, or an endowment fund for long-term building maintenance in addition to the cost of the bricks and mortar.

What is feasible? It may or may not be feasible to raise all the money that an organization needs for the project it has planned. Therefore, the fund-raising realities of the community, the reputation of the organization, and its readiness to solicit major gifts must be taken into account when setting the goal. If the organization's needs are higher than the amount that can be raised as projected in the feasibility study, the organization will have to develop a plan to finance the difference.

What will count? Although many people never stop to think about it, the campaign goal is determined in part by what is counted toward it. If, for example, an organization chooses to count a $250,000 bequest that will be applied to the project but that was received during the year before the campaign, the goal may be higher than if the bequest is not counted. Or if an organization includes three years of annual giving in the campaign goal, the goal (and scope of the campaign) will be different than if annual giving is not counted.

Who is committed? The courage and commitment of the campaign planning committee is an important element in determining the campaign goal. Although needs, feasibility, and knowing what will be counted are key factors in determining the goal, the courage, commitment, and enthusiasm of the campaign planning committee, though it defies quantitative measurement, can raise or lower the goal. Some planning committees decide to set a "stretch goal" and shoot for an amount well beyond that recommended by the consultant. Others choose a more conservative approach. Committee discussion of the campaign goal, particularly if it is accompanied by gift tables for various goals, gives each member of the committee an opportunity to consider quietly his or her individual gift. Often, potential lead donors on the committee understand where their gifts will fit in the giving pattern and guide the determination of the campaign goal according to the gifts that they have in mind.

When will the official goal be announced? A common practice to safeguard an organization's reputation is to determine a working goal for the campaign. This is a temporary, or provisional, goal used during the quiet phase of the campaign. It is not published in campaign material and appears only in material that is designed to be viewed by a select audience. Then, after the results of the lead-gift or quiet phase of the campaign become clear but before the campaign is made public, the campaign steering committee reviews the goal. If the advance-gift solicitations have proven disappointing, it might lower the public goal. If, on the other hand, the early phase has gone better than anticipated, it might raise the goal somewhat.

DEVELOPING NON-MONETARY GOALS

A campaign provides an excellent opportunity for an organization to articulate and achieve strategic non-monetary goals. These goals might be inside goals such as investing in new information systems or strengthening the development office, or improving communications between the public relations and development programs. Or they might focus on external issues, such as strengthening the volunteer leadership or increasing public awareness of the organization's programs.

Although some of these outcomes are likely to happen during the course of the campaign, articulating them during the planning process helps both staff and volunteers work strategically to institutionalize these changes. It also gives them an opportunity to reinforce and celebrate these accomplishments at the conclusion of the campaign.

THE GIFT RANGE CHART

Once the working goal for the campaign has been established, the campaign planning committee should review a revised gift range chart (see chapter 3). This chart will show a pattern of gifts that is reasonable to work toward given the goal, the history and culture of the organization, and the giving patterns in the community.

The gift range chart is an excellent tool to help staff and volunteers to grasp what will be required for a successful campaign. It will serve as a basis for much of the campaign planning. The chart will guide decisions about naming opportunities and donor recognition. It will provide a rational basis for developing the order of solicitation. And it will enable the staff to evaluate how many prospects and volunteers they will need to be successful.

DONOR RECOGNITION

Although it often seems remote during the campaign planning process, a clear plan for recognizing donors should be in place before the first gift is solicited (see Exhibit 5–2). Donor recognition will be discussed more fully in chapter 10, but the following three elements should be part of every campaign plan.

> *A **clear plan** for recognizing donors should be in place before the first gift is solicited.*

Giving Levels and Categories. Donors to most campaigns are distinguished and recognized according to the size of their gifts. Giving categories should be established for gifts in specific dollar ranges, and each category should be named in a manner that is appropriate for the campaign. Some organizations use such standard terminology as founder, patron, and contributor. Others take a more whimsical approach, with names that reflect the

Exhibit 5–2 Guidelines For Donor Recognition Planning

- Determine the number of naming opportunities available at each giving level.
- Provide one or more naming opportunities for each gift needed at a specific giving level.
- Determine the lowest gift amount for individual plaques.
- Plan a group plaque to accommodate all donors below the base amount for individual plaques.
- Once the plan is determined, do not negotiate with donors.

organization or the project. For example, an orchestra might offer the categories maestro, concertmaster, principal tuba, and so on. Donor recognition categories for a capital campaign should be different from those used for the annual giving campaign.

Donor Listing Practice. Typically, donors to a capital campaign are listed publicly in a number of ways, unless they request anonymity. The campaign plan should clarify whether and how public recognition will indicate the various giving levels. Many organizations elect to list donors alphabetically within broad giving levels. Generally these listings are organized to highlight lead donors, beginning with giving categories high enough so that the number of donors in the top range is small. Subsequent categories include larger number of donors. For example, a donor listing might look something like Exhibit 5–3.

Some organizations list donors alphabetically within giving categories but elect not to include the specific dollar amounts on wall plaques. Instead, they include them in programs or other campaign reports.

For reasons that stem from an organization's culture, some organizations do not sort donors according to giving levels, but rather by donor type—individuals, businesses, and foundations—and then alphabetically within each type. Still others prefer not to categorize donors at all and list them all alphabetically. For example, some religious organizations do not wish to highlight the social or class differences among the members of their congregations.

Strictly from a fund-raising perspective, listing according to donor category provides a strong motivation for people to give more than they might if their gift was not going to be made public. However, fund raising is only one aspect of the health and life of an organization and decisions about donor listings and recognition must be made in such a way as to build constructive long-term relationships between the donors and the organization.

The campaign planning process provides an excellent opportunity to discuss these issues and clarify them early in the campaign, thereby avoiding confusion during and after the solicitation process.

Plaques and Other Donor Listings. The campaign plan should also clarify the public posting of donor names. Most important in this area is a determination of who will be listed on permanent donor plaques. If, as is usual, donors will be recognized by giving level, the campaign plan should specify the lowest giving level that will be recognized on a permanent plaque. A campaign plan might also spell out the various print media in which donor lists might appear and the policy to guide the staff so that they know which names they may or may not publish. In general, it is good policy to ask donors for their consent to having their names used in the public media.

Although the campaign plan need not spell out the specifics of naming opportunities and commemorative techniques, it should indicate whether or not plaques that recognize donors or commemorate other individuals will be part of the donor recognition program. See chapter 10 for more detailed information about donor recognition.

Naming Opportunities

Many campaigns that raise funds for building projects—renovations or new buildings—offer wonderful opportunities for people to make gifts that enable them to have their name or the name of someone they care about inscribed on a plaque in a particular room or area. Although most people are quick to say that they have no interest in seeing their name "in lights," experience demonstrates otherwise. Though they may give to a campaign for reasons that have everything to do with the mission of the program and their desire to help the organization, a great many people also find pleasure in seeing their name or that of a loved one on the wall of a building.

Determining Giving Levels for Naming Opportunities

Contrary to popular belief, gifts made to name a specific room or space in a building do not actually pay for that particular space. Nor are the dollar amounts of those gifts determined by the cost of the space. Giving levels

Exhibit 5–3 Donor List

Founders ($250,000+)
Mr. and Mrs. Andrew Abelsmith
Mrs. Woodrow R. Blatsworthy

Master Builders ($100,000–$249,999)
Ms. Ellen Catting
Donald L. Cohen, Esq.
Samuel Wiffen
Mr. and Mrs. Robert W. Worthing

Builders ($25,000–$99,999)
Mrs. Thomas Esbenshade
Jessica Farthing
The Howing Foundation
Barbara and Benjamin Trestler
Mr. Chester Smith, III
Mrs. Trevor Training
Mr. and Mrs. Harvey Ulright

for naming opportunities are determined by the visibility, prestige, and emotional appeal of the space. Main lobbies are likely to have a higher price than even expensively equipped staff offices. The boardroom is likely to have a higher price than the training room. A chapel or meditation room is likely to be more valuable than a similar small meeting room.

The actual dollar amounts that are assigned to particular spaces should approximate the table of gifts being used in the campaign. The highest gift should correlate to the most prominent and prestigious space, the next two to the next most visible spaces, and so on.

The process of identifying spaces and assigning dollar values is generally accomplished by a small committee that includes the executive director, campaign leadership, and development director. The process works most simply if the development director prepares for everyone copies of the floor plans that indicate each of the rooms and spaces. Creativity is essential in preparing this list, for it is not only the standard rooms that can be named, but also flagpoles, entry porticos, garden areas, fountains, and all sorts of other architectural elements. Sometimes there is more than one way to name a space or architectural element—for example, with special stained- or etched-glass windows, either the individual panes can be given by several moderate donors or one donor can donate the entire collection.

Some campaigns identify naming opportunities for more than the largest amount on the gift range chart. For example, a campaign to raise $3 million for a new building might include a $5 million naming opportunity for the entire campus. Or a campaign to renovate a portion of a building might include an opportunity to name the entire facility. This practice raises the sights of staff, volunteers, and donors and highlights opportunities for people who may wish to consider making an extraordinary gift.

The discussions about what should be offered as a naming opportunity and how much it should be offered for are invariably interesting and lively. They result in an understanding on the part of both staff and campaign leadership of the complex nature of naming rooms and spaces in buildings and the appeal of making a naming gift. Sometimes the process of determining the naming opportunities actually raises the sights of the campaign leaders about their own gifts.

Once determined, the naming opportunity plan should be incorporated into the campaign plan. The dollar values placed on opportunities should not be negotiable. To change the value of a naming opportunity during the solicitation process devalues gifts that have already been made. In most cases, it is better to leave spaces unnamed than it is to devalue the naming process.

Exhibit 5–4 is a sample naming-opportunity list that was presented to prospective donors to help them envi-

Exhibit 5–4 Naming Opportunities

Hospice Center	$1,000,000
Center for Living with Loss	$500,000
Main lobby	$250,000
Entry portico	$250,000
Reception area	$150,000
Chapel/solace area	$150,000
Counseling wing	$150,000
Board/community room	$75,000
Multimedia training center	$75,000
Indoor garden	$75,000
Large conference room	$50,000
North team cluster	$50,000
South team cluster	$50,000
East team cluster	$50,000
West team cluster	$50,000
Facility-based care team	$50,000
Volunteer area	$30,000
Director's office	$30,000
Staff lounge	$30,000
Executive Director's office	$30,000
Chief Operating Officer's office	$30,000
Finance office	$30,000
Admissions area	$30,000
Named fund	$30,000
Counseling rooms (3)	$15,000 each
Patio with planters	$15,000
Personnel Director's office	$15,000
Vice President's offices (3)	$15,000 each
Medical Director's office	$15,000
Medical examination room	$15,000
Development office	$15,000
Small conference rooms (3)	$15,000 each
Window panels (30)	$6,000 each
Group plaque listing	$3,000 or more

sion the size and location of the space they were being asked to consider.

Naming Opportunities and Low-Level Gifts

Although most naming opportunities are designed to stimulate mid- and upper-level gifts, some campaigns use naming opportunities for lower-level giving as well. Architectural elements such as tiles in walls or brick walkways or seats in auditoriums provide a chance to incorporate the names of many people who give relatively low-level gifts to the building.

CAMPAIGN STRUCTURE

Another key element of the campaign plan is a chart of the campaign organization. The organization of every campaign, no matter how large or how small, is developed in a way that clarifies the order and organizational principles according to which gifts will be solicited. There are many ways to categorize solicitation groups and a wide variety of terms used in the fund-raising world to describe them. But two principles guide the fundamental decisions.

Principle #1: Soliciting from the Top Down

All successful campaigns are organized so that the top donors, those from whom approximately one-third to one-half of the campaign goal will come, are solicited first. A basic structure divides the giving levels into three categories: "lead gifts," "major gifts," and "general gifts." These levels are illustrated in Exhibit 5–5.

Exhibit 5–5 Top-Down Soliciting

Lead Gifts

Amount of Gift	Number of Gifts	Number of Prospects	Number of Solicitors	Amount Solicited in Gift Range	Percent of Total
$150,000	1	2		$150,000	
$75,000	1	2		$75,000	
$50,000	2	6		$100,000	
$25,000	6	18		$150,000	
Totals	10	28	7	$475,000	47%

Major Gifts

Amount of Gift	Number of Gifts	Number of Prospects	Number of Solicitors	Amount Solicited in Gift Range	Percent of Total
$10,000	10	32		$100,000	
$5,000	20	80		$100,000	
$2,500	40	160		$100,000	
Totals	70	272	68	$300,000	30%

General Gifts

Amount of Gift	Number of Gifts	Number of Prospects	Number of Solicitors	Amount Solicited in Gift Range	Percent of Total
$1,000	80	360		$80,000	
$500	160	640		$80,000	
Totals	240	1,000	250	$160,000	16%

> *Successful campaigns solicit lead gifts very early in the campaign. These are the gifts that set the pace of the campaign.*

Successful campaigns solicit lead gifts very early in the campaign. These are the gifts that set the pace of the campaign. They determine the standard of giving and establish the campaign's chances of success. Every campaign has a committee responsible for soliciting these top gifts. In some campaigns, this committee is referred to as the lead-gift division. This division is sometimes called the "pacesetter gift division" or "strategic gift division."

Whatever it is called, the lead-gift division assembles the organization's most powerful solicitors and donors around the task of raising these largest gifts. In the example in Exhibit 5–5, approximately seven solicitors will ask approximately 28 prospects for the top 10 gifts. If successful, these solicitors will be responsible for raising nearly one-half of the campaign goal.

Below the lead gifts but still extremely important are the major gifts. These gifts might constitute approximately one-third of the campaign goal and should be solicited in person. They are usually solicited after the public campaign has begun.

The general-gift solicitation reaches the largest number of prospects and brings in the smallest amount of money. Nonetheless, this portion of the campaign builds a base for continued giving.

Principle #2: Soliciting from the Inside Out

The size of the gifts is not the only factor determining the campaign structure. Successful campaigns build enthusiasm and attract volunteers to the cause by beginning the solicitation process from the inside, soliciting those who are closest to the organization, and proceeding outward to those less involved.

Although campaigns carry out this process in different ways, one way is to organize a "family division" that is responsible for soliciting gifts from those insiders not already being solicited by the lead-gift division.

The family division is likely to be responsible for soliciting the board, former board members, founders, key volunteers, former staff, and anyone else close to the organization. In general, solicitation of current staff is handled separately because of the sensitivities that often complicate that process.

Quiet Phase

The lead-gift and family divisions are organized during what is often referred to as the quiet phase of the campaign, before the campaign becomes public. Together, gifts solicited by the lead-gift division and the family division are referred to as *advance gifts*. The term refers to the fact that these gifts are solicited in advance of the campaign kickoff. These gifts constitute the campaign's *nucleus fund*. As it grows, this fund creates a sense of success and serves as a magnet for other gifts.

In some cases, of course, there will be an overlap between the family solicitation and the lead-gift solicitations. That is, some family members may be lead donors. Generally, all lead gifts are solicited by the lead-gift committee, whether they are insiders or not.

Major-Gift Solicitation Divisions

Because the best solicitations usually combine people of like minds, wealth, and position, mid-level solicitation divisions are often organized according to categories that best sort the constituency. Business people often succeed best by soliciting other business people; doctors solicit doctors; religious leaders solicit other religious leaders; residents of a particular neighborhood solicit their neighbors. Although it is sometimes difficult to determine the best categories around which to build the divisions, in many organizations the division categories will be obvious.

The solicitation divisions of a typical campaign for a community-based social-service organization might be structured as in Figure 5–1. The division categories should, of course, reflect the constituencies of the particular organization.

Non-Solicitation Committees

Campaign structures include more than solicitation teams. Volunteers often assist with many of the specific tasks that are necessary to a campaign. Task-oriented committees within the campaign structure help define the role of non-solicitor volunteers and clarify their relationship to the larger campaign. Common task-oriented campaign committees are the special-events committee and the public-relations committee. Some campaigns also have separate committees for cultivation and prospect rating.

The special-events committee is responsible for helping organize the various events that punctuate a capital campaign. The most common of these are the campaign kickoff, the ground-breaking (for building campaigns), and the final celebration of success. Occasionally, the special-events committee will organize other spirit-building events as well.

The public-relations committee helps develop a public-relations and media plan for the campaign. They work cooperatively with the staff person in charge of public relations. The public-relations committee also oversees

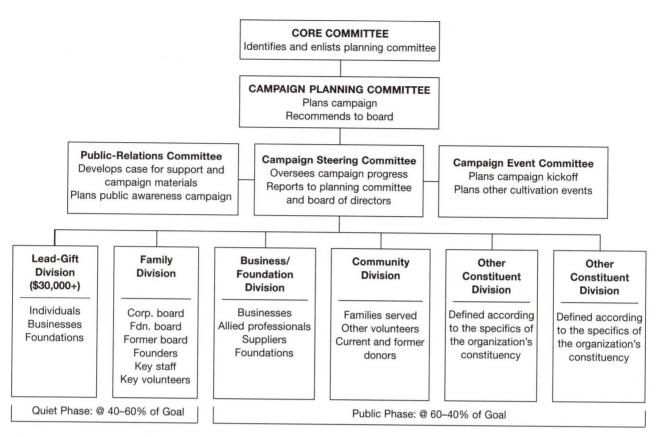

Figure 5-1 Sample Campaign Structure

the design and production of the solicitation and communication materials used in the campaign. These materials will be discussed in detail in chapter 9.

A cultivation committee can work wonders for a campaign by organizing an ongoing series of small events—luncheons, small presentations, tours of the facility, or other non-fund-raising contacts with prospective donors. In an ideal world, all of the cultivation will have been completed prior to the campaign, but in reality, most organizations only scratch the surface of this process; some never even think about developing an organized cultivation process.

Prospect screening and evaluation is an integral part of any campaign. Sometimes these tasks are organized within each division, and sometimes they are organized separately by staff members who recruit volunteers to review lists. For small organizations with limited staff time, it may be preferable to incorporate the screening process into the early divisional meetings, thus engaging the solicitors in rating and evaluating the set of prospects they will be soliciting.

Campaign Steering Committee

With a proliferating series of divisions and committees and a campaign planning committee that vanishes after three or four meetings, one might ask: Who actually oversees the campaign? As the campaign moves from the planning to the action stage, responsibility passes from the planning committee to the campaign steering committee. It is the responsibility of the staff and key leaders to enlist the steering committee. Ideally, this committee will include the campaign chairs, some of the most powerful members of the planning committee, and the chairs of each campaign division and committee.

The steering committee generally meets monthly or at least quarterly for the duration of the campaign. These meetings serve to inform people working on different committees or divisions of the progress in the entire campaign. It also provides an opportunity to get feedback and advice about inevitable unexpected issues that arise during the campaign.

This steering committee or campaign cabinet is composed of the various committee chairs and division leaders in addition to the campaign leadership team, the board chair, the executive directors and other appropriate staff members. The steering committee serves as the communications hub, enabling those heading up one or another piece of the campaign to learn what is going on in other areas. During steering committee meetings, each member has an opportunity to review the activity in his or her committee or division, and the campaign chair is able to discuss progress toward the campaign goal.

The steering committee also guides the course of the campaign. Its members evaluate the campaign's progress and are brought up to date on the solicitation of lead gifts. Using this information as a guide, the committee determines the timing of the campaign kickoff and makes a recommendation to the board for the level of the public goal before the general solicitation materials are printed.

PROJECTING A REALISTIC CAMPAIGN TIMETABLE

A campaign plan should, of course, include a realistic month-by-month timetable that clarifies the flow of work and provides benchmarks for the staff and the campaign leadership. The timetable must take many factors into consideration. Among them are:

- **Project dates.** Critical project dates such as the architectural-design schedule, zoning-approval schedule, and ground-breaking will figure importantly in the timetable. Sometimes the very nature of the project drives the campaign schedule. If, for example, money is being raised to rebuild a playhouse that had collapsed under the weight of a major snowfall, the internal exigencies of the project—opening night on June 17—will be the incentive for a quick and intense campaign. If, however, the campaign is to raise endowment and new venture funds, the timetable will have far more elasticity.
- **Staff availability.** The campaign schedule must reflect the amount of staff time and support available for the campaign. A campaign that will be run by a development staff member dedicated only to the campaign process can proceed more quickly than a campaign run by someone with other ongoing development responsibilities.
- **Geography.** The geography of the organization's volunteer base will also affect the timetable. When volunteers are far-flung and the campaign requires regional organization, such factors will most likely increase the length of the campaign. When volunteers are within a small geographic region and form a well-defined constituency—a church congregation, for example—the timetable might be shorter.
- **Weather.** Different climatic areas have different ideal solicitation periods. Communities where the winter is cold and snowy might choose to schedule the campaign so that the volunteer-intensive solicitation period takes place during the seasons when roads are clear and people of means have returned from their winter homes in warmer climes. In other communities the summer may prove difficult for solicitation if many families are away on vacation during the long school holiday.
- **Volunteer schedules.** The period between Thanksgiving and Christmas presents special challenges. Although the year's end continues to be a principal time for giving as people are reflecting and giving thanks in November and have gift giving on their minds anyway in December, it is an extremely challenging time for recruiting volunteers.

The Phases of a Campaign

Campaigns are punctuated by three major events that mark the beginning, middle, and end of the campaign. These events determine and are determined by the sequencing of many other aspects of the campaign.

- **The campaign planning process.** The campaign begins with the planning process. Once the planning committee has been assembled, there is no turning back, and a clear and timely sequence of events must unfold from that point if the campaign is to build momentum and retain the effective participation of the campaign planners and leaders.

- **The campaign kickoff.** The campaign kickoff marks the second critical point. Although campaigns are not closely guarded secrets before the official beginning, the kickoff commences the public phase of the campaign. The campaign kickoff occurs after enough of the money has been raised to provide reasonable assurance that the campaign will reach its goal. In some cases, this may be 40 percent, in others it may be as high as 60 or even 70 percent. The kickoff takes place after the volunteer solicitors have been recruited for the general phase of the campaign but before they begin soliciting gifts. The kickoff is an opportunity to build spirit, obtain media attention, announce the public goal and progress to date, and prepare the ground for the broad-based solicitation phase.
- **The campaign celebration.** Although campaigns always begin with clear definition and focus, they can easily lose their focus in the myriad details that must be attended to, often over a period of many months. To make the most of the campaign and to bring it to a fitting conclusion, a celebration that draws a campaign to a public close should definitely be on the agenda. Such a celebration bonds the leadership and volunteers to the organization even as it provides closure for their campaign responsibilities.

Presenting the Campaign Timetable

Because people absorb information in different ways, it is usually wise to present the campaign timetable in two ways—a timeline and a month-by-month schedule. A timeline illustrates graphically the duration of each major task of the campaign process with a bar on a chart, and is easily prepared with desktop publishing software. This format clearly shows the timing of the campaign kickoff in relation to the quiet phase of the campaign and enables volunteers to get a quick overview of the shape and timing of the campaign. Figure 5–2 shows a sample timetable.

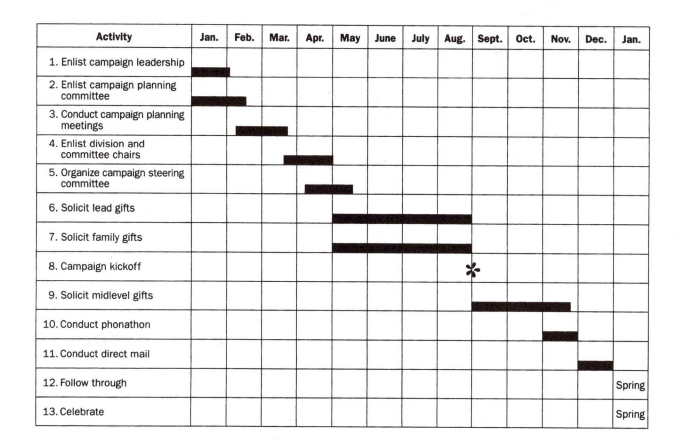

Activity	Jan.	Feb.	Mar.	Apr.	May	June	July	Aug.	Sept.	Oct.	Nov.	Dec.	Jan.
1. Enlist campaign leadership	▬												
2. Enlist campaign planning committee	▬	▬											
3. Conduct campaign planning meetings		▬	▬										
4. Enlist division and committee chairs				▬									
5. Organize campaign steering committee				▬	▬								
6. Solicit lead gifts					▬	▬	▬	▬					
7. Solicit family gifts					▬	▬	▬						
8. Campaign kickoff								*					
9. Solicit midlevel gifts									▬	▬			
10. Conduct phonathon											▬		
11. Conduct direct mail												▬	
12. Follow through													Spring
13. Celebrate													Spring

Figure 5–2 Capital Campaign Timetable

A month-by-month schedule lists the tasks to be accomplished during each month. Using this format, the campaign can be outlined quite specifically, including much more detail than a bar-graph timeline. The month-by-month schedule is also easier to use, adapt, and alter as the campaign proceeds. Exhibit 5–6 shows a sample month-by-month schedule.

Presenting Timetable Alternatives

It is sometimes difficult to predict accurately the schedule on which lead gifts might be committed to a campaign. To safeguard against a sense of failure, it is possible to present alternative timetables contingent on the actual timing of the advance-gift phase of the campaign.

Exhibit 5–6 Sample Campaign Schedule

January
- Enlist campaign planning committee
- Organize lead-gift prospect lists
- Prepare campaign planning materials
- Identify and enlist campaign chairs

February
- Conduct campaign planning committee meetings
- Conduct prospect-rating sessions

March
- Complete campaign plan
- Present campaign plan to board
- Organize lead-gift division
- Enlist leadership for committees and divisions
- Rate lead-gift prospects
- Prepare solicitation material for lead-gift solicitations

April
- Organize campaign steering committee
- Begin soliciting lead gifts
- Organize family-gift division

May
- Continue soliciting lead gifts
- Begin soliciting family gifts
- Organize special-events committee
- Organize PR/materials committee

June
- Continue soliciting lead gifts
- Begin to plan campaign kickoff
- Begin work on campaign brochure and materials

July
- Begin to organize midlevel gift divisions
- Continue work on campaign kickoff
- Continue work on campaign materials
- Continue lead-gift and family solicitations

August
- Complete lead-gift and family solicitations

- Complete campaign materials
- Complete campaign kickoff preparations
- Plan media approach for campaign kickoff
- Complete enlisting volunteers for midlevel solicitations

September
- Conduct campaign kickoff
- Begin soliciting midlevel gifts
- Follow through on unfinished lead-gift and family solicitations
- Campaign newsletter #1

October
- Continue soliciting midlevel gifts
- Begin to plan phonathon
- Plan direct-mail campaign

November
- Follow through with all unresolved lead-gift and family solicitations
- Continue midlevel solicitations
- Campaign newsletter #2

December
- Conduct phonathon
- Plan campaign celebration
- Follow through with midlevel solicitations

January
- Conduct direct-mail campaign
- Follow through with donors and volunteers
- Continue work on campaign celebration
- Campaign newsletter #3

February
- Review and plan donor recognition
- Follow through with donors and volunteers
- Celebrate success!

March
- Final campaign newsletter

One schedule might, for example, project a fall kickoff, with perhaps only four months for the advance-gift phase. An alternative schedule projecting a spring kickoff might be presented at the same time, providing a fallback position if the gift level is not high enough by the fall to warrant a public kickoff. Although this strategy may lessen the pressure to do what needs to be done for a fall kickoff, it might provide a necessary safeguard for an organization without a strong history of major-gift fund raising.

Timing Considerations

Campaign timetables can often be confusing. Because a campaign's phases will not run at the same time or for the same duration as either the pledge period or the period during which commitments made toward the campaign will count, it is important to clarify the meaning of a notion like that of the "three-year campaign."

Pledge Period

Most campaigns encourage donors to make financial commitments to be paid over a period of years. The pledge period is determined during the campaign planning process and is included in the written plan for the campaign. Although pledge periods for larger campaigns have been known to be as long as seven years, most campaigns today specify a three-year pledge period in their campaign materials but allow large gifts to be pledged over as many as five years.

Gift-Counting Period

Campaign plans often specify the period during which gifts made to the organization will count toward a campaign. Some campaigns choose to count gifts that were received prior to the beginning of the solicitation period or even before the work of the campaign planning committee began. Prior to the campaign, an organization might, for example, receive a large, unsolicited challenge gift that provides the impetus for the campaign. The campaign plan will specify that this gift, and perhaps others received prior to the campaign itself, may be counted toward the goal. The period of time over which gifts count toward the campaign goal will make an important difference in how much money is raised and how high the goal is set.

Solicitation Period

The solicitation period also has a timetable of its own that is distinct from the gift-counting period and the pledge period. In most community-based campaigns, gifts are solicited over six to twelve months.

So perhaps "How long will the campaign take?" isn't the right question. Instead, what will have to be determined are the answers to a host of questions that will define the campaign that works best for a specific organization.

- How long will it take us to become strong enough to undertake a campaign?
- How long do we need for campaign planning?
- How long do we anticipate for each phase of the campaign itself?
- How long will the lead- and advanced-gift solicitation process take?
- When do we think we will be able to announce the public phase of the campaign?
- How long a pledge period will we allow?
- When will we begin counting gifts toward the goal?
- How much can our campaign staff handle at one time and what consequences will this have on the timing of the general phase of our campaign?
- When do we think we will be able to announce our success?
- Have we planned enough staff time for cleanup and follow-up throughout the pledge period?

DETERMINING HOW GIFTS WILL BE SOLICITED

The campaign plan should describe general guidelines about how gifts will be solicited. Reviewing this process with the campaign planning committee prepares them for the solicitation process and prevents possible misconceptions. And misconceptions on this topic abound. (Chapters 6 and 7 cover the solicitation process in greater detail.)

The great majority of funds raised for a capital campaign are raised through personal solicitations. Indeed, the ideal campaign is a campaign in which every prospect is visited in person and invited to make a campaign gift. Of course, the real world requires us to compromise. Most organizations have limited staff time and a limited cadre of volunteers who are willing to solicit gifts. To establish an effective limit on the solicitation process, an organization should determine a dollar amount below which a prospect will not be solicited in person. This amount will vary from campaign to campaign depending on the campaign goal, the number of volunteers, and the amount of time allotted for the campaign. For many small to medium-sized organizations, individuals will be solicited only for gifts and pledges of $500 or more. For larger campaigns, this figure might be $5,000 or even $10,000.

The campaign plan should also clarify whether and how lower level prospects will be solicited. Some campaigns are designed to include only personal solicitations, with the lower level donors left for the annual campaign. Other campaigns solicit lower level donors through telephone solicitation and direct mail, thus providing an opportunity for everyone, no matter what their resources or giving history, to make a campaign gift.

DECIDING WHAT TO COUNT AND HOW MUCH IT'S WORTH

When to Start Counting

Although it seems obvious on the surface that campaign counting should begin once commitments resulting from campaign solicitation are received, in some cases a campaign may wish to include gifts made prior to the campaign. Occasionally, for example, a fund has been built over the years to help plan a new facility. It may be appropriate to count that fund toward the campaign goal even though the money was raised long before the campaign was planned. Or an organization might receive a challenge grant to stimulate fund raising for a new project. If an organization decides ahead of time to do so, it is appropriate to count that challenge grant in the campaign goal. Organizations run into difficulty when they neglect to clarify these guidelines in advance of the campaign.

> *Organizations run into difficulty when they neglect to clarify counting guidelines in advance of the campaign.*

What to Count

Gifts made to further the purposes of the campaign, in general, should be counted toward the campaign goal if they are made with the intention of being used for the campaign objectives. But gifts that might come in during the campaign period but that are designated to fund an unrelated project should not be counted. For example, an organization might be conducting a building campaign to renovate its headquarters and a donor might decide to give a major gift to the organization to open an off-site satellite office. This gift, because it was not made with the intention of helping to renovate the headquarters building, should not be counted toward the campaign goal.

An organization may receive a gift that was not specifically intended to further the campaign goals and did not result from a campaign solicitation. If such a gift was not specifically designated for another purpose, the board of directors may elect to assign the gift to the campaign and thereby count it toward the campaign goal.

Most campaigns count the full value of pledges that are committed for a multiyear period. The pledge period varies, generally from three to five years. Most commonly, a three-year pledge period is encouraged while pledges of up to five years are accepted for larger gifts at the donor's request.

How to Value Gifts

Many kinds of gifts may be contributed to an organization. To avoid confusion or the appearance of impropriety, the campaign planning committee should adopt a written set of policies outlining just how gifts of each sort will be valued. In an effort to standardize reporting practices by college and university development offices, the Council for Advancement and Support of Education (CASE) in conjunction with the National Association of College and University Business Officers (NACUBO) has developed a set of norms for fund-raising practices. These standards, Management Reporting Standards for Educational Institutions, are revised periodically and are available from CASE and NACUBO. The following summary addresses the kinds of gifts most often received through a capital campaign.

Gifts of cash and checks are clear and straightforward. They are counted toward the campaign on the day they are received, at face value.

Campaign gifts are often made in multiyear installments. The total pledge amount may be counted toward a campaign when a signed and dated pledge form has been received that indicates the total amount of the pledge and the anticipated payment schedule.

Gifts of securities are often given to campaigns. These gifts should be valued by the organization at market value on the date of their transfer. The value is established by averaging the high and low prices on that day. This amount may differ from the amount actually realized from the sale of the security, but neither gains nor losses nor brokerage fees should alter the counted value of the gift. Most organizations adopt a policy of selling securities as soon as possible and within a specified number of days after they are transferred. Securities may be held by the organization for a longer period only if instructed in writing by the donor. Most organizations cover the cost of the brokerage fees.

Gifts of readily salable or usable real estate, art, equipment, and other gifts in kind are usually credited to the goals of the campaign at the full fair-market value as determined by a mutually agreed upon independent expert appraiser. Small gifts worth $5,000 or less may be valued by the donor without a qualified appraisal. Donors must provide a qualified written appraisal for gifts of property exceeding $5,000. The donor is responsible for obtaining the appraisal because it is the donor who is responsible for reporting the value of the contribution to the Internal Revenue Service. The donor must include the appraisal with the required Form 8283, which the organization must sign if it receives property appraised at more than $5,000. In signing the form, the organization verifies that it received the property and agrees to file Form 8282 if it sells or disposes of the property. Note that the donor must have the property appraised by a bona fide appraiser. In general, that will include neither the donor himself nor the receiving organization.

Many organizations safeguard themselves against receiving unwished-for gifts of real and personal property by adopting an official policy that requires the board to review and accept gifts of real and personal property worth $5,000 or more. Policies of this sort are especially important for gifts of real estate, which sometimes bring major hidden liabilities to an organization.

In-kind gifts to a campaign are common. A graphic designer might contribute the design of the campaign material, a printer might donate the printing, a builder might even contribute a new roof. All gifts of this sort are counted at their full fair-market value as established by the donor and agreed upon by the organization.

Crediting gifts of life insurance can be tricky. Is the policy paid up? If not, will the donor or the organization be responsible for making payments? There are also different values for a policy—the cash-surrender value, the premium amount, and the amount that the donor can claim as an income-tax deduction. In general, when a donor makes a gift of life insurance to a campaign and names the organization as both beneficiary and irrevocable owner, the organization counts only the face value of the policy toward the campaign goal. However, Debra Ashton, in her excellent manual *The Complete Guide to Planned Giving*, describes four other options for crediting gifts of life insurance (1991, 133):

1. Credit for the cash-surrender value of a non-paid-up policy.
2. Credit for the cash-surrender value of a fully paid-up policy.
3. Credit for the amount of premiums paid directly to the organization (on the theory that the payment creates a capital asset).

4. Credit for premiums paid directly to the insurance company by the donor if the donor sends evidence of payment, usually in the form of a canceled check.

See also *Planned Giving Essentials: A Step by Step Guide to Success*, by Richard D. Barrett and Molly E. Ware, also in this series.

Unless a capital campaign has an endowment component, deferred gifts are usually not applied to the campaign. On occasion, however, an organization will receive payment from an unrestricted bequest during the campaign period. In these cases, the board of directors should have authority to determine whether those funds should be applied toward the campaign goal. Such decisions should be made on an individual basis.

Campaigns that have an endowment component will need guidelines for counting deferred gifts. In developing crediting guidelines for life-income gifts such as charitable remainder trusts, pooled income funds, and charitable gift annuities, the organization will need to think carefully about the implications of each crediting decision.

Charitable remainder trusts, pooled income funds, and gift annuities may be credited at fair-market value. In cases where a portion of the principal will be returned to a beneficiary, the remainder interest only may be credited. An exception to this rule is that some organizations choose to establish a minimum age base of 70 or 75 and credit gifts of donors who meet the age requirement at full-market value.

Charitable lead trusts are encountered occasionally. This is an arrangement whereby a donor makes a gift that provides the organization with an income for a specified number of years. At the end of the income period, the balance reverts to the donor or the donor's beneficiaries. Only the annual income that is received from such a trust may be included in the gift totals.

Crediting bequests that are received for the endowment portion of the campaign can be complicated because bequests are revocable and because the value of a bequest is sometimes difficult to determine, particularly if the bequest is a percentage of the donor's estate rather than a specific amount. Many organizations take the position that a bequest intention does not entitle the donor to a gift credit. Instead, they recognize bequest donors through a separate bequest society or giving club.

Other organizations have chosen to develop a type of compromise that gives donors beyond a certain age, usually 70 or older, full credit for their bequest intentions, contingent upon receiving a statement from the donor indicating the exact amount of the bequest. This amount is then entered into the organization's recordkeeping system as a pledge.

Because of their nature, bequests can be difficult to deal with during a campaign, and it may be less complicated administratively for an organization not to count bequest intentions at all as part of the campaign. If it decides to do so, however, it will need to establish strict guidelines within which bequests are to be counted.

THE CAPITAL CAMPAIGN AND ANNUAL GIVING

There are few topics in capital campaign planning that cause more consternation than that of the relationship between the capital campaign and the annual giving program. Volunteers who help with the annual campaign are often quite anxious about the potential effect of the capital campaign on annual giving returns even before the campaign has been planned. However, their fears of falling annual giving revenues during campaign years are rarely confirmed. In fact, it is more common for annual giving to increase during a campaign period as a result of increased prospect cultivation, organizational visibility, and donor commitment.

> *It is common for annual giving to increase during a campaign period as a result of increased prospect cultivation, organizational visibility, and donor commitment.*

There are two general approaches to handling the relationship between the capital campaign and annual giving: fold the annual campaign into the capital campaign or maintain the annual giving program wayside the capital campaign.

Fold the Annual Campaign into the Capital Campaign

Because it might be confusing and burdensome to both staff and donors to ask for two types of contributions during the same period, some organizations include the annual appeal in the capital campaign. In effect, they increase the campaign goal to include the funds that would normally be included in the annual campaign for the duration of the pledge period. The organization designates a specified amount from campaign revenues to cover annual operating expenses during the three years of the campaign period.

During the first year when capital campaign funds are being solicited, the organization does not conduct a separate annual appeal. Once the capital campaign solicitations have been completed, the organization reinstates the annual solicitation. Those who have made three-year pledges are not re-solicited for annual funds during the

following campaign pledge years, but those who have not given during the capital campaign are solicited together with new prospects when the annual campaign recommences following the completion of campaign solicitations.

For this model to be effective, the campaign planning committee must determine specific dollar amounts that the campaign will designate for annual operating expenses during each of the campaign years and then increase the campaign goal and broaden the campaign's objectives appropriately.

Maintain the Annual Giving Program Alongside the Capital Campaign

It is also possible and may in some cases be preferable to continue the annual giving program right through the capital campaign. This practice works best when the capital campaign will fund a project that is clearly distinct from the organization's ongoing operations. So, for example, a college or university is likely to blur the lines between the annual campaign's goals and those of the campaign by including new program funds in the campaign. But a small organization would be more likely to make a clear distinction between a campaign to build a new building and the annual support of its ongoing operations.

When the campaign's goals are clearly distinct from operational expenses, many donors will see the logic in making a special campaign pledge to boost the organization to a new level. At the same time they will continue their steady support to the organization's operations by maintaining or even increasing their gift to the annual campaign.

One common strategy for organizations that have decided to continue the annual solicitation process through the campaign period is the "double mention, double ask." With this approach, donors are solicited separately for the annual and capital campaigns. The campaigns are timed to provide breathing room between the solicitations, but each solicitation mentions the other campaign. In that way, donors are not surprised when they are asked to give again at a later time, and people who have given as a result of the earlier solicitation are acknowledged for that gift while being solicited again.

For more information about annual giving, see *Donor Focused Strategies for Annual Giving*, by Karla A. Williams, also in this series.

GIFT ACCOUNTING AND REPORTING

Finally, the campaign plan describes the roles and responsibilities for gift accounting and reporting. In most organizations, the burden of this responsibility falls to the development and bookkeeping staffs. In some small organizations, however, even these tasks are performed by volunteers. The campaign plan clarifies just who will tally gifts, keep the giving records, and handle billing for pledge payments.

Checks and Balances

In these days of growing cynicism about the honesty of large nonprofit organizations, it is especially vital that an organization be completely aboveboard when it comes to gift accounting and reporting. Whenever possible, someone on staff should tally gifts and send acknowledgments, and their tally should always be corroborated by someone else in the finance/bookkeeping department. For reasons of accountability, a staff person is always a better choice than a volunteer.

If the organization does not already conduct an audit each year, the campaign is a good excuse for beginning that practice. Financial audits not only ensure accountability, they also provide a thorough review of the organization's accounting practices.

Reports on campaign progress are a vital part of building and sustaining campaign momentum. The campaign plan should determine who is responsible for this process and in what forms and with what frequency campaign reporting will take place. Often the organization's staff will produce monthly reports throughout the quiet phase of the campaign for the campaign planning committee members and the campaign steering committee. Once the campaign becomes public, the public-relations committee may develop several issues of a campaign newsletter. Although the details of the reporting process need not be spelled out in a campaign plan, the plan should assign responsibilities for regular reporting and develop expectations about frequency and type of communication.

ESTIMATING CAMPAIGN COSTS

Finally, a campaign plan should include a campaign budget that outlines what the campaign is likely to cost. Capital campaigns are efficient ways to raise money. While direct-mail fund raising or special events can have costs that approach or even exceed half of their total revenue, the cost of running a capital campaign to raise $1,000,000 to $3,000,000 need not exceed 12 to 15 percent of the campaign goal. Because many campaign costs are fixed no matter what the size of the campaign, that percentage is likely to be significantly larger for small campaigns than for large campaigns. A campaign to raise $1,000,000 might cost 12 or even 15 percent, but a campaign to raise $10,000,000 should run no more than 4 or 5 percent of the total.

Campaign expenses are likely to break down as follows:

- 55% Personnel costs: consultants, campaign director, and support staff
- 15% Office expenses: supplies (including stationery, etc.), telephone, duplication, postage, travel and entertainment for donor cultivation, committee expenses
- 25% Communications and public relations: design and printing for brochures, direct-mail pieces, other presentation materials, and events
- 5% Contingencies: other miscellaneous expenses that are peculiar to your organization or community

These figures generally do not include the cost of a feasibility study that should be conducted prior to the campaign. See Exhibit 5–7 for sample methods for estimating a campaign budget.

A Complete Campaign Plan

If those who volunteer to serve on a capital campaign planning committee are the campaign's heart, then a well-conceived campaign plan is its brain. The plan outlines all the critical aspects of the campaign and provides a document that guides the many staff members and volunteers through a complex and demanding process. Without a clear and comprehensible plan, both staff and volunteers are likely to flounder in a sea of ad hoc decision making.

> *If those who volunteer to serve on a capital campaign planning committee are the campaign's heart, then a well-conceived campaign plan is its brain.*

Exhibit 5–7 Estimating Your Campaign Budget Using Standard Percentages

Campaign Size	Approximate Cost
Under $1 million	10%–12%
$1 million–$2 million	8%–10%
Over $2 million	5%–8%

_____ × _____ = $ _____
(Campaign Goal)   (% Cost)   (Estimated Campaign Cost)

Campaign Costs Broken Down by Expense Type

Personnel $_____
(campaign cost × 55%)

Office Expenses $_____
(campaign cost × 15%)

Communications and Public Relations $_____
(campaign cost × 25%)

Contingencies $_____
(campaign cost × 5%)

Estimating Your Campaign Budget Using Itemized Expense Projections

Expense Type	Estimated from Percentages	Projected Itemized Expenses
Personnel		
Consultant		$_____
Campaign director		_____
Clerical support		_____
Benefits		_____
Personnel Expenses	$_____	$_____
Office Expenses		
Telephone		$_____
Computer hardware/software		_____
Copy, fax, etc.		_____
Postage		_____
Committee expenses		_____
Office Expenses	$_____	$_____
Communications and Public Relations		
Letterhead/envelopes, etc.		$_____
Campaign brochure		_____
Presentation materials		_____
Direct-mail printing		_____
Cultivation meetings		_____
Campaign kickoff		_____
Celebration		_____
Communications and Public Relations	$_____	$_____
Campaign Expense	$_____	$_____
Contingencies (5%)	$_____	$_____
Total Campaign Expenses (Est. & Proj.)*	$_____	$_____

*These figures, arrived at in two different ways, will provide a cost range to help guide the budgeting process for campaign expenses. The expenses above do not include the cost of the feasibility study.

REFERENCES

Ashton, Debra. 1991. *The complete guide to planned giving: Everything you need to know to compete successfully for major gifts.* 2d ed. Boston: JLA Publications.

Barrett, Richard D., and Molly E. Ware. 2002. *Planned giving essentials: A step by step guide to success.* Gaithersburg, MD: Aspen Publishers, Inc.

Management Reporting Standards for Educational Institutions. Revised February 1996. Council for Advancement and Support of Education. Available from CASE by calling 1–800–554–8536 or through their Web site at www.case.org.

Williams, Karla A. *1997. Donor focused strategies for annual giving.* Gaithersburg, MD: Aspen Publishers, Inc.

Chapter 6
Who's Who? Prospect Research and Donor Cultivation

Chapter Outline

- Getting It Right
- Whither the Search?
- Where Not to Look . . . and Where to Look
- Building a Prospect List through the Research Process
- Setting Up a Prospect Information System
- Filling in the Details with Secondary Sources
- Knowing Right from Wrong
- Donor-Focused Development
- Patience and Practice

> Our Zoo's Director has been at his post for 18 years and joined the Zoo in the 1960s. His knowledge of our volunteers, past donors, and staff is extensive. At the beginning of our campaign, we gave Charlie lists of names. He reviewed name after name, telling us what he knew about the prospects. He knew all kinds of information that helped us understand our donors better and enabled us to do all of the "right" things with individual donors. His involvement in the research process was invaluable to me and to the campaign.
>
> —Prospect Research Manager

GETTING IT RIGHT

Campaigns succeed when the right prospects are asked for the right gifts by the right solicitors at the right time. To succeed, campaign managers must make many judgments about each solicitation. Who are the right prospects? What is the most appropriate gift for a particular donor? Who would be the right person to ask for that gift? To know the right answers to each of these questions requires information—lots of information. This chapter will attempt to demystify the area of fund raising known in large organizations as "prospect research" and will suggest simple, common-sense ways to gather, store, and make effective use of information about donors in ways that will benefit both donor and organization. This chapter will also review ways to shift the development emphasis away from organizational need and onto building partnerships with donors.

WHITHER THE SEARCH?

Prospect research is the process of gathering information about potential donors to determine as nearly as possible a prospective donor's giving potential, institutional interest, and readiness to contribute, and the person or persons who are best suited to cultivate and solicit the donor. Ideally, a development officer would like to obtain in-depth information about every potential donor in order to make the very best judgments about each of them. In reality, however, there will only be time and energy to gather information about a relatively small number of individuals. To use that time most efficiently, the development officer must work strategically, focusing on those individuals who are most likely to be helpful in making the campaign successful. But for small organizations with high staff turnover, little history of major-gift fund raising, and relatively low-profile prospects, information may be difficult to find.

The Search for Money

Unquestionably, money is a key ingredient in the success of a campaign. Where, then, does one find people with money? Who has given generously to the organization? Who has given consistently? Who in the community are the holders of wealth? Who has a reputation for a philanthropic spirit? Who gives to comparable organizations?

For a campaign to succeed, the organization must find enough such people—both those who have a prior history of giving to the organization and those who have a generous giving history in the community.

Some people give . . . and some don't. Giving patterns are rooted deeply in the human psyche. Some people develop the philanthropic spirit from their religion, others from their families, and some just seem to have been born with generous natures. Although there are examples of individuals who become donors in a rush of inspiration, most giving runs in predictable patterns. There are those who give small gifts to many organizations, and others who give a few large gifts. Some give often, others never give. Whatever a donor's pattern, however, it is a pattern not generally amenable to change, and so one should not conclude that every wealthy person can be converted into a donor. A donor must possess not only some financial resources but also a philanthropic mind and spirit.

> *Most giving runs in predictable patterns. Some people give small gifts to many organizations, some give a few large gifts, some give often, and some never give.*

The Search for Power

In the search for prospects, one typically looks for individuals with the resources to make a substantial gift. Often overlooked in the process is the value of searching out individuals with influence. For a successful campaign, it is important that organizations recruit not only people with the ability to give, but also those who have the power to encourage others to give.

Power is often defined as control or influence over others. In a campaign, however, power is also energy—the energy that accomplishes miracles and that turns a crisis into an opportunity, a quandary into a challenge, and caution into commitment. Power is acquired in many different ways. Some attain it through their positions, others because they have money. Some have it because of the circles in which they move. Still others owe their power to their excellent reputations. When looking for people with power, then, organizations must seek some combination of influence, affluence, and energy.

An organization's power base usually lies in no more than 25 people. In the case of a large organization, these may be people who can donate millions of dollars or who can attract major, national figures to the cause. In small organizations, the power list may include top donors who can give no more than $10,000. In either case, however, assembling a list of 25 names and learning as much as possible about those individuals will help the development staff assess its most important resource, a tool already at hand—the power of committed individuals.

The Search for Commitment

The process of researching, estimating, and analyzing the financial resources and power of prospective donors can become such an all-consuming task that one might easily forget that it takes more than money to make a major donor.

A major donor must not only have money but must also be inclined to part with it. Having the inclination to give is at least as important as having the resources to give. People with passion, inclination, and zeal can often find ways of giving that are remarkably effective even if their financial resources are limited. Sometimes they are willing to solicit wealthy friends or relatives to make deferred gifts or gifts of property, or perhaps to make large gifts pledged over several years. And sometimes people who appear to have few resources actually possess great wealth. It is important to remember that generous people who are committed to an organization are often more valuable than wealthy people with no inclination to give. Committed donors, even those without apparent major resources, breathe life into campaigns, drawing in other people with their energy, enthusiasm, and generosity. Conversely, small gifts from very wealthy

The Attorney Who Writes Children's Books

One day during a casual conversation with a board member, the director of a public library discovered that her friend, a successful attorney in town, had just published a children's book. Now, an interest in books ought to translate into an interest in libraries, and, more particularly, an interest in children's books ought to translate into an interest in the children's section of the library, whose renovation just happened to be the subject of the library's campaign. The director and the board member invited the attorney to lunch. Over lunch, the attorney informed them that although he had never been a donor to the library, he was exceedingly unhappy with the poor condition of the children's section and was very interested in helping raise money for the project. He indicated that he had a great many important contacts in the community that he was willing to cultivate on behalf of the project. He became an excellent solicitor (no pun intended) and made a generous gift to the campaign.

individuals set a low giving standard that can take the wind out of a campaign before it even gets started.

Although it is helpful to know who has resources, it is far more useful to identify those who are seriously inclined to support the organization's mission—those with passion and with the willingness to stretch generously for the organization's sake. Over the next few decades an unprecedented transfer of wealth will take place from the older generation to their children and grandchildren. In many if not most cases, people who inherit money do not change their lifestyles and the change in their financial status is invisible to development directors. A growing number of people who have been lower level donors will have tremendous potential due to this transfer of wealth. This will put the onus on organizations to redouble their stewardship efforts at all gift levels. If donors are treated well for their small gifts, when they inherit money they will be inclined to give at higher levels.

WHERE NOT TO LOOK . . . AND WHERE TO LOOK

Knowing Where Not to Look

Those new to prospect research often see it as the great panacea for fund-raising woes. They imagine that corporations, foundations, or even individuals somewhere "out there" are just waiting to be identified and asked to support a worthy cause. The overwhelming number of advertisements for corporate, foundation, and individual directories does little to disabuse the dreamers of this notion.

But think again! Virtually all gifts, whether from individuals, corporations, or foundations, come from persons who have a relationship with the organizations in which they show interest and who have a stake in the projects they fund. Although corporate and foundation fund raising may seem formal and impersonal, even in those organizations, decisions are made by individuals— men and women who are driven by many of the very same considerations that drive donors everywhere when they decide to make a gift. Whether or not they are giving away their own money or someone else's money, people give to credible causes that they support and believe in and to people in whom they have confidence. To paraphrase the head of a major foundation, "We look at the horse, but we bet on the jockey."

> *Virtually all gifts, whether from individuals, corporations, or foundations, come from persons who have a relationship with the organizations in which they show interest and who have a stake in the projects they fund.*

In the search for prospects, time is usually not well spent attempting to ask for money from wealthy individuals who have no affiliation with or reason to be interested in the organization.

Finding Money, Power, and Commitment Close to Home

An organization's very best, most generous, and most likely contributors are individuals, businesses, and foundations that staff and volunteers already know. A well-established annual fund program that includes some personal solicitation, telephone fund raising, direct-mail solicitations, and special events will already have a solid base of donors. These donors are the best starting place in the search for those who will be most likely to give generously to the campaign. Although they will vary in their resources, commitment, and generosity to an organization, among them will be the staunchest donors and volunteers. Somewhere in the organization's current or former donor lists are likely to be the people who will make the campaign a success by giving money and by raising money on the organization's behalf.

Finding those golden nuggets requires a transformation of the unwieldy and ill-defined list of cold, bloodless names into portraits of flesh-and-blood human beings. Good development officers evaluate attentively the lists of prospects to arrive at the most likely names and then move beyond the basic, impersonal facts to understand the values and interests of each donor. This knowledge will enable an organization to determine the right gift, the right time, and the right solicitor for that donor.

BUILDING A PROSPECT LIST THROUGH THE RESEARCH PROCESS

The Search for Insiders

A good way to begin the research process is by assembling a list of the organization's insiders—a list drawn from founders, current board members, former board members, major donors, volunteers, and staff members. This list may contain up to 200 or 300 names, depending on the organization's size and age. The development officer may already be familiar enough with the list to be able to identify the names of its 10 most powerful individuals without even looking at it.

The next step is to learn what information is already on file about these individuals. A complete profile will include a giving history, biographical information, a history of involvement with the organization, and press clippings, as well as anecdotal information about their families, education, religious affiliations, interests, and patterns of giving to other organizations.

A few surprises may surface with the information. There may be considerably more, or less, information in the files than one had assumed. Some surprising facts, hitherto unknown or perhaps long forgotten, about a particular individual may rise to the surface. Long-buried documents may be unearthed, identifying some of the organization's early founders or other individuals connected to the organization whose names have been lost.

The Past Paved the Way for a Gift

In preparation for a capital campaign, the development director of a private girls' school was delving through her files in search of information on the school's donors. She happened upon a dog-eared manuscript that turned out to be a copy of a speech presented by a long-retired headmaster at the dedication of a new library. By way of making some point or other—perhaps it was the relationship of love of learning to just plain old love—the headmaster recounted how Annie Day, a student at the academy almost a century earlier, had met John Frank, the son of the school's headmaster. The two young people fell in love, and, in 1871, they were married. We may assume that they lived happily ever after. Thirty years had passed since the dedication of the library, and during that time, the entire staff of the school had changed. There was no institutional memory of this love story, and it was just by chance that this speech had found its way into the development director's hands, for, as is usual with old files, those records had been consigned to the oblivion of deep storage.

Yet perhaps it was not entirely chance. The development director's well-honed instincts had directed her to that old filing cabinet in the dusty storeroom. Blessed with a historian's curiosity, she was intrigued by the story of Annie Day and John Frank, and she was aware of the Frank Foundation. Was there a connection? Indeed there was! That scrap of information about Annie Day led to a rekindling of the relationship that had lain dormant for more than 30 years between the school and the Frank Foundation, whose director was the great-grandson of John and Annie. That relationship grew and developed and eventually resulted in a leadership gift to the campaign.

The Search for Previous Donors

Although it may seem a monumental task, an organization must look carefully at its previous donor list. If well maintained, lists of names, addresses, and donation histories can reveal much about the strength of previous donors' commitment to the organization.

In her excellent set of videos, *Grassroots Fundraising Series* (1995), Kim Klein emphasizes that the real purpose of fund raising is not to raise money, but to acquire donors. The reason behind acquiring donors, of course, is to raise money, but the process of cultivating and acquiring donors and asking them again and again actually develops and cements a donor's relationship to the organization.

Many donors, says Klein, begin their relationship with an organization by making a small impulsive gift. By the time they have given several small gifts, they have begun to see the organization's cause as their cause. They pay more attention to the material that they receive from the organization, they become better informed about its mission, and they are more likely to champion the cause when speaking to their friends and acquaintances. If they are pleased with the material that they receive and the ways in which their commitment is acknowledged, they may begin to give larger gifts, thoughtfully rather than impulsively. Someone who gives gifts of $25 to many organizations may not give much thought to those gifts. But that same person, when asked to give $250 or $2,500, is probably going to consider the matter with some care. And when a donor makes a gift that stretches him or her to a new level, that is a signal that for some reason the donor has attained a higher degree of commitment to the organization.

Giving is a sign of commitment as well as a source of commitment. Donors who give again and again and who increase their gifts over time gradually embrace an organization more fully—they are the donors who make campaigns succeed. Figure 6–1 illustrates this continuum of commitment.

An examination of donor records of organizations that have asked for gifts early and often is likely to yield many individuals who have moved through the pattern described above. These donors often begin as casual acquaintances and impulse givers and move all the way through the sequence until they become thoughtful supporters and, finally, committed donors. A healthy group of committed donors—the fruit of years of hard work on annual giving programs—prepares an organization well for a capital campaign.

But what if an organization lacks a strong annual giving program? In today's fund-raising climate, the organizations that don't do a good job of asking, or don't ask often enough, or don't invite their donors to increase their gifts are likely to have flat donor patterns and only

Figure 6–1 The Commitment Continuum

Lowest commitment Lowest dollars → → →			Greatest commitment Highest dollars
One Impulse Gift $	Repeated Gifts $$	Increased Gifts $$$	Gifts + Involvement $$$$
Casual Acquaintance	Concerned Friend	Thoughtful Supporter	Committed Donor
One or Two Low-Level Gifts	Regular Pattern of Giving over an Extended Period	Increase in Dollar Amount + Gifts to Special Projects	Larger Gifts + Personal Involvement

a small group of thoughtful supporters or committed donors. Organizations with immature or inactive annual giving programs will have some catching up to do, and they may wish to delay a capital campaign until they can broaden their donor base and move donors up on the commitment continuum. Whether an organization begins the process now or in two or three years, the prospect of planning for a capital campaign will provide the impetus and the opportunity to examine, analyze, and strengthen the donor base.

Types of Donors

The best campaign donors are those with the greatest commitment. Founders, current board members, former board members, major donors, volunteers, and staff are the most obvious place to look. These are the people who, because of their proximity to and involvement with the organization, have had the opportunity to see firsthand how it accomplishes its mission, whom it serves, and how well it serves them.

More difficult to spot at first glance are the good donor prospects among the many who have given numerous small gifts to an organization over the years. Sometimes those prospects are individuals who have been served, or whose families have been served, by the organization. A pattern of repeated gifts, though they may be small, by a donor who has been helped by the organization may well signal a good prospect for a larger gift.

> *A pattern of repeated gifts, though they may be small, by a donor who has been helped by the organization may well signal a good prospect for a larger gift.*

These grateful donors also often make good helpers. Just as most people don't make financial contributions unless asked, most don't volunteer unless invited to do so. Many thoughtful supporters are ready to become volunteers—they just haven't been asked to help.

A capital campaign provides many opportunities to invite people to help. And because capital campaigns often boost an organization from one level of operation to another, helping an organization during these growth spurts builds enthusiasm and energy among its constituents far beyond what is possible in business-as-usual times. By inviting donors to help and helpers to give, an organization expands its base, strengthening the commitment of people who had previously been only marginally involved. A committed donor who is asked to help and is treated well as a volunteer is likely to become even more generous and committed—and those are the people who make generous gifts to capital campaigns.

Most donor lists have a large group of people who fall into the "casual acquaintance" or "concerned friend" category. This group includes individuals who have given again and again but whose donor records don't stand out in any other way. They have not been volunteers. Their giving has not made any notable leaps. They have not been served by the organization. Because there are often many donors of this sort, identifying the good prospects among them can be daunting. Rather than sorting through them one by one, an organization might design a way to encourage them to identify themselves. This might be done with a mail or phone survey that invites each person to respond with information that would help the staff better understand their commitment and interest in the organization.

The Search in Less Obvious Places

Often overlooked in the search for insiders are those who have been important to the organization in the past but who have slipped into obscurity. Those who work for an institution that has a long history should consider going on a plaque walk. This involves their taking a clipboard and walking the halls and grounds of the agency looking for plaques and portraits. Any names that appear on old plaques should be recorded, and likewise the names of individuals in the portraits. This can be an enjoyable process for those with a taste for amateur sleuthing or historical research. Although much of it may lead nowhere, the chances are good that something of interest or importance will turn up. There may, perhaps, be family names that also appear among those of the current insiders. Names, dates, locations of plaques, and any other information that seems significant should be written down. It may sometimes be helpful to take the plaque walk with a friend—someone to play Watson to your Holmes. Good-humored speculation about who these people were and what they did often sparks ideas that lead to important results. Those people whose names are commemorated on plaques were most likely very important at some point to the life of the institution. Descendants are often interested to learn about the important roles their forefathers and foremothers may have played and are pleased that someone has taken the time and effort to contact them.

Perhaps even more important is the process of scouring lists found in annual reports or programs of organizations with a similar mission or constituency. These sources can provide an excellent way of learning what might have become of lapsed donors, of seeing what an organization's donors are giving to other organizations, and of identifying new prospects with related interests.

A Gift from a Most Unlikely Source

There was a man who spent many years hanging around the law school of a major university. The school's administration tolerated his presence, turning a blind eye to his somewhat disheveled appearance. Over the years, he became something of a fixture at the law school, a sort of mascot for the generations of law students who came and went. This gentleman grew old at "his" law school, and at last he died. In his will, he bequeathed the school a considerable estate, much to the astonishment of the school's development director.

Looking to Others: Prospect Screening

One of the very best ways of gathering information about prospective donors is to ask their peers and colleagues to tell what they know. Most people know more about their friends, colleagues, and acquaintances than they would ever readily admit to. Although people seldom talk about their own wealth, they are very astute about recognizing signs of wealth in others. They notice neighborhoods, houses, cars, manners, interests, style, clothing, jewelry, travel, children's schools, and charitable causes supported, to name just a few. All of these are clues to power, wealth, and commitment. It is information that does not come in books, nor does it appear on lists. It comes through observation and conversations with other people.

Once information in the files has been organized into usable form, it is time for others to be invited into the research process. In fund-raising circles, this process is called prospect screening. Prospect screening occurs on three levels: one-to-one between a development officer and a volunteer; with small groups of high-level donors; and through cultivation events for larger groups of constituents.

The simplest form of prospect screening occurs when the development director or executive director asks a volunteer to review lists of other names and provide information about those people. These one-on-one conversations are an excellent way of learning about both the person who is helping review the lists and the people on the list. Information gleaned this way is often quite personal, and a meeting of this sort can lead to some excellent ideas about how to involve people in the organization.

> *By being alert and perceptive in observing others, one can learn an incredible amount, and be able to define tasks for individuals that they are likely to accomplish successfully. Sharp powers of observation will help make informed judgments, and well-informed judgments about people lead to successful campaigns.*

Small groups of people who are themselves major donors also make very good screeners. An organization might invite six or seven individuals who are likely to know one another to a meeting to review lists and to discuss other individuals they are likely to know. Not only is a great amount of information gathered about the target prospects, but the process is an excellent opportunity to involve people in the early stages of the campaign, thereby bringing them closer to the organization.

The campaign chair, if this individual has already been selected, should invite these people to a meeting to help the organization learn more about a group of prospects. (If the campaign chair has not yet been chosen, the board chair, fund-raising chair, or executive director can issue the invitations.) Screeners should be told that the organization is in the early stages of preparing for the campaign and that it needs help identifying those individuals who might be good workers, good leaders, and good donors for the campaign. The meeting might last one to two hours, depending on the size of the group and the number of names they will review.

The session will require a facilitator who understands the purpose of the session, who can keep things moving, who can keep attention focused on the task at hand, and who has a relationship with at least a few of the others who will be attending. A good facilitator can make the difference between an excellent screening session and a mediocre one, so this person should be chosen with care. Depending on his or her particular strengths and skills, the facilitator might be the board chair, the development chair, or the executive director. The development director should be on hand to take notes of what is said and by whom.

A small group can review approximately 40 to 50 names in an hour. For the meeting to be effective, the screeners must review lists of individuals they are likely to know. For example, board members might review lists of donors and former board members, major donors might look at major-donor prospect lists, staff members at staff lists, and so forth.

Although there are many ways to conduct meetings of this sort, the best information is often developed through discussion. To stimulate discussion, staff members should give each screener a profile of each prospect, which should present the existing information about the prospect without divulging sensitive or privileged information. For example, it is appropriate to share how many gifts someone has made to an organization over a period of time, and whether those gifts were small, medium, or large according to the ranges that the organization has set. But it is not appropriate to divulge specific dollar amounts. To avoid discomfort, some organizations delete the names of those who have been invited to attend the meeting in the material that is distributed to the screeners. Others, however, leave all of the names on the list and find it instructive to see how people rate themselves.

The sessions should focus on two questions: (1) What is the prospect's ability to make a financial contribution to a campaign? (2) What is this prospect's inclination to make a gift? In the answers to these two questions lies a wide range of information about each prospect. Buried in the rating of inclination are actually two factors: generosity and commitment to the organization.

Because people are often uncomfortable discussing dollars, salaries, and other specific aspects of wealth, it is useful to establish a code to sort the prospects from highest ability to lowest ability and from highest inclination to lowest inclination. It is easier, for example, for a volunteer to say, "Mr. Croesus's ability to give is probably a 5" (on a scale of 1 to 5) than to say, "I would estimate that Clyde Croesus makes upwards of $300,000 a year." For the purposes of this meeting, relative rather than absolute assessments are to be sought.

The words *ability* and *inclination*, together with the scale, can be posted in large letters on the wall in front of the meeting room:

```
ABILITY TO GIVE:
Rating Code: 1    2    3    4    5
1 is Lowest, 5 is Highest

INCLINATION TO GIVE:
Rating Code: A    B    C    D    E
A is Lowest, E is Highest
```

The prospect lists given to the screeners should include a place for the screener's name at the top of the first page and a place to indicate ability and inclination ratings for each prospect. See Exhibit 6–1 for an example.

The facilitator should go through the list and, allowing time for discussion about each prospect, collect and gather information to arrive at ability, inclination, and readiness ratings for each name. The scribe should capture as much anecdotal information as possible, such as children, schools, divorces, marriages, interests and hobbies, religious activities, reliability, apparent wealth, and so on. The screeners should write their own names at the top of their lists before turning them in, so that it will be clear who is to be contacted for additional information.

In many cases, prospect screening is a volunteer's first exposure to the campaign. This is a clear-cut, task-oriented meeting, and a simple agenda should be prepared in advance. The meeting should be well run, fun, and set a high standard of organization. If the group is diverse, time should be allotted for personal introductions.

In addition to learning a great deal about the screeners themselves during the meeting, campaign leadership will have also learned about the prospects. As soon as possible after the meeting, the staff must collate that information into a clear and manageable format. Once the information has been gathered, campaign leadership is ready to select those prospects who are likely to be the best campaign volunteers and donors. These individuals may themselves be willing to help identify and provide information about donor prospects.

When acceptances are received, targeted lists are devised for each attendee listing people they are likely to know. These may be assembled according to address, graduation year, fraternity or social club, business affiliation, or other common denominator. Each screener is given 300 to 500 names to review. The screeners' lists contain only names and addresses. Screeners are given an explanation of rating codes and they are asked to silently rate each prospect with regard to the individual's ability to give. The information gathered at these screenings provides an excellent guide for further research and cultivation.

Ratings

An organization that maintains ratings of all of their donors' ability, inclination, and readiness will be able to strategically allocate time and dollars, thereby putting the most resources into the prospects most likely to make a difference to the organization.

Sample Rating List			
John Jeffries	High Ability	High Inclination	Ready
Sally Jones	High Ability	Low Inclination	1 year
Jane Bolsom	Moderate Ability	Moderate Inclination	1 year
Sandy Santora	High Ability	Moderate Inclination	6 months
Tomas Brell	Low Ability	High Inclination	3 months

Looking at the list above, one can see how these ratings might organize the cultivation and solicitation process, not only helping to prioritize prospects but also developing an activity calendar. A system of this sort, however, only works when it is constantly being updated and adapted to fit the changing nature of donor relations.

Electronic Screening

If the internal prospect screening and peer reviews do not uncover a large enough pool of prospects for the campaign, a database screening might be the next best step. Several national firms have developed ways to screen large numbers of prospects to turn up indicators that might target them as major-gift prospects. These firms typically look at salaries, real estate holdings, and other asset information. Typically, a broad screening will turn up 1 to 3 percent of the records screened as major-gift prospects. When analyzed properly, a screening of this sort should identify dozens, possibly hundreds, of folks with means previously unknown to the organization.

For organizations with limited mailing lists, this process is usually prohibitively expensive. But for an organization with a mailing list of 25,000 or more, the investment is likely to yield enough results to be well worthwhile.

Looking to Community Leadership

All communities have a core group of individuals, corporations, or foundations whose names carry special weight and who often make or influence gifts to most of the community's major campaigns. These individuals have served on boards and campaign steering committees before. They know what that responsibility entails; and when they agree to help, they will usually understand that their commitment to the campaign includes a generous gift. Once associated with a project, these community leaders can be good sources of information. They will be excellent advocates for the organization's cause and the campaign's very best solicitors as well.

These individuals or organizations may or may not have a relationship with the agency that is planning a campaign, but as the campaign planning stage moves ahead, the organization must identify and cultivate them so as to increase the chance that they will assist and support the campaign. A sizable gift from a lead person or institution in the community early in the campaign will not only make a good financial start, but will also lend credibility to the entire campaign. Identifying and cultivating these individuals and organizations is, therefore, extremely important.

If the organization completed a feasibility study prior to embarking on the campaign, it may have included a good number of these leaders among those who were interviewed. The feasibility study may also have identified other individuals who are perceived as leaders. The organization should now take the time to identify, research, and cultivate community leaders before it develops its campaign structure.

If the organization is based in a large city with many diverse sectors and power bases, identifying the community power structure within that larger environment is a complex undertaking. In essence, an organization must look for individuals and organizations whose names bring credibility, whose interests dovetail with the organization's mission, and with whom it may find a common point of contact.

The search for community leaders may occur on many levels at once. Here are seven approaches worth trying.

1. Ask the most powerful board members for the names of the most influential people they know whose interests might overlap with those of the organization.

2. Ask major donors to assist in identifying and cultivating individuals.
3. Track local newspapers and other publications for clues about potential donors.
4. Research programs from the symphony, theater, and other organizations for donor lists. Find people whose names surface on the lists of organizations with related missions.
5. Ask colleagues for the names of their friends and acquaintances, who, in their opinion, really make things happen.
6. Study annual reports of agencies with related missions. Eventually, certain names will begin to pop up again and again.
7. Join community organizations in order to meet the heads of some of the large businesses and foundations in the community. People with power lead to people with power.

Throughout the research process, an organization should analyze the community's wealth. Where is wealth made? Who owns the means of production? Who controls the money that has been and is made? Which business sectors are profitable? And which are plowing their profits back into their own development? Which businesses are making real investments in the community? And which merely perch there without building lasting ties or investments? Answers to these questions, in addition to information gathered about the growing number of prospects, will make possible educated judgments about campaign leadership, prospect cultivation, and solicitation.

SETTING UP A PROSPECT INFORMATION SYSTEM

Prospect research can yield thousands, even hundreds of thousands, of pieces of information. This information is useless if it is not stored accurately and in a manner that permits easy retrieval. The time and resources that have been committed to gathering information about a potential donor will have been wasted if that information is inaccurate, or later becomes inaccessible or incomprehensible. See Exhibits 6–2, 6–3, and 6–4 for sample prospect charts for individuals, foundations, and corporations.

What makes an effective information system? First, it must hold the right information. Research will uncover all sorts of data, some of it relevant, some of it not. Sometimes it will uncover information that may be sensitive. Items about family discord, sexual behavior or preference, drug or alcohol addiction, financial scandal, or other closet skeletons might well be important information that would affect the manner in which the prospect

is solicited, but this information does not belong in open files.

When in doubt about whether information is relevant, consider the eight questions in Exhibit 6–5.

Information that helps in any of these ways is relevant, but when considering whether to include such information in the file, one should ask (1) Can this information be shared with a solicitor without violating the prospect's privacy? and (2) Is this information that one would feel comfortable sharing directly with the prospect?

If the answers to these two questions are "yes," then the information can be included. If, however, the information is important to the solicitation but has the potential of being hurtful or damaging, then it should not be included in the general file.

Organizing information in an easily accessible way is sometimes the most difficult part of prospect research. The time and money spent to set up a system that is easy to use and that permits accurate storage and efficient retrieval of all necessary data will be saved many times over in the long run.

Basic information should be maintained on the computer. Files kept this way can be updated easily, are accessible to several people, and are exquisitely easy to manipulate. In the last few years, organizations have been moving toward paperless record systems. Servers, Zip disks, and storage space on personal computers have made great advances, and today digital storage provides nearly unlimited "space" for information. And backup technology when used religiously greatly lessens the risk of losing data through computer crashes.

The Prospect Researcher's Dilemma

A young man attended a local college to which his father was a major donor. Unfortunately, not only was he a poor student, he also frequently found himself in trouble for drinking and cutting classes. When the prospect researcher was updating the donor's file for a solicitor, she added the information that his son attended the school but did not include any reference to the boy's difficulties. Instead, she prepared a private note about the student's problems for the solicitor and sent it along with the donor's file. She did not keep a copy or a record of the memo, reasoning that it would be helpful for the solicitor to know of the son's difficulties before he visited the father, but that in the long run such information, if kept in the files, might someday serve to mar the reputation of the father or the son.

Exhibit 6–2 Confidential Individual Prospect Information Sheet

Date Researched _____ Code _____

Updated _____ Solicitor/Organization Contact _____

Prospect's Name _____

Primary Home Address _____ Dates at this address _____

_____

Primary Home Telephone _____

Secondary Home Address _____ Dates at this address _____

_____

Secondary Home Telephone _____

Business Address _____

_____

_____

Business Telephone _____ Business Fax _____

Title _____

Personal

Birthdate _____

Spouse's Name _____ Anniversary _____

Children's Names and Ages _____

_____

_____

Other affiliations (clubs, board memberships, etc.) _____

Education _____

Giving information

Gift potential _____

Amount and date of largest gift to organization _____

Amount and date of last gift to organization _____

Special interests _____

_____

Other philanthropic interests _____

Indications of wealth _____

Cultivation information

Recent contacts (include date of contact, who made the contact, and result of contact) _____

_____

Additional information _____

_____

_____

_____

Exhibit 6–3 Foundation Profile

Date Researched _____ Code _____

Updated _____ Solicitor/Organization Contact _____

Foundation Name _____

Contact Person and Title _____

Address _____

_____

Telephone Number _____ Fax Number _____

Brief description of foundation _____

_____

_____

_____

Financial data for past three years

Year _____

Assets _____ Grants _____ Average grant amount _____

Year _____

Assets _____ Grants _____ Average grant amount _____

Year _____

Assets _____ Grants _____ Average grant amount _____

Interests _____

_____

_____

_____

Restrictions _____

_____

_____

_____

Officers/Directors _____

_____

_____

_____

Application information _____

_____

Sample grants to other organizations (include dollar amount, purpose, institution, geographic location) _____

_____

_____

_____

_____

Exhibit 6-4 Corporate Profile

Date Researched _____ Code _____

Updated _____ Solicitor/Organization Contact _____

Company Name _____

Contact and Title _____

Address _____

_____

_____

Telephone Number _____ Fax Number _____

Type of Business _____

_____

_____

_____

Address of Headquarters (if different from above) _____

_____

Financial data

Year Ending _____

Revenues _____

Net Income _____

No. of Employees _____

Senior Officers/Directors _____

_____

_____

Corporate giving program _____

_____

_____

Previous contacts with organization _____

_____

_____

Previous giving _____

_____

_____

Additional comments _____

_____

_____

_____

_____

_____

Exhibit 6–5   Is the Information Relevant?

1. Does the information help to understand the person's social group?
2. Does it give an indication of the person's wealth?
3. Does it help to reveal the person's interests?
4. Does it add information about the person's relationship to the organization?
5. Does it help to assess what sort and how big of a gift the person might make?
6. Does it provide information about family?
7. Does it provide clues as to how the prospective donor might wish to be treated?
8. Does it give information about giving patterns?

While there are software packages specifically developed for fund raisers, such a workable system can also be created in any relational database program. Beware, however—homemade systems tend to be jerry-rigged as the system needs increase. These personally developed systems are seldom effective for the long run and the more data there is in an idiosyncratic system, the more difficult and costly it will be to transfer it into a standard development package. Also, personally built systems are problematic when the person who built the system decides to leave. When they depart, any real understanding of how the system works leaves, too.

Simple Data-Capture Systems

Prospect information accumulates bit by bit over the years. Much valuable information is lost because it is not captured as it comes in. The development officer may have a conversation with a board member, for example, in which it is learned that a donor has just remarried, or moved, or changed jobs. Perhaps someone's sole remaining parent has recently passed away. All of these scraps of information are important, but all too often they go unrecorded.

The development officer is responsible for making sure that notes about any contact that takes place between the staff and a donor are added to the file. A steady stream of notes adds a wealth of information that may later prove important. Sadly, such information is often lost in the press of other tasks.

A workable system for gathering and storing such bits of information should be instituted. It does not have to be complex. Though it may seem outmoded, a file folder or even a shoe box might do the job quite well. Every time a salient fact about someone is acquired, the name of the individual concerned and the relevant information should be written down and placed in the research file. When the file is full, or once a month, or on what-

ever schedule is appropriate, the information should be logged in the database. Over time, this process will give the development director a wonderful sense of familiarity with the donor list. Those individuals will gradually begin to seem less like one-dimensional bits and bytes and more like real people.

> *Capturing bits and pieces of information about donors over a long period of time gives the developmental director a wonderful sense of familiarity with the donor list. Gradually, the donors seem less like one-dimensional bytes and more like real people.*

A key to making an information-capture system work is EASE. If it's not easy to capture information, it's not likely to get captured! Provide simple forms. Put the capture box in a central place that's easy to reach. Find ways to acknowledge and celebrate the people who regularly fill out forms.

Strategic Data Capture

Donors that are thought to have the greatest potential require a considerable amount of research. This is time-

The Major Donor and the Overdue Book
Imagine how embarrassing it was for the solicitor who went to ask a donor for a major gift for the library to find her fuming, "As for the library, you should hear about my experience! I was receiving a barrage of overdue notices for a book I had returned months ago. I telephoned the library to try to clear the matter up, and I was treated extremely rudely by a staff member." This woman had eventually discussed the issue with the director of the library, who succeeded in smoothing her ruffled feathers. But the director had failed to make note of the incident in the development files, and the unfortunate solicitor was completely unprepared for the onslaught she received about library employees' lack of consideration. This tale has a happy ending, however. The donor recovered her good humor about the situation, and the solicitation was successful. Nonetheless, the solicitor was rightly distressed by having been placed in a most awkward situation by a lack of information. Information can prevent catastrophe.

consuming and labor-intensive work, and most smaller nonprofit organizations do not employ a full-time prospect researcher for this work. Therefore, the development officer should make a list of the top 25 donor prospects and gather information on those individuals or organizations in a particularly disciplined way. When the first group of 25 is completed, the development officer can select another 10 prospects and then 10 more. Slowly, over time, a significant and impressive file of donor information on the best prospects will have been fashioned that will aid the organization in its preparations for a campaign, and indeed in its entire fund-raising effort.

Another approach is to engage the services of a freelance prospect research consultant. People in this field are equipped to unearth mountains of information about prospects quickly using the most up-to-date and sophisticated Internet links. Some researchers charge by the hour; others charge a flat fee per prospect depending on the level of research they are instructed to do. Prospect research consultants can also provide valuable advice on the intricacies of electronic screening and help assess whether it makes sense for an organization to invest in this kind of macro-research.

FILLING IN THE DETAILS WITH SECONDARY SOURCES

Most small nonprofit organizations have few resources for acquiring prospect-research tools. A research library is expensive, as are most online subscription services. However, over the last three years the number of free online research tools has grown rapidly. Today, with a good Internet connection, even someone without much experience can gather a remarkable amount of information quickly and inexpensively. To make more efficient use of their time, the development staff might enlist the goodwill and advice of a full-time prospect researcher. Most colleges, hospitals, and other large not-for-profit organizations have a full-time employee whose sole responsibility is prospect research. Such individuals are pros at acquiring information. They often have extensive research libraries in their offices that they are sometimes willing to share. But more important, they can provide advice about whom to ask and where to go for many kinds of information. Every community is different, so it is especially worthwhile to explore the local resources with a professional in one's own community.

Joining the Association of Professional Researchers for Advancement is another option for novice researchers. This professional association provides numerous resources for researchers in organizations of all sizes. It has local chapters in many cities and holds an annual conference.

In many communities, the local public library is an excellent resource. Today, most libraries have online reference services, and reference librarians can help track down information about individuals, corporations, and foundations. The librarian at the local newspaper office may also be a gold mine of information about individuals in the community. These reference people are well worth knowing, and if possible they should be engaged as volunteers in the organization's cause.

A rapidly growing area in prospect research is the use of electronic media. With a desktop computer and modem it is possible to access a vast array of research information without leaving the office. Through a commercial Internet service, one can access "prspct-l," a forum for prospect researchers. To sign on, one sends an e-mail message to http://groups.yahoo.com/group/PRSPCT-L. Subscribers to this list receive e-mail from prospect researchers from all over the world and are able to ask questions of professionals in the field. Although subscribing may result in an unwanted deluge of electronic mail, the forum can provide an excellent opportunity to become familiar with the field of prospect research and the use of the Internet to access information.

In addition to prspct-l, the Internet can be used to access information from a wide variety of sources. There are Internet White and Yellow Pages, Corporate Financial Online, PR Newswire, the Thomas Register of American Companies, the Directory of Funding Agencies, and many other such services, many of which are free of charge.

Hunting for information on the Internet can be daunting. The rapid improvements in search engines like www.google.com has helped bring more Web information more accurately to researchers' computer screens. Nevertheless, the right information is still not always accessible through search engines. To help improve the ability of Internet users to conduct effective searches, Gary Price has created a "list of lists" at http://gwis2.circ.gwu.edu/~gprice/listof.htm. These lists categorize many types of information that are useful in prospect research. If a search is not well-targeted, the Internet can be a sinkhole of time and energy. Rather than searching aimlessly, it is wiser to ask other experienced prospect researchers which Web sites and databases might be particularly helpful.

Many development directors who work in smaller, community-based organizations will find that their best information comes through conversations at screening meetings, informal discussions during social events, and one-on-one meetings. Most communities are small, and residents of small communities know remarkably much about other people's business.

To learn more about community leadership as well as the organization's donors, a good development director must play an active role in the community. By joining and becoming active in service organizations, reading the newspaper attentively, listening for clues that might indicate income—being particularly aware of discussions about vacation houses, art collections, exotic travel, antiques, or other such indicators—astute listeners can often recognize the signs of high levels of disposable income. As calculating as it may seem, development staff may want especially to look for people whose children have finished college or whose parents have recently passed away, since such individuals are frequently in a strong financial position and are just beginning to explore ways of using newly available resources. With these simple techniques and a good system for recording information, an organization will be able to assemble a remarkable amount of usable material about its best donor prospects.

A Cautionary Word

Word travels fast in small communities. It is not a good idea to poke around into other people's business in a way that donors may find offensive. The smaller the community, the more attention must be paid to not stepping over the line of propriety. People don't like to know that someone else is digging into matters that they consider private. For example, a prospect is not likely to look favorably on the local homeless shelter if his sister-in-law who works at the courthouse calls him one evening to tell him that the director of the shelter was trying to find out how much he paid for his house. However, more and more counties are placing their property appraisal and ownership information online and free to the public. See www.iaao.org for a detailed list of counties that offer this information via the Internet.

Researching Individuals

As mentioned above, a development officer can find out about a prospect in many ways—by listening to the prospect talk about himself, by listening to what others have to say about him, or by consulting secondary sources, such as newspaper articles and biographical references like Who's Who. There are benefits and drawbacks to each method of research, yet each is important, since information that is gathered one way might confirm or enhance information that is gathered another way. For example, if a volunteer mentions that she knows that a prospect is "some kind of dairy farmer," but doesn't know anything more about him, the staff can check various individual and corporate references. In doing so, the development officer might discover that instead of being just a dairy farmer, the prospect owns and operates one of the largest dairies in the state and has assets of well over $4 million.

When researching individuals, the goal is to provide answers to the following four questions:

1. What is the prospect's financial capacity?
2. What are the prospect's philanthropic interests?
3. How well does the prospect know the organization?
4. Who is the right person to ask the prospect for a gift?

Several secondary sources are available that provide information to researchers on financial capacity and philanthropic interests. A development officer may want to check the following four sources.

1. **Salary lists.** General salary range information can be obtained at a convenient, free Web site: www.salary.com. One might also look into *The American Almanac of Jobs and Salaries*, which is updated yearly. Another source is a company's proxy statement, which lists the compensation of its top officers. Finally, checking periodicals such as *Business Week* or taking a quick glance at the *Reader's Guide to Periodical Literature* or the *Business Periodical Index* will provide a wide range of articles on the subject of salary.

2. **Stock holdings.** While knowing a prospect's salary is helpful, it doesn't begin to give a complete financial picture. Most major donors will not make their gifts out of their salaries; typically, it will be financially more advantageous to them to make a gift of an appreciated asset such as stock.

   There are several ways to find information about a prospect's stock ownership. Securities and Exchange Commission (SEC) reports are a good place to start. If the individual is a director or officer of a corporation registered with the SEC, there are ways of ascertaining his or her stock holdings in that corporation. The SEC has proxy statements and a monthly publication available at a nominal charge to help in a search. Proxy information is online for free through www.sec.gov/edgar.shtml. One might also check www.freeedgar.com or www.tenkwizard.com.

   The SEC registers all corporations with 500 or more stockholders and at least $1 million in assets, as well as those listed on one of the U.S. stock exchanges. Stock holdings of the corporation's officers and directors are listed in its proxy statements. Frequently, the individual's salary and other compensation are also listed, as well as directorships held in other corporations. Some proxy statements also list director's trusteeships of educational and other nonprofit institutions. Proxy statements can be obtained from the corporation itself or from the SEC.

The Official Summary of Security Transactions and Holdings is a monthly publication of the SEC that lists all stock transactions of directors and officers for a given month, including the number of shares bought or sold, the price traded at, and the total shares held at the month's end. One should check through at least one full year of this publication when researching corporate directors and officers. Unfortunately, directors and officers are listed by company, so, in order to obtain a complete picture of an individual, a researcher will have to know each individual's company affiliation and look each one up separately. Many public and university libraries subscribe to this publication, and it can be ordered from the Superintendent of Documents.

3. **Real-estate holdings and other sources of income.** Because many counties now offer real estate information online for free, www.iaao.org is a good place to start. Yahoo also offers an excellent service that finds recent sales of homes near a target address or zip code (see http://list.realestate.yahoo.com). If information is not available online, county office buildings can be a useful source of information. The assessor's office can provide information about the value of the prospect's home and other personal property (automobiles, for instance) that is taxed. One should inquire as to how often assessment takes place and what percentage of the market value of the home the assessed value represents. This information is also available from the company Lusk and Sons, which compiles the information from assessors' offices.

4. **Courthouse records.** The county courthouse can also be a good resource. If a person's wealth is inherited, the county courthouse's probate records can be checked for a list of assets. Sometimes, depending on the circumstances, such records may be closed to the public, but it's worth a try. If the prospect has been divorced or involved in a civil suit, those records can be checked as well. Divorce records often contain financial statements. Civil cases often include information on assets and potential liabilities. These, too, may be closed, but this source of information is worth looking into.

To locate information on a prospect's philanthropic interests, researchers may want to check the newspapers and local magazines. The indexes of these publications should be checked to learn whether the prospect's name appears. Newspapers and magazines often profile community leaders, and such articles may indicate hobbies and interests. Annual reports and donor lists from other organizations also provide information. Published lists can sometimes give a good indication of the prospect's interests as well as the degree of financial commitment.

Researchers will need to keep in mind that unless a prospect is fabulously wealthy, his or her name is not likely to appear in directories of wealthy individuals. In community-based campaigns that rely on community leaders for major gifts, community resources are likely to be the best source of information.

> *In community-based campaigns that rely on community leaders for major gifts, community resources are likely to be the best source of information.*

Researching Corporations

Corporations are often easier to research than are individuals. Much information is available online at no cost. For example, www.hoovers.com, http://finance.yahoo.com, and the company's own Web site will provide a wealth of up-to-date information. Many corporations publish giving guidelines, so it is worth a call to the corporation to get the most recent version. Many companies also send press releases following a major-grant award, so when requesting giving guidelines, one should also request to be added to the company's press list. While many of these press releases won't be directly applicable to a fund-raising effort, a quick scan will provide an update on the company. More and more companies include this information on their Web site, so that's the first place to look.

Most smaller companies, however, don't have formal giving programs. In these companies, grant activities might be handled by the communications department, the personnel office, or even the president's office. When calling a smaller company for information, one should ask the receptionist who handles corporate giving. The receptionist may even be willing to share valuable information about how decisions are really made. The person in charge of corporate giving should be tracked down and asked for information about the company's giving priorities, schedule, and contributions budget.

To get a well-rounded picture of the company's history, current health, and outlook for the future, several sources are worth checking. Standard & Poor's Register of Corporations, Directors, and Executives is a basic resource that includes sales figures, number of employees, products, address and telephone numbers, and names of the company's officers and board of directors. It also includes a corporate family tree listing the company's subsidiaries.

Dun & Bradstreet Corporate Reporting Services is a service whose reports provide a summary that includes a financial-strength rating, along with the date the company was founded, a brief history, and information about its net worth, number of employees, and condition and outlook. There will also be a list of recent "special events" in the company's history and details on ownership.

Corporate Foundation Profiles is a reference book that gives in-depth analyses of the largest corporate foundations, including the types of organizations that they typically fund and the size and purpose of the grants.

Locating information on publicly held companies is fairly straightforward. It is not so easy to find information about privately held companies. A good place to start in such a quest is Ward's Business Directory of Major U.S. Private Companies. This volume includes an address and telephone listing for the company, sales figures, and a list of officers.

Community libraries often keep files on local companies. If these don't prove fruitful, one may want to check the company's articles of organization, which are the papers a company must file with the state when it incorporates. This document will provide the following information:

- the names and addresses of the company's officers and directors
- the purpose of the organization
- the amount and kind (common or preferred) of stock authorized
- the beginning and end of the fiscal year and the date of the annual meeting of the principals
- the amount of stock subscribed for each incorporator

Unfortunately, this information isn't uniformly required by each state. Sometimes the same information can be gleaned from a Dun & Bradstreet report, although such information may not always be on file for private companies.

Researching Foundations

Local charitable foundations are often a good source of funds. The development staff should compile a list of likely foundation prospects and gather information about each of them. What were the organization's previous foundation grants? Are those foundations likely to be interested in a particular aspect of the campaign? If so, they should be put on the research list and their most recent giving guidelines obtained.

Additional sources of foundation funding can be located in the state foundation directory, which gives brief descriptions of each foundation, including its giving priorities, gift recipients from previous years with the amount of the gift, names of trustees, and the name and address of the foundation's contact person. These list-ings are most useful if the researcher knows the donor list well enough to be able to recognize the name of a foundation board member as someone who has given to the organization. As with most fund raising, grants are made by people to people, and the ability to bring in a foundation grant has at least as much to do with the contacts that the organization has within the foundation as it does with the importance and credibility of its project. Special attention should be given to ascertaining who serves on which boards.

If the project will serve people primarily within a limited region, it is a waste of time researching foundations outside of the area, unless there is a compelling reason to do so. With the exception of the Kresge Foundation in Michigan, no other major foundation regularly funds building projects outside its own locality. If, however, the brother of the organization's board chair is married to a trustee of a major foundation elsewhere in the country and she invites the organization to submit a proposal, then that is another matter entirely.

The Foundation Center provides an excellent foundation search engine that provides information on the foundation's assets, grants awarded, contact person, interests, types of support, giving restrictions, application deadlines, board meeting dates, publications offered, foundation trustees, and information regarding proposal submission requirements. It also provides hot links to foundation Web sites. Although one must pay a fee to subscribe to FC Search, some public libraries provide free access to this service. Contact the Foundation Center at www.fdncenter.org. See the list of "cooperating collections" on the Foundation Center's Web site. Though some are more user-friendly than others, all of the libraries listed there have basic materials from the Foundation Center, including FC Search. Alternatively, a supportive development officer at local university, hospital, or other large nonprofit institution may be willing to provide access to FC Search. This service has effectively replaced The Foundation Directory, which for many years was a staple of the development research effort.

Another source of information about a foundation is its "990-PF," the form that every tax-exempt organization must file with the Internal Revenue Service. The 990-PFs can be found at the Foundation Center or at one of its library centers. The 990-PF forms are available at www.fdncenter.org, and much of the information will be helpful, depending on how much detail the foundation includes in reports of its grant activities. The 990-PF will report the foundation's geographic concentrations, assets, project interests, types of support, size of grants, diversity of grants made, and a list of its directors. Some foundations are much more forthcoming than others about their grant-making activities; many will provide more information than you will ever need, while others provide only the bare minimum.

A more descriptive (and sometimes easier to read) source of information may be a foundation's giving guidelines and annual report. In particular, the chairman's and/or chief executive's letter at the front of the report gives a development officer a feel for the foundation's priorities and future directions, as well as for the foundation's "corporate language" and style, which can be used when writing a proposal.

KNOWING RIGHT FROM WRONG

Before beginning prospect research and placing calls to board members or other volunteers to gather prospect information, the development officer must understand thoroughly the roles and responsibilities of a researcher. A development officer is not an investigative journalist, although some of the techniques are similar. Nor is the role that of government prosecutor, hunting for information on financial misbehavior that might lead to an indictment. The development officer is not a gossip columnist, sniffing out information of an embarrassing nature that could give the organization clandestine power. The development officer is, rather, a responsible professional, who, while collecting and analyzing information, always keeps the prospect's sensibilities in mind.

A development officer must use good judgment about whether to include certain information about a donor in the files and not only because the donor may ask to see the file someday. An effective development director and researcher respects every prospect. Insensitive or thoughtless treatment can be hurtful and damaging. When deciding whether or not to use a particular piece of information, a development professional must look at it from a prospect's point of view. Would the researcher want similar information included about him- or herself in an organization's files? If a researcher empathizes with and respects the individuality of every prospect, the donor records will paint an effective yet sensitive portrait of each person.

The development professional is responsible for creating a climate of trust and security in the organization. By example—when and how information about donors is shared—the development officer will establish an atmosphere in which volunteers will know what types of information are appropriate to share. If those involved with the organization observe that other people's confidences are respected and that information is used constructively, they will be willing contributors to the research effort. If, however, they hear that the development officer is broadcasting confidential information or gossiping about a prospect's problems, they will begin quietly to withhold information and gradually become less involved.

> *If those involved with the organization observe that other people's confidences are respected and that information is used constructively, they will be willing participants in the research effort.*

DONOR-FOCUSED DEVELOPMENT

All of the prospect research in the world will be useless unless the information gathered is used to move the prospects through a logical sequence that enables them to expand their commitment to the organization. The design of this sequence is based in part on the information that is unearthed through prospect research. The knowledge of prospects' interests, values, and giving patterns enables the prospect researcher to explore ways in which his or her organization serves the interests of its donors and to work with its donors to develop this intersection of interests.

This is not just a matter of keeping good files. Rather, it is a process of organizing and sharing information among the development team in such a way that those people become advocates for the donor as well as for the organization.

An excellent prospect researcher is a critical part of the development team. He or she not only unearths information about prospects but also shares that information with others who can help design a way to involve the prospective donor in serving the organization. The process works the other way, too. The more the prospect researcher is involved in major-gift strategy sessions, the more alert he or she will be to finding information that may be relevant to the project. Only when the en-

Eating Your Way to Success

The executive director of an organization was floored by the suggestion that he schedule at least one informal luncheon every week at his center with a couple of major-donor prospects. He simply had never thought that getting to know the donors was part of his job. In fact, he was quite sure that major-donor prospects would have no interest at all in getting acquainted with him. Although getting him to try it was like pulling teeth, little by little he became more comfortable with the process and just maybe he'll incorporate this practice as part of his regular schedule. If he does, his next campaign is likely to go way over its goal.

tire development team becomes committed to the idea of donor-focused development will the system begin to work at its best.

Managing the Process

Every organization needs an active prospect-tracking system. Once research identifies a lead-gift prospect, careful planning and action are required to move him or her from being a low-level donor to making a lead gift. This process takes the donor through a series of steps that draws him or her closer to the organization, gradually increasing the donor's knowledge, interest, and commitment.

When a staff person is working with a large group of prospects, it is very easy to let some languish while focusing all of one's energies on another. A good system of prospect tracking will provide the tools to manage and record the cultivation process with identified lead-gift prospects. It will help track cultivation activities, the level of donor readiness, the people involved in the cultivation process, next steps in cultivating the donor, and the solicitation process and results. A well-designed donor management system also enables a development officer to establish specific goals and project likely outcomes from active prospects. Finally, a prospect-tracking system will enable members of the development team to share updated information easily and accurately. For more information on prospect tracking, see "Informa-tion Systems: Managing the Database" by Scott Lange and Charles Hunsaker (1993).

Small organizations with very limited development staffing are unlikely to even think about any system of donor management. For them, just the process of gathering prospect names and doing basic research is often overwhelming. A campaign will force even a small organization to think strategically about developing a strategic pipeline for cultivating its lead-gift prospects and drawing them closer to the organization. For these small organizations, the campaign process itself provides the most effective strategic cultivation strategy they have ever used. Through the campaign, these organizations have an opportunity to see how such a system works and to understand the importance of continuing the effort long after the campaign is done.

PATIENCE AND PRACTICE

After several years of patiently pursuing a prospective donor, a CEO received a seven-figure gift for his organization and a lovely small plaque from the donor. That's right, the donor gave the plaque to the CEO! The plaque stated, "Patience is not a virtue, patience is a practice" (The Thompson Letter, 1989). Prospect research requires both patience and practice. By assembling piece after piece of information about its donors, an organization will know enough to enlist the right person to solicit the right gift at just the right time.

REFERENCES

Association of Professional Researchers for Advancement, 414 Plaza Drive, Suite 209, Westmont, IL 60559; 708-655-0177.

Klein, Kim. 1995. Grassroots fundraising series. The Head-water Fund. Videocassette. 612-879-0602.

Superintendent of Documents, P.O. Box 371954, Pittsburgh, PA 15250-7954; or 202-512-1800.

Thompson Letter, The. 1989. The Thompson Group, Nashua, NH.

Lange, Scott, and Charles Hunsaker. 1998. Information systems: managing the database. In *Capital campaigns, realizing their power and potential*, Andrea Kihlstedt and Robert Pierpoint, editors. San Francisco: Jossey-Bass.

Chapter 7
The Nucleus Fund

Chapter Outline

- The Nucleus Fund
- Soliciting Lead Gifts
- Special Techniques for Soliciting Foundations and Corporations
- Using Gifts Strategically: Challenge Grants
- The Power of Lead-Gift Fund Raising

After all of the preparation, planning, and research, the time finally comes to solicit gifts. This chapter sets the stage for the solicitation of the nucleus fund with basic information on donor and volunteer motivation. It then discusses board giving, staff giving, and the solicitation of lead gifts. The gifts raised from these groups during the quiet phase of the campaign constitute the nucleus fund. The chapter concludes with an exploration of the best uses of challenge and matching gifts to motivate other gifts.

THE NUCLEUS FUND

The "nucleus fund" is the pool of money that is committed to a campaign prior to the campaign kickoff. These funds are raised from the people with the closest ties to the organization and from those who can give the largest gifts. This is money that comes from the organizational family—board members, former board members, advisory committee members, and key staff members—and from the lead-gift donors (Figure 7–1). The standards of giving set by the nucleus fund establish the patterns of generosity and commitment that will permeate the rest of the campaign. This part of a campaign also provides excellent opportunities for the staff and key volunteers to practice the process of organizing solicitations and of soliciting gifts. This "practice" proves invaluable when the campaign broadens to include a far larger group of solicitors and prospects during the public phase.

Board Giving

Even though most boards of smaller organizations are not fund-raising boards, every board nonetheless has a financial responsibility to the campaign. Board giving is often an indicator of success for foundations or others who regularly give to campaigns. Major foundations often ask what percent of the board members have made a financial contribution to the campaign and keep track of the cumulative amount of money raised from the board. It is particularly important, then, that the board understand that they have an obligation to support the campaign financially. However, board members should not be placed in the untenable position of being expected to give more than they can. Karl Marx might have been describing board giving when he penned those famous words, "from each according to his ability. . . ."

From early in the campaign planning period, the board should be encouraged to discuss openly and fully the issue of board giving. The board should engage as a group in determining goals for percent participation and the amount of money that the board will collectively give. If possible, boards should try to get every board member to make a gift to the campaign. In some cases, this is not easy; however, the results are often worth the effort.

Developing Goals for Board Giving

Contrary to common belief, the appropriate level of board giving to a capital campaign is not a specific percentage of the campaign goal. Although one often hears consultants and others say that the board must give at least 30 percent of the campaign goal, such generalizations are appropriate only for boards who were recruited in part because of their financial strength.

Many social-service organizations quite appropriately build strong and effective boards that include very few people with significant wealth. These organizations are often more interested in having boards that will play a

NUCLEUS FUND =
LEAD GIFTS + INSIDER GIFTS

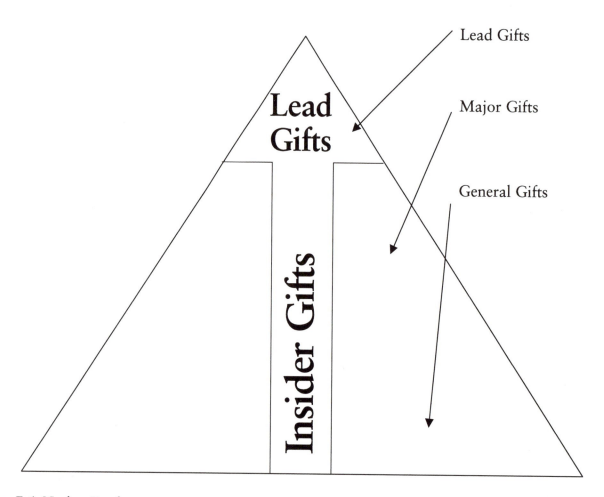

Figure 7–1 Nucleus Fund

hands-on role in conducting the work of the organization. They look for board members who represent different constituencies and ethnic groups. Unlike people of significant means, who are often asked to work on campaign after campaign and who are experienced donors, most midlevel board members are new to the capital-campaign process and are inexperienced as major donors.

For these working boards, the subject of board giving may be particularly uncomfortable. They are told again and again of the importance of board giving, yet they are intimately acquainted with the limitations of their own resources. And many of them have never considered making a charitable contribution of more than $250 or $500.

To further complicate the situation, many boards have had disagreements or even outright strife over their role in the annual giving program. Often board members have been recruited to the board without any clear statement of their financial responsibilities to the organization. When that happens, board members may believe that their gifts of time and expertise frees them from any financial obligation. For boards where these issues already exist, added pressure on board members to make a larger capital gift may result in resignations.

An upcoming campaign provides an excellent opportunity for a board chair and executive director to discuss and clarify the importance of board giving in general and more specifically the board's financial role in the campaign. When approaching the question of board giving to a campaign, it is wise to help the board determine a financial goal for the entire board. This process helps each board member assess his or her own gift and feel that he or she is part of a well-defined group endeavor with clear goals. Because board members are often unsure of the giving capacity of their follow board members, they are often at a loss as to what the board goal should be. However, it is possible to develop parameters that will help clarify the giving potential and thereby help each board member feel more comfortable about his or her gift to the campaign.

Small-Group Rating Session

The executive director or board chair should ask two or three of the most respected board members to rate each board member's perceived ability and inclination to give. The same process that is outlined in chapter 6 will work quite well. Any lead-donor prospects should be included in this rating committee. The names of the committee members should also appear on the rating sheet, so that each person will rate him- or herself as well as everyone else.

For a typical social-service organization planning a capital campaign to raise $2,000,000, the board rating material might look like Exhibit 7–1. The rating may be done by discussing each person on the list or by asking each person to review the list privately, depending on the culture of the organization and the courageousness of the leadership.

In either case, each board member reviews the list, filling in the codes for interest and ability. Each person should write his or her name at the top of the form. This can be done in a group or individually, but because the

Exhibit 7–1 Board Rating Example

Sample Giving Capacity Rating Codes

Code	Estimated Giving Capacity*
1	$500–$4,999
2	$5,000–$9,999
3	$10,000–$24,999
4	$25,000–$49,999
5	$50,000 and up

estimated giving capacity over three years

Interest Level Rating Codes

Code	Estimated Inclination To Give
A	Clearly enthusiastic; strongly inclined to give
B	Active and enthusiastic
C	Moderately active and interested
D	Minimal interest
E	Disenchanted; no perceived inclination

Sample List of Board Members

Name	Board Term	Giving History*	Interest	Ability
Joe Brown	1994–2000	15 gifts/$$$$$		
Jeff Solomon	1996–2002	4 gifts/$$$		
Sally Smith	1995–2001	22 gifts/$$$$		
Mike Stutz	1993–1999	6 gifts/$$		
Barbara Northrup	1955–(emeritus)	many/$$		
Peggy Manes	1997–2003	2 gifts/$$$$$		

Giving history is often shown according to the total number of gifts an individual has made to the organization and the relative gift range.

information and the process are somewhat sensitive, the board members should not take the lists out of the office.

A staff member should assemble the rated lists and collate the information into one master list with all the codes listed next to each name.

The list might look something like Exhibit 7–2.

The development director and board chair review the collective ratings—paying close attention to the self-ratings (indicated in boldface in Exhibit 7–2)—and make a judgment about the most likely gift range for each board member, thereby arriving at a list something like Exhibit 7–3.

Their judgments are guided by the information given on the rating sheets and also by any other information that the development director may have about each person's actual intention or ability to give. Often, when examining rating sheets, one learns a great deal about each of the persons doing the rating. Those who consistently rate others low are likely themselves to be low givers. Those who rate high are likely to give more.

Once each person on the board has been assigned a giving range, the low-end and high-end amounts should be separately totaled to arrive at a cumulative dollar range. For an entire board this range might be, for example, $400,000 to $550,000.

Self-Rating at a Board Meeting

The subject of a board campaign goal should be placed on the board's meeting agenda. At that meeting, each board member should be asked to rate him- or herself. Index cards should be distributed showing giving ranges within which each board member might choose to give. The cards might look like Exhibit 7–4.

Exhibit 7–2 Collated Ratings

Name	Board Term	Giving History	Collective Ratings
Joe Brown	1994–2000	15 gifts/$$$$$	A3, B4, **B4**, A2, B5, A4
Jeff Solomon	1996–2002	4 gifts/$$$	C2, **B3**, C4, C4, C3, B5
Sally Smith	1995–2001	22 gifts/$$$$	A3, A1, A2, B3, A3, **A2**
Mike Stutz	1993–1999	6 gifts/$$	**B3**, C2, C3, B3, C2, B2
Barbara Northrup	1955–(emeritus)	many/$$	A2, A5, A4, A2, A2, **A3**
Peggy Manes	1997–2003	2 gifts/$$$$$	C5, B4, B3, C4, C4, **A4**

Exhibit 7–3 Gift Range

Name	Board Term	Giving History	Potential Giving Range
Joe Brown	1994–2000	15 gifts/$$$$$	$10,000–$25,000
Jeff Solomon	1996–2002	4 gifts/$$$	$5,000–10,000
Sally Smith	1995–2001	22 gifts/$$$$	$1,500–$5,000
Mike Stutz	1993–1999	6 gifts/$$	$1,500–$5,000
Barbara Northrup	1955–(emeritus)	many/$$	$2,500–$5,000
Peggy Manes	1997–2003	2 gifts/$$$$$	$10,000–$25,000

Exhibit 7-4 Sample Self-Rating Card

Estimated Campaign Pledge over Three Years
$100–$499
$500–$2,999
$3,000–$4,999
$5,000–$9,999
$10,000–$24,999
$25,000 and up

Each board member should be asked to indicate which giving category reflects the gift he or she would consider making to the campaign over a three-year period. They should be asked to fold their cards without signing them. The cards should be collected and the giving ranges tallied. Estimated ranges for any missing board members should then be added to arrive at a board-giving range.

This range should be reported back to the board during the same meeting, and it should be compared to the range arrived at through the earlier rating process. It is helpful to post these two ranges on a large sheet of newsprint where everyone on the board can see them. Often the two ranges are quite close, but it is not unusual for the board to rate itself higher than had the smaller group.

This information now can serve as the basis for a discussion of the board's giving goal. The board chair should

The Campaign Chair Who Got Every Board Member to Give

Early in our campaign, the board met to determine their giving goals. After lots of talk, the board resolved that their giving goals would be 100% board participation and $120,000. I did my job and solicited every board member. Most of them gave promptly and generously, contributing more than the $120,000 they had committed to, but one board member didn't come through. As the campaign moved toward the kickoff I was determined to get this guy to give, so I wrote him a letter indicating that I would make a special gift to the campaign over and above what I had already given to match any gift he would make. The next week I happened to run into him. Though he looked a bit sheepish, he clearly was torn between not wanting to part with his hard-earned money and wanting to hold my feet to the fire by making me give more than I had bargained for. As I suspected, his inclination to be a nongiver swayed his gift more than his desire for revenge. He did give a gift. It was small, but with that gift we got our 100% participation.

—Campaign Chair

conduct an open discussion about where in the range the board would like to set its giving goal. Sometimes boards aim high; sometimes they are more conservative. No matter what the results of the discussion, it is important that the board arrive at a consensual goal through a participatory process.

At the conclusion of the discussion, the chair should request a motion that specifies a dollar goal for the board. Some boards also resolve to obtain the financial participation of every board member. If, as occasionally happens, someone on the board is unwilling to make a financial gift, such a resolution is not realistically attainable. Usually, however, a hesitant board member can be brought around through private conversations with the board chair, who might remind him or her that even a small gift would send a strong statement if it established unanimous board commitment.

Soliciting Board Gifts

The process of establishing a goal for board giving nicely sets up the solicitation process. Every board member who participated in determining the board goal expects to be asked for a gift, so before the fervor abates, the board should be solicited. The process for this is simple but important, as it sets the standard by which all solicitation for the campaign will be conducted. Every detail should be carefully thought through, and every loose end tied up.

Organizing the Board Solicitation Step by Step

- Enlist a small (four to five people) board solicitation committee.
- Develop board solicitation timetable (no more than six to eight weeks).
- Meeting #1: Committee members select prospects.
- Prepare proposal letter for each board member.
- Prepare blank statements of intent (see Exhibit 7–5).
- Meeting #2: Train board solicitors.
- Mail proposal letters.
- Track progress.
- Follow up when needed.
- Assemble report of board giving.
- Report progress and results to board.

This two-meeting process is the same process that will be used in many solicitation divisions of the campaign. It serves as a model for many of the other solicitation divisions. The two-meeting format provides enough time to cover the necessary material. At the first meeting, the solicitors learn about or are updated on the project itself and select their prospect names. At the second meeting, they have a chance to review the proposal letters that have been prepared and learn about the campaign and

Exhibit 7–5 Sample Statement of Intent

SAMPLE STATEMENT OF INTENT

I AM/WE ARE PLEASED TO STATE MY/OUR INTENTION TO MAKE A GIFT IN THE AMOUNT OF $_____ TO LONGBELL GENERAL HOSPITAL. THIS GIFT IS MADE FOR THE PURPOSE OF HELPING TO BETTER MEET THE HEALTH NEEDS OF WOMEN AND INFANTS THROUGH THE CONSTRUCTION OF A NEW WOMEN AND BABIES HOSPITAL IN LONGBELL, IOWA.

◆ ◆ ◆ ◆

DATE OF PLEDGE: _____

NAME: _____

ADDRESS: _____

_____

CITY/STATE: _____

PHONE: (DAY) _____ (EVENING) _____

MY/OUR GIFT WILL BE MADE IN THE FORM OF: CASH _____

SECURITIES_____

OTHER _____

I/WE PREFER TO MAKE PAYMENTS _____ (QUARTERLY, SEMI-ANNUALLY, ANNUALLY)

OVER _____ (1–5) YEARS, BEGINNING _____ (MONTH AND YEAR).

THIS PLEDGE IS _____ / IS NOT _____ BINDING ON MY/OUR ESTATE.

_____   _____
SIGNATURE   SIGNATURE

_____   _____
DATE   DATE

◆ ◆ ◆ ◆

ACCEPTED ON BEHALF OF LONGBELL GENERAL HOSPITAL:

_____   _____
JAY BOMBER, VICE PRESIDENT   DATE
LONGBELL GENERAL HOSPITAL

---

the solicitation process itself. By working with a committee rather than individuals, one has a chance to build an important esprit de corps that will inspire the campaign.

The proposal-letter method of soliciting gifts is somewhat controversial. The author of this book believes that when working with inexperienced solicitors it is wise to send proposal letters to prospects prior to the solicitation. The proposal letter is signed by the campaign chair and includes three things. It (1) summarizes the case for support, (2) requests a gift of a specific amount, and (3) indicates that a specific person will be calling to set up an appointment to discuss the gift. A letter of this sort prepares the prospect and the solicitor. Using a system like this, the solicitor is really just facilitating the gift rather than making the solicitation. Although not necessary for every solicitor, for a great many it eases the process. (See Exhibit 7–6 for a sample board solicitation proposal.)

Alternatively, one may send background information on the project and the campaign prior to the solicitation but not include the actual request, leaving that up to the solicitor. This method enables the solicitor to craft a request on the spot in direct response to the conversation with the prospect. Or, if the solicitor determines that the prospect is not ready to be solicited, he or she has the option of not asking for the gift at that meeting but instead identifying the next step in the cultivation process.

Soliciting Committee Members

All of the committee members should be solicited for their own gifts before they ask anyone else. This is easily accomplished. In general, it is the role of the campaign chair to solicit the board solicitors. A proposal letter should be prepared for each solicitor that will be mailed at the same time the other board proposals are sent.

Exhibit 7–6 Sample Board Solicitation Proposal

Dear _____ (personalize name):

I am writing to invite you to make a gift to the Art Museum campaign. More than a month ago you received a letter from Hans Greller reminding you of the power of art as only Hans can do. Now, we are ready to ask you to consider your gift.

So far, we've raised nearly $3 million from national organizations to help us expand our exhibition program, and we have embarked on a local campaign to raise $2.1 million to expand our building. Having solicited only those closest to us, we've raised more than $600,000. We are very pleased with our progress.

Before we expand the scope of the campaign, we are inviting the members of our advisory board to make a gift to the campaign. We hope that each advisory board member will make a gift to the campaign and that we will raise a total of $150,000 or more from this group of ____ individuals.

I invite you to consider making a gift of $_____, or $_____/year for three years. If you are in a position to consider a gift of more than that, we would, of course, be thrilled. If, on the other hand, a gift of that size does not fit your situation, we will be truly grateful for whatever contribution you feel is appropriate.

Gifts of $3,000 or more will be listed on a permanent plaque, which will be prominently displayed in the expanded building. Donors of $15,000 or more will be able to name a room or area. In case you should be interested in that option, I am enclosing a drawing of the building along with a list of naming opportunities.

Within the next week or two, <name> will be calling you to talk further about this campaign and your gift.

Please help us *imagine the possibilities* for the Art Museum!

Sincerely,

Catherine Tremble
Campaign Chair

The Staff Campaign

Every campaign should provide an opportunity for every staff member to make a campaign contribution. In many organizations, the staff campaign is the most sensitive facet of the entire campaign. Some staff members may be eager to support the campaign, but others may feel overworked and underpaid and resent any hint of being pressured into making a campaign gift. This is particularly true in social-service organizations, which are often staffed by people who feel that they already give their lives to the organization and receive little remuneration for their work.

Despite such sensitivities, a staff campaign should be part of every campaign for several reasons.

- Among most staffs there are some people who are able and eager to make significant gifts to a campaign.
- A well-designed staff campaign can help build spirit and enthusiasm for the campaign and the project that it will fund.

- Staff giving is yet another important gauge of an organization's health, and a strong showing in a staff campaign sends powerful messages to other funding sources.
- Every staff campaign should be designed to provide a way to enable every staff member to participate, no matter what their financial situation, but in no way should it pressure them to do so.

The most successful staff campaign involves key staff members in designing the campaign. It should be spearheaded by the development director (not the executive director) and should involve a handful of nonmanagerial representatives from the various parts of the staff. The selection procedure depends in part on the strength of the relationship between the development director and the rest of the staff. Some development directors ask each division of the staff to appoint a representative to help develop a staff campaign. Others select the individuals who they think would do the best job and be the most enthusiastic cheerleaders for the campaign. The staff-campaign coordinating committee determines goals for the staff campaign and develops a number of ways in which staff members can become involved. They also report to other members of their divisions and serve as spokespeople for them.

Many staff campaigns adopt dual goals. They determine a dollar goal that they believe is attainable but generous, and they adopt a goal for the percentage of staff participation in the staff campaign, which includes both financial contributions and campaign assistance. Adopting both dollar and activity goals defuses the pressure to make a financial contribution while providing other acceptable ways to give.

Successful staff campaigns often incorporate three aspects:

1. direct solicitation
2. staff-sponsored events whose proceeds are designated for the campaign
3. individual initiatives to raise campaign funds

Although staff members in management positions might well be personally solicited for the campaign, in no instance should a staff person be solicited by anyone who has managerial responsibilities over them. The staff-solicitation process should be organized so that staff members are solicited by their peers, not by their supervisors.

The executive director should make as generous a contribution as possible to the campaign. Because of the complicated politics of soliciting the executive director, a responsible and sensitive executive director will make his or her gift early in the campaign without being solicited.

The development director, working with the staff-campaign coordinating committee, then reviews the names of all staff members and determines those who should be personally solicited and the person most appropriate to conduct the solicitation. Every staff member who will not be solicited in person should receive a letter from the coordinating committee providing the opportunity to make a pledge to the campaign should they wish to do so. However, the letter should take care not to exert any pressure.

Some organizations give their employees the option of having their campaign gift deducted from their paychecks. This offers a convenient way for a staff member to make a pledge for a number of years. Other organizations believe that this method brings with it a pressure to give that they feel is inappropriate.

Many staff groups are experts on planning special activities. These might take the form of office bake sales, production and sale of a staff cookbook, bulb sales, a used-book exchange, or any number of other fund-raising projects. Some staffs design activities that are limited to the staff, others organize activities to raise funds from the community on behalf of their organization.

Some staff members prefer to design their own fund-raising activities to support the campaign. These individual efforts add to the general excitement that is generated by the staff campaign and often add a touch of humor as well.

Because staff members are part of a closed system, establishing deadlines, reporting progress, and celebrating success are extremely important. Establishing and clearly communicating a calendar for the staff campaign helps build activity timelines and staff expectations. Pe-

---

Sign On for Sit-Ups

One of our staff members—a slightly rotund, middle-aged woman—decided that she was going to raise money and get herself in better shape at the same time, so she organized her own sit-up campaign. She developed a sign-up sheet and asked everyone in the office to sponsor her. Each sponsor agreed to donate 25¢ to the campaign for each sit-up she could do at the office on a particular Friday morning four weeks hence. Then she set to work at home building up her abdominal muscles. By the day of her sit-up performance, everyone gathered to watch while she got down on the floor and began to do sit-ups—25, 50, 110 sit-ups! When all of the money was collected from the 30 sponsors she had signed up, she had raised nearly $500 for the campaign.

—Development Director

---

riodic reporting throughout the campaign period builds momentum as the campaign edges closer to its goals. And, of course, there are few better ways to develop team spirit among a staff than to support the process of celebrating once the goal has been achieved.

SOLICITING LEAD GIFTS

The do-or-die portion of every campaign is the solicitation of the 10 to 20 largest gifts. The solicitation pro-

---

Beating the Board

The board of our organization decided on a board-giving goal of $100,000 for the campaign. When the committee designed our staff campaign, they decided on a giving goal of $80,000. As the campaign moved along, the board crept toward their goal, but the staff campaign really caught on and in a few months we had gone over the staff goal. At one of our campaign-coordinating meetings, one of our members, disgusted at how slowly the board was moving, said, "I'll bet the staff can beat the board goal. That'd show them something!" So we took that idea to the whole staff, and some months later the staff had indeed raised more money than the board. The effort brought a great camaraderie to the staff and I think it embarrassed the board.

—Development Director

One by One

Our group of lead-gift solicitors was very small. In fact, it consisted of just me, our executive director, and one other volunteer. Our lead-gift prospect list was long, and the more we worked, the longer it seemed to get! Somehow I just couldn't enlist others to help very much. Occasionally, when I knew just the right person to solicit a gift, I'd ask them to help, and sometimes they did, but by and large the two of us volunteers and the executive director seemed to be the best solicitors for just about every prospect. In fact, we raised virtually all the lead gifts for the campaign. I'm not sure to this day (the campaign concluded successfully almost a year ago) whether we really were the best people for the job or whether I was just afraid to give up control.

—Campaign Chairman

cess of each of these gifts requires careful, individualized, strategic thinking. Some experts recommend that staff retain full control of the process by assigning solicitors to prospects based on information that is gathered during prospect rating and screening sessions. Others recommend that the campaign chair and a small subgroup of the steering committee be responsible for matching prospects and donors.

Soliciting the lead donors is one of the primary responsibilities of the campaign chairs. In many cases, the chairs have been selected specifically because of their knowledge of the people who have the potential to make lead gifts to the campaign and their potential influence on these individuals to make a generous gift. Often, of course, the lead gifts will be made by the chairs themselves.

Soliciting the Campaign Chairs

In any case, every lead gift should be specifically solicited. Every lead-gift donor should be treated with respect and care. And every lead-gift solicitor should be in frequent touch with the development staff so that they can provide encouragement, information about the prospect, and up-to-date reports about the status of the other lead-gift solicitations.

The very first gifts to be solicited should be those of the campaign chairs. If, as has been suggested, a discussion of each chair's gift was a part of the recruitment process, this subject may already have been broached. However, in many cases the initial discussion was rather general in nature and may not have resulted in a signed pledge form or letter of intent. Solidifying the chairs' gifts, then, is often the initial step in the solicitation process. This should be done by the chairman of the board, the executive director, or a combination of the two.

> *Resist the temptation to assume that campaign leaders will on their own make their gifts generously and early. Find the courage to solicit the campaign chair to get the campaign off to a rolling start.*

Those who solicit the chairs should view this encounter with the utmost respect and importance. The chair should be solicited at a meeting that has been set up specifically to discuss his or her gift. The solicitors should prepare for the meeting thoroughly and bring a table of gifts, a blank letter of intent, and the list of naming opportunities. If both the board chair and the executive director plan to solicit the gift, they should discuss their respective roles before the meeting. Often in such cases, the chairman of the board will run the meeting and so-

licit the gift while the director is on hand to provide specific information about the project, the organization, and the campaign.

Before the meeting, these two should discuss the gift and determine the amount that they wish to ask the campaign chair to consider. Also before the meeting, both the board chair and the director should discuss and make their own gifts. Although these may not be lead gifts, they should make financial commitments to the campaign that are at the upper levels of their financial ability.

In many cases, the campaign chair may arrive at the meeting with a specific gift in mind. Sometimes the chair may even arrive with a signed letter of intent. It is important, however, to discuss the gift in detail. How does the chair wish his or her gift to be acknowledged? Does the chair wish to name a room or a space? How and when will the gift be paid?

Not only will the early discussion of all of these issues get the campaign off to an effective start, but doing so will clear the air of some of the uncomfortable tensions that often poison a campaign.

If, as is common today, the campaign has more than one chair, the chair solicitation process should begin by soliciting the chair who is likely to be able to make the largest gift. That person then helps solicit the other chairs. Each chair should be solicited in a private meeting, in a clear and intentional fashion, and early in the campaign.

The Jittery Solicitor

We had asked someone to co-chair our campaign because we knew that she was a generous and experienced donor. She agreed to serve, making it clear that she would play a very limited role in the campaign. Our director and the other co-chair did talk with her about their hope that she would make a leadership gift, but they just couldn't bring themselves to discuss what her gift was likely to be. Then, once the campaign got rolling, the other co-chair, who himself was only able to make a small gift, got the jitters about asking for her gift, so he put it off and put it off. In fact, he never did actually solicit her and finally, just before the campaign kickoff, she sent a letter indicating that she would give $25,000. Now that was a welcome and even generous gift, but I suspect that she would have given significantly more had our co-chair screwed up his courage to ask her to consider giving $100,000!

—Development Director

Soliciting Other Lead Gifts

If the campaign chairs have been well selected and properly solicited, then the campaign will already have some momentum by the time the other lead gifts are solicited. Indeed, the process of soliciting these early gifts builds a lead-gift team to solicit the remaining lead gifts.

Many campaigns will have no more than 25 prospects for the top 10 gifts. Often, the best way to develop a strategy for soliciting each of these gifts is by establishing a small committee of lead donors. This lead-gift committee may meet weekly in the early stages of the campaign to review each prospect and determine the best way to solicit that individual. For each prospect, the committee will discuss questions in the following eight categories:

1. Who should solicit the gift?
   - With whom is the prospect friendly?
   - Who, if anyone, has recently been solicited by the prospect for another cause?
   - Whom does the prospect trust and respect?
   - Who among the group of possible solicitors is an effective solicitor?
   - Should more than one person solicit the gift?
2. What giving level should the prospect be invited to consider?
   - Has the prospect him- or herself indicated a giving range?
   - What has the prospect given to other, comparable projects?
   - What is the prospect's relationship and giving history with this organization?
   - What is known of the prospect's financial resources?
   - Where is the prospect likely to place him- or herself in a table of gifts?
3. What is the best solicitation approach?
   - Is there a specific aspect of the project that might appeal to the prospect?
   - Is the prospect likely to want to be seen as a leader?
   - Is the prospect likely to prefer to remain anonymous?
4. Should the solicitor suggest a specific naming opportunity?
   - Has the prospect named rooms in other projects?
   - Are there one or two rooms that might particularly interest the prospect?
5. When should the person be solicited?
   - When will the prospect be in town?
   - At what time might the prospect generally prefer to meet?

- Would it be possible and advisable to try to reach the prospect even though he or she is in Florida, for example?
6. How should the solicitation meeting be conducted?
   - Should the prospect's spouse or partner be included in the solicitation meeting?
   - Is the prospect likely to prefer a longer, more social meeting, or is the prospect likely to prefer a shorter, more businesslike meeting?
   - Where should the meeting take place?
7. What materials should be used to solicit the prospect?
   - What aspects of the project should the solicitation proposal stress?
   - Who should sign the proposal letter?
   - Should the proposal be sent ahead of time?
8. What are the action steps?
   - Who will call to set up the appointment?
   - Who will prepare the packet of materials?
   - Who will report to the staff on progress?

Sometimes the answers to these questions are clear, and the entire discussion about a particular prospect may take no more than 10 minutes. In other cases, after hours of discussion no clear approach emerges. In the latter instances, although it is tempting simply to assign the solicitation to someone just to have done with it, it is often a better strategy to hold off until more information can be gathered.

Soliciting the Lead Gifts in the Right Order

The sequence of soliciting lead gifts should be determined by both the size of the gift and the chances of the solicitation's success. If at all possible, prospects who are capable of making the largest gifts and who are seen to be most likely to make those gifts should be solicited first. Then come the lead-gift prospects for whom the solicitation strategy seems the clearest and most certain. Last come the prospects toward whom no one seems to know the best approach.

Ken Wyman, in his excellent manual *Face to Face: How to Get Bigger Donations from Very Generous People* (1993, 69), establishes a numerical system for prioritizing prospects, presented in Exhibit 7–7. Although in the lead-gift process most of the decisions are best made through discussion among peers, Wyman provides a quantifiable approach to prospect sequencing.

Lead-Gift Solicitation Material

The solicitation of lead gifts occurs early in the campaign, often before the campaign materials have been printed. While many people believe, quite understand-

Exhibit 7–7 Major Gift Prospects: Who to Ask First

Prospect's Name _____

Criteria	Points	Score
Prospect gave to us previously	100	
Prospect is rated to give a very large gift	35	
Prospect's gift will be easy to get	35	
Prospect's decision will influence others by example	35	
Prospect is or was on our board	25	
Prospect is known to make big gifts to other nonprofit organizations	25	
Prospect is or was a volunteer with us	20	
Prospect is or was a participant and we have stayed in touch	15	
Prospect is on the board of one or more other nonprofit groups	15	
We have a personal contact	15	
Prospect knows about and is interested in us	15	
Prospect is religious	10	
Prospect apparently has money to give	10	
Prospect is interested in our issue but apparently doesn't know about us	7	
Prospect has been given awards for community service	5	
Prospect has a high profile in the community	5	
Prospect is conservative (no matter how he/she votes)	5	
Prospect is over 55 years of age	5	
Prospect is in a professional or managerial occupation	5	
Prospect is an active volunteer with other groups	5	
Prospect is university educated	3	
Prospect is still married to first spouse	3	
Prospect has children	2	
Total Score (maximum 400 points)	**400**	

Source: Reprinted with permission from K. Wyman, *Face to Face: How to Get Bigger Donations from Very Generous People,* written for the Canadian federal government's Voluntary Action Program, available through Ken Wyman & Associates, 64B Shuter Street, Suite 200, Toronto, ON, Canada M5B 1B1, © 1993.

ably, that the solicitations for large gifts should be the most elaborate presentations, they in fact need not be at all elaborate; however, they must be comprehensible, professional, and personal. It is also a misconception to suppose that lead-gift proposals must be long, or weighty, or composed entirely of polysyllabic, erudite, recondite, recherché, abstruse, and sesquipedalian words. The very best lead-gift solicitation material is brief and simply stated.

The material used to precede or accompany most lead-gift solicitations is generally a brief proposal of two to three pages. The proposal usually is addressed to the prospect from the campaign leadership. It contains a simple statement of specific and relevant information including:

- the amount of the gift being requested
- a brief statement of what the gift will accomplish

- a statement of the campaign dollar goal
- an indication of where a gift of the suggested size would fit into the campaign
- suggestions about how the donor might be recognized for the gift
- specific information about who will follow up on the proposal

Effective proposals are written to reflect the point of view of the prospect. Each is individualized, connecting relevant information about the donor and his or her interests to the project and the proposed gift. If a donor has given to the organization previously or has been involved in its work, the proposal letter usually makes reference to such prior involvement. Some proposals are written in letter format, others in a proposal format with a simple cover letter. See Exhibits 7–8 and 7–9 for a sample proposal and cover letter.

The proposal is often sent with a packet of background information, thus enabling the prospect to read the letter quickly, understand what is being requested, and determine whether or how to proceed. It also provides enough supporting information so that the prospect will be able to review material that will assist in making an informed decision. Supporting materials often include some or all of the following:

- case for support (the simple three- to five-page document that has been refined through the campaign planning process)
- list of the organization's board of directors
- list of the campaign planning committee (if this is not already presented on the letterhead)
- project budget
- project timetable
- small versions of project drawings (floor plans and renderings)
- list of naming opportunities, highlighting the suggested gift and showing which spaces have already been taken
- table of gifts for the campaign goal
- highlights of the organization's operations and programs
- audited financial statement

Exhibit 7–8 Sample Lead-Gift Proposal

A PROPOSAL
to
THE JEFFREY B. SMITH FOUNDATION
and
THE ANNA F. SMITH FOUNDATION
from
LESTER GENERAL HOSPITAL
Lester, Pennsylvania

January 3, 2002

THE REQUEST

We are pleased to invite the Jeffrey B. Smith and the Anna F. Smith Foundations to consider making a lead gift for the construction of a new Women and Babies Hospital in Lester County. This new hospital will be the only medical facility in Lester dedicated solely to the health of women.

The women of the Smith family have been leaders in philanthropy—often setting a high standard for generosity and commitment. We believe that this project provides an exciting opportunity for the Smith family, and we invite you to consider making one of the following two gifts.

Gifts to this campaign may be pledged over as many as five years.

Option 1. Women's Health Pavilion

We invite the Smith Foundations to consider making a gift of **$1,000,000** to name the Women's Health Pavilion. This is one of four pavilions that compose the new Women and Babies Hospital. In this pavilion, women of all ages will be diagnosed and treated for gender-related medical problems including gynecology, breast care, hormonal changes, and osteoporosis.

A naming gift for this pavilion would be recognized with granite plaques installed over the exterior entrance of the building and over the entrance to the building from the main lobby of the Reception Pavilion.

continues

Exhibit 7–8 continued

Option 2. Main Lobby of the Foris Reception Pavilion

Alternatively, the Smith Foundations might consider a gift of **$500,000** to name the main lobby in the Reception Pavilion. The Foris Reception Pavilion is the central building of the hospital complex and its large lobby will serve as its hub. A high decorative ceiling will set this space apart architecturally from the rest of the hospital. The gift shop, education center, and administrative offices are adjacent to this lobby.

The plaque recognizing this gift would be installed in the lobby in a fashion that will do ample justice to the gift.

A CAMPAIGN TO RAISE $5.5 MILLION

<u>Though Lester General Hospital is operated as a successful business generating significant surpluses each year, it is in fact a not-for-profit institution that reinvests its surplus back into the community.</u> These surpluses, combined with generous contributions and bequests from many individuals, have enabled us to develop a state-of-the-art hospital. Now, for the first time in over 30 years, Lester General Hospital has launched an organized capital campaign to raise $5.5 million from the community toward this $17 million Women and Babies Hospital.

ON THE CUTTING EDGE OF HEALTH CARE

We are fortunate to live in a county that has a financially sound and forward-looking hospital. For the third year in a row, Lester General Hospital was named one of the top 100 hospitals in America. It has a strong reputation as a leader in many specialty care areas, including cardiology, trauma, neonatology, and neurosurgery. Many hospitals in the region refer patients to LGH for specialized care in these areas.

It is the responsibility of a fine hospital to stay abreast of the needs of its community and changes in medical care. In 1994 Lester General took a major step forward by opening the Health Campus for outpatient care. Though to some this project seemed radical, it has been successful in every way. Used by more than 3,000 people each day, the Health Campus gets rave reviews from patients and medical staff alike.

In 1995, we began to explore the growing demand for specialized health care for women. Through focus groups we learned that women not only want to have their babies in a family-oriented setting, but also want coordinated services for all of their gender-related health needs. The new Women and Babies Hospital both responds to their desires and reflects a national trend toward coordinated women's health care.

Both the Health Campus and the new Women and Babies Hospital enable us to renovate and expand the acute care capabilities of the downtown hospital.

THE WOMEN AND BABIES HOSPITAL

The Women and Babies Hospital will be adjacent to the Health Campus, directly across Good Drive from the Hospice of Lester County. Construction has been scheduled in two phases. The first three pavilions are currently under construction. They will include the Reception Pavilion, the Delivery Pavilion, and the Family Pavilion. These three pavilions will be ready for use by the fall of 2002. The second phase includes construction of the Women's Health Pavilion and a medical office building adjacent to the new hospital complex. These buildings are scheduled for completion in 2003.

The new hospital has been designed to welcome and encourage family participation in the birthing process. With an education center, play rooms for siblings, lounge areas for family members, and private birthing suites, childbirth will no longer be treated as a women's illness, but rather as a family transition. We anticipate that the new hospital will be the birthplace of more than 3,000 babies every year. In its first decade, enough people will be born there to populate an entire city.

Likewise, the Women's Health Pavilion will provide services for the entire woman, minimizing the compartmentalization that often characterizes our current health care systems. In this new 20,000 square foot facility, women will have access to diagnostic services as well as a range of doctors and medical personnel who specialize in the area of women's health. Women will be able to go to one location for diagnosis, treatment planning and education, surgery, and follow-up care. We anticipate that this convenient, coordinated care will reduce barriers that keep women from obtaining regular health screenings. It will also result in better, more timely communications.

The Women and Babies Hospital will cost $17,000,000 (including construction, furnishings, and medical equipment). Though Lester General Hospital is able to fund a significant portion of these costs, the Hospital is calling on members of the community to become financial partners in this project. This partnership will enable the Hospital to continue to be financially strong and to invest in the future health needs of our community.

OUR THANKS

We thank you for the opportunity to present this proposal to the Smith Foundations. We believe that the Raising Expectations Campaign provides an excellent opportunity for the women of the Smith family to continue their unique leadership role in the future of Lester County.

Exhibit 7–9 Sample Cover Letter

William Shirk
The Smith Foundations
8 West King Street
Lester, PA 17609

Dear William:

I am pleased to submit Lester General Hospital's proposal to the Smith Foundations requesting a naming gift for the Women and Babies Hospital. Because the gift we are requesting is significant, I hope that you will consider allowing us to make a brief presentation in person to the Foundation boards when they next meet.

As we enter the new year, our campaign is proceeding well. We have raised over $3.4 million. Of course, we have a long way to go to reach our $5.5 million goal. At the same time, construction on the new hospital is moving ahead on schedule. We are already receiving calls from women who wish to have their babies there in June of this year. We hope to complete our fund raising for that part of the project by that time.

Our campaign chair, Becky Burnam, will call you early next week to see if you have any questions and to discuss the possibility of our making a presentation to the Foundation boards.

Thank you so much for your interest in this project.

With best wishes for a happy and healthy new year.

Sincerely,

Mark Brokow
President

Much of this material may be generated on a computer and printed on a laser printer. It should be organized so that it is easy to understand. In some presentations the first sheet is a table of contents to the material that is included. This enables the reader to skim the list and go directly to the most relevant material.

When an organization has gone to the expense of having a color rendering prepared for the project, a presentation might include a color copy or photo of that rendering.

Pocket folders work well for organizing this material. Some organizations go to the expense of printing folders with the campaign logo and theme. This makes an attractive presentation.

Before sealing and sending a lead-gift proposal package, it's a good idea to take the time to review it as though one were a prospect looking at this material for the first time. Everything should be examined, beginning with the addressed envelope and continuing through each piece of material, viewing it all with a prospect's eyes.

First, put the completed package in its envelope on your desk. Does the envelope look professional? Are the name and address correct and accurate? Is the mailing label straight?

Second, pull out the packet. Is the proposal letter on top? Does it look inviting and easy to read? Does the folder look professional? Is the folder label personalized with the donor's name? Is the label on straight?

Third, read the cover letter slowly and carefully. Is the salutation appropriate for the person who signed the letter? After reading the first paragraph, do you know what it is about? Are there misspellings or other foolish errors? Has the letter been signed? Would you know how and when to respond?

Finally, open the folder. Can you see easily what information is included on each side of the folder? Is the proposal compelling? Does every piece of material look simple and clear? Does it all look professional? Do the numbers match? Is there anything that could be profitably omitted or simplified?

Such a thorough review seldom fails to turn up a need for last-minute corrections or amendments. Not only will the process improve the proposal package, but it will also increase the peace of mind and confidence of the staff member who is responsible for the proposal.

Building Confidence by Sharing Lead-Gift Progress

Because each lead gift helps to set the pace for the campaign, strategic sharing of information is of vital importance. The lead-gift solicitors are true campaign insiders. They are very much aware that the burden of the campaign rests on their shoulders. Every new lead gift that is committed to the campaign inspires and motivates other lead-gift prospects as well as their solicitors; thus, prompt and effective communication during this phase of the campaign is extremely important. The executive director, campaign chair, and development director must work as a team to make certain that information about each new lead gift is shared with the other lead-gift solicitors.

Sometimes donors who have already committed their own lead gifts can be very helpful in supporting other lead-gift solicitations. They might, for example, send a letter to someone they know who is being solicited for the campaign. (See Exhibit 7–10 for a sample supporting letter.) These extra letters can make a huge difference in the inclination of the donor. There's nothing quite like having a volunteer who has already made a generous gift to encourage similar behavior from another prospective donor.

Early in the lead-gift process, every lead-gift meeting should include an up-to-date accounting of campaign progress. Since lead gifts are large gifts, it doesn't take very many of them before the campaign has made sig-

nificant progress. It is also often helpful for lead-gift solicitors to be periodically updated on gifts in progress. A sample lead-gift update is presented in Exhibit 7–11. This sort of report, regularly updated for the lead-gift meetings, shows campaign progress quite clearly and motivates the solicitors to show activity on the solicitations to which they have been assigned.

Materials for Soliciting Lead Gifts

Each lead-gift solicitor should be acquainted with the material that might be used in soliciting lead gifts. In addition to the material that might be selected to send or present to each lead-gift prospect, every lead-gift solicitor will need additional information to facilitate the task of solicitation. Packets for lead-gift solicitors should include the following items:

- updated lists of the prospect's solicitation assignments
- letters of intent or pledge forms (see Exhibit 7–5)
- copies of proposals sent to their prospects
- solicitation call report forms for each prospect plus some extras (see Exhibit 7–12)
- thank-you note cards and envelopes
- campaign letterhead and envelopes
- an information sheet on each prospect to be solicited
- names and telephone numbers (home and business) of co-chairs, board chair, executive director, and development director or campaign director

Training Lead-Gift Solicitors

Lead-gift solicitors are usually a mixed group. Some have worked on campaign after campaign and are excellent solicitors. Others, though experienced solicitors, have adopted solicitation strategies that are ineffective. Still others have little solicitation experience. The task of the development director or campaign manager is to design an approach to solicitor training that will highlight the excellent solicitors in the group, reeducate those who are experienced but ineffective, and encourage and train those who are new to the field.

Because the lead-gift solicitors make up a small group, solicitor training can actively involve the solicitors. The training might effectively incorporate role playing and active discussion of specific prospects. This sort of participatory training really does help solicitors find and practice the words and phrases to use with their prospects. They will have a chance to think through responses to objections that their prospects might raise, and they will be able to experiment with different strategies for soliciting the gift.

Think Magnets

Once when I was a child my father brought home a magnet and a jar of iron filings. We sprinkled the iron filings on a sheet of paper and then, placing the magnet under the paper and moving it about, we were able to attract the iron filings and direct their course over the paper. To my child's mind it seemed like magic. The power of lead gifts is like the power of the magic magnet. These gifts draw people in and attract other gifts, directing the course of the campaign ahead in ways far more significant than the dollars they represent.

—Campaign Consultant

Exhibit 7–10   Sample Supporting Letter

Dear Don,

Boy, when Chuck sent me an e-mail asking if I knew Don Murtry I was instantly transported back 35 years to the "beachcomber" days at the lake! Well, I still drink beer and slalom water ski (less aggressive on both counts), but have grown up in some regards and one involves my penchant for helping kids get to know and love science and engineering, as it is my field of work, and investing in kids is better than gambling.

I was a Science Center Board member for many years—until I relocated to New York City two years ago (we love it down here, still have our farm overlooking the lake for retreating)—and really got into it. The Science Center has a vibrant group of people doing good work in the area of science education for all ages and especially kids 5–12 and their parents. Judy and I have pledged $30,000 (as we did back in construction of the first phase, which has been very successful) for the exhibits to be used in conjunction with the classroom/laboratory for which you have been asked to consider funding.

While Judy and I lived in Lennox for about 15 years, I represented the Cortland area on the Science Center Board. My company continues to be a supporter of the Science Center as a regional resource that invests in turning kids on to science and engineering as future employees and overall help the area economy. The Science Center is a one-of-a-kind nonprofit with tremendous volunteer and community support.

Please take a good look at this opportunity to join with me in supporting this next important expansion of the Science Center and its reach out to an expanded audience in the future.

Best of everything. I hope to see you some time (back East or there—my youngest daughter is second year at University of California at Berkeley).

John Smith

Exhibit 7–11   Sample Lead-Gift Progress Report

Lead-Gift Progress Report
January 4, 2000–January 18, 2002

Gift Report

Campaign goal	$1,000,000
Lead-gift goal	$475,000
Total gifts pledged as of January 4, 2002	$75,000
Gifts pledged since January 4, 2002	$50,000
Gifts pledged as of January 18, 2002	$125,000

Activity Report

Solicitations assigned	15
Solicitation meeting has taken place, gift made	3
No progress reported	5
Solicitation meeting set up but not completed	3
Solicitation meeting has taken place, decision pending	2
Solicitation meeting has taken place, gift refused	2

Although the next chapter covers solicitor training in detail, a few guidelines might be helpful to lead-gift solicitors.

- The more the prospect knows about the project, the more the prospect should be thought of as a partner in the process of determining the best gift for him or her and the organization.
- An excellent lead-gift solicitor listens for what the prospect wants to accomplish through the gift and then works with the prospect and the organization to accomplish those goals.
- Lead-gift solicitors are tenacious and creative.
- Lead-gift solicitations often require multiple meetings.
- Lead-gift solicitors must not become discouraged from soliciting others by a "no" answer from one prospect.
- Lead-gift solicitors often maintain contact with their prospects even after the prospects have made their gifts.

Exhibit 7–12 Sample Call Report Form

Solicitor's Call Report Form

Prospect name: _____

Contact: Phone call _____ Date _____

  Meeting 1 _____ Date _____

  Meeting 2 _____ Date _____

Prospect's attitude toward hospice: _____

_____

_____

Prospect's attitude toward the center: _____

_____

_____

Amount suggested: _____ Amount committed: _____

Type of gift: check _____ stock _____ other _____

Payment preference: number of years _____ payments/year _____

Other areas for involvement: _____

_____

Next steps: _____

_____

Solicitor's name: _____ **Date:** _____

Send, phone, or fax to: Susan Jones, Hospice of Aspen County
P.O. Box 555, Anywhere, PA 17606-5179
Telephone: 717-555-1234 Fax 717-555-4321

The Solicitation Process

Solicitation of gifts falls into four distinct phases:

1. setting up the appointment
2. preparing to make the solicitation
3. soliciting the gift
4. following through

Each phase presents its own set of challenges and requires discipline and attention to detail. Although solicitors focus most often on the actual solicitation of the gift, successful solicitors pay attention to all four stages.

Setting Up the Appointment

Once the initial letter has been received by the prospect, it is up to the solicitor to call the prospect to set up the meeting. For many volunteer solicitors, the phone call is the most difficult part of the process. The telephone becomes an enemy. The phone call provides the very first opportunity to be rejected. The specter of such early and summary rejection is at least as bad as the fear of any rejection that might come later. Indeed, many volunteers are so afraid of the initial phone contact that they sabotage the process and aren't even conscious of what they are doing. Take, for example, the volunteer who calls a prospect every day at exactly the same time though receiving no answer to any call. Or the volunteer who calls the prospect's work number in the evening. Or the volunteer who learns that it is a wrong number but somehow fails to take the initiative to get the right number. An anxious volunteer is perfectly capable of feeling justified in believing that every reasonable effort has been made but that the prospect just couldn't be reached.

More courageous solicitors overcome their initial panic and contact their prospects on the phone. Effective phone callers practice four strategies that make their calls successful.

1. The caller assumes that the donor will say yes.
2. The caller hears only what is actually said and neither embellishes nor reads into the conversation negative connotations stemming from the solicitor's own anxiety.
3. The caller always listens attentively and validates whatever the prospect says.
4. The caller keeps the initiative, suggesting dates and times for a meeting or asking for a better time to call back.

Read more on setting up the call in "Setting Up the Major Gift Meeting" (Klein, 1990).

Effective phone callers also know that it is not the end of the world if a prospect says no. Indeed, the expectation is that it takes two to five or more prospects to bring in a single gift, and experienced solicitors know that their personal worth does not ride on the success of each and every solicitation.

The telephone can be a trap. Successful solicitors phone only to make the appointment, and they do not let themselves be drawn into discussing the contribution over the phone. They hold out instead for a face-to-face meeting that will be set up specifically for the purpose of discussing the project. Lunch is generally not a great time to solicit someone. If the solicitation must be combined with a social call, the solicitor should meet early to get the business accomplished first and only afterward go for lunch or dinner.

Preparation

Gather information. Once the meeting date has been set, a solicitor will benefit by doing some homework before meeting the prospect. Solicitors should gather as much information as possible about the person being solicited. Often a few informal conversations with friends will provide valuable information to add to that provided by the organization. Before making the call, the solicitor should review all available information. What values are important to the prospect? How do those values relate to the project? What specific factors in the prospect's life are likely to provide a bridge to the project?

How Not to Solicit Gifts

I went to a dinner party recently and happened to sit next to the gentleman who is chairing a campaign in town. As we sat down to dinner, he leaned over and said to me, "I've noticed that you haven't made a gift to the campaign yet."

"I haven't been solicited yet," I replied under my breath.

"Well," he purred, "How about it?"

"How about what?" I shot back.

He gave me a quizzical look and then said, "You know, a gift to the museum campaign."

"I'll have to think about it," I replied, though I had decided right then on the basis of this exchange to give as little as I could decently get away with. In fact, I had considered giving that campaign a generous gift, but if the chairman didn't take me and my gift seriously enough to ask for it in a thoughtful fashion, well, there are many other places who will pay me the courtesy of a real discussion about my gift and its place in their project.

—A Lead-Gift Donor (to another organization)

Check the amount. Because most solicitations are preceded by a proposal letter suggesting that the prospect consider a gift of a specific amount, the solicitor should review the letter to make sure that the dollar amount that has been suggested remains clearly in mind.

Review personal commitment. Successful solicitors make their gifts to a campaign before they solicit anyone else. They understand their own reasons for supporting the campaign and are willing and ready to share them with the prospect. Often, personal stories are the most compelling parts of the solicitation process. Not only do they reveal something about the solicitor that helps bridge the distance between the solicitor and the prospect, but such a story might also reflect a specific aspect of the project in a new light.

Practice making the case. It is helpful to practice stating the case for the project before meeting with the prospect. Spouses, friends, or staff members make good audiences. It is not uncommon for someone to try stating the case three, four, or even more times before it becomes comfortable. Gradually, through practice, one learns what can be omitted and what is critical to the solicitation.

The Solicitation Meeting

Provide time for the dust to settle. Solicitation meetings often begin with general conversation about issues of common interest. This provides a period during which both parties can absorb information about the other person and the setting before bringing their attention to the task at hand. A solicitation call is not a social visit, however, and the solicitor is responsible for turning the conversation in due course to business.

Ask questions and listen. Without a doubt, asking questions and listening actively are the two most important skills of an effective solicitor. Before making a presentation on behalf of the organization and asking for the gift, effective solicitors draw out their prospects by asking open-ended questions that invite the prospect to express his or her values, opinions, hopes, and concerns. During this period, the solicitor turns the conversation to the project and then asks the prospect about his or her involvement, attitudes, and feelings about the organization or the project. Often prospects will articulate the reasons for their interest, thus laying the groundwork for discussing their contribution. During this discussion, the solicitor will also have an opportunity to answer any questions that the prospect may have about the organization and the project.

Make the case. Often the questioning and listening process leads quite naturally to the case for making a gift to the project. In the best instances, the prospect will make the case himself and the solicitor will have only to follow up by asking for the gift and organizing the details. In other instances, the prospect will not know enough about the project and will want to learn more. The solicitor then has an opportunity to summarize the specifics of the project and the campaign. This should take no more than 10 minutes.

Ask for the gift. If a proposal letter has been sent in advance, the gift has already been requested and the solicitor is responsible for restating the request. The dollar amount or range in the letter is a starting point for the discussion. The prospect may of course choose to give more or less. The solicitor might say something like, "I know you have received a letter from the campaign chair asking you to consider a gift of $100,000. Would you consider making a gift of that amount?" If no proposal letter has been sent, the solicitor should briefly ask for the gift.

After making the request, seasoned solicitors know not to say anything more until the prospect responds. It is tempting to continue speaking, but no matter how long the response takes, it is the donor's place to respond, not the solicitor's to interrupt.

Once again, active listening is all-important. The solicitor must listen carefully to the donor's response and hear accurately what he or she is really saying. It is not unusual for an inexperienced solicitor to be so anxious about the response that he or she hears a negative answer no matter what the prospect has really said.

When the prospect does respond, the solicitor must acknowledge the response positively and constructively. If the prospect says yes, the solicitor must express thanks appropriately and explore ways of finalizing the gift. If the prospect says no, the solicitor might suggest a different gift level or an alternative way of helping the campaign. If the prospect delays the decision, the solicitor must maintain the initiative and follow up again and again if necessary until the donor has either made a gift or has said no.

It is not unusual for the solicitation process to require several contacts between the donor and the solicitor. Solicitors should always remember that their job is to help the donor make a decision about the gift level. Both yes and no are appropriate answers, and solicitors have accomplished their goals when the donor's intentions are resolved either way.

The solicitor must determine how to proceed further before closing the solicitation meeting. If the solicitor receives a signed pledge form during the meeting, the donor should be informed exactly how the organization will follow up. If the prospect postpones a decision, the solicitor should specify a date and time when the donor will be contacted for a decision.

He Fell Asleep

I first learned how to solicit gifts when I became chairman of a campaign. One of the first calls I made was on a prominent couple in the community. I was terribly afraid that they would turn me down. I started talking and just couldn't get myself to stop until I looked over and realized that the husband had fallen asleep. I bumbled to a stop not knowing quite what to do. His wife quietly ushered me out, saying that they would let me know, but I knew for sure that my presentation had not been scintillating! Sure enough, it hadn't been. They did make a gift, but it was far smaller than it might have been. But I had learned my lesson. Near the very end of the campaign, when it had come down to the wire and we had to make our goal very soon, I made four brief calls in a week. I told each prospect that I myself had made a generous gift and had given a year of my time to this campaign, and I invited them to consider making a gift of a specific amount. Period. I just stopped and waited. All four donors said "yes"!

—Campaign Chair

Follow Through

> *Effective thank-you notes say something that is authentic and that relates specifically to the encounter with the prospect.*

As soon as possible after each solicitation visit, the solicitor should write a thank-you note to the prospect, whether or not a contribution was made, and complete a solicitation call report form for the development office, informing them of the results of the call. Most campaigns provide the solicitors with report forms to help them capture the most important information. See the sample report form in Exhibit 7–12.

Other Considerations

Soliciting in teams often strengthens the solicitation process. Sometimes a staff member who is intimately familiar with the specifics of the project will join a vol-unteer who has a strong relationship with the donor. Together, they are likely to be able to make a stronger statement than either of them could individually.

This team approach must be planned carefully in advance. The timing and strategy of the meeting should be well considered. Who will cover what material? Who will ask for the gift? Who will ask questions? Who will present the project? And who will close the meeting and determine the follow-up steps? If these issues are explored and discussed ahead of time, and if each person actually stays with the agenda, the team approach can be excellent, and it often reduces the intimacy and intensity of the interaction, thereby lowering the solicitors' anxieties. Care should be taken, however, that the soliciting team not gang up on the prospect. The prospect must be an active participant in the solicitation process, and the solicitors must leave room for the prospect to express his or her thoughts and ideas. If the prospect's role is brushed aside in favor of the choreography of the soliciting team, this approach will weaken rather than strengthen the request.

A good location for the solicitation meeting is often at the organization, where it should be preceded with a tour or a demonstration of some sort. The solicitation meeting itself should take place in a quiet and private meeting room. If the organization does not have an appropriate conference room or if such a room is not available at the right time, a tour or demonstration might be scheduled independently from the solicitation meeting.

If an on-site meeting is not possible, then other suitable options would be either a neutral location like a quiet club or the prospect's office or home. Although the latter may provide clues to the prospect's family and interests, it can be a problematic venue if the meeting is frequently interrupted by secretaries, telephone calls, or children. In the final analysis, the best place for a solicitation meeting will depend on what works best for the prospect and what best matches his or her style.

SPECIAL TECHNIQUES FOR SOLICITING FOUNDATIONS AND CORPORATIONS

Soliciting lead gifts from foundations and corporations is similar in many ways to the process of soliciting individuals. These solicitations, however, require some special attention.

Foundations

In a campaign, development staff will be responsible for securing funding from foundations. Most community-based foundations support only local projects. Raising money from this type of foundation is similar to raising money from individuals. In both cases, decisions are made by people who live and work in the community, who may recognize the need that the organization is addressing through the campaign, and who may have firsthand knowledge and experience with the organization. Just as with soliciting gifts from individuals, personal contacts with the donors are invaluable in these cases. These foundations include community foundations and family foundations. Their funding comes primarily from bequests and memorial funds, though they may conduct annual fund drives as well. These foundations often have specific funding guidelines, application forms, and submission deadlines.

Some family foundations support local community needs as well. Compared to the large national foundations, they have little bureaucracy, and the trustees are usually members of the family.

To approach these organizations successfully requires research about the funding patterns and guidelines of each as well as an understanding of the contacts and links that exist between the organization and the foundation. Volunteers are often useful in unearthing information about these foundations that will help the staff develop the best strategy for approaching each.

Staff members should request and study carefully a copy of the funder's current guidelines, proposal-submission requirements, and a list of recently awarded grants if they are available. If, as is often the case with small family foundations, there is no published information, either a staff member or a volunteer should contact someone at the foundation, present a brief explanation of the project, and ask whether their foundation would be interested in receiving a proposal. In most cases, the foundation contact will provide clear and appropriate instructions.

Corporations

Some local corporations also require a special approach. Many corporations give to organizations that serve their employees and in which their employees are involved. Organizations that think ahead often invite key corporate employees to serve on their boards well in advance of a campaign. Sometimes an organization will involve an employee of the corporation on the campaign planning committee. It will also help an organization to receive funding from a corporation if it can document the number of employees who volunteer for the organization or have benefited from its services.

Securing corporate contributions depends on knowing who makes the funding decisions. There are several ways to obtain such information. Some corporations publish giving guidelines that provide a clear outline of the decision-making process and a list of corporate of-ficers who are involved in the decisions. In some cases, however, this information is not accurate or up-to-date. Wise organizations develop personal contacts with the management of the corporation and use those contacts to learn the realities of how funding in that corporation is decided.

Organizations are often disappointed to learn that corporations with manufacturing plants in their community are not likely to be generous supporters. Unless an organization is headquartered in a community, funding for a substantial gift is likely to be funneled through the plant manager, who selects the projects that he or she will support and then submits them to corporate headquarters. The plant manager is often the gatekeeper for gifts, but often has little say over decisions made at headquarters.

Submit a Proposal

Rarely will a foundation or corporation make a grant without receiving a written proposal from the organization. A prospective funder will want one of two types of proposals. Many small foundations and corporations require only a two- to three-page letter containing a request and a description of the project. Other corporations or foundations may want to see a full proposal, which may include many of the following nine components:

1. A brief executive summary describing the request and the case for supporting the project
2. Information about the organization's history, background, mission, and services
3. The reason for the request
4. The project's impact on the community
5. A plan for evaluating the effectiveness of the project
6. A project budget and timetable
7. A listing of the key personnel who are involved in the project and a summary of their qualifications
8. The most recent audited financial statement
9. A copy of the IRS letter granting the organization its 501(c)(3) status

If an organization has done an effective job of preparing its case for support, preparing a proposal should not be difficult. If the organization has hired a campaign consultant, the consultant may be helpful in reviewing and critiquing the proposal.

Solicit the Gift

Some foundations and corporations welcome the opportunity to meet with volunteers and staff members who represent the organization to learn more about the project and to discuss a potential contribution. Others prefer that all communication be handled in writing. The organization should apprise itself of the preferred approach in each case.

Follow Up

Response procedures vary from funder to funder. Some corporations encourage applicants to follow up their proposals with meetings and phone calls; others prefer that applicants not contact them. Whatever the preferred procedure, a development officer must be prepared to provide additional information if asked for it, to arrange for particular individuals to attend a meeting if it is requested, and to be persistent in following up with a funder who has not responded in a timely manner.

If funds are granted, the development director also has the responsibility of making sure that the funder is thanked promptly and appropriately. Some funders prefer that their names not appear on any lists, while others want to be as visible as possible. Representatives from the foundation or corporation should receive newsletters, invitations to special events, and—most important—once the grant period is over, a report on how the grant has been used and its impact on the community. Good reporting is one of the most important ways to maintain a strong relationship between the funder and the organization.

If the funder denies the request for a gift, an organization should make the effort to find out why. The volunteer can talk "off the record" with the foundation or corporate contact, or the development officer might call the funder, ask why it was turned down, and inquire about whether the organization might submit another request in the future.

For more information on corporate and foundation fund raising, see *Corporate and Foundation Fund Raising: A Complete Guide from the Inside*, by Eugene Scanlan, another book in this series.

USING GIFTS STRATEGICALLY: CHALLENGE GRANTS

Sometimes lead gifts can be designed to provide incentives to both donors and staff alike. A gift can be designed to challenge others to give. Such gifts are generally the result of close collaboration between a donor and the development staff. A well-designed challenge gift requires thorough analysis and understanding of the campaign progress, the prospect base, and the aspects of the campaign that would benefit from external incentives.

Donors who make strategic gifts often give more than they might otherwise give because of the leverage value of their gift. A strategic gift also provides added incentives for other donors who respond to the challenge.

I Want the Campaign to Succeed!

When I approached the man who we thought could make the largest gift to our College's campaign, he told me that he was considering a $5 million gift but that he wanted the college to use his gift to leverage other gifts, thereby helping the campaign succeed. I knew the campaign needed a boost in two areas—gifts of $50,000 and more, and those gifts targeted specifically to the building projects.

I suggested to our donor that I draft a letter from him to the institution that would outline the terms of a matching gift that would help us in these areas. He would have a chance to discuss and revise the terms, but I would start the process with a draft. I went back to my office and wrote a letter outlining a gift of $5 million that would be matched 2:1 by all new gifts of $50,000 or more that were designated to the building projects outlined in the campaign objectives. His match would continue through the end of the campaign. I met with the donor to review the letter. He suggested some changes to the payment schedule. We revised the letter and he signed! Not only did we have our lead gift, but we had a wonderful way to make other people's gifts more valuable and to target the two areas in which we knew our campaign needed strengthening.

—College President

Strategic gifts present a challenge to the organization as well as to the donors. A donor pledges to make a gift if and only if the organization is able to fulfill the stipulated conditions of the challenge. These conditions usually include a dollar amount to be raised and a deadline. They may also specify a ratio of dollars to be raised for each dollar of the gift (e.g., 1 to 1, 2 to 1, or 3 to 1), a specific group from which the challenge must be raised, and/or a project that the challenge funds must be raised for. In some challenge grants, none of the challenge funds will be paid until the full terms of the challenge have been met. In other cases, the organization may draw down the gift as the match is raised, leaving open the possibility that the entire amount of the match might not be raised.

Why Do People Respond to Strategic Gifts?

1. **Leverage:** People like to know that their gift is important to the organization. Challenge grants provide powerful opportunities for a donor to use a gift to leverage other funds. They also make the matching gifts worth more than their face value.

2. **Credibility:** A strategic gift made by a person or organization of standing puts a stamp of approval on a project. The receiving organization is able to use an early gift from a credible source to convince others that the project is worthwhile and likely to succeed.

3. **Specific focus:** Strategic gifts enable an organization to focus on one aspect or objective of the total campaign. In doing so, the organization is able to reinforce the importance of particular types or sizes of gifts to the campaign and to highlight one or another aspect of the campaign.

4. **Deadlines:** Strategic gifts often provide important interim deadlines, and deadlines motivate people to action.

5. **Structure:** Strategic gifts impose an external structure on the campaign, making it easier to solicit gifts of a particular type in a defined time frame.

6. **Celebration:** Strategic gifts provide opportunities to celebrate success before the campaign is fully complete. Interim goals, deadlines, and celebrations can be used to maintain campaign momentum.

Ideas for Strategic Gifts

Strategic gifts come in many sizes and forms. A board member might make a gift that challenges the other board members to give at a higher level. Or a donor might structure his or her gift so that it requires the organization to match that gift in some proportion with gifts from others. A foundation might make a gift that challenges the organization to broaden its base of donors by stipulating that the gift be matched only by gifts from first-time donors. A corporation might make a gift that requires the institution to raise additional funds for a designated project within the objectives of the campaign. These are but a few examples of how a gift might be designed strategically to strengthen the organization.

Gifts designed with stipulations that require the organization to raise additional funds provide a call to action for both staff and donors. Most frequently, the donor and the development staff work together to develop the terms of a strategic gift that will best benefit the organization and work for the donor. Designing strategic gifts requires careful analysis of the strengths and weaknesses of the development program and of the needs of the campaign. These gifts should stretch the organization and provide incentives to help strengthen the campaign and the broader development effort; but at the same time, the goals they set forth should be achievable.

Some challenge grants are set up to increase the number of donors in a specific dollar range. A donor might, for example, make a gift of $100,000 if the organization matches the gift by raising another $200,000 in gifts of $10,000 or more. Another strategic gift might challenge

donors of a particular profile. These might be defined as graduates of a particular class, residents of a specific geographic area, staff members, members of a particular profession, or members of other identifiable groups.

Strategic gifts not only leverage funds, but they are often designed to create motivating deadlines. A donor might stipulate that he or she will match every gift made to the campaign before a specific date. This date motivates the staff and provides an excellent way of encouraging donors to make their commitments.

Kresge Foundation: Challenge Grantor Par Excellence

One of the most sophisticated challenge grant models has been developed by the Kresge Foundation in Troy, Michigan. Primarily interested in helping organizations strengthen their long-term development programs, the Kresge Foundation makes challenge grants to organiza-

---

Kresge: A Great Taskmaster

We really sweated to put our Kresge proposal together. We had never applied for a grant so big and, frankly, we weren't used to doing such careful planning. But we buckled down and developed a fund-raising plan we thought we could accomplish. It was frightening to project out nearly two years ahead, but we outlined what we would do stage by stage. Once we submitted the grant, we had to raise $600,000 before Kresge made their decision five months later. We realized then that our proposal sweats were just the beginning. We worked like mad to live up to the plan we had submitted to Kresge. Of course, we could tell our donors that if we raised $600,000 by June, there was a good chance that Kresge would award us a challenge grant of $350,000! That for us is one BIG gift and proved to be a major incentive for our donors. In June, we not only celebrated our interim success, but we also celebrated our Kresge award. That celebration coalesced our volunteers and got us great press to boot. Then of course we started sweating some more. This time, we had 15 months to raise $1,000,000. If successful, the Kresge grant would complete our campaign. Before we were done, we had turned over every stone there was to turn and asked everyone there was to ask. Our entire community rallied around our effort and, indeed, by June we had raised $1.2 million, bringing our total with the Kresge gift to $200,000 over our goal. Our sweat had certainly paid off.

—Executive Director, Science Center

---

tions all over the country. These grants are designed to encourage organizations to use campaigns and special-project fund raising to broaden their donor bases.

Kresge Foundation challenge grants provide the final dollars for a campaign. The Foundation makes provisional challenge grants to organizations after they have raised their lead gifts but before they have solicited the broad base of their constituencies. Though complex and demanding, the Kresge grant process provides excellent opportunities for community organizations. The application process forces an organization to analyze carefully their donor base and to outline an effective plan for raising the necessary funds.

The proposal outline from Kresge requires each applicant to describe its plan for raising funds both during the Kresge five-month review period and after a provisional challenge grant is awarded. During the review period, Kresge requires periodic progress reports. Grants are awarded in part based on the organization's ability to live up to its plan. This process not only forces an organization to plan carefully, but also provides an imposed timetable on the interim gifts, thereby enabling the organization to motivate donors during the middle period of a campaign—often a most daunting task. Then, if a provisional challenge grant is awarded, the terms of the grant provide a deadline to raise the Kresge Challenge. These timetables, and the positioning of Kresge funds as last-in, provide excellent leverage throughout the campaign.

Building Partnerships through Strategic Gifts

Development directors should look for opportunities among their own lead-gift prospects to shape strategic gifts that will help motivate donors, provide interim deadlines, and target specific aspects of the donor base that need additional incentives. Working together in creative partnership with lead-gift prospects often benefits both the prospect and the development staff. The prospect, in the process of shaping the gift, becomes an insider to the campaign, and the staff is forced to analyze rigorously the campaign process and define strategic initiatives that will move the campaign ahead. For more information on the Kresge Foundation Challenge Grants, see *Dynamics of a Challenge Grant* by John E. Marshall III and Eugene R. Tempel (1998). Or go to the Kresge Foundation Web site at www.Kresge.org.

THE POWER OF LEAD-GIFT FUND RAISING

The success of a campaign rests on its ability to secure lead gifts. While the concept of lead-gift fund raising can be daunting to those who have never dreamed of asking another person for a large gift, understanding the motivations that inspire donors and solicitors can help an organization use its volunteers in highly effective and successful ways. Armed with a broad understanding of the organization's mission, the campaign's purpose, and the elements of the solicitation process, solicitors can feel confident about their own ability to ask successfully for a major gift. Indeed, as a solicitor becomes empowered by affirmative responses, he or she may grow to understand that sharing his or her commitment to an organization with another person and then asking for a gift to support its work may lead to extremely rewarding and enjoyable experiences.

REFERENCES

Marshall, John E. III, and Eugene R. Tempel. 1998. Dynamics of the challenge grant. *Capital Campaigns: Realizing Their Power and Potential. New Directions for Philanthropic Fundraising #21*, Andrea Kihlstedt and Robert Pierpont, editors. San Francisco: Jossey-Bass.

Klein, Kim. 1990. Setting up the major gift meeting. *Grass Roots Fund-raising Journal* 9 (June): 1–6.

Marx, Karl. 1875. The critique of the Gotha program. In *The Marx-Engels reader*. Edited by Robert C. Tucker, 1972. New York: W.W. Norton and Co.

Scanlon, Eugene. 1995. *Corporate and foundation fund raising: A complete guide from the inside.* Gaithersburg, MD: Aspen Publishers, Inc.

Wyman, Ken. 1993. *Face to face: how to get bigger donations from very generous people.* Written for the Canadian federal government's Voluntary Action Program, available through Ken Wyman & Associates, 64B Shuter Street, Suite 200, Toronto, ON, Canada, M5B 1B1; 416–363–2926.

Chapter 8
The Public Campaign

Chapter Outline

- Going Public
- The Campaign Kickoff
- Media and the Campaign Message
- The Special-Events Committee
- Soliciting Major Gifts
- Soliciting the Broad Base
- Telephone Solicitation and the Capital Campaign
- Direct Mail and the Capital Campaign
- Welcome Relief after a Stressful Campaign

Once the majority of lead gifts and family gifts have been raised during the quiet phase of the campaign, it is time to broaden the focus and extend the solicitation process to more prospects. As the campaign extends its reach, the organization must spread the word about the project and the campaign and expand the volunteer base. The transition from the quiet phase to the public phase is marked by a campaign kickoff celebration. This event focuses media attention on the campaign and brings together all of the volunteers and staff members who will help make the campaign a success. After the kickoff, the work of soliciting the broader constituency begins. This chapter reviews the transition from the quiet to public phase and explores the process of soliciting major and general gifts.

GOING PUBLIC

Because of the strategic power of the top 10 gifts, these leadership gifts are solicited before the campaign is made public. In fact, the process of identifying, cultivating, and soliciting major-gift prospects constitutes the largest and most important part of any campaign. It is a quiet process, however, done before hosting a kickoff party and printing and mailing campaign brochures. It is also the process that determines the outcome of the campaign. During this period, commonly referred to as the "quiet phase" of the campaign, major-donor prospects develop a sense of ownership of the project and the campaign and are solicited for their gifts.

Once these gifts have been raised along with gifts from those closest to the organization, it is time to "go public." In most campaigns the nucleus fund will constitute from 40 to 60% of the campaign goal. For an organization with a broad donor base, a nucleus fund in this range should be enough to assure the success of the campaign. And once success is assured, it is time to kick off the public phase of the campaign. Although it is tempting to share an organization's needs with the world from the beginning in the hopes that new donors will respond generously, successful campaigns tightly control the flow of information and only publicly announce the campaign and its goal when success seems likely.

A public kickoff event marks the transition from the quiet phase to the public phase (see Figure 8–1). If staged at just the right time, this event celebrates the generosity and commitment of a campaign's leaders and insiders, prepares other donors to be solicited, announces the public goal, and gives the solicitors courage and confidence to complete the campaign.

THE CAMPAIGN KICKOFF

Campaign kickoffs take many forms. Large institutions are likely to organize spectacular events with lavish theatrical productions written to dramatize the campaign themes. Smaller organizations sometimes choose to host a simple, low-cost, wine-and-cheese gathering for press and campaign volunteers. Regardless of the size, lavishness, or type of event that the organization decides to host, the kickoff:

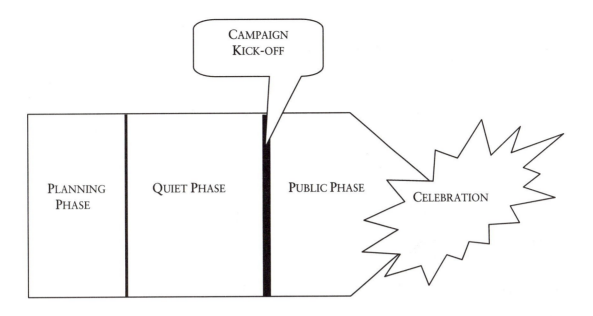

Figure 8–1 Campaign Phases

- Presents the public dollar goal of the campaign
- Recognizes generous donors and other individuals who have played important roles in the project
- Announces the campaign's progress
- Summarizes the case for support

The event creates a sense of excitement and enthusiasm for the project and for the campaign itself. It serves as a media event, providing a focus for the press. It celebrates the generosity of those who have already given to the campaign and focuses attention on the challenge ahead. Kickoff events are a time to celebrate and to muster energy for the final phase of the campaign.

The guest list for a campaign kickoff usually includes the following people:

- corporate, foundation, and individual donors and prospects
- former and current board members
- campaign volunteers
- public officials
- staff members
- media representatives

The Kickoff that Entertained, Astonished, and Informed

We were raising money for a women and babies' hospital. We knew our case was compelling, and we wanted a campaign kickoff that had more spirit and energy than the standard staid cocktail party or dinner. We wanted to explain our case in a way that was memorable. We decided to hire a local writer and actress to write a short monologue about the health care needs of women. She wrote and produced a 10-minute humorous piece in which she transformed herself using simple props into girls and women of different ages and performed skits related to the health needs of each age. It was funny, touching, and to the point. Our kickoff event was an 8 a.m. breakfast held in the unfinished lobby of the new facility. Everyone who came was entertained, informed, and astonished. We had many calls afterward about the success of our event largely because it was both interesting and unusual. I think we made our case in a most effective way.

—Vice President, Advancement

> *Beware of fund raising through special events for capital campaigns. They gobble up staff time. They are expensive. They are not often good cultivation events. They seldom raise significant amounts of money.*

Kickoff events are not fund-raising events. The expense incurred by the event should be part of the campaign budget and should not be raised by selling tickets to the event. In some cases, it may be possible to obtain a sponsor to underwrite the event, but more often than not the time and effort it takes to identify a sponsor would be better spent cultivating and soliciting a larger campaign gift.

The large campaign events—the kickoff, groundbreaking, and final celebration—focus attention on the collective accomplishments of the campaign, and in so doing, they lend credibility and importance to every small campaign meeting and phone call that has gone into making the campaign a success. These events move a campaign from phase to phase and create a public perception of progress and success that helps maintain or even increase the campaign's momentum.

> *Kickoff events do more than announce a campaign. They motivate volunteers, reinforce the case for support, inform communities, and provide a forum for acknowledging leadership gifts and volunteers.*

Preparing to Take the Campaign Public

Though the campaign kickoff occurs only after the largest gifts have been solicited, a great deal of work to organize the kickoff, develop campaign materials, and prepare for the broader solicitation must be completed prior to the event.

Revisiting the campaign goal: Throughout the quiet phase of the campaign, the goal has been stated as a "working goal." This indicates that it may be raised or lowered depending on the success of the lead-gift solicitations. By the time of the kickoff, however, one must take a stand and announce the campaign goal. If the lead-gift solicitations have been more successful than anticipated, this is the time to raise the goal. If they have been disappointing, an organization might decide to set more modest sights. Generally, the campaign steering committee helps make this decision.

Goal Escalation

We began with a $3.5 million working goal, but as we developed the case and began soliciting lead gifts, we found that we had sorely underestimated our potential. Not only were we able to tie down one gift of $1 million, but we suspected another such gift was likely. In addition, just about all of our lead-gift solicitations were either in line with what we had hoped or higher. We wrestled with how high to go, and as we prepared for the kickoff we had raised the goal to $5 million. We had a big banner printed with that amount to use at the kickoff, but the week of the event, we got another unexpected gift. Before the kickoff, we had raised $4.5 million! Clearly we needed to raise the goal again. We deep-sixed our lovely banner and announced in our press release that our goal was $6 million! Much to our amazement, by the end of the campaign we had raised $7.5 million. No one seemed to mind that we were so successful, because the entire project costs were $17 million. So there was no question about whether the money would be put to good use.

—Hospital Administrator

Preparing campaign materials: Though the solicitation of lead donors does not require a printed campaign brochure, this piece will be necessary for soliciting the wider constituency. As the solicitation process broadens and the campaign engages a growing number of volunteer solicitors, a simple and effective campaign brochure provides the volunteers with the material they need to guide them through a solicitation. By this stage in the campaign, every solicitation is no longer individualized and the staff is challenged to manage many volunteers who solicit a great many prospects. During the public phase of the campaign, a well-designed campaign brochure that provides the right information in a manner that is easy to comprehend is an important tool for the staff, volunteers, and prospects. See chapter 9 for more information on developing the campaign brochure.

Enlisting volunteer solicitors: When possible, the people who will solicit the midlevel gifts for the campaign should be enlisted prior to the campaign kickoff. Not only does the kickoff generate excitement and spark team spirit, but the media attention it will yield will prepare the prospects they will solicit. Therefore, the midlevel solicitations should occur as soon as possible after the kickoff event.

MEDIA AND THE CAMPAIGN MESSAGE

A campaign kickoff is a curious sort of event in that it reports on the success of the campaign at the same time that it proclaims the campaign to be beginning. It's rather reminiscent of that Boston marathoner who sneaked a ride on the trolley to the 15-mile marker.

> *A campaign kickoff is a curious sort of event in that it reports on the success of the campaign at the same time that it proclaims the campaign to be beginning.*

This seemingly cockeyed timing is actually a clever strategy for creating a sense of forward momentum and optimism at a crucial moment. The kickoff assembles a large and disparate group of campaign volunteers at one time and location around a shared goal, and uses that occasion to announce the specifics of the project to be funded and to recognize the campaign leaders who have already committed themselves to the success of the project. This all adds up to a compelling story for most community newspaper editors.

Coverage in the news media is most important at specific times during a capital campaign, and although standard press releases sometimes produce satisfactory results, a well-orchestrated event is far more likely to yield column inches and air time.

Waiting for the Right Time

A well-known gentleman in town sold us a large building at a price $700,000 below its market value. This was certainly news, and our benefactor would have been happy to have the publicity. However, our campaign was just in the planning stages and we didn't want to lose an opportunity for coverage later. So we asked him whether he would mind waiting several months until the campaign kickoff, when we could combine his gift with the gifts of many other community leaders. Together with the architect's renderings of the renovated building, we would have a story that could be a really big splash. Our donor agreed, and as long as the reporters don't decide to jump the gun, we'll be able to show him in a truly wonderful light!

—Campaign Director

In the Newspaper when It Counts

Last summer I volunteered to solicit five gifts for the library's campaign. The solicitation process was scheduled for September. I attended a meeting or two to learn about the project and get the material I needed. I knew it was time to begin making my calls. On Sunday morning I was amazed to open the local paper and find a big article on the front page about the library's project and the campaign. That really motivated me to get going. I knew that my prospects would also have seen the article and would be well prepared for my call. It really worked. Of five solicitation calls, I brought back four gifts. Everyone I spoke with already knew something about the project and they were happy to get my call.

—Campaign Volunteer

Although the kickoff serves several purposes, it is often a media event designed to interest the press in a story about the capital campaign and the project it is to fund. This event is designed to obtain media coverage in the broader community just before the solicitors begin to make their calls. A front-page article about the campaign and the project lends them credibility and visibility. And good press just a few days before the solicitors are to telephone their prospects gives courage to the solicitors and prepares their prospects to be solicited.

THE SPECIAL-EVENTS COMMITTEE

Campaigns are punctuated by events, some large, some small. The campaign events committee helps plan and implement these events. Often the events committee provides an ideal opportunity for those who are uncomfortable with soliciting gifts to be involved in the campaign in an important and visible way. Event planning is time-consuming and requires great attention to detail.

A strong events committee expands volunteer opportunities in the campaign and thereby adds energy, expertise, and enthusiasm to an important part of the campaign. Committee members are given time-specific, clearly defined assignments, thus avoiding much of the special-events burnout that can result when the same committee members are responsible for multiple events.

The mere thought of a special event gives some people a four-aspirin headache. For them, special events mean lots of work with little reward. They shudder as they anticipate mediating endless disputes about table linens, and about whether it should be fish or chicken, chocolate mousse or tiramisu.

Others thrive on the complex logistical planning and plotting; the minuscule details; the haggling with caterers, florists, printers, public officials, and other key personnel; and recruiting underwriters for the event. These people may be exhausted when the event is over, yet after a good night's sleep they are ready to tie up the loose ends and move on to the next event with renewed enthusiasm.

It's usually easier to find a special-events "natural" than a solicitation "natural." A person who hates special events should not be saddled with the task of planning them. Special events are demanding and time-consuming, and require a great deal of skill and know-how. Most communities have many such experts as potential volunteers. Organizations that do not have a special-events natural in their ranks should take the time to cultivate one early in the campaign. The participation of such an individual can add zest and sparkle to an important aspect of the campaign.

General Event-Planning Considerations

Before planning the campaign kickoff and other campaign events, an organization should consider the following suggestions (see Exhibit 8–1).

First, clarify goals, objectives, and tasks. Every event should have clearly defined goals and objectives that have been understood and accepted by everyone who is working on the event. Before the first committee meeting, the staff should draft a statement that describes the purpose of the event and its function in the capital campaign. Such a statement will enable the volunteers to plan the event so that it will serve its intended purpose. A statement of purpose for a campaign kickoff might be drafted using the guidelines in Exhibit 8–2.

This draft document should outline the goals of the event and provide a framework from which the committee designs the specific character, type, and style of the event. Beginning the planning process with a written

Exhibit 8–1 Event Guidelines

- Clarify goals and objectives
- Develop a realistic budget and stick to it
- Involve volunteers and board members
- Attend to details
- Recognize the event planners
- Be true to the organization
- Reinforce the organization's message
- Evaluate

Exhibit 8–2 Campaign Kickoff Planning Outline

Purposes:

- energize campaign volunteers
- obtain press coverage for the campaign and the project that the campaign will fund
- recognize the campaign's lead-gift donors

Timing:

- kickoff date

Suggested Attendees:

- major donors
- major-gift prospects
- community leaders
- campaign volunteers
- key staff members

Target Budget: $15,000

description of the event's purposes will help everyone work from the same set of assumptions, thereby smoothing the planning process. A checklist of decisions to be made, such as the one in Exhibit 8–3, is sometimes helpful in presenting the questions and issues that must be addressed.

Second, develop a realistic budget and adhere to it. The process of building a budget will help an event-planning committee understand and explore realistic options. The staff member who has been assigned to the project should present a preliminary event budget that fits within the budget for the entire campaign and then work with the committee to refine it as the event takes shape. This will put reasonable limits on the committee's decisions.

Third, involve volunteers and board members. Board members and volunteers are often responsible for the success of an event. They invite friends and colleagues, they provide in-kind donations, they make financial contributions toward the cost of the event, and they help run the event.

Fourth, attend to details. In planning any special event, it's the details that make all the difference. Many a well-conceived event has fallen short of its goals because its execution was sloppy. Taken one at a time, the myriad detailed decisions seem relatively unimportant, but together they create the climate for the event. Guests often aren't conscious of every detail of appearance and organization, but they do absorb the overall ambiance, and they notice all too well when a number of little things are awry.

Exhibit 8–3 Sample Kickoff Checklist

Fundamentals
- ☐ Date
- ☐ Time
- ☐ Number of people
- ☐ Guest list
- ☐ Description and timing of event

Location
- ☐ Parking
- ☐ Handicapped accessibility
- ☐ Size
- ☐ Appearance
- ☐ Liquor license
- ☐ Insurance

Invitations
- ☐ Design
- ☐ Production
- ☐ Addressing
- ☐ Date for mailing
- ☐ Return mechanism

Food and Drink
- ☐ Type of food
- ☐ Type of drinks
- ☐ Provider (caterers, local restaurants, etc.)
- ☐ Wait staff

Setup
- ☐ Linens
- ☐ Centerpieces
- ☐ Flowers
- ☐ Table arrangements
- ☐ Chairs
- ☐ Stage

Program
- ☐ Speakers
- ☐ Drafts of speeches
- ☐ Presentations
- ☐ Music
- ☐ Displays

- ☐ Slide show or video
- ☐ Other

People Management
- ☐ Volunteer roles
- ☐ Welcome table
- ☐ Name tags
- ☐ Seating chart
- ☐ Committee seating
- ☐ Prizes or other "take-homes"

Cleanup
- ☐ Pack and cart materials
- ☐ Draft report on event
- ☐ Final committee meeting
- ☐ Thank-you to volunteers

A List Maker's Heaven

I am by nature a compulsive list maker, so I was in my element when it came to planning the campaign kickoff. I set up a form for the master to-do list on my computer—with a line for each job, who was going to do it, and when—and then added a line where we could check off each item as it was completed. The form could be easily updated and printed before each planning committee meeting so that everyone would know who was responsible for doing what.

Then I bought a big calendar for my wall and put each task in its proper place on the calendar. Keeping track of everything two different ways gave me an overall picture of the process while simultaneously letting me focus on each task as it needed to be done.

—Development Director

Fifth, thank and recognize event planners. Getting volunteers involved in special events is one of the best ways to solidify relationships with those volunteers. A volunteer may have worked hard for months to build a special event, and when that event succeeds, the volunteer feels a closer sense of belonging to the organization. However, these volunteers are not likely to put themselves forward to be recognized and rewarded at the event on which they have worked. Staff members, therefore,

should make sure that all of the volunteers who worked on the event are properly thanked and recognized for their labors. You might use one or more of the following methods to do so:

- Include the names of the event planners in the printed program.
- Make a special presentation to the event chair during the event.
- Invite the event chair to make a brief speech during the event.
- Ask volunteers to stand and be recognized during the program.

Sixth, be true to the organization. Events should be in keeping with the style, capabilities, and traditions of the organization. Planners should not be carried away by the lavish event at the Metropolitan Museum of Art featured in the last issue of *Town and Country* when the organization lacks the experience, resources, and constituency to carry off such an elaborate production.

Seventh, reinforce the organization's message. While most of those who will attend campaign events are likely to know a good deal about the organization's mission and purpose, retelling the organization's story generates excitement and often shows the organization's work in a new light.

Finally, evaluate. After every event, the planners should take the time to evaluate its effectiveness. Evaluating an event and preparing a report are often useful when planning the next event.

For more on the nuts and bolts of event planning, see *Successful Special Events: Planning, Hosting, and Evaluating*, by Barbara R. Levy and Barbara Marion, another book in this series.

SOLICITING MAJOR GIFTS

The campaign kickoff occurs when the solicitation process is expanding from its tight focus on soliciting the nucleus fund to soliciting a broader number of mid-level or "major" gifts (see Figure 8–2). Ideally, by the time the kickoff takes place, the major-gift volunteers have been enlisted and they are ready to make their solicitations. The solicitation of major gifts requires extensive organization. The number of prospects to be solicited is far larger than in the lead-gift process, and a larger number of volunteers is required to solicit the prospects. Exhibit 8–4 demonstrates a method for calculating the number of solicitors needed to raise $300,000 in a major-gift campaign.

An Overview of the Major-Gift Solicitation Process

Although the meeting between the solicitor and the donor is the core of the matter, in reality this encounter is embedded in a much larger organizational framework that has been established to increase the chances of that encounter's success. This section describes the various preparations and activities that support and surround the major-gift solicitation. The example used here has been developed for a small campaign; however, it can be easily adapted for a campaign of any size. The table of gifts that was developed in chapter 3 and refined in chapter 5 provides the information on which the sample major-gifts division is planned.

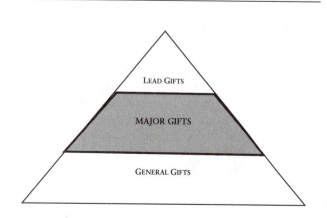

Figure 8–2 Moving Down the Gift Range Chart

Exhibit 8–4 Calculating Prospects and Solicitors Needed

LEAD GIFTS: 2–3 prospects/gift

Gifts Needed	Amount of Gifts	Prospects Needed	Gift Range
1	$150,000	2	$150,000
1	75,000	2	75,000
2	50,000	6	100,000
6	25,000	18	150,000

Lead Gift Totals: 10 gifts, 28 prospects, 6 solicitors

MAJOR GIFTS: 3–4 prospects/gift

10	$10,000	30	100,000
20	5,000	80	100,000
40	2,500	160	100,000

Major Gift Totals: 70 gifts, 270 prospects, 54 solicitors

GENERAL GIFTS: 5–6 prospects/gift

80	$1,000	400	$80,000
160	500	800	80,000
300+/-	<500	1,500	65,000

General Gift Totals: 700 gifts, 2,700 prospects; to be solicited through phone and mail

Total: 780 gifts, 2,998 prospects needed

Identifying Qualified Prospects

In the process of planning for the campaign, the organization has conducted several screening sessions to learn more about its prospects and to determine the appropriate request level for each. In preparation for the major-gift division solicitations, the staff has reviewed the database and has identified approximately 400 donors who might reasonably be invited to consider a gift in this range. This judgment has been based on the ratings of inclination and ability by other volunteers, staff evaluations, patterns of prior giving, and the prospects' history with the organization.

Designing the Division

The organization knows from the table of gifts developed in the campaign plan that it will require approximately 70 gifts of between $2,500 and $10,000 to raise $300,000. It also knows that each gift will require three or four solicitations and that consequently this division will need approximately 272 solicitations. If, on average, every volunteer will make five solicitations, this division will require 54 volunteer solicitors (272 ÷ 5).

To organize the division into manageable segments, the division will be divided into teams of six solicitors, one of whom will be designated team captain. In this example, the volunteers are divided into two sections and each section is organized into five teams of one team captain and five solicitors. Each section will comprise 30 volunteers (in addition to the section leader or division chair) and will be responsible for up to 150 solicitations. While this structure in theory provides 300 solicitations, or 28 more than necessary, in practice the actual numbers of volunteers will fall somewhat short of the goal because some team captains may not be able to find enough solicitors to fill their teams and some solicitors probably won't follow through. And, if for some reason everyone is successful in their recruiting, the organization will only benefit from the additional solicitors. This structure is illustrated in Figure 8–3.

Enlisting the Volunteers

Enlisting volunteers for the division proceeds from the top down. The campaign chair enlists the division chair. The division chair enlists the section chair. Section chairs enlist the team captains, and team captains enlist the volunteers. It is important to coordinate the selection of volunteers so that one volunteer is not recruited by several team captains. The simplest way to avoid overlap is to invite all the team captains to a meeting to discuss and clarify their role in the campaign. They will be invited to review lists of prospective solicitors and to place their names next to those whom they would like to recruit. Beyond the initial selection, the names of potential recruits should, if possible, be cleared through the development staff before they are contacted. Although it is sometimes helpful to define the teams according to their town or neighborhood, thereby reducing the potential for overlap, team captains usually prefer to recruit their friends and acquaintances, and patterns of friendship no longer commonly reflect neighborhood or community boundaries.

Soliciting the Solicitors

Every volunteer solicitor should be solicited before that solicitor solicits others. Although many campaigns assume that solicitors will make their gifts without being solicited, this is rarely the case, and this phase of the solicitation process is most effectively accomplished by organizing a clear and explicit schedule by which every volunteer is solicited by the person who recruited him or her. Not only does this address the issue of solicitor giving in a straightforward manner, as it should, but it gives every volunteer an opportunity to practice the solicitation process with a fellow solicitor. If handled properly, each of these solicitations can be not only a fund-raising call but also a chance to talk about the solicitation process—about what worked and what didn't. This method eases the tension for both volunteers. In some cases, the section leaders and team captains have their own solicitor-training session. This prepares them to be good solicitors and good coaches for the solicitors they have recruited. In other cases, they are trained alongside their fellow solicitors.

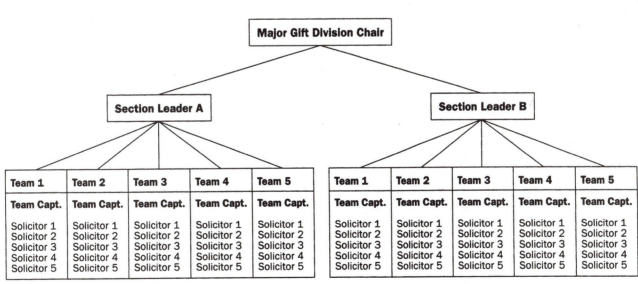

Team captains solicit team members. Solicitors each visit five prospects. Each team will be responsible for approximately 30 solicitations.

Figure 8–3 Sample Major Gift Division Structure

Matching Prospects with Solicitors

With 400 qualified prospects and roughly 56 solicitors, one needs a simple mechanism for pairing each solicitor with the five most suitable prospects. In the lead-gift solicitation process, solicitation strategies are determined prospect by prospect. With the larger numbers of prospects and solicitors in the major-gifts division, such an approach is not feasible.

The following prospect-selection strategy accomplishes the task in a way that:

- pairs each solicitor with the most likely prospects
- avoids duplication
- highlights the prospects who are most likely to make a gift
- provides information for the staff about who is soliciting whom

The volunteer solicitors all attend the prospect-selection meeting. The meeting should take approximately one and one-half hours and should be convened in a room large enough to seat all the volunteers classroom style, with a speakers' table and/or podium at the front and several long tables around the perimeter of the room for displaying prospect cards.

For some solicitors, the prospect-selection meeting will be the first opportunity that they have to become familiar with the campaign in an official setting. Many of them are likely to know the organization from previous contact, and all of them will have had conversations with their team captains or section leaders, though many will have only a passing understanding of the goals of the campaign and what is expected of them. The prospect-selection meeting provides an opportunity to inform and instruct the volunteers.

A typical agenda for the meeting might be organized as follows:

1. welcome and review of the meeting agenda and contents of packets (campaign chair)
2. mission and accomplishments of the organization (executive director)
3. summary of campaign goals (campaign co-chair or other)
4. description of division goals and the solicitation process (division chair)
5. instructions for selecting prospects and reminder of the next meeting (staff)
6. prospect selection (group)

Questions and discussion should be encouraged throughout the meeting.

Prospect cards should be prepared well in advance of the meeting by the staff. Each card contains the prospect's name, address, phone numbers, and a code that indicates the prospect's level of prior giving and relationship to the organization. The ideal system uses duplicate cards attached by a perforated edge. A sample is given in Figure 8–4.

The 3 × 5 cards that are used for tractor-feed printers work well. They are perforated and can be pulled apart in sets of two. Because many computer programs will not print duplicate information in the correct order, organizations often print two sets of mailing labels with the appropriate information and affix them to the cards. The cards should be kept in alphabetical order unless there is a particular reason to do otherwise. Every solicitor will thus be able to find the cards of specific prospects or institutions whom they have decided in advance that they wish to solicit.

Sometimes prospects whose names have surfaced in the lead-gift-rating sessions are for one reason or another not solicited in that division. These cards might then be included with those that have been identified for the major-gifts division. These special cards and any others that have been deemed particularly important should be identified with a special mark. One might, for example, place a gold star on each half of such priority-prospect cards.

Mrs. Elvin Strassner (Susan)
348 East Chestnut Street
Lancaster, PA 17602
717-333-8990

$$$$ Former board member, volunteer

- -

Mrs. Elvin Strassner (Susan)
348 East Chestnut Street
Lancaster, PA 17602
717-333-8990

$$$$ Former board member, volunteer

Figure 8–4 Sample Prospect Card

The cards should be set out on the tables around the room prior to the start of the meeting. They should be arranged alphabetically, and large signs showing the alphabetic categories of each table should be displayed on the wall above each table or on the tables themselves.

Information packets should also be prepared prior to the meeting for each solicitor. Simple pocket folders work well. Some organizations invest in folders specially printed with the campaign name and logo, while others put campaign mailing labels on the outside of the folders. As in most details of small campaigns, presentations need not be extravagant or glossy to be effective.

Material in the folder should include:

- the meeting agenda
- background information about the organization and the project being funded
- a description of the role of the volunteer in the campaign
- information about the volunteer's team: names and phone numbers of teammates, team captain, and coordinating staff member (a diagram of the campaign showing divisions, sections, and teams is helpful)
- a list of key dates for the division
- a copy of the proposal letter to be used in the solicitation process
- call report forms (see Exhibit 7–12)

Prospects are selected at the conclusion of the meeting when volunteers are requested to pick five prospect cards from among the cards laid out on the tables. If possible, solicitors should give special priority to the cards with stars but nonetheless should select individuals whom they know or with whom they share a contact. After selecting their cards, they should print their first and last names on the front of each half of the cards. They may take one half of the card home for reference and return the other half to a staff member before leaving.

Team captains usually contact absentee volunteers after the meeting to help them select their prospects and review their packets. If the team captain is unable to do this, a staff member will have to pick up these loose ends.

Assigning leftover prospect cards should wait until the first round of solicitation has been completed. To give the volunteers a wide enough selection so that they will be likely to find prospects whom they know, it is ideal to have more than five times as many qualified prospects as solicitors. This means, however, that some prospect cards will remain after the selection process is complete. Although solicitors should be encouraged to select starred cards first, if there are any leftover starred cards, they should be assigned in a second round to the most successful solicitors. Other remaining cards might be added to the prospects for another division or added to the list of phone solicitation or direct mail prospects.

Preparing Proposal Letters

Every solicitation should be preceded by a written proposal letter. This letter should be no more than two pages long, and it should be personalized for the specific prospect. The proposal letter includes four important elements:

1. a summary of the case for the project
2. a statement that a specific volunteer will be calling to set up an appointment
3. a request that the prospect meet with that volunteer
4. a request that the prospect consider making a gift of a specified dollar amount or within a specified range

The letters should be signed by the campaign chair. People are often confused about this strategy, wondering why the letters don't come from the solicitor. That the proposal letters are signed by the chair serves as an indication that the request for support comes from the campaign rather than from the volunteer solicitor. Through this strategy, the prospect is asked to support the goals of the campaign rather than to give based on his or her friendship with the volunteer. This approach also removes the burden of stating the actual amount of the request from the shoulders of the volunteers, many of whom feel uncomfortable doing so. Because the letters will be sent over the signature of the campaign chair, the salutation must match the chair's relationship with each prospect.

The proposal letters also motivate the volunteer solicitors to complete their calls. If solicitor Cecily knows that the campaign chair, a person of influence in the community, has sent a letter to Mr. Ernest Worthing informing him that a Ms. Cecily Bracknell will be calling him to set up an appointment, chances are good that Cecily will follow through.

Exhibit 8–5 is a sample proposal letter that was created for a fictitious organization. Much of the language in this letter was developed for the case for support and then adapted for many campaign communications. The letter should be short, easy to read, and non-bureaucratic. It should get to the point in the first paragraph and draw the reader inexorably through to the end. After reading the letter, the prospect should know what the project is about, who will call, what the call will be about, and what size gift the organization is asking him or her to consider.

Timing is crucial. Proposal letters must be prepared between the prospect-selection meeting and the solici-

Exhibit 8–5 Sample Proposal Letter

Salutation is appropriate for Sam Smith, the campaign chair, who signed this letter. He knows them well.

Dear Jennifer and Steve:

Letter begins with a remainder of what an important resource the library is

The County Library is one of the busiest places in downtown Lancaster. Every year, more than 400,000 people come to the library to borrow books, get information, study, do research, or just browse.

Highlights benefits of project to library users

This year the Lancaster County Library is getting ready to computerize its collections. Instead of struggling with the old microfiche system, you'll be able to find any book easily and accurately by typing key words into a computer. Every book and resource in the library will be coded, and scanners at the check-out desk will enable you to check out books easily and quickly.

With the new system, all sixteen county libraries will be linked to one computer system so that you will be able to get up-to-date information about whether a particular resource is anywhere in the library system, where it is, and whether or not it has been checked out. The library staff will be able to tell you what books you already have checked out and when the book you are waiting for is due back in. In short, the library will be able to serve you and your family better.

Positions the project as a public/private partnership. This is important for libraries!

To make this a reality, we need your help. Our County commissioners and many other generous individuals and corporations have already pledged more than $1 million toward the $1.8 million it will take to complete this project. We are now asking each of our library donors to consider making a special gift to help raise the remaining $800,000 before the end of the year.

States total goal

Highlight amount left to raise

Although we have no way of knowing whether or how much you would like to contribute to the campaign, we hope you will consider making a pledge of between $500 and $1,000 per year for up to three years. If you are in a position to consider a gift of more than that, we would, of course, be thrilled. If, on the other hand, a gift of that size does not fit your situation, we will be truly grateful for whatever contribution you feel is appropriate.

Mentions pledge period

Gently requests a gift in a specific range

Within a few days, Barbara Johansen will call to set up an appointment to talk with you about this project. I hope that you will take the time to meet with her and consider a generous contribution to the Open Sesame Campaign.

Sets up expectation that Barbara will call

The health of our public library reflects the values of our community. Please join me in helping to make sure that our county library remains strong well into the next century.

Indicates Sam's commitment

With sincere appreciation,

Puts request in larger context

Sam Smith
Campaign Chair

P.S. The enclosed brochure will give you a more complete picture of the project. This brochure was contributed as a campaign gift by a generous area designer and printer.

Often in small campaigns, people are uneasy about spending money to raise money tor-training meeting. The cards that are collected at the conclusion of the prospect-selection meeting provide the staff with the name of the solicitor—the final piece of information that they need to prepare the solicitation letters. The staff prepares drafts of the letter for each prospect prior to the solicitation-training meeting. The drafts of the letters to their prospects are given to each solicitor at the training meeting so they have a chance to review them for content and accuracy before they are sent. This helps the solicitors to become familiar with the contents of the letters, allows them to review (and occasionally alter) the amount of the gift being requested, and increases the chances of catching any errors in spelling or grammar that may have snuck by the in-house error sleuths.

Training the Solicitors

The solicitor-training meeting marks the beginning of the actual solicitation process, and all volunteers in the division are expected to attend. At that meeting they not only learn how to solicit a gift but they also receive copies of the proposal letters that have been prepared as well as all other material that they will need to solicit their prospects.

This meeting usually lasts about two hours. It should be held in a room large enough to accommodate all of the solicitors, staff, and other speakers in a seating format that encourages participation. Ideally, the solicitors from each team should sit at a round table with their team captains. A refreshment table should be located in an area where people can mingle, and a speakers' table or podium should be at the front of the room.

For this meeting, each solicitor should receive a prepared name tag from a table by the door. Depending on the time of day, simple but attractive refreshments give people a chance to relax and break the ice as everyone arrives.

Information packets for team members should be given to each team captain to distribute at the table. Extra information from the last meeting should be on hand for those who forgot their packets.

The agenda for this second solicitors' meeting might be as follows:

- welcome and introductions (campaign chair or board chair)
- review of purpose of meeting (campaign chair)
- review of campaign goals and progress to date (campaign co-chair)
- review of division goals, structure, process, and timetable (division chair)
- distribution and review of drafts of proposal letters (team captains and solicitors)
- solicitation training (consultant)
- distribution of other material (staff)

By reviewing the draft of the proposal letter before it is sent, the volunteer is able to make adjustments. Any volunteer who on reviewing the draft letters to his or her prospects finds an error in the letter should be instructed to mark the error or any other suggested changes directly on the letters and return them to the staff. Or if a volunteer disagrees with the amount of the gift that has been suggested in the proposal and believes that a higher (or lower) amount would be more appropriate, that too should be noted.

The staff will make all corrections, have the final letters signed, and send final copies to the solicitors at the same time that the letters are sent to the prospects. Solicitors should be instructed to begin calling their prospects to set up appointments when they receive copies of the final proposal letters in the mail.

Some campaign managers prepare simple spiral-bound handbooks for their volunteer solicitors. The handbook might have a nice cover with the campaign name and logo. This handbook format helps solicitors keep the information that they will need in a well-organized, easy-to-use format. A volunteer handbook might include the following:

- statement of campaign objectives
- campaign goal and table of gifts
- rules of thumb for soliciting a gift
- guide to a successful solicitation
- answers to tough questions
- ways to give to the campaign
- relationship between annual giving and the campaign
- gift-crediting guidelines
- donor recognition opportunities
- names and telephone numbers of staff resource people

Maintaining Contact during the Solicitation Period

Volunteers are usually expected to complete their solicitations in four to six weeks. The division structure establishes a clear pattern for communicating with volunteers during the solicitation period, and effective team captains call each of their solicitors every week to check on their progress and to see whether they need help or advice.

It is also helpful to schedule two or three informal reporting meetings for team captains, section leaders, and the division chair. These meetings might be organized as drop-in meetings during a specified afternoon or evening in which people stop by with their updates, signed pledge forms, and questions. These meetings are most effective if they are scheduled for one hour every week during the solicitation period. They provide an opportunity for team captains to hear what is happening in other teams, for the section leaders and staff to track progress, and for the staff to provide assistance and advice as needed.

Throughout the solicitation period and often well beyond, solicitors must be informed when someone whom they have solicited sends in a gift. Although solicitors are strongly encouraged to keep control of the pledge form until it has been signed, in practice many solicitors are unable to stand firm on this dictum and are likely to leave a pledge form with their prospect. When pledge forms are sent to the office, someone on the staff must be responsible not only for acknowledging and thanking the donor and recording the gift but also for informing the solicitor that the gift was received.

As the solicitation period proceeds, the staff might prepare brief, written progress updates reporting on how many calls have been made and how much has been raised by the division to date. These serve as reminders and motivate solicitors to complete their visits.

The solicitation process has a way of beginning with a bang and ending with a whimper. The organization should make every effort to highlight the timetable and to encourage the solicitors to complete their calls by the end of the solicitation period.

Completing Unfinished Solicitation

At the end of every solicitation period there is an untidy group of unfinished calls. Some volunteers could not reach one or another of their prospects. Some volunteers just didn't follow through. Some prospects asked for time to consider and then the volunteer didn't get back to them. Sometimes a prospect will make a verbal commitment to the solicitor but not sign a pledge form. Occasionally, a pledge form is returned with an amount different from that reported by the solicitor. No matter how you look at it, cleaning up unfinished calls is time-consuming and messy.

The first stage of the cleanup falls to the team captains. They review their lists of prospects and get in touch with their solicitors to determine the best strategy for completing each call. Sometimes the team captains themselves complete an unfinished call. Sometimes, however, this process gets passed to the staff member in charge of the division. The staff member, through phone calls, personal visits, or letters, wraps up the process, bringing any open solicitations to a close.

Reporting Success, Thanking Solicitors, and Acknowledging Donors

No solicitation process is really complete until everyone knows the final tally; the solicitors are thanked by the campaign chair, the section leader, and the team captain; and every donor has been thanked by the solicitor, the campaign chair, and the director of the organization.

Coordinating this entire process is usually the responsibility of the development staff.

Summarizing the Process and Meetings

There is a great deal to keep in mind in organizing a solicitation division. The outline of meetings and tasks in Exhibit 8–6 may help to crystallize the process. This outline may be effectively adapted to any division in any campaign. Following the list of tasks in order from beginning to end will help ensure that the right solicitor solicits the right donor for the right gift.

Job Descriptions for Division Leaders, Team Captains, and Solicitors

Although the structure and timing of each piece of a campaign is extremely important, a campaign must also recruit effective division leaders, team captains, and solicitors if it is to succeed. Entire teams and even divisions have failed to raise as much money as they otherwise might have because one solicitor in a lead position did not follow through, became dissatisfied and slacked off, or was perhaps diligent but nonetheless ineffective.

> *The success of any committee or division is often shaped by the effectiveness of the volunteer leaders.*

One way of avoiding such misfortune is to specify the role of these leaders in advance so that they know what will be expected of them before they agree to take the job.

Simple job descriptions outlining the tasks as clearly and specifically as possible often provide the necessary focus, enabling a volunteer to look realistically at other commitments in light of the campaign calendar. Although some volunteers may turn down the job once they know what is involved, those who agree to help will know just what they are getting into and so will be more likely to do the job well.

Job descriptions for division leaders, team captains, and solicitors should include information about the purpose of their part of the campaign, the number of meetings that they will be expected to attend, the tasks for which they will be responsible, and the projected timetable and duration of their involvement.

Exhibits 8–7 and 8–8 are sample job descriptions that may be adapted for other divisions and other campaigns.

Solicitor Training

Soliciting gifts takes courage. Development directors should develop a sympathetic understanding of the fears

Exhibit 8–6 Outline of the Solicitation Process

Task	Responsible Persons
☐ Enlist division chair (DC)	Staff and campaign chair
☐ Rate prospects	Staff and volunteers
☐ Design division structure	Staff, consultant, DC
☐ Enlist section leaders (SLs) or team captains (TCs)	DC
☐ Schedule division meetings	DC and SLs
1. Solicitor training meeting for DC/SLs/TCs	
2. Prospect selection meeting	
3. General solicitor training meeting	
4. Report meetings for DC/SLs/TCs	
☐ Enlist team captains	SLs
☐ Enlist solicitors	TCs
☐ Plan prospect selection meeting	DC, SLs, and staff
1. Plan agenda	
2. Prepare prospect cards	
3. Assemble packets for solicitors	
4. Prepare speakers	
5. Prepare room	
6. Send reminder notice	
☐ Conduct prospect selection meeting	All
☐ Prepare proposal letters	Staff
☐ Plan solicitor training meeting	DC, SLs, and staff
1. Plan agenda	
2. Arrange for room setup and refreshments	
3. Send reminder notices	
4. Prepare speakers	
5. Enlist consultant as trainer	
6. Organize campaign material for solicitors	
☐ Conduct solicitor training meeting	All
☐ Prepare and send final proposal letters	Staff
☐ Solicit campaign volunteers	DC, SLs, and TCs
☐ Solicit proposals	Solicitors
☐ Track solicitation progress	SLs, TCs, and staff
☐ Conduct report meetings	SLs, TCs, and staff
☐ Close all open-ended solicitations	SLs, TCs, and staff
☐ Thank volunteers	TCs, campaign chair, and staff
☐ Thank donors	Solicitors, campaign chair, and executive director
☐ Report success	Staff

that swirl around the gift solicitation process. Understanding and acknowledging the discomfort that is involved and celebrating the extraordinary courage that solicitation requires heartens solicitors far more effectively than simply telling them not to be afraid.

While effective solicitor training does not eradicate fears, it does prepare solicitors to solicit gifts in spite of their anxieties. Training sessions provide a safe environment in which solicitors are able to learn and to practice their art. Because most people learn best when they participate actively in the learning process, the best solicitor training provides every solicitor with opportunities to find the right words and to practice the solicitation process. By practicing in a safe environment, volunteers begin to find the words, phrases, and approaches that ring true for them, and as that happens, they develop the confidence to help them overcome their fears.

Fund raising is high-stakes behavior. When creating a campaign structure, one therefore works to build safe environments that foster confidence.

Exhibit 8–7 Sample Division Chair Job Description

Job Description
Business/Foundation Division Chairperson

Division Goals: To identify, cultivate, and solicit business and business-related foundations that may be able and willing to make contributions of between $1,200 and $30,000 to the Hospice campaign. The financial goal of this division is $220,000.

Primary Time Period: July through December

Responsibilities of the Chairperson:

√ Help identify and enlist eight to ten individuals to serve on a business-division committee
√ Solicit business-division committee members
√ Conduct two division meetings to organize the business-solicitation process
√ Attend and chair two meetings for business-division solicitors
√ Serve as advocate for the campaign and committee
√ Serve on the steering committee, which will meet monthly throughout the campaign
√ Make a gift to the campaign

Staff Support: The staff of hospice will work with the chair of this committee to organize the business division, provide lists and solicitation material, maintain effective communication and follow-through for all aspects of the committee's work. The campaign consultant will conduct a solicitor training session for the business-division solicitors.

Exhibit 8–8 Sample Solicitor Tasks

Responsibilities of a Solicitor

1. Attend one meeting on March 20 from 4:00–5:30 p.m. to obtain background information and select prospect cards.
2. Attend a meeting on April 10 from 4:00–6:00 p.m. to review proposal letters and become a trained solicitor.
3. Solicit five prospects between April 15, 2001 and June 1, 2001.
4. Report results of solicitations to team captains during the solicitation period.
5. Deliver completed pledge cards to the team captain or to the development director by June 15.
6. Make a financial contribution to the campaign.

Before describing effective approaches to solicitor training, it may be helpful to have a reminder of just what it is that solicitors fear.

Fear of Fund Raising

It is rare to find a person who is not afraid to ask others for money. Even those who solicit gifts year after year have to resist the natural anxiety that comes from putting oneself on the line.

Although it doesn't make the fear disappear, understanding and acceptance of the many facets of these fears help one to act in spite of, or even because of, that fear. In soliciting gifts, one can learn much about oneself that is enlightening and that transfers to many other endeavors in life.

Perhaps the most common fear is that of personal rejection. People confuse the word "no" with the phrase "I don't like you." Most people find it hard to separate a request on behalf of an organization from a request for personal approval. And to be fair, some people do say "no" in an insensitive way, giving the impression that he or she is angry with the solicitor, rather than just declining the invitation to give.

Many solicitors are afraid that they don't know enough about the project and the organization to do a good job. They worry that they will present the case incorrectly or unconvincingly, that they will not know the answers to questions that the prospect raises, and that they will respond in a way that loses the gift. Soliciting is indeed a heavy burden, and although it seldom requires as much learning as the solicitor might fear, it is easy to understand the concerns of volunteers who are only occasionally involved in the solicitation process.

Most people are afraid to fail—we tie our self-esteem to success. And as has been discussed earlier in this book, capital campaigns are designed to incorporate a great deal of failure. With only one gift expected from four solicitations, three of those four solicitations should fail! Of course, such a lighthearted attitude toward failure may be fine in the campaign planning phase, but those who solicit those three prospects who decide not to give are often left feeling as though they have contributed to the failure of the project rather than to its success.

In soliciting gifts, volunteers must not only put forward the general case for the organization and the project, but they are actually required to ask their prospects for specific amounts of money. For those who grew up in a society in which discussion of money is considered much more personal than a discussion of, say, sex, it is no wonder that the solicitor fears embarrassment.

The experience of soliciting is not unlike that of attending a concert that one has particularly enjoyed and being the first to rise during the applause. The potential embarrassment of not being joined in a standing ovation keeps many a concertgoer from rising early no matter how much he or she liked the concert. The act of initiating a standing ovation is implicitly an invitation to others to join you in supporting the performer. And if they don't join in, then the inference is that they disapprove of your sentiment and of the action you took.

Asking for money requires similar courage. One takes a stand on behalf of an organization and through the solicitation process invites others to do the same. This public commitment on behalf of a specific project can be especially difficult if one has lingering reservations about the project—and it is a rare project indeed about which one has no reservations!

Solicitor-Training Workshops

Solicitor training is a small but important aspect of capital campaigns; and as with many parts of this complex process, there are many ways to train solicitors. Usually the solicitor training is designed by the consultant and/or the development staff, whose approach reflects their specific style as well as the logistical realities of assembling the solicitors at one place and one time. For community-based organizations, logistics are relatively simple, and the solicitors can be expected to attend a training workshop lasting two to three hours. If the solicitors are traveling across the country, however, they will be likely to attend the workshops only if the workshops are embedded in a larger schedule of events.

The workshops will also vary depending on the number of participants. If volunteer training is done division by division or even section by section, each training workshop may have no more than 15 or 20 participants. Although that is an ideal size, it is possible to design an effective workshop for 50 or more people.

Consultants have varying opinions about the style and length of the training process. Some believe that volunteer training is best and most simply accomplished by a lecture-style motivational presentation delivered at the campaign kickoff. Others believe that every volunteer solicitor should attend a workshop of two to three hours that both presents the necessary information and actively engages the volunteers. Although each approach has been used successfully, the latter is probably better. See Exhibit 8–9 for a sample outline of a solicitation workshop.

Adapting the Process to Specific Constituencies

The major-gift strategy generally works best when the prospects have been organized by like kind, and volunteer solicitors from within that group are recruited to serve their peers. The model described above for soliciting major gifts can be adapted for any specific group of prospects. One might organize a business division; a division of parents, alumni, neighbors, congregants, people within a specific profession; or other sub-grouping. Businesses are the most common division grouping in a community-based campaign. Business people in a community tend to know one another through participation in groups like Rotary or Chamber of Commerce. Because of their ongoing involvement in soliciting for the United Way, many business people are experienced solicitors. And, although nationally business giving is declining, locally-owned business are often generous sources of campaign funds for community organizations. See Exhibit 8–10 for a sample listing of responsibilities of a team captain for a business division.

SOLICITING THE BROAD BASE

In this section, we focus our attention on the bottom section of the gift range chart, the general gifts (see Figure 8–5). At this level, when the financial stakes are lower and the numbers of solicitations are much higher, we turn to solicitation mechanisms that are less personal and take less volunteer effort. Using a campaign with a goal of $1,000,000 as a model, we will explore the best ways of soliciting donors capable of giving $1,000 or less to the campaign. As Exhibit 8–11 shows, the campaign will require 80 gifts of $1,000, 160 gifts of $500, and approximately 300 gifts of under $500 to raise the $225,000 needed from the general gifts level. Using a multiplier of five or six prospects/gift, the campaign will need between 2,700 and 3,240 prospects. While an organization may elect to organize personal solicitations for the gifts in the $1,000 range, many of these solicitations will take place by phone and/or mail. This section reviews effective strategies and techniques for raising money for capital campaigns through these less personal, but important, techniques.

Exhibit 8–9 A Solicitation Workshop That Works

Duration: one and one-half hours to two hours

Room Arrangements: one large oval or rectangular table to seat everyone, one flip chart at the front of the room, and enough space to form six seating clusters of three chairs each.

Meeting Agenda:

- welcome and introductions
- objectives of the meeting
- presentation on how to solicit gifts
- finding one's own words
- practicing the solicitation process
- objections and responses
- key points to remember
- next steps

Meeting Outline:

1. Welcome and Introductions (15 minutes)

Even a simple, "Hello" and "Thank you for coming" from the campaign chair should convey excitement and urgency as well as to highlight the importance of the volunteers in completing the campaign.

A simple introductory exercise can ease the initial tension and help the solicitors get acquainted. The participants should be asked to introduce themselves by giving their names and perhaps sharing their history with the organization or relating one positive fund-raising experience that they have had.

2. Objectives of the Meeting (5 minutes)

The objectives of the training meeting will include:

- helping each volunteer understand how to solicit gifts
- helping solicitors find and practice their own solicitation styles and words
- identifying likely objections and appropriate responses
- clarifying the next steps for the solicitors

3. Presentation on How to Solicit Gifts (15 minutes)

The consultant and/or the development staff will present material on the solicitation process. A discussion of the following elements is essential:

- understanding why donors give
- setting up the solicitation
- preparing for the solicitation
- conducting the meeting
- handling objections
- closing
- following up

4. Finding One's Own Words (10 minutes)

While everyone is sitting around the table, ask each volunteer to write down two or three sentences that best describe his or her own reasons for supporting the project. Invite them to share their reasons while the facilitator writes them down on the flip chart. This process will give the group a look at the many reasons others have for supporting the project, while clarifying and putting words to their own reasons. The newsprint sheets are then taped to the wall where they will remain visible during the role-playing exercises.

5. Practicing the Solicitation Process (30 minutes)

Divide solicitors into pairs. Every person will play the roles of both solicitor and prospect. The prospect may assume whatever identity he or she chooses, including his or her own. Each solicitor is given five minutes to solicit the prospect. At the conclusion of each five-minute period the pairs discuss what worked and what didn't. Switch roles and repeat.

6. Handling Objections (15 minutes)

The group reassembles around the table. On a flip chart, list the objections that came up in the solicitations. Invite the group to suggest responses to each of the most commonly encountered objections.

7. Key Points to Remember (10 minutes)

Ask each person to complete the following sentence: "When I go to solicit my prospects, I want to remember to…". Ask each person to read what he or she wrote.

8. Next Steps (5 minutes)

The training concludes by reminding the volunteers of what they should do next, reviewing the solicitation timetable, and answering any questions.

TELEPHONE SOLICITATION AND THE CAPITAL CAMPAIGN

After face-to-face solicitation, telephone is the most personal and effective approach to solicitation. Although some people find telephone solicitation intrusive, if organized correctly telephone solicitations can provide an extremely rewarding way to reach donors who would otherwise be relegated to the mail.

Carol Blanton's article "The Pitfalls and the Promise of Telephone Fundraising" (1994) describes the results of a test that was conducted by the Nature Conservancy of California to measure the effectiveness of telephone fund raising against the response rate of a two-letter direct-mail appeal. The results show telephone fund raising to have 10 times the response rate and less than half the cost of the direct-mail appeal! Although this test was carried out in the context of an annual giving program, it is consistent with results that the author has seen in phonathons conducted to solicit lower-level gifts for capital campaigns. Through telephone solicitation, an organization can significantly increase the returns from a group of donors, both in the number of gifts and the amount per gift.

While it would be wonderful if a trained volunteer could personally solicit every prospective donor, the large

Exhibit 8–10 Responsibilities of a Team Captain for a Business Division

---

Goal of the Business Division

The Business Division of the Day Care Center Campaign is charged with raising $250,000 by soliciting 140 identified area businesses.

Description of Tasks

Prospect Type: Area Financial Institutions

The task of the financial institution team within the business division is to:

1. review and evaluate the list of 28 currently identified financial institutions
2. add financial institutions that may have been left off the list but may be deemed good prospects
3. enlist people to solicit the financial institutions (approximately one solicitor per five institutions)
4. solicit the financial institutions

Requirements

1. Attend one meeting of team captains to review and evaluate prospect lists.
2. Enlist team members (solicitors), each of whom will visit five prospects.
3. Attend one meeting with team members to learn about the project and select prospect cards.
4. Attend one solicitor training meeting.
5. Solicit team members.
6. Maintain contact with team members during the solicitation period.
7. Attend two report sessions during the solicitation period.
8. Complete unfinished solicitations.
9. Attend wrap-up meeting of the business division.
10. Make a financial contribution to the campaign.

Anticipated Timing and Duration of Business Division:
March 1, 2002–May 30, 2002

Figure 8–5 Moving Down the Gift Range Chart

Exhibit 8–11 General Gifts Needed to Raise $1,000,000

GENERAL GIFTS: 5-6 prospects/gift

Number	$ Amount	Prospects	$ In Range
80	$1,000	400	$80,000
160	500	800	80,000
300+/-	<500	1,500	65,000

Totals: 700 general gifts   2,700 prospects needed

---

number of prospects usually makes such an approach impractical. Various combinations of mail and telephone solicitation produce results that directly correlate to the extent of the personal relationship developed between the solicitor and the prospect. Yielding the highest returns, of course, are personal solicitations preceded by a personalized proposal letter. The next most effective approach is a proposal letter in conjunction with a tele-phone call from someone who is known and well respected by the prospect. Less effective is just a phone call from a friend, and so on down the effectiveness ladder. The following list shows the order of effectiveness, from most to least, of various types of solicitation combinations:

- proposal plus face-to-face solicitation from a respected friend or acquaintance
- face-to-face solicitation from a stranger
- phone solicitation by a respected friend or acquaintance
- phone solicitation by a stranger
- mailed appeal with personal note from a friend or acquaintance
- mailed appeal with no note

Many organizations regularly raise money through direct-mail solicitations, but they resist telephone solicitation. Not only is organizing telephone solicitation more demanding than assembling a mail campaign, but many people are so bombarded by telephone sales calls that board members and staff hate to burden their donors with yet another dinnertime phone call. However, prospects do make contributions as a result of telephone solicitations, particularly if they feel that their opinions are being heard and their questions are being answered by knowledgeable and informed volunteers.

Telephone fund raising serves an important function in a capital campaign. It provides an opportunity for the organization to make personal contact with the most likely remaining prospects who weren't solicited earlier in the campaign. Since the phonathon takes place near the end of the campaign's public phase, most of the organization's prospects have read about and heard about the campaign through the newspapers, on television, or from friends. Since they have been donors to the organization in the past, these people may actually be waiting to be solicited. Telephone fund raising gives these donors the opportunity to speak directly with someone who represents the organization to learn more about the campaign, ask questions, and make a campaign gift.

Volunteers vs. Paid Solicitors

Telephone solicitation in the later phases of a capital campaign is most commonly organized through a phonathon, in which volunteers gather in one location with many phone lines to make telephone calls on behalf of the campaign. Some phonathons last for three evenings, some as long as a week, some even longer.

Phonathons are a tidy way to complete the best remaining prospect solicitations. Many volunteers who feel intimidated by the idea of making face-to-face solicitations are willing to participate in phonathons. The phonathon process is more controlled, and many volunteers find it to be a comfortable way to help out in the campaign.

Phonathons often return more than money to the campaign. Through conversations with its constituency, an organization can get immediate feedback on its programs and learn firsthand about the prospects' interests and ideas.

Rather than using the staff time and energy that are needed to coordinate a phonathon, some organizations hire a telemarketing firm to conduct the telephone solicitations. Large organizations with tens of thousands of prospects use them regularly; small to medium-sized organizations must carefully weigh the costs and benefits of employing a telefundraising firm. For organizations with unsolicited prospect lists that are smaller than 6,000, using a telefundraising firm is probably not cost effective.

Volunteer-staffed phonathons have three important advantages over those run by paid telemarketers:

1. Volunteers have a genuine and often heartfelt connection to the organization and enjoy sharing their stories about it with others.
2. Volunteers may know the people whom they are calling, increasing the chances of obtaining a pledge.
3. Volunteer-staffed phonathons cost a fraction of those done using a telefundraising firm.

Organizing the Volunteer Phonathon

Determining Whom to Call

At this late stage in a capital campaign, phonathons are used to reach the most likely prospects among former donors who have not yet been solicited for the campaign. Often these donors will number in the thousands. Two or three hundred names may be those of individuals who were earmarked for face-to-face solicitation but whose cards were not selected. The rest will be names of donors who have given before but who were not targeted in this campaign for personal solicitations. Although most organizations also have long lists of constituents who are not donors, these people are not usually included in campaign phonathons.

Lists of donors still to be contacted should be organized into categories ranging from most likely to least likely donors. Some organizations color code the prospect forms according to these categories so that the callers can easily see who should be contacted first.

Once the phonathon list has been determined, the staff must find the phone numbers to match the names. Some organizations regularly gather and update phone numbers from checks, pledge cards, or other information sources, and already have telephone numbers for the majority of their donors. Other organizations may have no phone numbers at all. Some organizations contract with an outside agency to provide phone numbers. Others have staff members and volunteers who are willing to look them up in the directory. On average, an organization will be able to find phone numbers for approximately 60 percent of the names on its list. The remainder of the prospects will have to be solicited by mail.

Recruiting Volunteers

Organizations are often able to recruit excellent phonathon volunteers during the concluding phases of a campaign. By this time, many people have solicited gifts face-to-face and have become more comfortable with the solicitation process. There are also many people who will agree to help because they are aware that they had not helped earlier and they are safe in the knowledge that their time commitment will be limited. The goal is near and people are often willing to sign on to help for the final push.

Anyone who is committed to the organization and is able to use the telephone can be an effective phonathon volunteer. Often board members, those who volunteer in other aspects of the organization's programs, staff members, professionals who have played a role in developing the campaign project (architects, graphic designers, attorneys, contractors, and so forth), and people who have volunteered for earlier phases of the campaign are willing to sign up for a calling session.

Campaign phonathons are often staff driven, although if the staff member plans far enough ahead, engaging the help of several volunteers may broaden and in some cases strengthen the phonathon. Volunteers may help the development staff member find an appropriate space, identify and enlist phonathon volunteers, and provide refreshments and prizes to motivate the callers. It is not unusual by the late stages in the campaign, when volunteers and staff members are weary, for a staff member not to rely on a volunteer committee to organize the phonathon. Some organizations even choose to hire a part-time staff person just to plan and coordinate the phonathon.

In any case, each calling session will require one set of volunteers to make the calls and another set of clerical volunteers to collect the paperwork, write notes, address envelopes, and keep track of gifts and pledges for the calling session. Generally, more callers and support people than needed should be recruited for each calling session to provide the necessary leeway for the individuals who invariably don't show up.

Although there are many ways to recruit phonathon volunteers, many organizations recruit two phonathon chairs whose job it is to recruit the volunteers. The staff provides them with a list of those who have volunteered in the past, and the chairs set up the calling teams by dividing up the lists and contacting prospective volunteers. If time permits, it is also effective to circulate sign-up sheets showing the dates and times of each session with a blank space for each volunteer who is needed. The sign-up sheets might be circulated at board meetings, staff meetings, volunteer meetings, and campaign meetings. The staff should then thank each person who signs up for a slot and confirm the dates and times in writing. Staff members also often send a reminder notice or make a reminder call just prior to the date of the calling session.

Determining the Duration

The size and shape of the phonathon emerges from the number of solicitations to be made. We know from experience that on average, one volunteer can make approximately 15 calls per hour. We also know that the average prospect will need to be called twice before being reached. So if the staff has identified 750 names of people who should be called during the phonathon, the phonathon should be designed to make 1,500 calls. In addition, most phonathons schedule calling sessions that last two hours, with an additional hour for training and distributing materials. Therefore, if each volunteer can make 30 calls in one calling session (15 calls x 2 hours = 30 calls per calling session) and if the organization has access to a good location with 10 phone lines and 10 desks, then the phonathon will require approximately five calling sessions (1,500 calls ÷ 300 calls per session = 5 calling sessions).

> *A basic phonathon planning guide is that one volunteer makes an average of 15 calls per hour, and each prospect will have to be called twice. Phonathon sessions are usually three hours long—one hour for training and two hours for calling.*

Setting Dates and Times

Campaign phonathons must be scheduled for just after the completion of all the face-to-face solicitations so as not to conflict with the organization's regular annual giving program. Seasoned phonathon planners find the calling response rate best on midweek evenings, although some organizations also find Sunday evenings productive. A long phonathon, one requiring six or eight calling sessions, may be scheduled over two or even three weeks, with two or three calling sessions per week. Smaller phonathons are best scheduled during a one-week period to simplify the mailing of pledge forms and follow-up letters to those who were not reached and to focus the energy of staff and volunteers.

Calling sessions are often scheduled between 6:00 p.m. and 9:00 p.m. This gives the volunteers a chance to assemble, receive their materials and training, and begin making calls by 7:00 p.m.

Finding a Suitable Location

A suitable phonathon location has approximately 10 telephone lines and 12 or more desks or tables assembled in an open space. Although organizing a phonathon on site is most convenient, many small nonprofits do not have the requisite large open area nor the multiple phone lines and desks, so they must borrow other space. Banks, insurance companies, travel agencies, and other businesses that rely on phone sales often have such configurations and are willing to donate the use of their space.

A central and open space for phonathons creates the right mood. When staff and volunteers are close enough to communicate easily with one another, they can generate a sense of excitement and camaraderie. As they make calls and begin to get results, they can easily share information, celebrate successes, and laugh together over difficult calls.

> *On the last night of the phonathon, it's a nice touch to have each phonathon volunteer leave a thank-you note to the person whose desk they used.*

Sending a Pre-phonathon Mail Appeal

Many organizations send every prospect a letter approximately two weeks before the phonathon. The letter summarizes the case for support in one or two brief paragraphs, suggests a giving range that the prospect might consider, and lets the prospect know that a volunteer will be calling during the week of the phonathon.

Opinion varies on whether to make it easy for people to respond to the letter by sending a gift and preempting a phone call. In its favor is the fact that some people would like to make a contribution but resent phone calls. Against this practice is the fact that people are likely to give larger gifts if they can be actively engaged in a conversation about the project.

Preparing Supporting Materials

Supporting materials include:

- prospect information forms
- pledge forms and response envelopes
- scripts, talking points, and common questions
- completed-call folders
- instructions for clerical volunteers
- instructions for solicitors

Off to a Strong Start

After going back and forth on whether we should send the pledge form along with the letter we sent out before the phonathon, we finally decided that we'd send both a pledge form and a return envelope. We even put a P.S. on the letter, telling people that if they didn't want to be called, they should send a gift by return mail. I didn't know what to expect, but I sure didn't expect what happened. We sent the letters on Friday. By the following Tuesday, we had received more than $10,000 back, and before the beginning of the phonathon people had sent in nearly $20,000! This turned out to be one-quarter of the total phonathon gifts, and at least one donor thanked me personally for giving her the mail option.

—Development Director, Hospice

Simple, well-organized, color-coded materials help clarify the phonathon volunteers' tasks. Some of the material may be adapted from the campaign material that has already been designed, but some pieces will have to be created specifically for the phonathon. All of the material should highlight the campaign theme and logo, thereby distinguishing it from the organization's annual giving solicitations.

Prospect information forms should provide a place for name, address, telephone number, and giving history, as well as information, if any, about the relationship between the prospect and the organization. This information should be incorporated into a larger document (8-1/2" x 11" works well) that provides space for the volunteer to keep track of what transpired during the call and also to take notes. Some organizations are able to design the form directly on the computer and print out a form for each prospect. Others design a form with a space for prospect labels, and then duplicate the forms and add the labels. Copying these forms onto color-coded paper according to request level provides the callers with a simple way of knowing whom to ask for what amount.

Pledge forms should be large enough to permit a brief handwritten note from a volunteer. These notes are often added the night of the calling session and sent out the next day. To facilitate the process, a volunteer also writes out by hand the address on a campaign envelope. Unlike annual giving phonathons, campaign phonathons encourage people to make multiyear pledges. The pledge form must reflect this option. In addition, more organizations today are finding that their donors are happy to use their credit cards to make pledges. Although this option will cost the organization a small percentage of the pledge, it will also prevent unpaid pledges—all in all, a good investment!

Scripts help those volunteers who feel most comfortable with some appropriate written words to guide them through the call. Others find a script limiting and stilted and prefer to find their own words. To accommodate all styles, volunteers should be presented with a script, as well as a set of talking points and a set of common objections and the responses to them. Because volunteers are likely to feel most comfortable with information placed prominently in front of them while they make their calls, a placemat-size sheet, with the information well organized on it in large type, provides background support for volunteers as they make their calls. In this larger format, the information does not get lost among the other sheets of paper. It fits well on a desk, and it can be read at a glance.

Folders for completed calls help keep volunteer callers from feeling inundated by paper. A system of color-coded file folders helps callers keep their prospect forms organized. One might, for example, give each volunteer four folders—a green one for complete pledges, a red one for rejections, a blue one for prospects who need more time or information, and a yellow one for prospects whom the caller was unable to reach.

Written instructions help volunteers understand what they are to do before they begin calling, help clarify any questions that they might have, and can be referred to as needed throughout the session. Although the instructions are also covered verbally during the training session, some people absorb information more effectively when it is also in writing.

Solicitor training should precede each calling period. Usually these training sessions take approximately 30 to 45 minutes and are conducted by the development director or phonathon coordinator. They incorporate the following three elements:

1. **Review basic instructions.** Discuss the specifics of telephone operation, location of rest rooms, goals for the evening, dinner schedule, process and procedures, and prizes.
2. **Review the telephone solicitation process.** Discuss how to make a phone solicitation, the case for support, the pledge period, using a script, listening, summarizing from talking points, responding to common objections, and asking for the gift.
3. **Review material.** Distribute packets to each volunteer and then review the material, giving specific instructions about capturing and managing information.

Motivating Volunteers

There is nothing like food to help make people feel welcome. Because most phonathons take place over the dinner hour, organizations often provide pizza or sandwiches or other simple sustenance. Many people also use prizes to encourage the volunteers. Often, one volunteer is assigned the task of "cheerleader," whose job it is to dole out encouragement and prizes. The prizes are sometimes simple and silly, sometimes larger and more serious. Prizes are given for getting the highest number of gifts and the lowest number of gifts, for getting the most dollars and for getting no dollars at all, for completing the most calls or being the most cheerful, and so forth.

The cheerleader circulates around the room to collect forms from completed calls. This keeps the paper process moving throughout the period. Some development directors find it helpful to keep a running tally of the evening's progress on a large board in a central location.

Following Through

A great deal of the follow-up information can be prepared by the support staff during the calling period. Notes can be written directly on pledge forms, addresses handwritten on mailing envelopes, return envelopes enclosed, and even postage affixed so that those who have made a pledge will receive their confirmation within two days. Names of prospects who couldn't be reached should be placed back in the pile of calls to be made for the next night.

From the office the next day, letters should be sent to individuals who declined to make a contribution, thanking them for their time and, if necessary, addressing any concerns that they may have articulated during the conversation with the caller. Thank-you notes should also be written to the volunteers, giving them a preliminary report of their accomplishments.

At the conclusion of the entire phonathon, letters should be sent to every prospect who was not reached. The letter should indicate that the organization was not able to reach them, and it should ask for a gift. This letter most certainly should include a prospect pledge card and a reply envelope.

After the phonathon, the staff must prepare the cumulative phonathon report, which includes each night's total and totals for the entire phonathon.

Reporting Results

Effective reporting practices are important not just for the staff, but also to let all the volunteers know what they have accomplished. The sample phonathon report form in Exhibit 8–12 helps all involved to understand the results of the phonathon.

Exhibit 8–13 is a sample phonathon planning checklist.

DIRECT MAIL AND THE CAPITAL CAMPAIGN

Capital campaign fund raising does not rely on mail as the primary method of soliciting gifts, yet the mail serves an important role throughout the campaign. Most, if not all, solicitations for campaign gifts begin as written proposals. The proposals are individualized, some are even unique. And—at least as important—the mail transports multiple thank-you letters for every gift.

More and more people are using newer forms of communication such as e-mail and fax. However, "snail mail"

Exhibit 8–12 Sample Phonathon Report Form

Report of Dollars Raised and Expenses

Total Dollars Raised		_____
Total Dollars Expenses		_____
Printing	_____	
Postage	_____	
Food	_____	
Prizes	_____	
Phone	_____	
Net Return		_____
Number of Pre-phonathon Letters Sent		_____
Total Number of Gifts Pledged		_____
No. of gifts sent prior to phoning period	_____	
No. of gifts made during phoning period	_____	
No. of gifts sent after phoning period	_____	
Average Dollar Amount Per Gift		_____

Report of Activity Levels

Total Number of Calls Made		_____
Number of people reached	_____	
Number of people not reached	_____	
Number of rejections	_____	
Number of multiyear pledges	_____	
Number of gifts still pending	_____	
Total Number of Volunteers		_____
Number of volunteer callers	_____	
Number of support volunteers	_____	
Total Number of Staff Hours Spent		_____

Exhibit 8–13 Phonathon Planning Check List

Prospect Names
☐ Select names
☐ Research phone numbers
☐ Prepare prospect forms

General Plan
☐ Determine number of prospects to be called
☐ Determine number of callers needed
☐ Determine number of calling periods
☐ Determine number of phone lines and desks needed
☐ Determine number of clerical volunteers per session

Location
☐ Check availability
☐ Review layout
☐ Determine available parking
☐ Check accessibility

Dates and Times
☐ Decide on times of day
☐ Select days of the week
☐ Determine duration of volunteer sessions
☐ Determine duration of calling periods

Recruiting Volunteers
☐ Recruit phonathon chairs
☐ Develop lists of volunteers to call
☐ Print sign-up sheets
☐ Prepare follow-up letters
☐ Plan reminder notices or calls

Pre-phonathon Mail Appeal
☐ Draft letter to send prior to phonathon

Support Materials
☐ Purchase folders
☐ Prepare prospect information forms
☐ Write telephone script
☐ Draft letter to be sent afterward to those not reached
☐ Outline talking points and common questions
☐ Prepare instructions for clerical volunteers
☐ Prepare instructions for solicitors
☐ Print pledge forms and response envelopes
☐ Print mailing envelopes

Training
☐ Outline training session
☐ Organize materials

Motivation
☐ Plan and arrange for refreshments
☐ Plan prizes

Follow-up
☐ Send thank-you letters to volunteers
☐ Mail letters to those not reached
☐ Send pledge reminder notices
☐ Prepare phonathon summary report
☐ Send thank-you letters to location host and organizing committee

still carries most solicitation letters, and these days truly personalized letters and envelopes stand out.

The great majority of the gifts made to a campaign are not made as a direct result of a mail solicitation; they result from personal contact made over the telephone and in face-to-face meetings. In fact, most gifts, particularly the larger ones, result from multiple contacts made in a variety of ways. Though it is rare for a campaign to keep track of the number of contacts it has taken to tie down each gift, such recordkeeping would likely reveal that each significant gift (and some not-so-significant gifts) takes between five and ten contacts. Some, of course, require many more.

However, as the campaign draws to a conclusion, the mail solicitation acquires more importance. Throughout most of the campaign, staff members and volunteers do their utmost to maintain the initiative during the solicitation process. Each proposal letter begins what is often a long series of contacts and communications between the organization (through staff and volunteers) and the donor. Mail used at the end of the campaign turns the initiative over to the prospect. No longer are letters followed up with phone calls and visits. No more is the staff beginning a series of initiatives with every letter. At this stage in a campaign, letters close open-ended loops. They give people who have been solicited in one way or another earlier in the campaign one final chance to make a gift. And they reach out to people more tangentially related to the organization who have not yet been solicited.

Why Mail?

The long and uncertain strands of prospect contacts that weave together during a campaign can frustrate even the most steadfast development-staff members. Early in the campaign, each contact invariably brings with it more work, more anxiety, and more bits of information to track; thus, staff members often feel relieved when they can begin to complete the giving exchanges.

Direct-mail appeals late in a campaign serve four important purposes:

1. Letters provide a way to tie up loose ends.
2. Letters can reach people who were not reachable any other way.

3. Letters provide the organization's donors who were not solicited in any other way a chance to make a gift.
4. Letters enable an organization to broaden its base of support by reaching out to constituents who are not yet donors.

The solicitation process of many campaigns ends with a direct-mail appeal. Direct-mail appeals are typically sent to four types of prospects:

1. those who have been solicited but who haven't said yes or no
2. those who were not reached during the phonathon
3. those who are on the donor list but for whom a telephone number couldn't be located
4. everyone else on the mailing list who hasn't been solicited in another way

Occasionally, if the campaign is still some distance from its goal, letters will also be sent to those who have already made gifts but who might consider giving more or giving again.

Reaching Closure

Campaigns begin with a bang and inevitably end by petering out. The campaign has involved hundreds of volunteers, and thousands of prospects have been contacted; it is no wonder that as the campaign nears its goal, many people may feel ill-informed and out of the communications loop. Thank heaven for computers and thank heaven for mail, because with those two helpers an organization can tidy up many loose ends, thereby helping staff, volunteers, donors, and prospects take part in the successful conclusion of the campaign.

Before turning to a broad direct-mail appeal, the development staff, campaign leaders, and executive director should take one last look at the names in the still-pending list. Are there people on that list who should be visited one more time? Are there people on the edge of a decision for whom an informal call from the chair would make the difference? Is there anyone on that list who really doesn't want to contribute but who could be helped to a resolution with a final personal contact? Is there someone important who for some reason hasn't been called?

As the pressure mounts to bring the campaign to a conclusion, a final review of the prospect lists will yield a set of people who should be called or visited rather than solicited by mail. These will be those who for some reason of history or financial capability have a larger-than-average stake in the project. Each of the cleanup visits should aim at closing the process, finding out if the individual intends to make a gift and getting the pledge

or helping that person to say no. At this stage, each person is contacted as a courtesy so that the relationship between that person and the organization can continue to be a healthy one—whether or not he or she makes a gift.

Direct-mail appeals do have a place in most campaigns. However, their place is at the very end when the campaign goal is in sight. A campaign far from its goal will not be able to make up with a mailing what the face-to-face solicitation process has failed to accomplish. If a campaign has gone more slowly than expected, its conclusion should be delayed, and soliciting people one-to-one should continue until the campaign has concluded all solicitation except that at the very lowest level of giving. Then and only then has the time for direct mail arrived.

If the campaign has progressed well and the goal is within reach, as it should be, the direct-mail solicitation can benefit from the natural momentum that builds as the finish line draws near.

Refocusing the Case for Support

With success within reach, the case for supporting the campaign often shifts. No longer is there a question about whether the campaign will succeed, for success is virtually in hand. The final appeals invite people to help close the gap, to be among the heroes who made the campaign successful. Strange as it may seem, the opportunity to jump on board an enterprise that is sure to succeed motivates many people who, until momentum was high, had stood on the sidelines. The direct-mail campaign, then, is an invitation to climb aboard a winning project. Everyone who gives before the campaign is over will be able to feel his or her heart swell just a little bit when driving by the organization's new building or reading an article about the organization's success.

> *The direct-mail campaign is an invitation to climb aboard a winning project.*

As the motivation shifts, the emphasis of the case for support moves from the project to the campaign itself. As the campaign draws to a close, the case shifts to emphasize its remarkable success to date and to tell donors how they can help take the campaign over the top. Of course, the real story for the project continues to be an important element in the case for support, but at this point it shares the stage.

When possible, these final appeals target a closing date for the campaign. This is easy when deadlines are determined by matching or challenge grants that impose the dates from the outside (so long as the dates are feasible).

But when external deadlines are not imposed, an organization should determine an internal deadline, based on the date of a groundbreaking, a moving day, or some other visible event that will give the deadline credence.

When the end is in view, deadlines motivate staff, volunteers, and donors. Though they may complain and squirm under the pressure, if the deadlines are reasonable—tight enough to create some discomfort, but long enough to be doable—everyone will work more efficiently and cheerfully when they know exactly when the end really will arrive!

Special Characteristics of Direct Mail for Capital Campaign Appeals

In many ways, direct-mail appeals for campaigns are the same as direct mail used in annual giving, and an organization that is expert in this area should rely on their previous experience and knowledge to guide them in the specifics of writing, design, response pieces, mailings, and so forth. However, there are some ways that capital-campaign direct-mail appeals should be different from their annual appeal siblings.

First, the appeal should look different. Because the capital campaign is a distinct and special campaign, and because the donors should understand that it is different from annual giving, the campaign mail appeal should look and feel distinct. It should repeat the themes that were used in the rest of the campaign material. By engaging the same graphic designer who developed the

---

The Last Minute . . . Is Now!

We were just $120,000 from our $1.8 million campaign goal and it was October. Our Kresge grant didn't have to be met until the following April, but another foundation challenged us to finish by November 1. We knew we wouldn't make their deadline, so we asked them if they would give us two more months and let us use their gift to highlight a December 30 deadline. The theme of the direct-mail appeal was "The last minute . . . is NOW!" We asked the people on our mailing list to help us get over the top by the end of the year. We sent out a large mailing the second week of December and were flooded by responses as the year drew to a close. When we were finally down to the wire, we found that we were still $60.58 short of our goal. We passed a hat at the staff meeting and went over the top!

—Executive Director

---

campaign material to design the mail appeal, an organization can often give some added zip to that appeal.

Second, it should sound different. The writing style for a campaign appeal should have more punch and energy than many annual appeals manage even in their heroic attempts to stay fresh year after year. Capital-campaign appeals really are "once and done," and that very fact should inspire almost any author.

Third, it should ask for multiyear pledges. Unlike annual contributions, capital campaigns can ask donors to make gifts over as many as three or even five years. Because many people are not in the habit of making multiyear pledges, this request should be highlighted in the letter, or perhaps included in the P.S., which most people actually do read. The multiyear pledge option should also be emphasized on the pledge form.

Fourth, it should ask prospects to consider gifts in a specific range or amount. Although some organizations use the practice of asking for specific gifts in their annual appeal, many do not. For the capital campaign's direct mail, requesting a specific amount is even more important because it requests a multiyear pledge somewhat larger than gifts usually given to an annual campaign. This further separates it from the annual appeal. Someone who has given an organization $25 per year for the past 10 years is likely to continue in that pattern unless specifically asked to change it. A specific request helps the prospect understand the "appropriate" level for a capital campaign gift.

Finally, it should tell donors how they will be recognized. Because capital campaigns are often associated with building projects, donors of a certain amount may see their names on a permanent plaque. If the lowest amount for being listed on a plaque is within the range of possible direct-mail gifts, the appeal should be sure to mention this option. Although few people ever say that they want their names on a plaque, when they are listed they are likely to point it out to their children, grandchildren, and friends when they walk by!

Segmenting the Mailing List

Many organizations today are quite sophisticated in the way in which they can segment their mailing lists so that they can send special letters targeted to specific groups. Effective capital-campaign mail appeals also rely on segmented lists so that every prospect receives a letter that fits his or her relationship to the campaign. A campaign mailing list might be segmented in the following four ways:

1. People who have been asked for a campaign gift but have not responded. These are truly cleanup letters and must be worded accordingly. A donor who has been solicited earlier and then receives a

letter that does not acknowledge the prior solicitation is likely to become irritated. However, if the same donor understands that the organization is merely trying to find out whether or not he or she intends to give to the campaign, then the donor is likely to recognize that this letter will conclude the process and will therefore feel relieved!

2. Former donors who have not yet been asked for a campaign gift. One might further subdivide the list according to former giving patterns or according to specific relationships that the donors might have to the organization. For example, a school might choose to send a different letter to an alumnus than to an area businessman.

3. People who are on the organization's mailing list but who have never become donors. In this list are the seeds for future giving. Even if the organization does not ordinarily send its annual appeal letter to all these people (the numbers in this category are often large), an organization might use the campaign as an opportunity to reach them. Although this is not likely to bring in major gifts to the campaign, it may turn up new donors who will then continue on as donors to the organization for many years.

4. People who have already given a small gift of cash to the campaign. Some campaigns write to donors who have already given, asking them to extend their gift at the same level for each year of the pledge period. This second appeal offends some but works for others, and the decision about whether or not to use this approach will probably depend on how much money is yet to be raised.

Celebrate Success with a Last-Chance Appeal

As the campaign glides over the top, those with great stamina might send one last letter to all previous donors who have not yet given, inviting them to get on board before the celebrating begins. This letter should be short, low pressure, and light in tone. Responses to these very last appeals tend to trickle in over a remarkably long time. See Exhibit 8–14 for simple reminders about direct mail appeals.

WELCOME RELIEF AFTER A STRESSFUL CAMPAIGN

Most development directors are familiar with that mixed feeling of apprehension, excitement, and dread that greets the daily mail delivery following a broad-based appeal. At the conclusion of a capital campaign that has gone well in its early stages, these mail runs are often particularly exciting and rewarding. Each pledge form closes a relationship and helps close the distance to the goal. Every acknowledgment note brings with it a lighter heart and every dollar the anticipation of being closer to the goal.

Telephone and direct-mail fund raising provide excitement, relief, and comfort at the conclusion of a long and stressful campaign. Embedded in this low-end fund raising are often the seeds of a reinvigorated annual giving program for many years to come.

Exhibit 8–14 Simple Reminders about Direct Mail

Direct mail appeals should be:

- Clear
- Attractive
- Distinctive
- Compelling
- Eye-catching
- Well-written
- Focused
- Targeted
- Individualized
- Celebratory
- Upbeat
- Specific
- Easy to respond to

REFERENCES

Blanton, Carol. 1994. The pitfalls and the promise of telephone fundraising. *Grassroots Fundraising Journal* 13 (December): 3–6.

Levy, Barbara R., and Barbara Marion. 1997. *Successful special events: planning, hosting, and evaluating.* Gaithersburg, MD: Aspen Publishers, Inc.

Chapter 9
Campaign Communications

Chapter Outline

- Campaign Communications
- Developing a Communications Plan
- Managing Campaign Announcements
- The Power of Materials in Positioning a Campaign
- Using Communications Professionals
- Campaign Theme and Logo
- Campaign Materials
- Miscellaneous Materials
- Spinning the Campaign

CAMPAIGN COMMUNICATIONS

The planning and solicitation discussed in the previous chapters is truly the "meat" of the campaign. Just as important, however, are the opportunities to communicate the excitement of the project and the progress of the campaign. Without a well-conceived communications plan that covers both internal and external communications, even a very successful campaign will not fully capitalize on the process. This chapter discusses many aspects of campaign communications, from reporting about campaign progress to the board and other insiders, to managing the announcements of gifts, to developing campaign letterhead, brochures, and other campaign material. This chapter opens the door to creative approaches to campaign materials and encourages readers to be receptive to new ideas, styles, and formats.

Effective communications enable an organization to use the campaign to build excitement and support, both among insiders and throughout the broader community. These communications "spin" the campaign success into a web that enhances the image of the organization throughout the larger community.

DEVELOPING A COMMUNICATIONS PLAN

Perhaps because communications and public relations are often not the direct purview of the development de-

---

The Tzarina of Communications

Our organization is large and complex with many people in charge of very diverse programs. As we got going on our campaign, I realized that the person working on campaign communications needed the support of the membership director, the director of programming, the marketing director, and several other people who controlled one aspect or another of our organization's communications. We needed them all to understand and incorporate the messages of the campaign into their communications. In short, we needed them to jump to our tune. But they weren't used to jumping to our tune. I realized that we needed a Tzarina of Communications—someone who could call the shots about communications across organizational lines. In due time, I became that Tzarina and was able to get the job done well. All of the many communications pieces that our organization used during the entire campaign, the membership brochure, the program guide, the annual report, the newsletter, and the campaign material were all conceived and designed with the campaign in mind. We raised far more money than ever before with 10 times the number of donors. I know our coordinated communications effort made a big difference

—Director of Communications

---

partment, in many organizations the strategies for communicating about the campaign are piecemeal and sporadic. Most organizations know that they must develop a campaign brochure, newsletter, and final report. Few take seriously the opportunities afforded by a carefully developed campaign communications plan.

Who Develops the Plan?

Campaign communications is a polyglot process requiring collaboration and coordination among many people in an organization. The development staff drives the campaign and will play an important role in developing the communications vehicles that are specifically designed for the campaign. But the public relations staff will plan, coordinate, and implement all aspects of campaign communications that interface with the regular public relations vehicles. While it may be relatively easy to convince the executive staff and board to hire additional staff for the development office, it is often far more difficult to make the case for hiring additional communications personnel. Yet an organization that uses the campaign to reach out to all of its constituencies is likely to increase the financial capacity of the campaign and strengthen the long-term fund-raising program. But the importance of campaign communications is often underestimated or simply not considered at all, and it is difficult to convince the board and executive staff to invest resources in additional communications staff just for the campaign. The result is that there is seldom enough staff to absorb the extra burden.

Ideally, an organization will have a full- or part-time staff person (depending on the size and complexity of the organization) who is responsible solely for developing, coordinating, and implementing a campaign communications plan.

Great Learning, High Tolls

I was pleased when my boss encouraged me to be the person responsible for campaign communications. I figured it was a great way to learn. What I didn't figure was that it was very nearly a full-time job. . . and I had to do it in addition to my other responsibilities. Yes, the learning was great, and now that we're done the satisfaction is tremendous. But the personal tolls were too high. My marriage suffered, my children were neglected, my exercise regime was abandoned. Next time I'd fight harder to hire additional staff.

—Communications Director

The Elements of a Campaign Communications Plan

A campaign communications plan organizes every aspect of campaign communications. For the purposes of communications, the campaign falls into four phases: quiet phase, campaign announcement, public phase, and conclusion. Each of these phases requires a distinct approach. During the quiet phase, the organization will communicate primarily with those constituencies that are relatively close to the organization—staff, board, advisory board, major donors, and lead-gift prospects. The messages focus on the case for support, articulating clearly and consistently what the organization will be able to accomplish when the campaign is successful. These messages answer the tough questions "So what?" and "What now?" in a clear and compelling manner. Exhibit 9–1 outlines a communications plan.

The messages used for the campaign announcement include the core case messages, but they add messages that capture the success of the early stage of the campaign. The audiences in the announcement phase become broader as the campaign reaches out to constituencies that will be solicited during the public phase, while still maintaining contact with the insider groups. During the public phase, communications blossom and every vehicle is pulled into play. The messages reinforce the vision and case, but as the campaign approaches its goal, the messages convey the excitement of going over the top and

---

Exhibit 9–1 Outline of a Communications Plan

    I. Goals
   II. Audiences
       External
       Internal
  III. Strategies
       Messages
       Vehicles
           Existing
           New
   IV. Campaign Phases
       Quiet Phase
       Campaign Announcement
       Public Phase
       Conclusion and Follow-up
    V. Design Implementation
       Theme and logo
       New vehicles
       Gifts/mementos
   VI. Communications Implementation
       Calendar
       Workplan
       Budget

reaching a successful conclusion. Finally, when the campaign is over, the audience is at its broadest and the messages capture the vision, celebrate the people and groups who have made the campaign successful, recognize both donors and volunteers for their roles, and tie the campaign vision back in with the ongoing communications program. See Exhibit 9–2 for a simplified communications planning chart.

Several other planning tools will be helpful. Developing a complete and specific list of all of the organization's audiences and constituencies along with the communications vehicles most appropriate for them will help set the stage for developing the entire plan. Assembling this list is an excellent task for brainstorming with a group of people who know the organization and the community. The same group will also be helpful in clarifying the core campaign messages. One or two meetings of an ad hoc volunteer committee can be invaluable in conceptualizing the communications plan.

The communications aspect of the campaign will also need a budget. Although most campaign budgets include line items for the primary campaign materials (brochure, newsletters, and final report), few budget for other communications expenses. Perforce, these expenses are often squeezed out of other office budgets. In particular, campaigns seldom budget for photography—and excellent photography can make a huge difference in the quality and effectiveness of the entire communications process. The photography budget should be high enough to cover the cost of a fine photographer to take pictures of the people served by the organization, the campaign leadership, and numerous donors who will be highlighted in various campaign publications.

MANAGING CAMPAIGN ANNOUNCEMENTS

Although it is tempting to share an organization's needs with the world from the beginning in the hopes that new donors will respond generously, successful campaigns tightly control the flow of information. Effective campaign planning requires that an organization wait before publicly announcing the campaign and its goal until success seems likely. A public kickoff event, staged after 50, 60, or even 70 percent of the campaign goal has been raised, celebrates the generosity and commitment of a

Exhibit 9–2 Campaign Communications Planning Chart

	QUIET PHASE	ANNOUNCEMENT	PUBLIC PHASE	CONCLUSION
Audiences	Insiders Lead-gift prospects	Insiders Lead-gift donors Lead-gift prospects Major-gift prospects General-gift prospects	Insiders Lead-gift donors Major-gift donors General-gift prospects All constituencies	Insiders All donors All constituencies Community-at-large Visitors
Messages	Case/vision	Case/vision Donor examples Building success Gap to goal Celebration	Case/vision More donor examples Closing gap to goal	Vision to reality Donor examples Success D/V recognition Celebration
Vehicles	Draft case Logo/letterhead Proposal material Staff/board updates	Campaign brochure Party mementos Campaign video Campaign newsletter	Campaign brochure* Campaign newsletter Regular newsletter Radio/TV spots Newspapers Events Bumper stickers, etc. Lobby displays Print ads Telephone greeting Member letters	Campaign report Radio/TV spots Newspapers Events Lobby displays Mementos Banners Annual report Print ads Telephone greeting Member letters Pledge reminder letters Billboards, etc.

*A campaign with a large, expensive brochure may elect to produce a smaller brochure for the public phase of the campaign.

Exhibit 9–3 Sample Campaign Report

IMAGINE THE POSSIBILITIES CAMPAIGN,
January 2001

1.	**Campaign Working Goal**	$	2,100,000
2.	**Raised to Date**		
	Cash received	$	475,550
	Pledges		1,040,107
	In-kind received		120,966
	In-kind pledges		10,000
	Endowment received		5,099
	Endowment pledges		50,000
	Total Raised	$	1,701,722
3.	**Percent of Campaign Goal Reached**		81%
4.	**Percent of Campaign Period Elapsed**		62%
5.	**Number of Gifts Pledged or Received**		152
6.	**Number of Gifts of $30,000 or more**		20
7.	**Major Proposals in Progress**		
	Number		12
	Amount	$	402,000
	Anticipated return	$	137,000
8.	**Board Member Gifts**		
	Number		21
	Amount	$	565,000
9.	**Number of First-Time Donors**		30

Courtesy of Todd Lindsley of Lindsley Consulting Group, Lancaster, PA and Charlie Trautmann, Executive Director of the Sciencenter, Ithaca, New York.

campaign's leaders and insiders, prepares other donors to be solicited, and gives the solicitors courage and confidence to complete the campaign. Prior to that kickoff, however, effective communications among insiders is critically important.

Insider Communications

Campaign Reports: Long before the campaign becomes public, it is important to communicate effectively with board members, campaign planning and steering committee members, and other people who are close to the organization. Perhaps the most important, if mundane, aspect of insider communication is a regular, well-organized campaign progress report. Although there are many formats for campaign reports, the report in Exhibit 9–3 highlights all of the important information that should be tracked throughout the campaign in a fashion that is clear and easy to decipher. This report, when developed monthly over the duration of the campaign, provides an effective way for key insiders to understand the campaign's progress and to track it in the context of the entire campaign timetable. This simple report tracks every aspect of the campaign. Line 1 restates the campaign goal. The second section of information tracks the total of funds pledged to date, breaking this figure down according to cash received, pledges received, and endowment commitments.

The campaign progress is also reported in terms of the percent of the goal pledged and the percent of the campaign period that has elapsed. These two figures together provide a clear reminder of the work to be done and the time left for doing it.

Line 6 provides a count of lead gifts. In this relatively small campaign, they have tracked gifts of $30,000 or more. For this organization, which has little history of lead gifts, the growing number of lead gifts surprised board members and advisory board members and encouraged them to think differently about the organization's potential to raise larger gifts. With 20 gifts of $30,000 or more, there is no doubt that more than a few people believe that this organization is worth a healthy investment.

Line 7 shows the state of the funding pipeline. In any campaign, tracking gifts in progress is just as important as tracking pledges received. By watching the in-progress figure, the staff and board will have a sense of what is possible over the next month or two. When the pipeline or gifts in progress are small, the short-term prognosis for the campaign is poor. A regular tracking system draws a clear line from current effort to future pledges.

Line 8, board member gifts, reminds people of the importance and progress of board giving. Often these figures are surprising for their generosity, and including this number in the campaign report highlights the board commitment.

Finally, in line 9, the report tracks the number of first-time donors. This figure points the way to the future. Every donor who enters an organization's ranks through a campaign gift becomes an excellent prospect for the annual fund and for future campaigns. At the end of a campaign, some organizations actually project the long-term giving potential of these first-time donors. These figures make a strong statement about the power of a capital campaign long after its conclusion.

Using a program like Excel or another relational database, it is easy to develop this report on the computer with an input screen that allows simple monthly data entry and that automatically transfers the information into the standard report format.

Some organizations distribute the report to their board at their regular board meeting. This simple, clear sheet enables board members to easily compare the figures from month to month and to keep track of the campaign progress.

Insider Bulletins: In addition to regular campaign reports, the early phases of the campaign should be punctuated with frequent updates for those people whose efforts are making the campaign's progress possible. Sharing early information with key insiders is an excellent way to solidify their relationship to the organization and the campaign. This information might be conveyed personally via e-mail or telephone, or through a faxed or mailed campaign newsflash.

Organizing and managing this process is simple but important. The campaign manager should maintain a list of insiders who will be kept abreast of campaign news. Many organizations have two or even three lists of names targeted to different levels of campaign communication. One list might be those people who should be informed immediately and personally about campaign progress. This list will probably include the campaign chairs, the board chair, and perhaps major donors who have already contributed to the campaign. A second, broader list might include the campaign planning committee members and board members. A third list might add members of the advisory board, former board members, key community leaders, and perhaps some donor prospects. The lists will vary according to an organization's size and characteristics. In every case, however, information about the campaign should be used to maintain contact with the community of insiders. A wise development director will maintain a mailing list of those who have a special stake in the campaign and will be able to get out a bulletin in a short time and with limited effort. Preparing several sets of addressed envelopes to the insiders in advance facilitates the process even more.

Though the most effective news is good news, even disappointments or knotty problems can be used to advantage by seizing them as opportunities to invite people to help wrestle with challenges. If shared, these unwelcome episodes—for example, gifts that don't come through, rejected zoning appeals, or estimates that come in way over budget—sometimes yield opportunities that lead to the success of the campaign.

Insider Newsletters: For the largest group of campaign insiders, the staff may wish to prepare a regular, informal newsletter to keep people abreast of progress. These are often designed in-house and produced on a laser printer. Such instant newsletters let people know about major gifts as they come in, progress or changes in the status of the project, special efforts that someone may have made on behalf of the campaign, or any other special and late-breaking campaign news. These newsletters should be in keeping with the overall look of the campaign, presenting a consistent and integrated appearance. Attentive directors or campaign chairs may choose to add small personal notes to some of these communications, helping people feel even more connected to the project.

If insider newsletters are distributed prior to the campaign kickoff, they should all be stamped CONFIDENTIAL to remind people that the campaign is not yet public and the information should not be broadcast.

E-Communications

This relatively new mode of communication has wonderful potential during the campaign. More and more people use this as the preferred mode of communicating for both their personal and professional lives. It has the great advantages of being inexpensive, easy, and immediate. There are few things as satisfying as writing a memo and, with the push of one button, sending it to all the people you know. From the receiver's perspective, e-mail is also full of blessings. No insistent ringing telephones . . . no rambling voice-mail messages in which the caller's telephone number is spoken too fast to write down. . . no need to grab for a pen and paper to take notes from a phone call. Yes, for many people e-mail is not only the preferred way of sending messages, but also the preferred way of receiving them. Convenient, quick, cheap, non-intrusive. . . and easy to disregard!

And it is this last quality that must shape the role of e-mail in capital campaigns. Use it to inform and update, to remind people of meetings, to help schedule meetings, to ask simple questions that require simple answers. Use it to facilitate the process of asking several people to edit a document. But *don't* use it to do anything that requires serious attention or a personal exchange, or to obtain a serious commitment. Don't use it, for instance, to invite someone to serve on a committee, or to solicit campaign gifts, or to enlist a committee chair. E-mail is wonderful for easy communication but it is not wonderful for serious discussion, for securing commitment, or for soliciting major gifts.

Some organizations have explored the possibility of soliciting low-level gifts via e-mail. This technique is slowly gaining acceptance in annual giving. But for capital campaigns, where people are invited to make larger, special gifts, e-mail is unlikely to be an effective mechanism for solicitation.

It is important to remember that not all people are comfortable with e-mail or check it regularly, and that you may not be informed of changes in e-mail addresses. Every campaign manager should be sure to get information from donors and volunteers about whether they would like to be communicated with via e-mail, U.S. mail, or phone.

THE POWER OF MATERIALS IN POSITIONING A CAMPAIGN

The spirit and heart of a capital campaign are captured by the materials that are developed for them. These materials give a campaign its unique style and appearance. They provide a distinctive character that helps focus the many elements of the campaign around a common theme. The materials that support the work of a capital campaign take many forms over the course of the campaign. Campaign materials provide a critical and solid foundation that supports and facilitates the solicitation process as well as many other campaign activities.

Excellent campaign materials have a look and a feel that tell the tale and powerfully express the importance of the campaign in images and words. With every written communication, the power of the case is restated. Through every image, the unity of the campaign is reinforced. While poor, unprofessional materials raise doubts and anxieties, excellent campaign materials empower and embolden staff members and volunteers. They symbolize the quality of the enterprise and the importance of the campaign's mission.

Campaign materials work hand in hand with the effective organization of volunteers, active face-to-face solicitation, responsible follow-through, and donor rec-

ognition to weave the strong fabric of professionalism and commitment that is needed for successful campaigns.

USING COMMUNICATIONS PROFESSIONALS

Marketing communications strategists and graphic designers are the unsung heroes of campaign materials. A talented communications team is able to assemble concepts and images into a form that captures the spirit of the campaign within the value structure of the organization. They are trained to understand the importance of language and the nuances of visual images, type, and layout. Through their work, the themes that for most people are verbal are expressed and organized visually.

Although we seldom stop to reflect on it, the work of marketing and communications professionals permeates our culture. Advertisements, product packaging, billboards, Web sites, and magazines are just a few of the many areas through which they shape the cultural environment.

Campaign materials are usually designed by advertising, public-relations, or marketing-communications firms. And because these professions are so important in our society, most communities have a healthy selection of firms to choose from. Every firm has its own particular style, so an organization is well advised to spend some time exploring the available talent pool and determining who is likely to work best with them.

Ideally, the marketing-communications team creates the messages as well as the design, since in most cases neither staff nor volunteers are trained in copy writing for persuasion. And even good graphic design loses its effectiveness if the words aren't chosen carefully. But communications firms vary in their strengths and abilities. Every firm has a different aesthetic sensibility and writing style. A thorough review of their work on other projects will present a clear account of their preferences and styles.

Designers or Communicators

A marketing-communications team specializes in finding just the right combination of word and image to communicate clearly. They are more than artists. They are communicators as well. Not only do they understand how to add an image to an idea, but they are experts in the organization and flow of ideas—how they can be arranged on a page to encourage reading and increase comprehension. They often pare away words, leaving only those that are essential to the concept that is being communicated.

In the author's experience, graphic designers might be categorized according to whether they are primarily designers or primarily communicators. Some are wonderful designers but are less interested in communication and therefore, perhaps, less able to communicate clearly. Others understand the need to communicate, but in doing so they sometimes compromise their aesthetic standards. The ideal designer places equal value on both communication and design, and insists on doing them both well.

The telltale signs of an artist who doesn't communicate well are

- the use of small and light typefaces that look beautiful on the page but are difficult to read
- a propensity toward odd sizes and shapes that stand out visually but interfere with communication
- overprinting of one image or block of text onto another image in a way that is striking but confusing
- organization of the material on a page so that it looks elegant but on closer inspection does not flow logically

The telltale signs of a communicator who compromises on the art are

- text-heavy pages that flow well but are not visually inviting
- very little white space on each page
- sloppy spacing and placement of text blocks on the page
- lack of an overall unifying design concept

Tombstone Graphics

With the proliferation of desktop publishing in recent years, the field of graphic design has become open to many people with little or no artistic training or ability. This has led to the rise of what is sometimes referred to as "tombstone graphics." This style, characterized by blocks of text bordered by single or double lined squares or rectangles, is typical of self-taught graphic designers and is generally not of a standard or quality that is suitable for the design of capital campaign materials. People who are untrained in graphic design but who dabble nonetheless often reveal themselves by their clumsy, random use of multiple typefaces. Though it is tempting to pretend to be a designer, the campaign manager should remember that good design is a highly sophisticated enterprise that requires training and experience. The design of effective campaign materials should be left to professionals.

Selecting a Communications Firm

A firm should be selected after a thorough review of its work. To review a firm's portfolio effectively, one must spend enough time to consider and read each piece. A quick glance at a glossy portfolio provides only the most cursory sense of the firm's style. A thorough examination—reading all the text and understanding the purpose of the piece—is likely to reveal the abilities of the designer. However, when reviewing a portfolio, an organization must be sure that they are examining the work of the person or team of people who will be responsible for their work. In larger firms, the portfolio might be a collection of work by various designers who may or may not be working on the campaign materials.

What to Consider when Looking at a Portfolio

- Do the pieces reflect the character of the projects they describe?
- Is the message, both verbal and visual, consistent with the campaign and/or the organization's position?
- Can you understand what the objectives of the communications campaign were—who the audience was? What the desired result was?
- Are the materials well organized and easy to follow?
- Are they appealing to the eye with plenty of white space?
- Are the materials all similar in style or do they show a range of styles and character?
- Is the writing clear and effective?
- Are the typefaces used easy to read?

Because capital campaigns involve the leadership of a community, design or advertising firms often donate design services for campaign materials, charging only their out-of-pocket expenses. This goodwill gesture helps spread the reputation of their firm. Most campaigns count the value of these services as an in-kind campaign gift and acknowledge the contribution of the firm on the campaign brochure itself.

Clarifying Responsibilities and Schedules

Before interviewing a firm, it is helpful to draft a list of the materials that it will be asked to develop and a preliminary timetable of when they will be needed. Such a list will help the communications firm understand the universe within which each piece will fit and prepare them to develop basic design concepts that can be adapted to a wide range of pieces. The list is likely to include the following pieces:

- campaign positioning logo and theme
- campaign letterhead
- campaign brochure
- pledge form

- thank-you note cards
- mailing labels
- campaign folders
- kickoff invitation
- format for an insiders' newsletter
- four to six issues of a campaign newsletter
- design for printing on promotional items
- celebration invitation
- direct-mail solicitation piece
- all necessary envelopes

In addition, the communications firm should be asked to play a role in developing the public relations and publicity plan, electronic communications, TV and radio communications, and perhaps even event planning.

The creative director usually coordinates all aspects of producing the materials. He or she selects and collaborates with photographers, artists, typesetters, and printers. The creative director recommends paper types and colors and helps an organization understand the alternatives and benefits of one selection over another.

CAMPAIGN THEME AND LOGO

The old adage "One picture is worth a thousand words" expresses the spirit and importance of capturing the campaign theme in a simple and compelling logo or visual identity. The logo might be a drawing or graphic image, or it might be a distinctive typeface that presents the campaign theme. Whatever the means, the logo should provide an image that encapsulates the concept behind the campaign. Although the logo or image should be in keeping with the standards of taste and style generally used by the organization, it should be distinct from the image of the organization itself.

The campaign logo is most often developed from a *positioning statement* that distinguishes the organization and the campaign. The positioning statement is an internal document but should be tested with those close to the organization to make sure it captures the right spirit and content. It emerges from the many discussions, drafts, and rewritings of the case for support and gives a common ground to all who read it. The strongest, most compelling aspect of the campaign is clarified here. The fundamental concept developed in the positioning statement will underlie all of the campaign communications, and should be captured in a campaign name and logo.

Examples of good campaign themes and logos abound, as seen in Figure 9–1:

Figure 9–1 Sample Logos for Capital Campaigns

She Got the Message Right from the Start

We really lucked out. One of our PR committee members wanted to hire a small graphic design firm in town. They came to strut their stuff and just rubbed our director the wrong way. They didn't ask questions, and when he spoke they didn't listen. We almost hired them anyway because our volunteer had recommended them so highly, but at the last minute, I convinced the committee to interview a design firm that was located just a few miles away. The minute Elizabeth walked in, everyone (including the volunteer who had recommended the first firm) knew she was right for us. She had asked me many questions over the phone and came to the meeting with a sincere interest in learning about us and our project. We knew that the concepts she came up with for us would really reflect who we are. We hired her, and the materials she produced inspired volunteers and donors alike. The material also won several regional and even national design awards, which made us all feel proud!

—Director of Development, Planned
Parenthood Center

- A Spanish American Civic Association chose the campaign title "Building Bridges" and used a multi-colored rainbow as the campaign logo.
- A day-care center used an image of a child's hand-print and entitled its campaign "The Campaign for the Next Generation."
- For the campaign to automate its card catalog, a library used the theme "Open Sesame" and developed an image in the form of a bookplate showing treasures behind a computer screen.
- For its building renovation campaign, a Planned Parenthood center used the phrase "Moving Ahead with Our PLANned Parenthood" together with a simple image of a partially completed building.

Campaigns need names. Although it is easy to say, for instance, "I'm working on the campaign for the hospice" (and indeed, some organizations choose such simple and straightforward names), a compelling name that captures the essence of the project will promote the campaign theme every time the name is mentioned. For example, it is far more powerful to speak of the Building Bridges campaign for the Spanish American Civic Association than it is simply to mention the Spanish American Civic Association campaign. In the theme of bridges is embedded the powerful concept of creating opportunities for individuals in a minority culture to become integrated into mainstream society. Painfully aware of the problems that come from belonging to a ghettoized minority, the people who created that logo provided a simple image for a broad theme that helped motivate business leaders and other donors to contribute to the campaign.

Certain words and themes occur over and over in capital campaigns. Words like *cornerstone*, *foundation*, *century*, *opportunity*, and *investment* pop up in campaign after campaign. These words are used with such frequency because they are strong and powerful, though they tend to lose power over time due to overuse.

Coming up with the right words or logo can be a great challenge. Sometimes the right words simply emerge from informal discussion. Sometimes they come from meetings that have been organized for the explicit purpose of determining the campaign theme. Yet other times a graphic designer or advertising firm will be hired to present a variety of ideas for an organization to choose from. Whatever the process, the theme and logo must be circulated among the key campaign volunteers and staff members before it is adopted. If someone in a leadership position strongly opposes the first choice, the organization should try again.

The most frustrating aspect of developing the theme and logo is that what rings true for one person might not entirely please another. This is yet another instance when one becomes aware that in capital campaigns not all opinions carry equal weight. The ins and outs of these

Open Sesame

We had been mulling over many possible choices for a name for our campaign to automate the library systems. "Information Superhighway" was a buzz phrase in the media at that time and we tried to incorporate those words. If we didn't automate our library, we knew that we would soon become a dinosaur, and we thought about using the image of a dinosaur with a diagonal red line through it. But the idea of a prohibition seemed too negative. We knew that people responded positively to the argument that automation would benefit the children of our county, so we wanted something that would get that message across. We explored the idea of using the image of a computer, but the project really wasn't about computers, it was about accessing information. And the computer part of it actually frightened many of our older patrons. Somehow, the many suggestions that we floated just didn't catch on until one day our consultant called to say that the name had just come to her! She thought we should call the campaign "Open Sesame." It had the advantage of being a literary theme, right out of the Arabian Nights. Anyone old enough or young enough to have encountered Ali Baba and the Forty Thieves knew that "Open Sesame" was the magic spell that offered entry into a cave filled with riches, just as our new automated systems would provide magical entry to the world of information available in our library system. In one flash of inspiration we had our campaign name!

—Library Director

decisions may require sensitive and politically astute maneuvering by the organization's staff. It is seldom a mistake, however, to engage in a great deal of communication. Even when some individual's opinion does not prevail, that person will have been pleased to have been included in the debate. The development of a positioning statement helps move the discussion out of the realm of personal taste to a more objective discussion of what will move the target audience.

> *In capital campaigns, not all opinions carry equal weight.*

Once a campaign has settled on a positioning statement, the visual and verbal identity of the campaign can be developed. Graphic designers are experts in this field. They understand the visual world in the same way many others understand the verbal world. Here are some simple guidelines to keep in mind when considering a campaign logo.

- It should be graphically simple enough so that it reads well even when rendered in a small size, such as used on a business card or novelty item.
- It should read well in black and white, even if it will most often be depicted in three or more colors.
- It should have enough contrast to show well when run through a copier or fax machine.
- It should be distinctive.
- It should be in character with the organization's culture and purpose.

CAMPAIGN MATERIALS

The Power of Campaign Letterhead

Every campaign needs its own letterhead. Letterhead is the most basic of the campaign materials. Literally thousands of letters are sent during a campaign, and if it is designed well, the letterhead itself will send a power-

---

I Hate Maroon!

Just what is the difference between maroon, dark red, and aubergine? Our campaign chair had approved our logo and theme. In fact, he was delighted with them. But he was out of town when we picked the official campaign color, and when the letterhead arrived from the printer, the first words out of his mouth were "But I hate maroon! Maroon was the color of my old high school gym shorts, and I can't bear to look at it." Never mind that we thought the color we had chosen was aubergine. The chair said it was maroon. To be honest, it was rather more maroon than anything else. But by then it was too late, and we had to make do. We spent the rest of the campaign teasing one another about the color maroon (with what color would you choose to be marooned on a desert island?), but I felt bad about it the whole time. If I could replay the campaign, I would have waited to select a color until our chair returned. Saving a few days was far less important than making sure that the chair felt good about every aspect of the campaign materials!

—Executive Director

---

ful message, enhancing the impact of the text of the letter.

Campaign letterhead should include the campaign logo, title, name of the organization, address and phone number of the organization, and the names of those who serve on the campaign committee. Sometimes the names of the entire board of directors or trustees are included if they are people of influence. Although it may at first seem insignificant, the letterhead is a powerful communicator, setting out the theme of the campaign, presenting the campaign's most important information, and establishing credibility by presenting the team of the campaign's most important players.

People will comment on a campaign brochure, yet they seldom comment on the campaign letterhead. Nonetheless, the importance of the letterhead is not to be underestimated, for it adds significant information to every piece of campaign correspondence, builds credibility, and communicates its message directly and with immediacy.

Several common issues often arise as the letterhead is being developed.

Listing the names: The campaign letterhead should include the names of the campaign chairs and the names of those who serve on the campaign committee. It is a seemingly simple task, yet the listing of names always requires great care and attention. Not only does everyone have a particular preference as to how his or her name should be listed, but many people feel quite strongly indeed about exactly how their names are to appear. One person always uses a middle initial. Another never does. Connie wants to be addressed as Mrs. David Z. Kutler, Jr., while Susan will be certain to take offense if her name appears with her husband's surname; she is Susan Lansdown-Worthing—always has been, always will be. Such personal preferences are further complicated by the loosening of social conventions in recent years. What used to be guided by Emily Post is, in our post-Emily world, guided largely by personal preference.

The other question that arises in developing letterhead is whether or not to include the business affiliations of those whose names are listed. Including them makes for a text-heavy, cumbersome appearance, but the members' affiliations may well lend credibility to the campaign. In some cases, a blue-ribbon group will need no identification beyond their names. If business affiliations are included, one then struggles with the identification of those with the less prestigious identifiers. "Housewife" or "Community Volunteer" pales beside "Chief Operating Officer" or "Senior Vice President." Finally, it is wise to check with each individual about how he or she wants to be listed—or, perhaps more expeditiously, to send or fax a draft of the letterhead before it is printed to each person for approval or corrections.

Although there is no right or wrong way to decide these issues, the decision should be based on the specific requirements of the planning committee and the organization. If the organization is struggling for credibility and the planning committee members are credible but not well known in the community, their affiliations should be included. If the members are active community leaders whose names are often seen and recognized, then their affiliations may not be necessary.

Size: Occasionally an overzealous graphic designer will try too hard to make an organization's campaign materials stand out. One way that is sometimes suggested to accomplish this laudable goal is to create square or oversized letterhead. Although this strategy does separate an organization from the pack, it can do so in a negative way. Standard business practice in the United States employs 8–1/2" x 11" format almost exclusively. File folders, briefcases, business portfolios, and even most piles of papers on desks are designed to accommodate the standard size. Letterhead that is smaller or larger than the standard size loses a subtle sense of professionalism. Large-format letterhead may indeed attract attention, but having to fold it to fit into an envelope diminishes its appearance and may actually prove irritating. Smaller-than-normal letterhead, on the other hand, gets lost amid its standard-size brethren, and can accommodate only short letters without requiring a second page. Although the standard format may seem mundane, and mundane is not the ideal for capital campaign materials, this is one area in which the standard solution invariably works best.

Layout: Successful letterhead design leaves enough room for a reasonable amount of text. As obvious as that seems, in their search for good design or their desire to incorporate more and more material, some people forget the primary purpose of letterhead, which is for writing letters. Before sending the letterhead to the printer, make several trial copies of the letterhead layout and print letters of different lengths on them to see how the letterhead will look when it is actually used.

> *Before sending the letterhead to the printer, make several trial copies of the letterhead layout and print letters of different lengths on them to see how the letterhead will look when it is actually used.*

By adhering to certain standards of layout, the letterhead can retain its function while still being attractive. In general, the logo and campaign title belong somewhere near the top of the page. Although there are many excellent creative options, placing them anywhere on the page that will require special layout for the text of the letter is inconvenient and may not be worth the fuss. The list of names should be spaced down the left-hand margin and

should be set in a typeface and style that keeps the lines of type reasonably short. The organization's address and phone number often appear near the top with the logo or title. If placed across the bottom, they should be well down on the page, leaving as much room as possible for text. When the campaign office and phone number differ from that of the organization, the campaign information should be used on the letterhead. See Figure 9–2 for sample layouts of successful letterhead.

Paper: The quality and color of the paper make a big difference in the impression that the letterhead will make. Paper color and texture should be chosen to complement

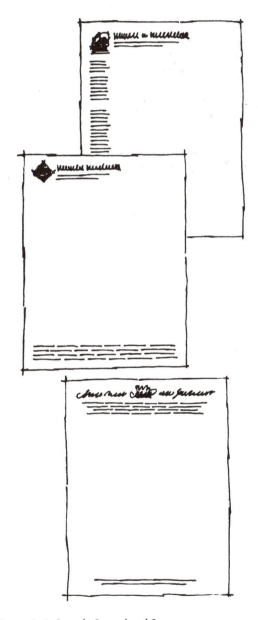

Figure 9–2 Sample Letterhead Layouts

the design, and the designer is the best person to make these recommendations. All too often an organization will go to the time and trouble to procure well-designed letterhead and then decide to save a few dollars by printing it on poor quality paper. The look, feel, and weight of the letterhead affect people's perception of an organization. While there is no need for a modest institution to use the most elegant heavy paper stock—in fact, that can be counterproductive—a medium-weight paper of good quality is well worth the expense. The color should be light enough so that photocopies will not look streaked or gray.

Note Cards, Pledge Forms, Envelopes, and Mailing Labels

If letterhead is the most important piece of campaign material, note cards come in a close second. Although many campaigns actually neglect the design and printing of these cards, printing special cards for campaign thank-you notes emphasizes most appropriately the fundamental importance of saying thank you. From the very beginning of the campaign planning to the bitter end (well, we hope it's not bitter), there will be things to thank people for. Little things such as "Thank you for attending that meeting," big things such as "Thank you for that half-million dollar gift," and all sorts of medium-sized things in between. By providing campaign notes for staff and volunteers, a campaign will send a strong signal to everyone who is involved that saying thank you is a vital part of the campaign.

The note cards should be reasonably sized, so as to accommodate a brief note. They should be printed on a good-quality card stock that can be put through a laser printer but that also lends itself to handwritten notes. It should incorporate the campaign logo and theme so that those being thanked will know at once that the thanks is not just from the volunteer but represents a thank-you from the campaign as well.

Note cards sometimes double as invitations. If they can be run through a laser printer, such cards may serve as excellent invitations to small gatherings, or even as catchy reminder notices.

Every campaign requires pledge forms, although early in the campaign before the campaign material has been printed, it is common and acceptable to use laser-printed letters of agreement.

Printed pledge forms are generally used for most of the campaign gifts. The pledge form usually incorporates two types of information—information that instructs and assists the donor, and information that is received from the donor.

Information for the donor includes

- a one-sentence statement of the goals of the campaign
- information about required gift size for being listed on the group plaque
- sample payment schedule for the pledge period and payment options for the campaign
- giving levels and giving categories, societies, or clubs (if relevant)
- specific information about how checks should be made out
- instructions for gifts of securities
- address and phone number of the organization

Information from the donor includes

- total amount of the pledge
- number of years over which the gift will be paid
- reminder-notice schedule preference
- date and year of first payment
- information about employer's matching gift program, if any
- information about how the donor wishes to be acknowledged
- printed name and signature
- date
- address
- phone number

Like letterhead, pledge forms have a specific function. It is, therefore, always surprising to see pledge forms that may look fine but don't function well. By following some simple guidelines, an organization can make sure that its pledge form will work for the solicitors, the donors, and the organization.

The most effective pledge cards are large enough to accommodate all of the information listed above without looking crowded and confusing. The donor information space and signature line should be large enough so that someone can fill it out easily and legibly with a felt-tip pen.

A pledge card should be small enough so that together with a return envelope, it can be enclosed with a letter in a standard #10 business envelope.

Many donors are of middle age or older, and their eyesight is perhaps not what it was. The type on pledge forms should be large enough and dark enough to be read easily.

Both donors and solicitors generally prefer pledge forms that fold inward so that the information the donor provides is concealed. This accommodates many people's sense that money is a private matter, and it helps solicitors control their urge to give the form a sidelong glance as the donor is handing it over.

The layout of material on a good pledge form looks simple. In fact, a great deal of disparate information must be carefully organized in a relatively small space. This is no task for amateurs. The pledge form should be designed by professionals who know how to use layout to lead a reader through complex material. See Exhibit 9–4 for a sample pledge form layout.

Exhibit 9–4 Sample Pledge Card

pledge card
With your gift, we can help our children meet the challenges of tomorrow.

Naming Opportunities

Donors of $15,000 or more will be able to name a room or area in the expanded Sciencenter. Please call the development office for a list of naming opportunities.

Donor Wall of Scientists

Gifts of $3,000 or more will be recognized on Scientist Plaques. Each plaque will include information about a respected scientist and the name of the donor/honoree. Plaques will be on permanent display at the Sciencenter and sized according to giving category:

Inventors	$15,000	or more
Explorers	$10,000	– 14,999
Investigators	$6,000	– 9,999
Researchers	$3,000	– 5,999

Sample three-year payment schedule

Pledges may be made over three years and paid in annual or semi-annual installments.

Total gift	Annual	Semi-annual
$30,000	$10,000	$5,000
$15,000	$5,000	$2,500
$7,500	$2,500	$1,250
$6,000	$2,000	$1,000
$3,000	$1,000	$500
$1,500	$500	$250
$600	$200	$100

The campaign welcomes gifts of cash, securities, or other negotiable instruments. For instructions on stock transfer, please contact Mary Helen Cathles, Campaign Manager, at (607) 272-0157.

Sciencenter

I / we agree to contribute $_____ to help meet the goals of the Sciencenter.

This contribution will be paid over a period of: ❑ 1 year ❑ 2 years ❑ 3 years ❑ other_____

I / we would like to begin payments on _____ (month) _____ (year)

and request reminder notices as follows: ❑ annually ❑ semi-annually

❑ My employer _____ will match my gift. I will initiate the procedure right away.

Select payment method

❑ Check enclosed

Credit card: ❑ Mastercard ❑ VISA

_____
Card number   Exp. date

_____   _____
Signature   Date   Name

_____   _____
Please print your name(s) as you wish to be acknowledged   or   ❑ Check if you wish to remain anonymous   Signature

_____
Address   City   State   Zip   Phone

Please make checks payable to the Sciencenter, 601 First Street, Ithaca, NY 14850.

A summary of our registration and financial information may be obtained from the Office of the Attorney General, Charities Bureau, 120 Broadway, New York, NY 10271 or from the Sciencenter directly.

Courtesy of the Sciencenter, Ithaca, New York.

Every campaign needs envelopes—envelopes for mailing letters, return envelopes for pledge forms, envelopes for large proposals, envelopes for thank-you notes. Fortunately, campaign envelopes can and should be relatively simple and straightforward mailing envelopes. Campaigns generally do not use the window envelopes or response envelopes that are often employed in annual campaigns.

Many campaigns have found it worthwhile to print self-adhesive mailing labels that incorporate the campaign logo and theme. These may be used on large, unprinted mailing envelopes for proposals and other campaign materials. They can also serve double duty on unprinted folders, thereby creating campaign folders at little extra expense.

The Campaign Brochure

The most visible and impressive of the campaign materials is the campaign brochure. It gathers and summarizes information about the project, the organization, and the campaign into an attractive and readable format. In images, captions, and headings, it should convey enough information so that someone with only a casual interest in the project can absorb its essence and importance after scanning the brochure for a minute or less. Because most organizations are pleased to share their campaign material with others in the field, it is easy to assemble a collection of campaign brochures. As you prepare for your campaign, collect campaign brochures. You will learn what is effective and what is not, preparing yourself to guide the development of a successful brochure for your campaign. Perusing 10 or 20 campaign brochures of different styles will help you determine what will and what won't work for your campaign.

> *As you prepare for your campaign, collect campaign brochures. You will learn what is effective and what is not, preparing yourself to guide the development of a successful brochure for your campaign.*

Timing: Campaign brochures are usually unveiled and presented at the campaign kickoff, when the campaign is officially announced. The brochure presents the project and the campaign in their official format. By the time the brochure has gone to press, the building plans have been fine-tuned, the public goal for the campaign has been established, the campaign theme and logo have been settled, and the case for support has been finely honed. In some sense, the campaign brochure brings together in simple form the many months of work that went into preparing the project and the campaign.

Purpose: Campaign brochures are sent to prospective donors together with proposal letters. They should be attractive, eye-catching, and easy to read. When the brochure arrives in the mail, together with a personal letter requesting a gift, it focuses the attention of the prospective donor on the project and the campaign.

Much more important, however, is the brochure's function as a tool for the volunteer solicitors. Volunteer solicitors are anxious—they are afraid that they don't know enough about the project, that they won't be able to make the case effectively, that they will get the facts wrong, or that they will forget what they are supposed to say. In short, many volunteers feel as though they are about to take an examination but haven't studied enough! The campaign brochure makes the solicitation process an open-book exam. It arms the solicitors with the facts, figures, words, and pictures to guide them through a successful solicitation visit.

These two functions—informing prospective donors and guiding solicitation meetings—overlap but are not the same. An understanding of both functions will have important consequences for design and layout. As a conveyor of information, the brochure should contain detailed information about the project, enabling a prospective donor to become thoroughly informed by reading the text. In its function as a solicitor's guide, it should be organized into talking points that will lead logically and smoothly through the solicitation process. Each point should be highlighted by headings in large type, with charts, drawings, or illustrations where they will graphically clarify or elucidate every concept to be covered during the solicitation.

Formats: The most common format for a campaign brochure is an 8 1/2" × 11" stapled (saddle-stitched) booklet of eight to twelve pages. However, there are many brochure formats that work just as well and may even be preferable for small or medium-sized campaigns. Brochures in traditional format usually work better as information pieces than they do as solicitors' guides. A prospective donor is able to sit and read or at least skim the booklet from cover to cover, absorbing the images and reading the headings and text. For a solicitor who is guiding a prospect, however, this format works less well since it requires the volunteer to turn pages while walking the prospect through the presentation. An easier solicitation format is one that opens to a larger size and presents all the important information on one page so that the volunteer can refer to particular topics and areas without having to flip back and forth.

Sometimes these campaign booklets are designed with pockets in the covers to hold pledge forms and other materials.

Occasionally, a graphic designer is able to develop a campaign brochure that accomplishes both ends equally well. One satisfactory format is 8 1/2" × 34" and is folded three times, accordion style. This provides eight panels, and can be either held and read like a booklet or spread out to full length and placed on a table. Although this large size is difficult to produce, it functions extremely well.

Some campaigns use even larger formats that fold down to smaller sizes. These too can work well if the material is organized effectively. Examples of three formats are found in Figure 9–3.

Style: Campaign brochures range from extremely simple one- or two-color pieces all the way to elaborate four-color presentations. The only important determinant of style is that the format and degree of lavishness of the brochure match the mission and general values of the organization and the amount to be raised. Undoubtedly, it is appropriate for an art museum to tip the scales on the artistic side, pulling out all of the stops for elegant design and high visual impact. On the other hand, the very same sort of brochure prepared for a small day-care center campaign would be inappropriate and consequently ineffective.

Social-service organizations are often afraid that their donors will disapprove of money spent on good design and printing. While this concern does contain a kernel of truth, a well-designed campaign brochure that is simple, clear, and attractive almost never engenders a donor's ire. Donors dislike wasted money, not well-designed brochures. Well-designed brochures, however, even if simple, require the assistance of excellent designers, good paper, and quality printers.

The use of poor photography often undermines what might otherwise be a strong campaign brochure. Sometimes, in a misguided effort at economy, an organization will elect to snap its own shots for the brochure. What usually results is a collection of stilted or uninteresting photos in washed-out tones of gray that communicate nothing specific about the case or the organization. Dollars spent on excellent photography are often some of the very best dollars spent. Although a picture sometimes is worth a thousand words, a bad picture is worth no words at all.

Occasionally an organization has an opportunity to highlight the work of a locally known artist in its campaign material. Although some brochures make powerful use of good photographs, others rely on artists' renderings and paintings. If an artist is well known in the community and willing to support the campaign, that individual might be willing to create a limited number of

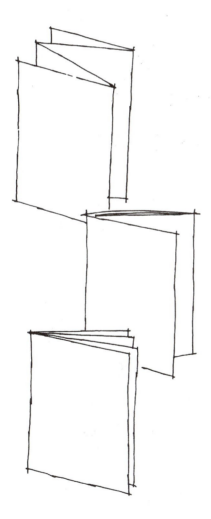

Figure 9–3 Examples of the Accordion Format, Folded Format, and Booklet Format for Brochures

Limited Edition

For our campaign brochure, we commissioned a well-known local artist to paint a watercolor of the building we were going to renovate with campaign funds to become the offices for our chamber of commerce. His painting provided the main visual image of the entire brochure. He then worked with a local printer to create an edition of 250 four-color prints on high-quality paper. He signed 100 of these and we presented those to our largest donors. Those signed prints hang on office walls all over town. Since then, the artist's work has become quite valuable. The donors who received a signed print through the campaign ended up with an even better investment than they had thought!

—Director, Chamber of Commerce

prints of the artwork that is used in the campaign brochure. Matted and framed, these make wonderful gifts for major donors and key campaign volunteers in appreciation for their part in the campaign.

Content: The content of the campaign brochure differs little from the information that is contained in a lead-gift solicitation package. It contains information of three types:

1. **Background information** should include summary information about the organization's history, mission, programs, and goals; a board of directors list; the address and phone number of the organization; and the name of the executive director.
2. **Information about the project** should include the case for support, highlighted with headings; drawings of the building or project; floor plans; a map showing the project location; a project budget; and a timetable.
3. **Information about the campaign** should include the names of the campaign leadership and the campaign planning committee; the campaign goal; the table of gifts, giving categories and donor-recognition opportunities; ways in which to make a gift (cash, pledges, securities); and a sample payment schedule.

The brochure should, of course, incorporate the integrated marketing-communications message into the design, and where possible should clarify and emphasize the message, through photos, drawings, or other images.

Campaign brochures are sent to everyone who will be personally solicited for the campaign. Enough brochures should be printed for every solicitation, plus a healthy surplus for various public-relations uses. Sometimes organizations print enough to send a brochure along with the direct-mail solicitation that concludes the campaign. More often, an organization will develop a different, smaller brochure for the end-of-campaign mailing. This smaller piece can create a final burst of energy and urgency by highlighting a looming deadline or the push for the end.

Direct-Mail Brochures

For organizations that have a large mailing list that includes many who have not been personally solicited, it makes sense to develop a special direct-mail piece for the broad-base solicitation. By the direct-mail phase of the campaign, the remaining donor prospects usually have little direct connection with the organization. This list will include people who are low-level donors as well as those people whose names are on the list but who have never given to the organization. Sending these

people a complete campaign brochure is often inappropriate and expensive.

A specially designed, eye-catching, direct-mail solicitation will usually pay for itself many times over and will attract new donors to the organization. Be sure to include a donor response card and return envelope. It is not uncommon to have different donor cards for different sets of prospects showing different levels of giving.

Campaign Videos

Videotapes are becoming more common in capital campaigns. Before deciding to invest in a videotape for a campaign, one must understand fully what they can and cannot accomplish.

Videotapes can

- present an organization in a lively and engaging fashion
- build credibility by using people who are well-known and respected in the tape
- give a personal and human touch to the case for support
- create an easy way for a prospect to experience the case for support

Videotapes cannot

- solicit gifts
- replace face-to-face discussion

Two for One

Approximately 400,000 people have library cards in our county. When we automated the library system, we had to send each of our cardholders a new bar-coded library card. We decided to develop our final campaign appeal in conjunction with our library-card mailing. The appeal was actually the carrier for the new card, so everyone who received a new card also had an opportunity to fill out one flap of the flier and send it back in a return envelope with their gift to the campaign. This approach was very successful. It cost us very little, as we had to do the mailing anyway, and it combined the request with a tangible sign of what the new system would accomplish for the donors. Months later, we are still getting gifts from our library-card mailer. All together, we've added hundreds of new names to our donor lists, and many of these people may continue as regular contributors!

—Library Director

An organization that has many prospective donors who live far away should seriously consider developing a videotape for the campaign. Although a video is not nearly as good as a personal visit to the organization, a good videotape can do a respectable job of bringing the organization and the project to the donor in an engaging and entertaining fashion.

On the down side, video is a demanding and complex medium requiring specific expertise, technical sophistication, and elaborate equipment. Unless an organization is willing to spend the time and money that is necessary to develop a high-quality product, it would be better off not using video. Bad, boring video presentations are far worse than no videos at all.

Because of our experience with television and movies, people in our culture have come to expect professional-quality videos. We want attractive images, good lighting, clear color, well-timed dramatic effects, and professional graphics. And professional-quality videos are demanding, expensive, and time consuming to make.

If an organization is fortunate enough to have the resources to produce a high-quality videotape, its use should be carefully determined beforehand. No matter how good a video is, solicitors should not take it along to play during the solicitation meeting. Although a tape may be sent in advance or left with the prospect after the solicitation meeting, the time that the solicitor spends with the prospective donor should be used exclusively for active and personal interchange.

Power Point presentations and interactive CD-ROMs are often more effective than video in today's environment. They are more interactive and can be customized to different audiences with different messages.

Campaign Newsletters

Campaign newsletters keep information flowing, and the flow of information builds energy and enthusiasm for the campaign. Campaigns often use two types of newsletters—informal, brief news bulletins for the campaign insiders, and more elaborate newsletters to communicate with all volunteers, donors, and other constituents.

Official campaign newsletters vary in number. Most campaigns produce at least four to six campaign newsletters. These are often designed to have a special campaign look that is different from that of the organization's regular newsletter. The campaign newsletter features the integrated marketing-communications message developed for the campaign and presents only campaign-related information.

A series of campaign newsletters might cover the following material:

- **Issue #1:** Pre-announcement of Campaign (one to two months before the campaign kickoff). Presents the organization's vision for the future, plans being developed to accomplish that vision, and plans for the campaign. This first issue should present the project and create a sense of anticipation.
- **Issue #2:** Campaign Kickoff (just after the campaign kickoff). Contains information about campaign organization, leadership, goal, and kickoff event. This second issue often acknowledges key campaign volunteers and contains more specific information about the project.
- **Issue #3:** Progress Report (two months after campaign kickoff). Reports on success and forward momentum of the campaign, including lead gifts and early results from the general solicitation process. This third issue contains news about volunteers and news about the project.
- **Issue #4:** Progress Report (two months after issue #3). Continues reporting on campaign progress. This fourth issue highlights special gifts or grants and creates a sense of urgency about reaching the goal.
- **Issue #5:** Victory Issue (when goal is achieved). Announces that the campaign has reached or gone over its goal. This fifth issue recognizes donors and volunteers, lists names of donors, and announces the campaign celebration. If there is still time remain-

An Unfortunate Cure for Insomnia

An organization that provides transition housing for indigent people engaged my firm to help them prepare for a campaign. They gave us the videotape that a proud board member had just produced to tell the story of their organization. Later the same day, happy to have a chance to get away from my desk, I popped the tape into the VCR and sat back to watch. After 10 minutes, my eyes began to close. After 20 minutes I was sound asleep. When I awoke sometime later, I remembered nothing. This video had done a great job of helping my insomnia but no job at all of presenting the organization in a way that engaged my attention and interest. Later, as I spoke with several board members, I learned that other people were affected by the video in the same way. The organization had spent more than $6,000 and had accomplished less than nothing!

—Campaign Consultant

ing in the campaign, it might report on how additional funds will be used so those who haven't yet given are still encouraged to do so.

- **Issue #6:** Wrap-Up Issue (after campaign celebration). Reports on the campaign celebration and the projects made possible by the campaign. The final issue provides a transition from the campaign communication back into the organization's standard communications pieces.

The content and timing of these broadly distributed campaign newsletters will vary from organization to organization depending on staff time and the funds that are available. Effective communication with donors, prospective donors, and volunteers is an important way to build team spirit and spread an aura of success and accomplishment.

Web Sites

An organization's Web site is an excellent place to highlight the campaign. Images and themes captured in the campaign brochure and newsletters can be added to the site along with campaign updates and stories about generous donors. The Web site should also provide a simple online way to make a campaign contribution.

MISCELLANEOUS MATERIALS

Many campaigns develop a whole host of other secondary materials to support the campaign. These may include campaign buttons, tote bags, T-shirts, paperweights, and banners. Although not necessary, these items can add enthusiasm and energy to a campaign. Before investing in any promotional items, the staff should develop a well-considered plan for distributing the items. Sometimes people get caught up in their own enthusi-

asm and decide to invest in one item or another only to find that they have no effective way of distributing them beyond a relatively few volunteers. It is not uncommon for boxes of campaign buttons or T-shirts to remain under a table in the workroom for years after the conclusion of the campaign.

Progress Thermometers

Many organizations develop a visible symbol of their campaign progress that lets the public see the climb to the goal. While these signs do keep the campaign in the public eye during the final phase of the campaign, they require frequent updating. If the campaign goes through a stagnant period, the public thermometers broadcast this fact, too!

SPINNING THE CAMPAIGN

A thorough and well-planned communications plan that is integrated into the campaign and the organization can make the difference between a campaign that is merely successful and a campaign that transforms an organization. Early in the campaign, clear communications with key staff and volunteers build confidence that the campaign will be successful. The campaign materials help volunteers do a good job of soliciting gifts. And the public-relations and media effort take the progress and eventual success of the campaign and broadcast it far and wide, radiating an aura of excitement that tends to serve as a magnet for gifts and volunteers alike. In a world in which many people measure success by money, an organization that has completed a major campaign is seen in a different light. And a powerful communications program will not only spread word of that financial success, but will also show how the money raised will help the organization transform the community it serves.

Chapter 10
Practicing the Discipline of Gratitude

Chapter Outline

- The Discipline of Gratitude
- Saying Thank You
- Recognizing Donors and Volunteers Publicly
- Plaques
- Reaping the Rewards of Gratitude

THE DISCIPLINE OF GRATITUDE

It may seem unusual to think about gratitude as a discipline to be practiced. But those who understand that gratitude is a discipline and that discipline requires practice learn to incorporate gratitude into their lives and the lives of their organizations. For these people, the discipline of gratitude yields constant and unexpected rewards. For them, the focus of a development program is as much about what they can give back to their donors as it is about what they can get from them. A genuine and disciplined emphasis on giving, surprisingly all too rare in the nonprofit world, creates an environment that encourages true philanthropy.

This chapter reviews many aspects of expressing gratitude in the context of a capital campaign. Campaign volunteers and donors can be thanked and recognized through means as simple and inexpensive as making thank-you phone calls and sending brief notes to techniques as complex and costly as installing donor plaques on a new building. In this chapter we will explore many aspects of a topic that all too often is assumed to involve nothing more than plain common sense. These topics may well be common-sense, but they are nonetheless far from obvious, and more than any other topic in fund raising, more than any technique for increasing gifts, more than any information about campaign structure, a disciplined approach to gratitude and recognition is a true investment in an organization's future.

SAYING THANK YOU

The Many Places for "Thank You"

How many times a day does the average person say "thank you"? "Please" and "thank you" are certainly common occurrences in everyday parlance. We use these phrases to ask for and to acknowledge the small kindnesses that add so much to the quality of our lives. They are embedded in our speech patterns in much the same way as "How are you?" or "Good day." To thank someone is to express gratitude for something that he or she has done. Of course, using formulaic words of gratitude is often not the same thing as a sincere expression of appreciation. For example, we usually thank a sales clerk after making a purchase. We may be happy to have obtained the item, but we are not really grateful to the clerk for selling it to us. We may be grateful for efficient and businesslike behavior, but often we don't even have that to be grateful for. We often say "thank you," simply because in our culture "thank you" is an acceptable way to indicate that a transaction has been completed.

Thank-you notes for gifts also bring a transaction to a close. They let the donor know that a check or pledge has been received and that someone in the organization has recorded it and responded to it. But the function of thank-you notes as indicating the completion of a transaction is just the beginning. Gratitude, real gratitude, connects people. It holds up and celebrates the best of human behavior, and in doing so it reminds us of the ways in which we would like to behave. To practice the discipline of gratitude, one begins by looking for what is real and good in other people and figuring out ways to recognize and acknowledge it. Real thank yous—the ones that inspire a tear or a lump in the throat—connect the gift and what it makes possible with what is special in the giver.

The Many Faces of "Thank You"

The variety of ways to thank people is limited only by the imagination. One need not succumb to the power of social conditioning that predisposes most people to act only within a limited range of options. Gratitude may be expressed effectively through something as simple as a casual thank you that is spoken in passing or as elaborately as a bronze plaque that dedicates a building in someone's name. The wide range of alternatives in between makes it possible to find just the right way to thank a specific donor for his or her particular contribution. Finding the right way to thank someone is just as personal and idiosyncratic as finding the right solicitor to ask for the right gift in just the right way.

A review of the most common ways of saying thank you yields a range of options from which one, two, or even more ways to thank a particular donor or volunteer can be selected. As readers review these familiar mechanisms of gratitude, their own creativity will help them find other ways to thank their donors and volunteers. Here are just some of the ways one might thank a donor for a gift:

- verbal thanks in person
- verbal thanks over the telephone
- handwritten thank-you notes
- typed thank-you notes or letters
- typed note with personal, handwritten note appended
- notes from the beneficiaries of the gift
- notes from the head of the institution
- notes from a friend
- personalized updates about the success of the project or program
- special humorous awards
- special serious awards
- personal invitations to dinner or another thank-you event
- flowers, candy, champagne, or some other extravagance
- personal invitations to visit the program or facility
- nonpersonalized tokens of appreciation
- personalized tokens of appreciation
- public acknowledgment from the podium
- public acknowledgment in the press
- permanent public acknowledgment (plaques, signs)
- a work of art commissioned to capture an image of the project
- artwork (photo, drawing, painting) of the building, mounted and framed along with personalized message

The Need for Honesty and Authenticity

In reviewing this far-ranging list of recognition techniques, it is important to remember that the effectiveness of a gesture is based more on the honesty and authenticity of the feelings that are motivating it than on the lavishness of the gesture itself. An authentic expression of gratitude for a gift can make the smallest of thank-you gestures effective, while a vacant or dishonest gesture can diminish the value of even the grandest form of recognition.

> *Honesty and authenticity are the sine qua non of effective gestures of gratitude.*

Most people know only too well the disappointment that comes from a thank-you note that doesn't connect with its recipient. While most donors do not wish to be thanked excessively for a small or medium-sized gift, most people do want to know that someone noticed that *they* gave!

Thanking Donors Personally

Without doubt, the most powerful forms of gratitude are personal gestures. Donors who are acknowledged by someone whom they know, in a way that reinforces the importance of their gifts, feel truly appreciated. Small

---

The Best View in the State

Our campaign chair had his name on the reading room in the new library. When I took him up to check it out (on the day before the formal dedication), he stood in front of the window, got big tears in his eyes, and whispered, "This is the best view in the state." It is a beautiful view down the main green, past the chapel, and out toward the mountains. So, for his "thanks for being our chairman" gift, we had a photographer take a color photo of that view and make an 8" x 10" print. We had a calligrapher mount it on an 11" x 17" board and letter underneath our words of appreciation for everything he had done. The best part was that under the picture I had the artist letter "The Best View in the State." We had it all matted and framed, and we gave it to him at the campaign celebration. He loved it. He still says it is the most meaningful thing he's ever been given.

—Development Director

and insignificant as they may seem, personal notes and phone calls specifically for the purposes of thanking a particular donor often leave a more lasting impression on a donor than the most deeply etched plaque.

Small notes, phone calls, or other gestures are effective when they are thoughtfully prepared. They need not take long or be particularly artistic, but they must come from the heart and reflect on specific characteristics of the donor. It is not enough, for example, to write a note that thanks the donor in a neutral, matter-of-fact way. It must mention something specific about the donor that bears on the gift and the organization. Such personalized comments let the donor know that the writer has actually thought about him or her as a particular individual. And knowing this, the donor feels a personal sense of connection.

Consider, for example, the sample letters in Exhibits 10–1 and 10–2 that might be written by an executive director of a children's center to the son of a long-time supporter, now deceased.

Neither of these letters is bad, but the first one captures the spirit of Dave's father and, in doing so, it lets Dave know that his gift will accomplish what he is really after—making sure that his father's memory is kept alive at the center. The second letter appropriately tells Dave that his gift will help the community and that it will help attract other gifts to the campaign, but it says nothing that lets him know that Dorothy really understood the motive behind the gift. The first letter is donor oriented, the second is organizationally oriented.

Writing donor-oriented thank-you letters is much easier when one knows the donor. With just a little practice and discipline, it is possible to put oneself in the shoes of the donor and envision the real reason that underlies the gift. Thank-you letters that actually address those underlying reasons often ring true and communicate effectively, even when the reasons are not the usual ones.

Consider, for example, the donor who gave a generous gift not because of the specific project, but because of who asked for the gift. The correspondence in Exhibits 10–3, 10–4, and 10–5 stands out because of its candor and good humor. The proper tone of a correspondence is established by the relationship between the donor and the organization. Ideally, every lead-gift donor has had an opportunity to build a relationship of trust and respect with the director of the organization, and the specific style and patterns of that relationship dictate the content and style of the letter more than any particular rules of fund raising.

These letters reflect a genuine relationship among Dave, Anne, and William. The first letter from Dave to William does not make more of the relationship between William and the center than is real, though it certainly expresses appropriate gratitude for the gift. The letter from Dave to Anne gives her credit for both her own and William's gifts; it lets Anne know that Dave is sensitive to her need to acknowledge her deceased husband through this gift, and it acknowledges the risk Anne took in asking William for such a large gift. The third letter from Anne to Dave lets him know that both her gift and William's were made because of her confidence in him.

Correspondence of this sort reflects honest relationships between the donor and an organization that have been built over a period of years. The gifts were really the culmination of these relationships, and the thank-you notes are strong in part because they recall the underlying motives all around.

Personally Thanking Donors One Doesn't Know

If one is not acquainted with the donor and knows nothing except his or her name, address, and gift amount, it is more difficult to write a letter that is donor oriented. Nevertheless, by sharing one's real feelings, it is possible to write a note that has a good chance of creating an authentic connection with the donor. Thank-you notes that reveal something personal about the author or something immediate about the organization, particularly as they relate to the gift, help the donor feel that he or she has not been relegated directly to the computer's form-letter software module.

The success of thank-you letters really does depend on their authenticity. Exhibits 10–6 and 10–7 illustrate simply the style and content typical of effective thank-

Exhibit 10–1   Donor-Oriented Thank-You Letter

Anytown Children's Center

535 Lewis Lane, Kidsville, Maryland 20917
(301) 555–6432

Dear Dave:

Your pledge to the campaign just arrived today, and it made my heart soar! I can't wait to tell Mary that you've decided to name the Center's library in memory of your father. He really believed that knowledge and information gave people power, and he spent countless hours reading to our children over the years. He would be so pleased to know that the library will be called the John Davison Memorial Library. How wonderful of you to help us all remember the lessons your father lived so well!

Thank you so very much for your gift. As we get a bit further along with the campaign, I'll call to set up an appointment so we can begin to talk about the specifics of the signage and plaque wording.

Although words can't express the depth of my gratitude for this gift and what it means to the library, please know that your generosity has brought tears to my eyes, both because of what it will do for the library and for the memories it brings back of your father!

With appreciation,

Dorothy

Exhibit 10–2   Organizational-Oriented Thank-You Letter

Anytown Children's Center

535 Lewis Lane, Kidsville, Maryland 20917
(301) 555–6432

Dear Dave:

Thank you so very much for your generous gift naming the center's library in memory of your father. Not only will the gift help renovate this important area of the center, but it will set the giving standard for the leadership division of our campaign.

The center continues to work to help young people in the community. The renovations will enable us to serve more than twice the number of families we have served in the past, and your gift gets us off to a great start.

We are in the process of developing a plan for donor recognition, and I will contact you soon to discuss the wording on the plaque for the center.

Sincerely,

Dorothy

Exhibit 10–3 Letter #1

Anytown Center

678 Capital Street, Some City, PA 17087
(718) 555-1234

Dear William:

Today in the mail I received your pledge for $250,000! Now, I know that you are a generous person, and that collectively your gifts make possible much of what is good in our community, but I also know that you have no particular reason to be passionate about our organization. So you can imagine how surprised (and delighted) I was that a leadership gift should come from your foundation. I guess I really owe Anne a special thank-you as well. I knew she was taking you to lunch to call in some favors and I guess she did just that! Perhaps your real return from this gift is having evened the score with her! In a world where what goes around comes around, you've made a full circle, and our organization is the thrilled beneficiary.

Thank you so much for your generous gift. It will go a long way toward providing a new fitness center in our community. People from all walks of life will have access to a well-equipped and furnished center. Older citizens will be able to use the new therapy pool, and young children will be taken care of in the child-care center while their parents participate in our programs.

Perhaps you didn't know this, but the expanded gym will be fitted out for indoor tennis courts in the winter. When you come to visit, why don't you bring your racket and we can try it out!

Again, William, thank you so very much for your generous gift. We understand our good fortune and are indebted to you for it.

Sincerely,

Dave

Exhibit 10–4 Letter #2

Anytown Center

678 Capital Street, Some City, PA 17087
(718) 555-1234

Dear Anne:

You have certainly wrought a miracle! With just your gift and William's, we're about halfway toward our goal. What a true pleasure it is to know that someone is willing to go out on a limb for our center. Your lead gift got the ball rolling, and your solicitation of William has set the standard for the entire campaign. I look forward to the day in not too many months when we can dedicate the new gymnasium to Sam's memory. That will be a day for all of us to celebrate the completion of a project that you really extended yourself for.

Thanks so very much.

Warmly,

Dave

Exhibit 10–5 Letter #3

Anne Markham Spencer

18 Montgomery Place
Some City, PA 17204

Dear Dave:

I've seldom had more fun than I did at lunch with William. I knew and he knew that he had asked me more than once for a big gift and that I had come through. He knew and I knew that I wanted a return favor for the center. I hemmed and he hawed, but in truth, I think it was done before we ever met for lunch. I guess I see myself as part of a small team in this county of people who are fortunate to have enough resources to give away. Those of us on the team work together in an informal way to get the things done that are really important. So, although William and I seldom talk about it directly, we both know that we'll always help each other. That way, we both can accomplish even more!

Thanks so much, Dave, for being such a good manager and for making sure the center is worthy of our support. I, too, look forward to the dedication ceremonies. I wish Sam could be there to enjoy it too.

Sincerely,

Anne

Exhibit 10–6 An Effective Thank You to a Stranger

Dear Mr. Janus:

What a pleasure it was to find your pledge of $300.00 for our campaign in today's mail. Your gift was among the very first responses we had from the letters we mailed last week. You must have sent it by return mail! For us, therefore, your gift had extra significance. It meant that the letters actually got where they were supposed to go and people like you responded immediately.

The campaign is in its final stages. We still must raise $220,000 before the end of the year, but if the early response to this phase is any indication, we should be able to reach our goal in time.

Soon it will be time to plan a celebration. You'll get an invitation in the mail as soon as we've gone over the top!

I hope to meet you in the new year, and I send my sincere thanks for your pledge to our campaign.

Sincerely,

Joan Dresser
Executive Director

Exhibit 10–7 An Effective Thank You to a Stranger

Dear Mrs. Keener:

Thank you so very much for your pledge of $300.00 to the center's capital campaign. I was working with the architect to finalize the details of the new classroom when our development director put it on my desk, and I felt reassured that money was coming in even as I was planning how to spend it!

Through these last five months when all of us here have worked so hard to develop the building plans and manage the campaign, gifts like yours have buoyed our spirits. You remind us that there are people whom we haven't had the pleasure of meeting yet who care deeply about the center and give their hard-earned money to help us move ahead.

Thank you again. I look forward to writing to you before the end of the year to let you know that with your help, we've achieved our goal.

Sincerely,

Joan Dresser
Executive Director

Exhibit 10–8 A Thank-You Letter that Doesn't Work

Dear Mr. Jamison:

Thank you very much for your generous pledge of $300.00 to the center's capital campaign. We are truly grateful for your support.

The campaign must raise another $230,000 to get us over the top. This money will fund the renovations to our building. This program will grow and be sustained by your generosity and that of many other donors.

I've enclosed an official receipt for your records. Thank you again for supporting the center's capital campaign.

Sincerely,

Sonya Green
Chair, Capital Campaign

you letters. Exhibit 10–8 is typical of a letter that doesn't work.

In Exhibit 10–6, even though Joan does not know Mr. Janus, her letter speaks directly to him. It highlights his rapid response time. It lets him know that his gift stood out. It also tells him that his gift made a difference to the emotional state of the staff as well as to the cam-

paign itself. It informs him about how the campaign is doing and lets him know that Joan would like to meet him.

The letter in Exhibit 10–7 is simpler, but it still works. It acknowledges the gift and the special role it played when it was received. It lets the donor know that not only does her money count, but that her commitment to the center counts, and it looks ahead to a successful campaign.

The letter in Exhibit 10–8, which for many organizations is standard, falls well short of the mark. The word *generous* in the first line presumes information about the donor that the author does not have and thereby immediately strikes a false note. There is nothing in the letter that lets the donor know that Sonya Green specifically acknowledges this particular donor. Indeed, with a change of name this letter could be sent, and in fact probably was sent, to every campaign donor. Even though the letter is signed by Sonya Green, when Mr. Jamison reads it, he will have no sense that Sonya actually noticed his gift. This letter also reveals nothing about its author. In fact, it was probably written by the development director and simply signed by Ms. Green.

Campaign thank-you letters prepared by the staff for the campaign chairs to sign need not be so bloodless. If the staff takes the time to work with the campaign chairs to find the style and content that actually reflects their voices, even routine, staff-prepared letters can sing and speak from the heart.

The Number of Thank Yous for Each Campaign Gift

Every campaign donor should be acknowledged at least three times soon after the receipt of the gift—the donor should receive an official thank you from the executive director that states the amount of the gift or pledge, a thank-you letter from the campaign chair, and a thank-you note from the person who solicited the gift.

Artful Thanks

A day-care center decided to involve the center's children in the process of preparing the thank-you notes for their campaign. They gave pieces of card stock to each of the art teachers and asked them to have the three- to five-year-old children draw and paint on them. They then mounted these small works of art on brightly colored folded paper and glued white paper on the inside to use for handwritten thank-you notes. These were used as one type of thank-you note to campaign donors. Thus, in addition to an official typewritten thank-you letter, each donor received a handwritten thank-you note that came inside a unique work of art created by one of the children at the center. These notes brought the donor into contact with the children and gave the children a role to play in the campaign.

Over a longer period of time, donors should be thanked in other ways as well. Thanks might be extended with personal notes that accompany periodic progress reports or newsletters. Or donors might be recognized in less personal ways at special events or in the organization's newsletter.

Personal thanks might also be extended through phone calls from board members to campaign donors. These calls, though inexpensive and easy to make, nonetheless send a powerful message to the donors. It gives them an opportunity to speak directly to one of the organization's leaders, ask questions, express their opinions, and feel personally acknowledged for their participation in the campaign.

Special Gifts and Lasting Mementos

Small gifts or gestures of appreciation that are given at unexpected times can sometimes have great meaning. Some people seem to have a particular knack for spotting just the right thing for the right person. Gifts and gestures must be appropriate to be effective. If they are either too lavish or given insincerely, the result can be worse than no gift at all.

Some campaigns go to the expense of creating mementos, often with the campaign logo, for volunteers and donors. Paperweights, tote bags, prints of fine art, tie tacks, pins, or even coffee mugs are sometimes presented to campaign workers and donors as tokens of thanks and as a remembrance of the campaign. For some campaigns, these items do indeed seem appropriate and well received, though for others they seem an unnecessary expense. The decision to invest in lasting mementos should be determined according to their appropriateness for the particular organization and whether the director and campaign chair feel comfortable with such an expenditure.

For donors of larger gifts, personalized tokens of appreciation that donors can display in their homes or of-

---

Say It with Chocolate

A development officer for an organization in Hershey, Pennsylvania, started every meeting with a donor with a small gift of chocolate. Sometimes it was a large canister filled with Hershey Kisses and sometimes it was just a Hershey bar. This small gift immediately sent the donor into a good mood, started the meeting with a sincere and palatable thank you, and allowed the development officer to leave a "sweet" reminder of her visit.

---

fices are common, and they are usually appreciated. In the effective practice of gratitude, every major donor should have a personal reminder of the gratitude of the organization. There are many ways to provide take-home versions of plaques for donors. Some organizations actually have replicas of the plaques made for their donors. Others photograph donors with their plaques in the named room or building and then frame the photo with an inscription of gratitude. Still others assemble scrapbooks for donors showing the construction of the building and culminating with photos of the donor at the building dedication. Whatever the gift, it should be an appropriate one, and specific to the particular donor.

Acknowledging Non-Donors

Although it is often not done very well, thanking donors is commonplace. Less common is the practice of thanking non-donors, but much goodwill might be reaped by this simple gesture. In every campaign there are people who feel strongly about the organization but who for one reason or another are not sufficiently moved or just not able to make a campaign gift. It is tempting to view these people as stingy or as the organization's second-class citizens. In truth, however, many non-donors wish to remain friends of the organization and may even become generous donors at another time. Post-campaign letters to non-donors help keep the door open for building stronger relationships in the future. Consider, for

example, how a non-donor would feel receiving one of the letters in Exhibits 10–9, 10–10, or 10–11.

People who have written note after note in the course of their jobs as directors of agencies find that there are two ways in which one can accomplish this sometimes overwhelming task. One can think of it as a formal activity—one that simply needs to be done—or one can actually use it as a chance to connect with the many people who help in one way or another to make the organization strong. If one takes the former approach, one is relegating a substantial amount of one's time to routine work. If, however, one is able to grasp these small opportunities to communicate, the process of thanking people, though it need not take any more time, becomes a creative and personally rewarding assignment.

RECOGNIZING DONORS AND VOLUNTEERS PUBLICLY

Mixed Motives

The more public the recognition, the more mixed the motives for both the organization and the donors or volunteers. Organizations often recognize their most powerful donors and volunteers publicly because they want the community to know that these people have aligned themselves with their project. Many donors and volun-

---

Exhibit 10–9 Letter #1

Campaign for the Counseling Center

Dear Sue:

You've been such a good friend to the center for so many years that I thought you might want to join us for a tour of the newly renovated center on March 1 from 3:00–4:00 p.m. We're inviting a small group of people who have been our long-time supporters to take a look at what we've accomplished and to see the amazing differences it will make in the way we are able to serve our patients. Please call Mary in the office (334–8758) and let her know if you'll be able to join us.

I hope to see you then.

Sincerely,

Janet Moss
Executive Director

Exhibit 10–10 Letter #2

Campaign for the Counseling Center

Dear John:

I know you had reservations about the building project and chose not to give to it. And indeed, we really did go so far out on a limb with the project that even I felt uncomfortable at times. But now that it's over and the mission accomplished, I'd love to show you around and talk about how we might expand programming in the future. That's really your specialty, and I hope to be able to pick your brain for some ideas.

I'll call you next week to set up an appointment. I look forward to speaking with you.

Sincerely,

Janet Moss
Executive Director

Exhibit 10–11 Letter #3

Campaign for the Counseling Center

Dear Ken:

I just wanted you to know how much I enjoyed our meeting yesterday. We've sat in the same boardroom for months and have seldom had a chance to get acquainted. So, finally to have a chance to learn about you and your extraordinary service in our community felt like a reward indeed. Although I am sorry you won't be able to join Doug and me in making a leadership gift to the center's campaign, your clear thinking and suggestions about developing the case for support have already gotten us going in the right direction. I hope you'll be willing to continue to guide me through this—it's my first campaign and I will truly need your advice!

Thanks so much for the many things you do for the center and for this community.

Sincerely,

Barbara McMillen
Campaign Chair

teers are pleased to receive public recognition because it may increase their influence in the community. Other donors and volunteers, though they may personally shy away from such coverage, understand its effect in the community and are willing to exert their influence to help the campaign.

However, public recognition is no substitute for personal recognition. Rather, public recognition most often stems from a collaboration between the donors and the organization to further the cause of the organization. When the donor is genuinely pleased with broad visibility, everyone wins. When the donor would rather remain private, his or her willingness to assume a public presence for a campaign is yet another reason for a private thank you.

Public Recognition and Commitment

It is easy to forget the discomfort that comes with public visibility. On the one hand, it is gratifying to be known for one's good works and generosity, but on the other hand, people in the public eye sometimes become the target for others' jealousies or irrational anger. By becoming publicly aligned with a particular campaign, one also accepts responsibility for its success or failure. If it fails, its failure will be your failure! If it succeeds, then, of course, that success is yours, too. People who have never experienced public visibility often overlook the downside and ignore the need to recognize donors and volunteers for their willingness to assume such a role.

Sometimes the process of becoming a public figure actually helps an individual become more committed to the campaign. Such a person gradually becomes drawn in until finally his or her name and face have become publicly associated with a particular cause or campaign. And now, having publicly thrown in his or her lot with the campaign, this individual swallows all reservations

and does whatever is needed to make sure the campaign succeeds.

Effective executive directors and development directors make sure that volunteers are presented in the very best light. They go to great lengths to get good photographs of key volunteers. They help draft public statements for campaign leadership. They work with volunteers to polish their presentations. And they do whatever is possible to protect volunteers from any negative coverage or publicity. Staff take the blame when things go awry and give credit to volunteers for what goes right.

> *Staff take the blame when things go awry and give credit to volunteers for what goes right.*

The Desire for Anonymity

Some donors truly wish to remain anonymous. They don't want their names to appear on plaques or even in donor listings. Sometimes they don't want anyone but the campaign chair or executive director to know about their gift. More often, however, donors who wish anonymity are pleased to be recognized in nonpublic ways. While they shy away from publicity, they appreciate every personal thank you and gesture that lets them know just what their gift meant.

Misunderstandings around the expectations of the anonymous donor arise when the organization does not trouble itself to discuss these issues with the donor. Does he or she really want no one to know? Is it all right to share information about the gift with the organization's board and the campaign steering committee? A few specific questions posed to the donor will clarify his or her intentions and desires, which then should guide the way that donor is recognized. Lastly, it is well to remember that few if any donors—even the most anonymous—would prefer not to be thanked!

Ceremonies

Large institutions usually have the staff, facilities, budgets, and traditions that support effective recognition ceremonies. Unfortunately, it is common for smaller, lean-staffed organizations to make short shrift of recognition ceremonies. These organizations often find themselves so bogged down in moving and getting their new programs under way in the increased press of activity that often accompanies the completion of a major project that they overlook the importance of these ceremonies for both donors and staff.

These ceremonies provide both public and private opportunities for thanks and recognition. Donors and staff alike come together around a job well done. For

---

A Campaign Chair's Biggest Fan

The other morning at breakfast, my four-year-old daughter asked me when my picture was going to be in the paper again. The week before, my picture had been in the paper because I am the chairman of a capital campaign. My daughter had taken my picture to school with her and had proudly told her classmates that her daddy was helping raise money. Though underneath I had had mixed feelings about being so public about it, when I realized what an object lesson it was for my daughter, my ambivalence faded fast!

—Campaign Chair

such an event, they are no longer staff members or volunteers; rather, they are people who have worked hard and have accomplished something significant for their community and their organization. These opportunities for recognition and gratitude are every bit as important as the plaques, thank-you letters, gifts, and mementos. They bring people together and give each of them a moment when they can enjoy knowing that their work counted.

PLAQUES

A Selling Tool or a Recognition Device?

Some campaigns and some solicitors use the list of naming opportunities as a primary solicitation tool. Others take a low-key approach and encourage donors to name a space only toward the conclusion of the campaign. The first approach capitalizes on an interest in having permanent recognition for a gift. The latter uses naming opportunities to strengthen relationships with people who are already donors, recognizing them in ways that they themselves might not have initiated.

Organizational Culture and the Role of Plaques

These different approaches often reflect variations in organizational culture. For some organizations, plaques and permanent recognition have always played an im-

---

The DRAFT Plaque

At the suggestion of our consultant we had our sign maker install a temporary donor recognition plaque in the lobby of the new building. Though we listed donors according to giving categories, we did not state the gift amounts on the plaques. Shortly after the plaque was installed, I was surprised when I started getting calls from people wanting to know how much it would take to get on the donor plaque. Between that time and the installation of the final plaque three months later, we had eight donors make significant gifts to our campaign just for the privilege of having their names listed on the plaque. Oh, and by the way, we did have several cases where we had to change the names of those already listed on the plaque. There's no question in my mind that it was worth the expense of installing a "draft" plaque.

Mixing Mission with Appreciation

A small science center in an academic community was sure that its donors were not interested in having their names on plaques. Furthermore, if their names were on plaques, they should be listed alphabetically rather than according to giving category. I wasn't so sure that the people who lived in this town were so different from those in the other communities where I had conducted campaigns. We wrestled and tugged about whether to have a plaque wall and what it should look like. Finally, we determined that the plaque wall should honor both the accomplishments of scientists and the generosity of donors. We worked with the architect and the graphic designer to design a large wall in the new community room to suit our needs. What emerged was a plan that enables every donor of $3,000 or more to select the name of a noted scientist. A scientist plaque will be designed for each, incorporating the photo of the scientist and a quotation and/or a brief description of his or her accomplishments. The name of the donor or someone else they choose to honor will be included on a bar at the bottom of each plaque. All of the plaques are the same size, but they will be color coded according to giving level. The entire area will include 120 plaques and the science center will continue to raise money with this until every plaque is taken. If the campaign is completed first, the remaining funds raised will be placed in the endowment fund. As of this writing, it looks as though we won't have many plaques left over. The people in this town are indeed not so unlike the people in other towns!

—Campaign Consultant

---

portant role in the institution. A walk around the grounds and buildings of an organization is likely to turn up plaques of all kinds. In organizations with a "plaque culture," plaques tend to be well cared for and carefully displayed. Brass is polished, outdoor plaques are cleaned regularly, and photos and oil portraits of founding fathers and mothers are proudly and prominently displayed.

In other organizations, one is struck by the occasional and haphazard use of plaques. There may be none at all, or there may be a few that are so poorly displayed that they radiate the organization's discomfort with the practice. Bronze is tarnished; one or two small plaques might hang by themselves in the middle of a large blank wall. Paintings of founders hang crookedly in their dirty frames.

> I didn't think I cared much about plaques. I had given a gift to the little museum in my community and the director twisted my arm to have me name a space. I decided to name one of the small galleries in honor of my mother who had taught me to love art. But when I walked into the finished building and saw her name on a beautiful plaque displayed at the entrance of the gallery, my heart sang. I know she would have been proud to have her name displayed in that way, and it keeps her memory alive.
>
> —A Generous Donor

If plaques are not a part of an organization's culture and history, it may be difficult for the leadership of that organization to commit the time, effort, and resources that it will take to use plaques effectively. Few things are more destructive to donor relationships than a promise of recognition that is not followed through with or that is carried out poorly, so the decision to use plaques should be made along with a long-term commitment for their display and upkeep.

In the short term, good plaques take thorough planning and a significant outlay of resources. It is not uncommon to spend $10,000 or more to design, prepare, and install donor plaques. Although plaques need not be bronze or marble, they do need to be well designed, attractive, and well placed.

However, plaques are also for the long term, and any organization that decides to offer naming opportunities to its donors must accept the long-term responsibilities of maintaining the plaques in such a fashion that the donors whose names they honor and represent—and their descendants—will be proud to be a part of that institution.

Location and Design of Plaques

To develop a program for recognition through plaques that really works well, a campaign should begin during the planning process when the architects are planning the building. Alas, often plaques are mere afterthoughts. Not that they are conceived as development tools after the fact, but the specifics of their size, materials, design, and location are afterthoughts. Many a prestigious institution spends ample time poring over floor plans and assigning dollar values to spaces, but neglects to discuss the specifics of plaque size, design, and location with the architects or interior designers. Then, two months before the building dedication, the development director is assigned the task of getting plaques made for the building—a project far outside the expertise of most people in development. It is little wonder, then, that plaques often look out of character and ill placed.

Think ahead to avoid the problem of poorly planned plaques. One need only think ahead and incorporate a scheme for donor plaques into the design of the building. Qualified architects and interior designers, if given the assignment early in the design process, are capable of incorporating plaques into their design schemes in a way that pays respect to the donors and enhances (or at least does not diminish) the building design.

When the issues of size, design, and placement of plaques are sprung on architects and interior designers at the end of a project, these professionals are likely to see these plaques as detrimental to their design. As a consequence, they often relegate them to the fire extinguisher–exit sign cluster. Such conflict is less likely if expectations are presented early on and the designers have an opportunity to design around the needs of the campaign.

Conflicting Goals

One of my clients recently presented their need to recognize donors on plaques to their design team just as construction was nearing completion. She was very surprised to find that the architects and interior designer found these plaques a distinct inconvenience. Their solution was to incorporate all the donor names into an etched window, which would minimize their visual impact in the overall building. Of course, that worked for the design team but did not work for my client, who realized that the donors expected their names to appear prominently on walls in or near the rooms they had designated. A prolonged and unpleasant battle ensued. The design team strongly objected to individual plaques, strewn, as they put it, all over the building. The development director felt strongly that every person who had given with the intent of naming a space should be recognized at or near that specific location. A satisfactory compromise was finally reached that clustered plaques that named the rooms in a particular wing on the wall of the entry to that wing. Great care was taken in informing the donors of the design decision, and, in the end, everyone was pleased. However, the road to compromise was littered with considerable argument and dissension.

Just as people seldom think about plaques in a timely fashion, they also tend to ignore the need for incorporating directional and labeling signs for the building (both inside and out) until after the designers have completed their work. A building for which the design of both plaques and signs has been planned from the perspective of complementing the architecture is one that truly stands out. There is, however, nothing like tacked-up, poorly planned signs and plaques to make even the most competent building renovation look shoddy immediately.

In order to be able to inform donors accurately about just what it will mean to them to "buy" a naming plaque, the development director should work with the designers, director, and campaign leadership to determine policies about donor plaques. These policies should be outlined in writing as explicitly as possible during the planning phases of the campaign. They should include decisions about the following questions.

Group Plaques

- Will there be a group plaque listing the names of all donors (except those who wish to remain anonymous) of gifts over a certain amount?
- How much must a donor give in order to be listed on the plaque?
- Will donors be listed according to gift amount or alphabetically within category?
- Will the amount of the gift be listed on the plaque?
- Where will the group plaque be located?
- What will it look like?
- Will donors be able to specify the wording of their name(s) on the group plaque?

Individual Plaques

- What does it mean to "name a space"?
- Does naming imply any sort of ownership or proprietary benefits?
- Will donors be able to name spaces within wings named by other donors?
- Will the space actually be named for the donor (e.g., the Weisman Room or the Stengle Chapel)?
- How large will plaques be for each giving level?
- Who will determine the wording on each plaque?
- Will donors have a say in the design of their plaques?
- Will plaques be located within the named room or clustered with other plaques?
- What will plaques be made of, and what will they look like?
- What will happen to the plaques and to the name of a particular space if the building is ever renovated or demolished?

But I Thought It Was My Wing

A major medical center put up a new building. One wing was dedicated to cancer research and a donor decided to name that wing by giving $1 million. The wing included many laboratories and offices. Using that lead gift to spark their campaign, the development officer and campaign leadership were able to raise many generous gifts from other donors to name each of the laboratories in the cancer-research wing. Everything seemed to be going well and on course until shortly before the building dedication, when the first donor visited the new building and was shocked to find other donors' names in "his" wing. In his mind, his million-dollar gift had actually bought that wing. And by selling off pieces of his wing, the campaign had diminished his gift. Now it looked as though he had not really donated the wing, but only in conjunction with all those other donors. If the donor had been better informed at the time that his gift was being solicited, then this problem never would have arisen. Of course, there would then have been the possibility that the donor might not have given such a large gift. He might, however, have given an additional $1 million to "buy up" all the real estate in his wing.

Wording on Plaques

Wording on plaques is more difficult and sensitive than one might imagine. Group plaques often recognize all donors to a project who have given over a certain amount. This contribution level is often $1,000 but may be higher or lower depending on the size of the campaign and the number of donors. Most such plaques list donors by name alphabetically within giving categories. Some group plaques specify the dollar ranges indicated by the giving categories, but more often, the dollar range is omitted and the giving level is simply indicated by placing the highest giving category at the top of the plaque and listing the remaining giving categories in order of descending amount.

The wording of names is often suggested by the institution to the donors. It is often simpler to establish a preferred manner of listing and then to ask each of the donors if he or she is willing to be listed that way. By suggesting, for example, that every donor will be listed by first name, middle initial, last name, without titles such as Dr., Ms., Mr., or Mrs., one is able to develop relatively consistent text for the plaque. When someone wishes to include a spouse, the organization should suggest the order and manner of the listing. A couple might, for example, be listed in any of the following ways:

- Mr. and Mrs. Anthony Partner
- Susan B. and Anthony Partner
- Anthony G. and Susan Partner
- Susan Blain Partner and Anthony Partner
- Susan Blain and Anthony Partner

Of course, decisions such as these must be guided as well by the preferences and standard practices of each couple, and one must not be rigid for the sake of consistency.

Most group plaques begin with an expression of thanks to the donors of the project. The wording should be relevant to the project, and should be an honest expression of gratitude. In general, simpler and shorter phrases are better than long, flowery ones.

Every group plaque should be dated and should state the name of the project or the campaign so that it will speak clearly throughout the future history of the organization.

Finding the right wording for individual plaques can be a challenge. For larger gifts, it is common to name a room for the donor and to indicate this by incorporating the donor's name into the building. So, for example, the waiting room might become the Arthur Judson Waiting Room, or the boardroom might have a sign on the transom that says "Bellows Boardroom." In some cases, the donor is further recognized with a plaque in the room as well as a sign that names the space.

When gifts are made in memory of loved ones, donors often have proprietary feelings about the message on the plaque. It is not uncommon to have a donor write a note with his or her pledge form asking that the plaque read something like the following:

> In loving memory of Agnes, who was a wonderful wife and an outstanding mother. Her contributions to this agency over many years served to make it strong, and her unflagging enthusiasm provided hope for many of the patients served here.
>
> John Jamison, Cathe Jones,
>
> Jim Jamison, Jonathan Jamison,
>
> Mary Kreege, and Kristie Jamison Kelly

Of course, those kinds of heartfelt sentiments are lovely, but they are generally too long for a 6" x 8" plaque. Showing donors standard-wording options and plaque

sizes early in their deliberations helps keep them from being disappointed or disillusioned later.

Approval from Donors

Donors must have a chance to see the wording, size, and design of their individual plaques in advance. They should have a chance to see a life-size drawing of their plaque and should be asked to indicate their approval. Some organizations send mockups of plaques to the donor with a response form that the donor is asked to sign and return. Other organizations invite donors to visit the site to review a mockup of the plaque in its proposed location.

Timing

Once the plaques have been designed, the process of finalizing the wording, checking with donors, and fabricating and installing the plaques can easily take two or three months of dedicated work. For plaques to be ready and installed by the building dedication, work should begin on plans for the plaques well before the building is complete.

REAPING THE REWARDS OF GRATITUDE

The better one becomes at the discipline of gratitude, the easier it is to practice it! People who have made a habit of recognizing others for what they do well find that this practice repays them many times over. Not only

---

The Value of Try-Outs

When a new summer playhouse was constructed, the final bronze, group-donor plaque could not be ordered before the building dedication because gifts were still coming in. For the dedication, the campaign chair decided to have a local artist make a simple painted wooden replica of the final plaque, and it was hung with a sign indicating that the final plaque would be cast in bronze. As it turned out, that temporary plaque served two purposes. Several people saw the temporary plaque and decided to make gifts so they could see their names in bronze. And several others found misspellings in their names on the wooden version and were able to correct the errors before the bronze was cast.

do those who practice gratitude learn to focus on the good things that people do rather than the bad, which in itself is a gift, but practitioners of gratitude also find that people are happy to work with them again and again.

Fortunate is the staff member whose supervisor recognizes and acknowledges the many things he or she does for the organization. Fortunate is the director who works with a board chair who sees and cites his or her effectiveness. And fortunate are the volunteers who help in a campaign where they are appreciated, whether or not every one of their calls brings in a gift!

Capital campaigns are strategic moments in the life of an organization. Although we tend to focus on the dollars that are raised through these campaigns, the long-term strength of the relationships that are built through a campaign have consequences far stronger than the money raised. The effective practice of the discipline of gratitude builds those relationships and strengthens the ties that shape an organization's future.

Chapter 11
Beyond the Campaign

Chapter Outline

- Finishing the Campaign
- Evaluation, Reporting, and Stewardship
- For the Record
- Institutionalizing the Power of the Campaign
- Looking Ahead
- Campaign Lessons

FINISHING THE CAMPAIGN

While for the volunteers the campaign wrap-up celebration signals the end, for the development staff it is merely a transition. After the champagne has been drunk and the streamers cleared away, there is still much work for the development staff in cleaning up odds and ends and making sure that pledge-payment systems are working. It is also time for the development staff to begin thinking about how to capitalize on the lessons from the campaign, adapting the major-gift orientation to the annual fund. And, of course, it is time to figure out how to build on the deep commitments donors made during the campaign, strengthening their relationship to the organization in the future.

This final campaign period, which often lasts several months, provides a transition for both staff and board during which the excitement and struggles of the campaign gradually take their place in the history of the organization, and the organization begins once again to look to the future. This transition period is often ignored, but if consciously incorporated into organizational planning, it will provide a healthy conclusion to an important episode in the life of the organization and the beginning of the next phase in the life of the organization.

This chapter covers the final, wrap-up phase of the campaign, emphasizing the importance of tying up loose ends, both externally and internally. It also draws attention to the importance of institutionalizing the powerful

lessons learned from campaign fund raising and realizing the potential of major-gift fund raising long after the campaign is finished.

Is It Ever Really Over?

It is far easier to know when a campaign begins than when it ends. Most campaigns seem to go on and on . . . and on. Even campaigns that have struggled hard to reach their goals seem loath to stop soliciting merely because the goal has been reached. There are always more calls to be completed and more people to be solicited. In fact, in the last weeks of the campaign, it is quite common for a foot-dragging executive director, campaign chair, or development director to find "campaign religion." Perhaps the certain success of the campaign emboldens them, or perhaps their guilt about their earlier procrastination finally motivates them. Whatever the reason, many campaign workers find new zeal in the last days of the campaign that often carries them along until one or even two months after the official end of the campaign.

> *It is far easier to know when a campaign begins than when it ends.*

In some sense, the campaign can be considered to be over when the staff and volunteers wind down and when every solicitation that was initiated during the campaign has been completed, either in person or by telephone or mail. But this ending is just one of many, for long after the final solicitation has been accomplished, the development staff still collects pledges, thanks donors and volunteers, and prepares final reports on the campaign for the staff and board. And even when all of the cleanup activity is over, the campaign doesn't really end until the staff and board can begin to move on and once again begin to plan their organization's future.

Gifts and Pledges Just Keep Coming

Although the torrent of gifts and pledges that come in as the campaign reaches its goal gradually subsides, it is common for gifts to trickle in for months after the campaign has concluded. One by one, all those donors who had put off writing their checks or filling in their pledge forms find the time to sort through the stacks of papers on their desks, and then they finally get around to doing what they had always intended to do. To many donors, the decision to give is made when an organization's pledge form and envelope are put on the to-do pile rather than deposited in the circular file. The timing of their gifts depends on their internal timekeepers rather than the campaign schedule. Most of these late-arriving gifts are small, but occasionally a large gift comes in as well. Although these gifts after the fact often seem like magic, they are nonetheless the result of the cumulative efforts of everyone who worked on the campaign.

When the campaign has gone over its goal and donors keep sending gifts, the organization may elect to let these donors know of the extra things that their gifts will make possible. Some campaigns use such an "extras" strategy to squeeze the last bit out of the campaign. They prepare a brief case for the extras—perhaps landscaping or furnishing a specific area or something else that wasn't included in the original budget—and then they write to everyone who has not yet given, soliciting a special final gift.

Collecting Pledges

Verbal pledges are common in capital campaigns. An individual promises to make a contribution but then never sends in the pledge forms. If left unresolved, this incomplete transaction is likely to irritate both parties. The donor feels uneasy, the development director annoyed— both would like to complete the process one way or the other. Before a campaign is over, the solicitor, director, or campaign chair should call to check on every pending gift. The context of concluding the campaign often enables a solicitor to focus on completing the request rather than on pressuring the donor into a gift. This change in focus often gives the donor the requisite feeling of autonomy to actually make a gift.

Once the active portion of the campaign is over, an organization might consider using its pledge reminders and thank-you notes as opportunities to keep their donors informed about the progress of the project that their gift is helping to create. A simple update that is changed every month might be enclosed with each pledge reminder and thank-you note, or receipts for checks that are received might incorporate some specific information about the project. The long-distance telephone company Working Assets uses their monthly invoices as an opportunity to inform their customers about issues they support. This idea can be applied to the billing process for capital campaign pledges.

Defaults occur in every campaign when a small group of donors do not make good on their pledges. Some people just pay late, and though they may have missed their quarterly payments, at year's end they send in the entire amount due. Others make pledges but then never send in any payments at all. Most organizations send second notices and even third notices, and when the donor still fails to respond, the executive calls the donor to discuss the situation. Organizations seldom resort to the courts to resolve these situations and rely instead on moral suasion; if that doesn't work, they write the pledge off. The great percentage of gift defaults are for relatively small gifts, so even if the number of defaulting donors seems large, the dollar value of such pledges seldom amounts to as much as five percent of the total amount of campaign gifts and pledges.

Pledging is a practice most campaigns encourage. Donors make their contributions over a period of several years (three to five years is the most common range), but pledge payments are likely to arrive in a somewhat different pattern. Although the specifics of payment will vary according to the vagaries of the individual donor, the donors for every campaign fall into three categories— those who prepay their pledges, those who pay exactly as they have indicated on the pledge form, and those who pay later than they indicated. Figure 11–1 illustrates

---

The Defaulting Donor

It doesn't happen often, but every once in a while a major donor defaults. For our campaign to expand our day-care center, our principal donor was a philanthropic leader in our community. The head of an international corporation headquartered in our community, he had established himself as a generous patron of many of our community's arts and social-service organizations. True to form, he pledged the lead gift to our campaign. We raised the rest of the money and thought we were sitting pretty, until one day we opened the newspaper to learn that our benefactor had been exposed as a scam artist and that the house of cards he had constructed over the years had collapsed, almost taking a major British armaments company down with it. His pledge to us was worthless, and we wound up $50,000 short. The gentleman in question has since taken up residence in a federal penitentiary.

—Executive Director, Day-Care Center

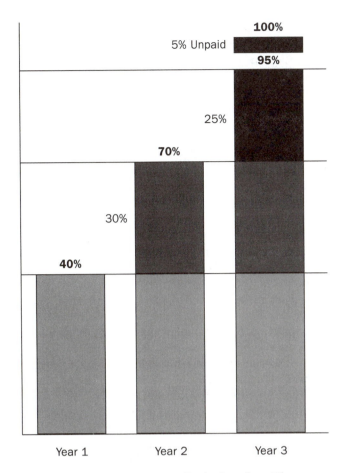

100%
5% Unpaid
95%

25%

70%

30%

40%

Year 1   Year 2   Year 3

Figure 11–1 Common Payment Projections for a Three-Year Campaign

a common pattern of actual payments for a campaign with a three-year pledge period. Keep in mind that this typical pattern may be skewed substantially by one or more major donors who select a different payment schedule.

Celebrating the End of the Campaign

After the goal has been reached and the solicitation and cleanup activity has died down, it is important to spend time and resources to celebrate the campaign's success. For many campaign volunteers, the celebration marks the end of the campaign. This is the time for small acknowledgments, special lunches, bottles of campaign champagne, and large parties that help draw a campaign to a successful close, completing the long journey for staff, donors, and volunteers. These activities highlight all the many positive aspects of the campaign. They recognize volunteers for their hard work, they applaud donors for their generosity, and they acknowledge staff

members for the thousands of hours of organization and coordination that made it all possible. Such gestures help coalesce all the many acts of commitment that make a campaign successful, and in so doing they erase the memory of the things that didn't go quite right.

Campaign celebrations serve another important function. As the campaign draws to a close, staff members and volunteers often experience a sense of emptiness and loss. Suddenly the overwhelming burden and anxiety of the campaign has evaporated, the phone is quieter, the to-do lists are shorter, and meetings are less frequent. Celebrations help staff and volunteers wind down constructively. They can put their energies and minds into one more campaign event, one that brings a sense of completion.

Campaign celebration parties are primarily for all the staff members and campaign volunteers who helped to make the campaign a success. Of course, the celebration should include all the major donors as well. Often such parties take place at an elegant restaurant or country club. But inexpensive celebrations in simple locations work well, too.

As with any special event, planning the campaign celebration requires a great deal of time and attention to detail. Because most nonprofits are expert at planning special events, and because events are covered in some detail in chapter 8, what follows are only some ideas and guidelines specific to campaign celebrations.

The guest list should focus on the campaign staff, volunteers, and major donors. This is not the time for a huge event attended by every donor.

A location should be chosen that will not offend people. If the country club has exclusive membership policies, it may not be wise to use it for the campaign celebration.

A memento from the campaign is a nice way to recognize all those who helped it succeed. For the rank and file, one might give printed tote bags, T-shirts, or mugs. Some organizations prefer the more traditional engraved paperweights, certificates, wall plaques, or coffee-table statues. The best presents for campaign chairs are those that are specific to them and their role in the campaign.

A new beginning comes with the campaign celebration, which marks the end of the campaign for donors and volunteers. The end also begins a new phase in donors' relationships with the organization. Every organization should use the celebration event to engage donors and volunteers in the process of looking beyond the campaign. The celebration should thank them for their help and paint a picture of a future exciting enough to get them thinking about wanting to stay on board.

A short and sweet program works best. Thanks and speeches are an important part of these events, but it doesn't take long before they become stale to a large crowd who would rather be socializing.

EVALUATION, REPORTING, AND STEWARDSHIP

No campaign is complete without an evaluation of the results and a report on its successes. A structured evaluation process provides the opportunity to reflect on what actually took place and analyze the results. A judiciously worded report can solidify and reinforce the organization's image and reputation in the community.

> *A judiciously worded report can solidify and reinforce the organization's image and reputation in the community.*

Taking time to think critically about the campaign after it is over may seem a daunting task, but it is nevertheless a key component in ensuring that the lessons learned during the campaign carry over into the organization's development program, strengthening it and preparing it for the organization's next phase of growth. Usually the development director manages the evaluation process, with the assistance of the campaign consultant.

Evaluation

Campaign evaluation has two components—the objective collection of facts and information, and the subjective analysis of what worked well and what worked less well. Both are important pieces of a complete evaluation and should be assembled into a report that will be included in the written documentation of the campaign. (See more on that subject later in this chapter.)

At the conclusion of the campaign, the development staff should prepare a report that documents the quantifiable results of the campaign. Sometimes assembling this document produces surprises for both staff and board, revealing patterns of giving that previously had been only hunches.

The campaign evaluation should contain at least the pattern of campaign gifts, categorizing of gifts by donor type, the number of gifts, the number of gifts made by volunteers, and the campaign costs.

Find the pattern of campaign gifts by using the original table of gifts as a model. Giving information should be collated to show how many gifts actually came in at the various giving levels. This process requires some interpolation, as actual gift amounts seldom coincide exactly with the amounts on the table of gifts, but with a bit of stretching and contracting one way or another it is usually possible to compare the actual results of the campaign with those projected on the gift table. Exhibit 11–1 shows an example of a final report on the pattern of campaign gifts.

Examining the final pattern of giving in this way directs attention to specific areas of the campaign. The table in Exhibit 11–1 shows a campaign in which the lead gifts and general gifts exceeded the original expectations, but the midlevel gifts fell short of the target goals. A pattern like this may reflect a structural weakness in the campaign—perhaps a division head who didn't follow through, or relationships with midlevel donors that had not sufficiently matured prior to the campaign. Identifying the specific causes might be helpful in pointing

Exhibit 11–1 Actual Pattern of Gifts

Number of Gifts	Amount of Each Gift	Actual Number of Gifts	Projected Amount from Level	Actual Amount From Level
1	$150,000	1	$150,000	$150,000
1	75,000	2	75,000	150,000
2	50,000	2	100,000	115,530
6	25,000	7	150,000	177,486
10	10,000	7	100,000	69,843
20	5,000	14	100,000	71,345
40	2,500	23	100,000	57,500
80	1,000	46	80,000	46,622
160	500	76	80,000	39,520
many	under $500	436	65,000	143,423
	Totals:	614	$1,000,000	$1,021,269

the way to strengthening the organization's development program.

One might also choose to analyze the reasons for the campaign's success in the lead-gift area. In this case, the strong showing of lead gifts came from the fact that the two campaign chairs both made lead gifts themselves and through their own commitments were able to leverage gifts from other major foundations and individuals in the community. The success of the bottom end of the campaign resulted from a major foundation that challenged the community to match its substantial pledge two-to-one before it would actually commit the money. This challenge, coupled with an excellent direct-mail package, brought in a significant number of gifts of under $500.

A discussion and analysis of the actual giving pattern helped the campaign staff and leadership understand the correlation between their work and the pattern in which the gifts came in.

Categorizing gifts by donor type is also an instructive way to analyze a campaign. Tallying the amount of money raised from each type of donor—board, staff, volunteers, former donors, new donors, businesses, and foundations—indicates strengths and opportunities for future development initiatives. Various organizations are likely to categorize gifts in different ways. A school, for example, might look at alumni, parents, and grandparents; a medical facility at patients and patient families; a library at regular borrowers and volunteers.

It is often helpful to know the total number of gifts and pledges that were made to the campaign and how many of these were made as one-time gifts and how many as multiyear pledges. In addition, one may wish to look at how many gifts were received from regular donors, how many from lapsed donors, how many from new donors, and how many from campaign volunteers.

Volunteer activity and campaign gifts are often revealing (and surprising). Some organizations that are good at gathering information report not only on how many volunteers actually worked on the campaign and how many campaign gifts they made, but they also estimate how many volunteer hours were spent.

The objective evaluation part of the report should also summarize the actual cost of the campaign. It is often helpful to compare actual campaign costs with those that were budgeted. Consistency is important in this analysis. Many questions often arise about what does or does not count as a campaign cost. For example, an organization that has combined its campaign newsletter with the regular newsletter must determine what portion of the newsletter costs to apportion to the campaign and what to its regular operating costs. Another gray area is whether and at what level to allot a portion of the salaries of the executive director, development director, and development assistant to the campaign. Colleges and universities have tried to standardize the practices by which organizations determine their campaign costs. However, simplicity, clarity, and internal consistency in reporting should guide the practices of most smaller institutions.

Subjective opinions are an important component of the campaign process. The campaign evaluation should also incorporate feedback from the primary campaign volunteers. Some campaigns ask each campaign chair, committee chair, and division head to fill out a written evaluation of their portion of the campaign. The types of questions that are asked might include some of the following generic questions, as well as others that reflect the specific campaign.

General evaluation questions

1. Did you understand what would be expected of you when you accepted your campaign role?
2. Did the staff support you in carrying out your tasks?
3. Overall, was this campaign a positive experience for you?
4. Do you feel that campaign meetings were well organized and productive?
5. What would you have needed in order to carry out your responsibilities more efficiently?
6. Which were the most challenging aspects of your tasks?
   - enlisting volunteers to help you
   - rating prospects
   - soliciting prospects
   - keeping in touch with other solicitors in your division
   - working with the staff
   - other
7. What were the most rewarding aspects of your involvement?
   - furthering the organization's cause
   - making new friends
   - learning about capital campaigns and fund raising
   - getting recognition and visibility for your work on the campaign
   - other

Campaign materials and public relations

1. Do you feel that the campaign materials were clear?
2. In your opinion, were they well written and attractive?
3. Do you think that they presented the case effectively?
4. Was the pledge form easy to understand and use?
5. Did you want to read the newsletters?

6. Do you feel that the campaign received adequate publicity?

Solicitation training

1. Did the trainer present the material thoroughly?
2. Was the training too long? Too short?
3. Was it engaging and interesting?
4. Did it provide the information that your volunteers needed to solicit their prospects?

Follow-up

1. Were you and your volunteers well informed about the results of your solicitations?
2. Was material sent out to prospects and volunteers in a timely fashion?

Campaign events

1. Were campaign events consistent with the character of the organization?
2. Did they add to the momentum of the campaign?

Written evaluations from the campaign consultant often provide a broader perspective. At the conclusion of the campaign, the campaign consultant should be asked to submit a final written report. Most consultants do this as a matter of course, but because consultants sometimes conclude their work with an organization before the conclusion of the campaign, the consultant's report and the campaign's end sometimes do not dovetail. Because consultants are outside the organization and have experience with many other campaigns, their opinions are often valuable additions to the final report. Some organizations actually contract with their consultants to help design and manage the entire evaluation process.

Finally, the staff often helps in evaluating the campaign. The role of staff is often complicated by the political realities in an organization. It is not uncommon for a staff member to have been dissatisfied with the performance of a colleague throughout the campaign. Perhaps the development director believes that the executive director did not pull her weight during the campaign, or perhaps the executive director despaired about the development director's lack of follow-through or inattention to detail. It is equally common for staff members to blame the board for any weaknesses of the campaign.

The campaign-evaluation report is not the appropriate mechanism in which to raise these issues. Rather, an executive director might incorporate these discussions into the regular performance evaluations with staff or discuss board issues in the course of private meetings with the board chair.

Of course, staff members should be invited to contribute their ideas about the campaign and the lessons learned from it that might be incorporated into the culture of the organization.

Some campaigns prefer to gather information from their campaign leaders and key volunteers through a meeting called specifically to discuss various aspects of the campaign. Although an informal evaluation meeting is often a good way to help complete the campaign experience for both staff and volunteers, such a meeting must be organized to focus attention on the positive rather than providing a forum for chewing over the negative. An evaluation meeting might pose questions such as:

- What are the most important things you have learned through this campaign?
- What are the lessons this organization should take from the campaign?
- How can we apply the lessons of the campaign to the future of the organization?
- Which campaign volunteers would be good candidates to involve further in our organization?
- How in the future might our organization do a better job of involving volunteers?
- What have you learned about your own strengths through this campaign?

Some organizations ask key campaign volunteers to fill out written forms and then use the collective results and feedback as a basis for group discussion.

Reporting

A written evaluation report should be prepared and shared with the staff members who worked on the campaign, with the board, and with the campaign leadership. The written report should frame weaknesses and criticisms as opportunities for learning and growth, using them to guide the organization into the future rather than trying to affix blame for past transgressions.

Once key staff members and campaign volunteers have had a chance to review the report, the staff should determine in what form to report the campaign evaluation to the full board, campaign planning and steering committees, and other campaign volunteers. Some organizations distribute the complete evaluation report, others excerpt from it and distribute a summary report.

Because various constituencies have differing interests and goals, an organization might excerpt different elements from the report for different groups. For example, a campaign-evaluation report for the full board might summarize the campaign statistics, board giving, and opportunities for strengthening the development program, or include other aspects of the report that they might use in the future. A report for the campaign steering committee might focus in greater detail on the successes of the campaign and the involvement of volunteers.

The results of the campaign should be reported more broadly as well. Every volunteer who worked on the campaign and every donor should be informed that they were part of a winning team. As the reporting process broadens beyond the leadership, the message must be tightened and the medium must be more focused. Although campaign volunteers who made five solicitation calls want to be informed of the success of the campaign and to be recognized for their part in that success, those volunteers do not want to read pages of text analyzing the campaign. Rather, such individuals would be happy with a simple letter, note, or card telling them that the campaign has gone over the goal and thanking them for their contribution to the campaign's success.

Campaign Reporting and the Annual Report

Most organizations also produce final campaign reports that list all the donors by giving category. These are generally printed reports similar to an organization's annual report. Some organizations produce a separate report for the campaign, others combine the campaign report into the annual report, including special articles about the campaign and a separate list of campaign donors. A combined report might highlight the campaign, using the campaign logo and theme on the cover and giving the campaign priority billing.

Over the Top

Our campaign was blessed with a wonderful graphic designer. She had helped us put together a package of campaign materials that got the message across, maintained the use of the campaign theme, and caught everyone's eye. When the campaign went over its goal, she designed a large postcard that incorporated the campaign logo with a great photograph of the executive director, the board chair, the two campaign chairs, and the honorary chair. The text said, "Over the top. Thanks to your generous support and commitment we have met our capital campaign goal, raising $1.8 million dollars. Now we can move ahead with our plan. Thank you. Thank you. Thank you." We sent it to all volunteers and donors. For those who had played special roles in the campaign we added personal notes. It was simple, eye-catching, and effective.

—Development Director

Many organizations miss the chance to get the most out of their successful campaigns because they run out of steam at the final lap. A successful campaign casts the glow of success and accomplishment over the entire organization, often boosting its stature and reputation in the community. The success of the campaign should therefore be announced as broadly as possible in the community. This takes a bit more time and energy just as other future-oriented pressures begin to mount. But even though they may be tired and ready to be done with the campaign, the public-relations staff and committee should muster one final blitz of the local media to spread news of the organization's triumph and the consequences of the campaign's success throughout the community.

Stewardship

As the money that was raised is applied to the campaign project, the organization must keep its donors informed of its progress, letting them know that the organization has been and continues to be a good steward of their money. Informing donors of the consequences (both short- and long-term) of their gifts is every bit as important as thanking them. If done well, it will solidify the relationship between donor and organization and begin preparing every donor to contribute to the next campaign. Good stewards report not only on how the money has been used but also on the consequences of their investment to the community.

FOR THE RECORD

What to Include

When all the celebrating, evaluating, and reporting are done, the development director and executive director have one final task. It is up to them to store the campaign for future reference. This requires going through and cleaning out campaign files, storing what's important, discarding what's not, and assembling a paper record that will make sense years and even decades later to those who have had no contact whatsoever with the campaign.

All pledge cards and copies of checks should be dated and stored for a period of five years.

Even if these records are maintained on the computer, the hard-copy record of the campaign should include a list of all donors to the campaign and the amount of each gift or pledge.

Records of all substantive correspondence with every donor should be kept, as well as copies of all correspondence with donors of middle- and upper-level gifts. The organization should determine the dollar levels for which all donor correspondence is kept.

The record should contain documents that describe the plan for the campaign. These should include the campaign structure, names of campaign leaders and planning committee members, campaign policies, campaign timetables, case for support, and division and committee planning documents.

The record should include one copy of each piece of campaign material: letterhead, envelopes, brochure, invitations, note cards, announcements, newsletters, internal newsletters, campaign reports, and so forth.

Also to be included are the campaign evaluation and the mechanisms used to report on the campaign to the various constituencies.

The names of the staff members who worked on the campaign should be included, as well as the length of their work on the campaign and the positions that they held.

A three-ring binder with front and back pockets is an effective mechanism for assembling the campaign record. It should be clearly titled with the name and dates of the campaign, and organized into effective categories so that someone who has played no role in the campaign can learn about the campaign just by paging through the notebook.

What Not to Include

Not every piece of paper kept in the campaign notebooks must be preserved for the long-term file. Meeting agendas, hand-scrawled notes, multiple copies, early drafts, and interim progress reports might well be discarded as part of the effort to consolidate the final record into a meaningful and effective historical document.

INSTITUTIONALIZING THE POWER OF THE CAMPAIGN

Changes Brought about by a Capital Campaign

Capital campaigns are usually times of organizational change. Not only are organizations often rapidly growing or evolving when they consider a campaign, but campaigns usually push organizations to a more effective level of operation. Volunteers must be involved at exceptional levels of performance and with greater intensity. Executive directors and development directors must face any latent fears about major-gift fund raising and learn to

ask courageously for large gifts. Donors of major gifts often begin to help shape the future direction of the organization. Everyone works harder and as a result either becomes more committed to the organization or decides that it's time to leave.

Although staff and volunteers are happy to see the end of the increased tensions and greater workloads that accompanied the campaign, many of the changes wrought by the campaign greatly strengthen the organization and should be incorporated into its ongoing life and development patterns. The following are some of the changes that many nonprofits seek to make in their development operations.

Donor recognition and stewardship. The campaign having created a group of major donors, each with considerable clout, an organization can no longer afford a hit-or-miss attitude toward donor recognition and stewardship. Major donors want to know that their gifts are appreciated and being used well. One result of a capital campaign is that most organizations become far more sensitive to this aspect of their development program.

Board building. Capital campaigns push many organizations to build stronger boards. No longer are they content with their working boards. After a campaign, the staff and board leadership understand far better the potential of a fund-raising board, and they have had an opportunity to develop relationships with excellent candidates for future board membership.

Relationship building. After a campaign, development professionals begin to understand the importance of building relationships with individuals who can affect the future of their organizations. Gone are the days when a director could run the organization as a sole-proprietor enterprise. Moreover, today's directors are under considerable pressure to serve as advocates for their or-

---

Our Board Didn't Do Fund Raising

One of the most important lessons that I learned from my organization's capital campaign was the importance of a board that was willing to raise money. Our board didn't do much fund raising during the campaign. As the campaign progressed, our volunteer solicitors resented doing all the "hard" work of asking for gifts while the board did none. As a result of that lesson, we are now recruiting new board members who understand and embrace their roles as fund raisers. While this process will take some time, we will be better prepared, at least from a board perspective, for our next campaign.

—Development Director

ganizations, constantly seeking new friends and developing new contacts.

Major-gift fund raising. Most smaller nonprofit organizations shy away from major-gift fund raising until they are forced into it by a capital campaign. Through the campaign experience, many executive directors and development directors not only lose their fear but even become impatient with the bottom-end fund raising that has until now shaped the bulk of their annual giving campaigns. Suddenly, the potential for requesting and receiving larger gifts for specific programs or needs alters the focus of the development effort.

Role of the executive director. It is also quite common for an executive director who has had little or no interest in fund raising to learn through the campaign that major-gift fund raising is an avenue to power and potential for the director as well as the organization. After a campaign, many executive directors become hands-on development professionals, looking for special projects to be funded, building relationships with individuals in the community who can help make them happen, and participating in activities in the community that make them more visible. This change in roles necessitates a change in the relationship between the executive director and the development director. No longer do they operate quite so independently of each other. After a campaign, they often become partners in the process of major-gift fund raising.

Reframing the operating budget. With new attention turned to major-gift fund raising, the design of the operating budget takes on new meaning. No longer does an organization see the budget simply as line items and dollar amounts, but the budgeting process becomes a way to find opportunities for major donors. The standard line for equipment now translates into a form that might interest a donor. For example, the amount that is budgeted for new playground equipment might be higher than otherwise if a donor can be identified who would love to purchase something special that catches his or her fancy. The line item for the organization's radio program now looks different because the director knows that a donor is particularly interested in helping to spread the word about a particular program over the airwaves. No longer is lack of money an acceptable reason for why things can't happen. The reason now that some things don't happen is that the executive director and the development director just haven't yet found the right person to give the money that will make it possible.

Redesigning the Annual Giving Program

All the changes mentioned above have profound consequences for an organization's annual giving program. No longer can it rely on letters and a few special events. Those bottom-end fund-raising methods must now serve the larger goals of identifying and cultivating donors for a major-gifts program. Moreover, the major-gifts program should become the centerpiece of the entire annual giving initiative. A new focus on major-gift fund raising will compel an organization to redesign its annual giving program. Sometimes this requires reformulating the composition and function of the development committee. It may even require a change of development staff. But if the annual giving program is not redesigned to accommodate the new focus on major gifts that the capital campaign has made possible, those important lessons will be lost within one or two years, and the organization will fall back to its former reliance on bottom-end fund raising.

Picking Up Where the Capital Campaign Left Off

We finished a very successful campaign three years ago and realized that the development program was languishing so we decided to apply some of the campaign lessons we learned to our annual giving program. We created a special Sylvan Society for annual donors of $1,000 or more. We got a few of our most committed capital campaign donors to collectively pledge "seed" money for our Society. We promised that we would match every $1,000 of seed money with a gift of $1,000 from an individual donor. Our seed money donors are the Sylvan Society Founders, and our Development Committee is now the Leadership Council of the Sylvan Society. We have created three giving clubs within the Sylvan Society: Mulberry Grove for donors of $1,000 through $4,999, Cherry Grove for donors of $5,000 through $9,999, and Sassafras Grove for donors of $10,000 and above. Each Grove has different benefits.

The result is that we've successfully shifted the focus of our development program. Our development committee is actively helping with major gifts just as they should be. We've created a growing group of theatre "insiders" who are serious investors in the company. And, yes, we've raised far more money than ever before toward our annual fund, with every expectation that this program will continue to grow.

The benefit of this restructuring may be worth far more for our company in the long run even than our great capital campaign!

—Vice President for Advancement,
Theatre Company

Planned Giving and Endowment

A successful capital campaign paves the way for a planned giving program and increased emphasis on raising funds for an endowment fund. At the conclusion of a campaign, organizations have an excellent opportunity to shift the campaign focus to the endowment. Donors who have made major gifts to an organization are often the same donors who will consider gifts to an organization's endowment. For many of these donors, a planned gift or endowment gift is a logical next step in their relationship with the organization. If their campaign investment yields significant results and if they have felt very good about their relationship with the organization through the campaign, they may be willing to consider making another large gift long before the next campaign.

To take advantage of these opportunities, an organization should consider boosting its efforts around the planned giving program in the years following the campaign. They may find that some of the campaign donors are not only willing to consider making a planned gift, but these same people may also be willing to serve as volunteers in developing this program.

LOOKING AHEAD

Planning

When a campaign draws to a close and staff and volunteers breathe sighs of relief, it is time to begin looking ahead. No longer are the projects funded by the campaign out in some hazy future. They are at hand, and the future once again beckons! Following a break that is long enough to let staff and volunteers recharge, an organization should begin developing a long-range, or strategic, plan. Without doubt, the best and most exciting fund raising is always done as an organization moves ahead. Effective fund raisers have little time to rest on their laurels. Indeed, in effective organizations, there is little time for repose of any sort. Organizations must always be looking ahead, not necessarily to grow, but to remain vital, changing with the times to improve programs and find ever better ways to serve their constituencies and their communities.

> *The best and most exciting fund raising is always done as an organization moves ahead.*

Another Campaign?

For many staff members who have just completed a campaign, the very thought of another campaign is unthinkable, but with good planning and stewardship, a community organization might consider conducting a second campaign within a 10-year period. Many colleges and universities, for whom capital campaigns are a way of life, schedule their campaigns more tightly, planning the next campaign even as an earlier one concludes. But unless there is a compelling reason to move more quickly, smaller, community-based organizations should probably let at least three or four years elapse between the end of the pledge period and the start of planning for the next campaign.

A breathing period between campaigns provides a time for community donors to take care of some of their other favorite organizations and keeps an organization from appearing greedy in the eyes of those donors who are expected to fund most of the capital campaigns in their community. It also enables the organization to build new relationships and to institutionalize the lessons of the campaign.

CAMPAIGN LESSONS

Capital campaigns are replete with many of the lessons for life that people learn again and again. Campaigns are based on enabling people to use their resources effectively to accomplish something important and lasting in their community. Through campaigns, organizations build relationships and make friendships that endure far beyond the duration of the campaign itself. In many cases, friendships among staff members, volunteers, and donors begun during a capital campaign last a lifetime and evolve and grow through other campaigns and other organizations.

The lessons of a campaign are simple lessons that remind us of the power of positive human interaction. They call on each of us to find and share our own humanity, our commitment to helping others, and our ability to be generous in many ways. The lessons are many and varied. But they are important lessons that if taken seriously and practiced steadfastly will enrich our lives.

Involving Other People

Although the simplest course is often to work alone on a project, the results of solo work are seldom as effective as those obtained if one takes the time and finds the patience to ask for the help of others. In doing so, one will learn about other viewpoints and become exposed to new ideas. Through the collaborative process, one's own ideas are led into new, richer channels.

Sharing the Ownership

The more one shares ownership, the more of a project one owns, for one cannot share something one does not own. Sharing ownership also increases the chances of success, for people seldom accept ownership of something that they don't wish to see succeed.

Practicing Gratitude

The practice of gratitude brings powerful returns to its practitioners and to its recipients. The grateful person has the opportunity to observe and remark on a worthy act. The person who is recognized for a worthy act knows that he or she has had a positive impact on someone's life.

Looking Forward

There is more to be gained from looking forward than from looking back. Looking back encourages one to place blame for things that didn't go well, while looking forward encourages the projecting of the positive lessons of the past into the future. People are usually happy to become part of an organization that is moving forward, and happy to abandon one that is not.

Celebrating Success

All too often in life we chew over our failures and discredit our successes, but the balance between success and failure can be radically altered by recognizing and celebrating every success and acknowledging and learning from and then letting go of every failure.

Recognizing Your Own Power

As you harness the abilities of other people around a common goal, you will come to recognize your own power. Because of our insecurities, we all too often forget that by our actions, efforts, and commitments we have the power to make our organizations strong. Many staff members come to recognize and understand their own power and potential through their work in a capital campaign, and this new awareness can have far-reaching consequences.

Doing the Right Thing

Successful capital campaigns and successful lives are built on honesty and integrity. When in doubt about how to present something or how to act, always make the choice that will let you sleep at night. Those choices may cause short-term stresses. They may even cost your organization a major gift or you your job, but the long-term returns will be worth the short-term costs.

Appendix A
Troubleshooting Guide to Capital Campaigns

No matter how carefully one plans and prepares a capital campaign, challenges always arise, and although one would like to think they should not happen, when they do occur, one wishes for guidance in designing a constructive solution. The author has relied on personal experiences and those of many other professionals in the field to determine the most commonly encountered campaign difficulties to include in a troubleshooting guide. Most of the situations described below are complex and confusing and seem to have no right answer. However, in every case, opportunities are hidden in the obstacles, and a positive approach that looks for and magnifies those hidden opportunities will be the key to developing an action plan.

Perhaps one of the greatest lessons to be learned through capital campaign fund raising is that very few obstacles and challenges are big enough to stop a campaign. Persistence, good humor, and an unflagging commitment to making the campaign succeed can carry one through, under, around, or over virtually any brick wall. When one stops seeing brick walls as obstacles and begins seeing them as life-enriching puzzles, then one is able to continue forward with glee even when presented with what would otherwise seem to be insurmountable challenges.

The collection of challenges below have been adapted from real campaigns.

Campaign challenges fall roughly into seven major categories:

1. dollar goals
2. people (volunteers, staff, and donors)
3. specific gifts
4. public relations
5. organizational issues
6. project difficulties
7. national calamities or acts of God

A general discussion of each category follows, along with a variety of specific stories adapted from real campaign difficulties and food for thought about how one

might deal with each. The author presents no formulaic answers, but does offer ideas that might help clarify the issues in hopes of stimulating the reader to find his or her own solutions to fit the actual situation, specific personalities, and tolerances of the people involved.

The reflections below are intended to encourage the development professional to explore creative ways to approach each challenge. There is no one correct solution to any of the situations, and very few solutions are absolutely wrong. If one is guided by a commitment to honesty and integrity, if one is willing to communicate openly, and if one has the patience to evaluate results over the longer term, the paths taken through the complex terrain of a capital campaign will almost inevitably lead to a successful conclusion.

CAMPAIGN GOAL CHALLENGES

"We are not interested in the possibilities of defeat."

—*Queen Victoria*

Problems relating to campaign goals fall into two categories. Sometimes goals appear to have been set too high, other times too low. Of course, goal difficulties are merely the reflection of a campaign that has not progressed as anticipated. In the case of the too-high goal, the campaign has not raised as much money as was originally targeted; if goals have been set too low, the campaign did better than anticipated.

The real goal of every capital campaign should be to raise as much money as possible to accomplish a specific project in a way that develops strong and healthy relationships among the organization, its donors, and its community. The dollar goal, then, is just one aspect of a campaign goal, and although the dollar goal is the one most commonly highlighted, every decision about goals must be considered in its broader framework.

Story #1. The Campaign Is Just a Little Short

Our campaign has gone well. We hired a consultant, recruited a good campaign chair, and developed a strong case. We were to have finished the campaign by December 30, and indeed by mid-November we had completed the lead-gift and major-gift solicitations and were busy soliciting the broad base of donors in our community. But it's December 20, and we are still about $60,000 shy of our $1.5 million goal. What should we do?

- A torrent of gifts often comes in at the very end of the year. The $60,000 may still roll in before the deadline.
- The shortfall provides a wonderful opportunity to breathe a final spark of energy into the campaign. Meetings with several major donors asking them to close the gap might do just that. Or a letter inviting all donors who have made one-time gifts to extend their gifts with a second- or third-year pledge may yield strong results.
- The shortfall also enables a campaign to go back to donors who have been solicited but have not yet made a commitment and let them know that they have an opportunity to take the campaign over the top.
- Although specific deadlines are important, within reason, for a campaign, people are far less concerned about the specific date than about the overall success of the campaign. If December 30 comes and goes and the campaign has not quite reached its goal, it does not mean that the campaign has failed. Especially over the holiday season when people are busy, mail is even slower than usual, and staff is burdened, campaign leaders are generally unworried, even if the campaign doesn't actually go over its goal for two or three weeks after the deadline.
- Relatively small distances to the end of the campaign provide opportunities to create a hero! In one of our campaigns, the steering committee met just before the end when there was still a $30,000 gap. At that meeting, the steering committee member who had made the very first gift to the campaign pulled out his checkbook and wrote a check for $30,000, saying that he would have to refinance his mortgage to cover the check but would do so if necessary. He asked every person in the room to do their part in closing the gap, but said that his check would close the gap if need be! His generosity sparked others to increase their gifts. In the end, the donor did not have to go to the mortgage company, but his commitment made him one of the heroes of our campaign.
- As the finish line of a race approaches, spectators cheer, runners go faster, and enthusiasm builds. It is

possible to build the same momentum and enthusiasm for a campaign even though people are not standing at the finish line to actually witness the end. To do so, however, the organization must keep as many people as possible informed as the campaign runs toward its goal.

Story #2. The Campaign Is Far Short of Its Goal

Most of the donors have been solicited and the projected end of the campaign is in sight, but the campaign has raised only $700,000 of its $1.2 million goal. Volunteers and staff are disheartened and tired.

- The situation described above is probably the result of poor campaign preparation and planning. If the campaign is short because it missed some major leadership gifts, either the goal should have been lowered before the campaign became public or the kick-off should have been delayed until more leadership gifts could have been secured. If the campaign was successful in raising its leadership gifts but fell short in soliciting midlevel and lower-level gifts, the table of gifts probably did not accurately reflect the realities of the organization. Nonetheless, organizations do find themselves in situations like this, and staff and board members must find creative and constructive ways to turn potential failure into success.
- If one sees virtually no prospect of finding the remaining dollars, one must stop weeping and begging and take stock! Assess just where you are and what your various options are, and develop a plan that is embraced by the steering committee and the board. Grasping at straws saps energy and destroys an organization's credibility. But since everyone who has been involved in the campaign would like it to succeed, everyone will be relieved to understand the options and embrace a new plan that will enable the campaign to succeed even if on a different timetable and for modified goals.
- An organization might hire an outside expert to take stock of the realities of the situation by interviewing key donors, staff, and board members; look at what has and has not been accomplished through the campaign; and work with a group of committed volunteers to fashion a plan. The plan might include developing phases, lowering the goal, extending the time frame, and/or exploring other ways to finance the project.
- Along with the need to develop a well-conceived plan to get beyond being stuck, the organization will need a public-relations plan to reposition the campaign and the project in the eye of the broader community. While the campaign may have fallen short of its goal, it should be possible to focus attention on

the first phase of the construction project rather than on the campaign's failure.

- It is not wise to throw the campaign on the mercy of the community. It is tempting to believe that people will send in money if they know an organization is in trouble. The reality is that while people will often send money if they read a heart-wrenching story about people in trouble, they are seldom inclined to support a failing campaign or a failing organization.
- If major donors have given well short of their abilities, many donors have not yet been solicited, and/or many solicitations have not been completed, it may be possible to raise the remaining money without going back to the drawing board. One might go back to committed leadership donors to ask them to increase and/or extend their commitments. One might extend the campaign timeline and organize another solicitation effort. Or one might find other solicitors or approaches to help close pending solicitations.

Story #3. The Campaign Reaches Its Goal before Everyone Has Been Solicited

Although our building was projected to cost nearly $4 million, our consultant estimated that we wouldn't be able to raise more than $2 million, so we adopted that number as our campaign goal and arranged for long-term financing to cover the rest. Everything went pretty much as planned. We raised $1.2 million in leadership gifts, announced a $2 million goal, and set to work soliciting the midlevel gifts. But not long after the campaign kickoff, one of our solicitors asked a prospect who had given small gifts to us for many years for a pledge of $15,000 and came back with a gift of $500,000! Suddenly we have raised more than $1.7 million, we've just barely scratched the surface of the midlevel solicitations or the lower-level giving, and our campaign is scheduled to continue for another six months. What should we do?

- Because the project costs exceed the goal by $2 million, the organization might shift the campaign emphasis from the campaign goal to the project costs. It would be compelling for donors to know that the remarkable generosity of the community has enabled the organization to shoot for raising the entire amount of the project cost, leaving the organization debt free.
- One might consider asking the donor to frame the $500,000 gift as a challenge grant, requiring the organization to raise $1 or even $2 in new money for every one of hers by a certain date. This approach engages the donor in stimulating additional gifts from the community and would result in at least $3.2 million.

- Another approach would be to discuss with the donor the possibility of using her gift to create a special endowment fund that would support a particular aspect of the new facility, thereby separating it from the stated campaign goal.

PEOPLE PROBLEMS

"What really matters is what you do with what you have."

—*Shirley Lord*

Some of the most challenging and common campaign problems arise from the idiosyncrasies and varying capabilities of both staff members and campaign volunteers. Without doubt, the most common cause of all people problems is poor communication. People often simply don't communicate, and when they do, they often communicate incompletely or inaccurately. Communications difficulties are two-sided, being as much the fault of the receiver as the fault of the sender. Not only do many people not organize and impart information effectively, but most people don't read or listen carefully, often missing a large percentage of the material that has been presented.

But people problems are not just a result of poor communication. They also result from people who are unable to follow through on commitments that they have made in an effective and timely way. These performance problems are compounded by a common tendency not to accept responsibility for one's own weaknesses. It is quite common, for example, for a staff member or volunteer who has not done his or her job to assign blame for his or her poor performance to someone else.

Sometimes people problems arise from more extreme causes—a staff member quits, a campaign chair dies, a donor winds up in jail. These events cause unanticipated and often unpreventable disruptions to the flow of a campaign, and as unlikely as they seem at the start, these extraordinary events occur in more campaigns than one might imagine.

All of these people problems have profound consequences on capital campaigns, but whether the effect on the campaign is beneficial or adverse depends on how they are handled.

Story #1. The Campaign Chair Doesn't Solicit His Prospects

Our campaign chair does a wonderful job of presenting the campaign and the organization in public. He is handsome, speaks well, knows the organization thoroughly, and is a real advocate for the cause. Unfortunately, he does less well soliciting gifts. Actually he would do it very well if he ever got around to it, but the calls he's supposed to make just get put off and put off. What should we do?

- Some years ago when the author was nagging an unresponsive volunteer more and more, a sage advisor gave her the following advice: "Andrea," he said, "turning up the volume is fine for a start, but if it doesn't work, try changing the channel." So one might begin by making a couple of follow-up calls to the chair asking him if he has a solicitation date yet, if he would like you to go along, or if you can send a proposal letter to the prospect. But once he starts avoiding your calls, turning up the volume is no longer working.
- To change the channel you might ask a peer of his who is already involved in the campaign to offer to make the calls with him. Or you might ask the chair if he would feel more comfortable if you reassigned the prospects.
- Some people only work to deadlines, so it might help to call a lead-gift report meeting of all of those volunteers who are making lead-gift solicitations. Most people will produce when it gets to the wire and they know that they will have to report to their peers. The downside of this strategy is that if the chair doesn't perform his tasks before the meeting, his nonperformance will negatively affect the momentum of the entire group.
- Scolding generally doesn't work. People who put themselves in a position of being nagged or scolded generally do so because it satisfies something in them. At some subconscious level, the attention of the scolding itself is often a greater reward than the completion of the task.

Story #2. The Executive Director Doesn't Perform

As we began to plan the campaign, it soon became clear that our executive director was better at finding reasons not to do campaign assignments than she was in figuring out how to do them. Every time the consultant or a board member suggests an action, the director either derails the idea or says that she doesn't have time to carry it out. Often others pick up the slack for her, but gradually we all see what is going on and little by little we become less willing to work hard ourselves. The poor campaign consultant is stuck in the middle. Suggestions?

- Usually when a staff member doesn't perform effectively during a capital campaign, his or her behavior is merely an exaggerated form of the way that person has been performing the rest of the time. During normal times, however, it is possible to over-

look mediocre performance. During campaigns it is not.
- As the campaign heats up, and the conflicts with the consultant grow, the director is likely to be less and less comfortable in the role and may leave of his or her own accord.
- There are at least two ways to deal with every staff problem. One can try to change the source of the problem either by strengthening or replacing the nonperforming staff member or by shifting the staff member's responsibilities away from the tasks of critical importance and reassigning the responsibilities to someone more effective.

In a real-life situation like the example above, the consultant pushed and pushed the director. Her nagging produced an intolerable tension between the two of them, and the director up and quit, much to the relief of the consultant and the board.

Story #3. A Board Member Rebels

We've been planning our building renovation for years. Various committees of the board have worked actively on many aspects of the project. We developed architectural plans, conducted a feasibility study, and are nearing the successful conclusion of our campaign. The board has been informed at every turn and officially approved the campaign and the building project. Last week our campaign chair (a former board chair), who solicited each board member in person, followed up with one board member who had not yet made his gift. At that meeting the board member informed the campaign chair that he had given the building project careful thought and not only had he decided not to make a campaign gift, but he was going to make a motion at the next board meeting to put the renovation project on hold for an indefinite period while the climate around the medical professions stabilized. What should the campaign chair do?

- The real risk of this situation is that this board member will unnerve other board members, and, if he works hard to bring people to his opinion, he might be able to derail the project. But if the current board chair is solidly behind the project, such a dire consequence is unlikely.
- The campaign chair might express his disappointment that the board member will not make a gift and might suggest that the board member contact the current board chair to discuss his views well before the next board meeting. The campaign chair should then call the board chair to alert him or her to the views of the board member.
- In the real situation from which this story was taken, the executive director documented all board involve-

ment with the building project—at which meetings it was presented, what votes were taken, and when board members had opportunities to discuss the project. His documentation was extensive and reminded the board that they had owned the project at every step. He distributed his list to board members at their meeting. By the time of that meeting, the dissenting board member elected not to say a word.

Story #4. A Major Donor Dies

Our campaign chair was a wonderful and generous man. Early in the campaign planning process, he let us know that he intended to make a gift of $250,000 to name the chapel in the new facility. We were thrilled and proceeded with the campaign, which went quite well until our chairman became ill and was diagnosed with leukemia. To us it seemed that all of a sudden he went downhill. He seemed well one day and deathly ill the next. In fact, he died within six weeks of being diagnosed. During that time, we realized that we did not have a signed pledge form for his gift, but once he was so ill, we felt uncomfortable asking him to sign one and he died without having done so. What should we have done?

- It's not uncommon for those closest to a campaign to be too relaxed about filling out pledge forms. Because these people are in constant touch with the organization, handling pledge forms for other donors all the time, and meeting perhaps daily with the executive director or development director, once the amount of the gift has been established verbally, everyone simply assumes that the corroborating paperwork either has been or will be submitted.
- In these situations executive directors are often uncomfortable asking the chair to sign a pledge form because of what might be perceived as an underlying mistrust.
- Once a donor has become critically ill, it becomes even more difficult to ask him or her to sign a pledge form. Suddenly one is aware that priorities might have changed and that the solicitor might appear to be a waiting vulture even by bringing up the subject with the donor or the family.
- It is easier to discuss these issues from the perspective of wanting to be able to fulfill the donor's wishes rather than wanting the donor to make good on his or her pledge.
- This organization was fortunate that the family was willing to honor a verbal commitment for such a large amount. That is probably the exception rather than the rule. However, signed pledge forms for specific gift amounts are considered obligations against the estate in most states.

- The campaign has an excellent opportunity to create a lasting memorial to the deceased donor. Not only would this be a fitting and appropriate gesture for the organization, but it would help build a relationship between the organization and the donor's family.

Story #5. We Can't Find a Campaign Chair

We spent hours deciding who to invite to serve as campaign chair and planning our approach to our nominees. We came up with three people who would make excellent campaign chairs, but as we made the rounds, one by one, they all said they'd help with the campaign but they would not serve as chair. We have no choice, we have to move ahead. The building project is under way, the campaign is being planned, momentum is building . . . but no campaign chair! What do we do?

- One might consider the team approach to campaign leadership. If the burden of chairing the campaign is too heavy for one individual, a shared responsibility might be more manageable. Perhaps a former board chair or even a current board chair might agree to co-chair the campaign and then invite one of the others to join him or her.
- One needs to guard against panic, which leads to asking people who may be willing but are unqualified for the job. Stop! Take stock of the situation. Examine why the first three said no. Consider what you really need from a campaign chair. Before you ask another person, raise your sights. Just because the first three said no doesn't mean that everyone of their stature—or even higher stature—will say no. In fact, someone of greater stature in the community may have more wisdom and say yes!

Story #6. We Can't Recruit Enough Volunteers to Solicit All of the Prospects

We did fine gathering the people to solicit leadership gifts and the family division. Those solicitors were the people who were actively involved in planning the campaign and who are in our organization. But when we began to broaden the effort and enlist the teams for the community division, we came up short. We had a hard time finding team captains, and the team captains had a very difficult time finding enough solicitors. In the end, we managed to get enough volunteers to solicit only about half of the prospects whom we had identified for that phase of the campaign. Are there things we might have done to increase the number of volunteers? And how should we deal with the shortfall?

- With two-income families, who have less time for volunteer activities, and with more and more campaigns looking for solicitors, many organizations are having difficulty finding volunteer solicitors. The further in advance an organization begins to enlist volunteers, the more it will be able to find. Not only does planning ahead provide more time for the enlistment process, but the longer the time between asking someone to do something and the date on which it must be performed, the greater is the likelihood that the person will say yes.

- The best way to build a base of solicitors is by involving potential solicitors in the life of the organization well before the actual campaign. Organizations with large and vital volunteer programs tend to have an easier time than those that do not regularly use volunteers.

- All is not lost because enough volunteers couldn't be found. One might ask each solicitor to take more cards. Or, once the solicitors have completed their first round of solicitation calls, one might invite those who have been successful to take another set of cards.

- If the division will not be able to solicit all of the prospects who have been identified, it becomes more important to highlight the cards of those prospects who are most likely to make a gift so that the personal solicitations are used to maximum effect.

- The cards that are not selected even after a second pass might be targeted for priority attention in the phonathon. Generally, it is easier to enlist volunteers for a phonathon than it is for personal solicitations. And the better the prospects who are left for the phonathon, the better its results.

Story #7. Board Members Resent the Campaign Steering Committee

When we were able to recruit some really powerful people for our campaign steering committee, I was sure the board would be thrilled. Here, finally, we had been able to involve some of our community's largest donors and most credible names in shaping the future of our organization. I could just taste the long-range potential, not only to our campaign, but to our entire organization! So I was taken aback when board members began to question the decisions of the steering committee and even question the wisdom of the whole campaign. I think that the board members were actually jealous of the steering committee. The obvious power discrepancy between the board and the steering committee made board members feel as though they were being phased out, and some of them didn't want to go! What might we have done?

- This situation is not unusual, although it is often overlooked and almost never discussed.
- Most people are uncomfortable with others of dissimilar backgrounds, financial resources, and levels

of power. So it is not surprising that a working board would feel uncomfortable when paired with a fundraising board. This organization might have avoided some of the problems had it taken steps early in the campaign planning process to make sure that the two groups interacted in some way and that key members of the board felt included in the campaign.

- Perhaps the campaign chair and two or three other board members well respected by the rest of the board should have been included in the campaign planning committee. Early in the campaign, the board might have hosted a cocktail party or other event for the full board and steering committee to thank the steering committee members for their assistance and to facilitate some informal communication among members of both groups.

- Some of the steering committee members might have created a task force with some board members to explore ways in which the board might actively participate in the campaign.

- Boards of directors are often not well informed about campaigns; and in a vacuum of thorough information, they become anxious. They are painfully aware that the results of a failed campaign will end up in their laps—not the laps of the steering committee—and are therefore anxious about the progress of the campaign. The campaign chair, working in coordination with the board chair and the executive director, should put special effort into keeping the board informed. This might be done at regular board meetings, at periodic special meetings, or in writing.

- No matter what the steering committee accomplishes, never forget that the board of directors is really responsible for the health of the organization.

- If an executive director is frustrated with his or her board, it would be easy for him or her to express those frustrations to the more powerful members of the steering committee. The director must remember, however, that the steering committee is actually an ad hoc group with no authority. The director must resist the temptation to talk down the board to the steering committee.

GIFT PROBLEMS

"All that glitters is not gold."

Some campaigns face difficult and even embarrassing situations that stem from difficulty around specific gifts—anticipated gifts that don't materialize, multiple gifts intended to name the same area or room, or the gift with strings attached.

Worries about specific gifts have kept many development directors and campaign chairs awake at night.

When all of the process of the campaign—the committees and divisions and solicitation teams—is done, the success of the campaign hinges on whether or not the gifts come in. And a problem around one of the top 10 campaign gifts has the power to tip the balance from success to failure or vice versa.

Most gift problems arise because of misunderstandings. But sometimes donors make commitments that they are unable to make good on, and sometimes organizations do the same.

Story #1. The Retracted Major Gift

A donor gave a major gift to our institution and to confirm the gift he sent a signed letter stating his intentions. All was well and the campaign proceeded according to schedule. At the campaign kickoff we announced our goal and publicly honored our donor for his leadership gift. About a month later, while the general phase of the campaign was in full swing, the donor was diagnosed with cancer and his wife sent us a letter saying that in light of his illness he would be unable to honor his commitment. What should we do?

- Although written pledges giving the date, signature of the donor, amount of the gift, and terms of payment usually serve as legal contracts and in most states stand up in court, most community-based organizations hesitate to use the legal system as a way of forcing payment. The consequences of negative publicity and ill will caused by an aggressive approach are often seen as being too detrimental to the long-term reputation of the institution.
- The organization might try to meet with both the donor and his wife to review the commitment letter, discuss the gift, and determine the donor's intentions. If, at such a meeting, it becomes clear that the donor himself has had a change of heart and would like to change the gift, it may be possible to find a way for him to change the type or terms of the gift so that they work better for him in his current circumstances.
- One might involve other people in the community who have a close relationship with the donor and his spouse to learn more about the facts of the case. Is the wife estranged from her husband? Is she being pressured by children who are hungry for the estate? Are there real financial hardships? An organization would be better able to find a workable solution if it had a thorough grasp of the situation. Unfortunately, when a family is in distress, the facts may be colored by emotion that is difficult to unravel.

Story #2. The Wealthy Campaign Chair Who Makes a Small Gift

We were so pleased when one of the wealthiest members of our community agreed to chair our campaign. Although he did not have a strong history of giving, his family had been active in our organization's programs. We did not know him well, but we felt that the ties were strong enough to make him a reasonable campaign chair. When we recruited him, we talked about the importance of his making a leadership gift, though we were not specific about the actual dollar amount of the gift. We were shocked when, early in the campaign, he sent in his pledge form making a gift of just $10,000 toward our goal of $2.2 million. His stature in the community and his perceived wealth made that gift seem like a slap in the face to us, and we are worried about how effective he will be as a lead-gift solicitor.

- There are few things more disheartening than receiving a small gift from a wealthy campaign chair early in the campaign. We suggest a good night's sleep before starting the search for the best way to turn this disaster into an opportunity. Then consider the following as just a few of the many ways one might choose to proceed.
- Meet with him to discuss the strategic importance of his gift and figure out a way to serve both his financial situation and the campaign. He may increase his gift by extending the pledge period, make an entirely different kind of gift, delay his gift, or simply increase it. Just remember that he may not have thought through the negative effect of his gift. Do not make assumptions! Talk clearly and openly and listen carefully! Together you and the chair will probably be able to turn the problem around.
- Suggest that he hold off on his gift until later when some of the other lead gifts have been solicited. Then make sure that several of the major gifts are in before soliciting him. Some of the large donors might participate in the solicitation and ask him to match their gifts.
- Meet with some of his family members who have been actively involved in the organization to find out whether they would consider pitching in to make his gift part of a larger family gift.
- The table of gifts for the campaign can serve as an excellent tool to help facilitate the discussion of his gift.
- This story is a reminder once again of the importance of early and specific discussions about the role of campaign leaders—before they sign on.
- The fact that the important money matters were not discussed in advance does not mean that they can-

not be discussed later. Clear, nonassumptive, open discussion about the campaign, the role of campaign leaders, and the campaign chair's interests and intentions can often solve such problems. Indeed, through the discussions, the campaign chair is likely to learn to be an effective solicitor—and that's the silk purse that might be gotten from the sow's ear!

Story #3. The "Sure" Gift That Didn't Come In

For many years our largest gift had come from one donor. Year after year she supported our organization to the tune of approximately $10,000 each year. She had told us clearly that she preferred giving away her money while she still lived. When we began our campaign she was in her nineties and her health was beginning to fail. We went to her in the spring to ask for a campaign gift of $100,000. In her usual fashion, she listened and told us that she would consult her attorney and let us know by September. September came and went but we received no word from our donor. Our board chair knew her attorney and called him, only to learn that he was concerned about our donor's declining health and need for round-the-clock care and was advising her against making any more large gifts. It looked like our sure leadership gift was not so sure after all.

- The frustrations of this story are twofold. Not only has the gift not been made as anticipated, but there is simply no clear word at all.
- Sometimes elderly people become virtual prisoners of their caregivers, attorneys, and accountants. It would help to gather as much information as possible about her situation from the community grapevine. Is she making large gifts to other organizations? Are other organizations getting the same feedback? Is she still seeing people? Does she still like company even though her health is not good? How much of a say does she still have in giving away her money? Unless one knows the answers to these and other questions, it is difficult to determine the appropriate strategy.
- Sometimes one does miss a gift because of timing. If her health is truly failing and she has decided not to make a gift, the organization might shift its focus from trying to tie down a campaign commitment to doing nice things for her that will help enrich and soften the end of her life. Even in campaign times, organizations should not lose track of what is right— and if right is letting go of the gift and supporting a loyal and generous friend, that is what you should do.

Story #4. The Lead-Gift Donor Doesn't Pay Up

Our campaign went over its goal and we celebrated with great glee. We then heaved a sigh of relief and dove headfirst into constructing the addition to our building. All was fine until several months later when one of our major donors missed his first payment of $10,000 on a $50,000 pledge. At first I thought it was just an oversight, but when my calls weren't returned and no check showed up, I began to think that he made his contribution for show and has no intention of making good on it. How would you handle this?

- People generally behave consistently, so it might help to track down some other information about this donor's patterns. You certainly do not want to assume that he is defaulting on his gift if in reality he intends to pay. By checking around with other organizations and other people in the community, you might find that he has done the same thing before only to pay off the whole amount in one lump sum at the end of the year. Or, you may find that he has defaulted on other gifts. Whatever the pattern, knowing it might help you determine the best course of action.
- When someone makes a commitment for a campaign gift in writing, in most states that document serves as a contract under the law and one might consider bringing suit against him for the gift. Although for large gifts this is certainly a strategy to consider, sometimes even then the ill will that such an action engenders and the time and energy it takes may not be worth the return.
- Sometimes people default on or delay payment of gifts because their financial situation has suffered an unforeseen blow. It is not uncommon for people who have fallen on hard times to be sensitive and awkward about their reduced means. If this is the case, your donor may appreciate a face-saving strategy. You might send a letter inviting him to redesign his gift to the organization. He might choose to alter the payment schedule or even lower the amount of the gift. By offering him a way out, you might retain him as a donor even though you may not get the full gift.
- If you get no response from the donor, it is sometimes possible to engineer a conversation with his spouse or other family member to try to get more information about what is going on. If someone in your organization is friends with the donor or the spouse, you might share the basics of the situation with him or her and ask if he or she could try to find out what is going on. One must use careful judgment about what information to share and what

should be kept confidential. The grapevine is often a good source of information, and a few well-placed queries might unearth answers to many of the questions.

Story #5. The Campaign That Received Two Gifts to Name One Library

In the course of soliciting lead gifts we invited three people to consider making gifts that would name the library in our building. We thought we would be lucky if one of the three donors would make a gift of the size it would take to name that space, so we were surprised, delighted, and dismayed when two of the donors promptly responded with pledges to name that space. How should we have dealt with the situation?

- Most people are flexible in their preferences for naming a space. You might open a conversation about alternative spaces with the donor who has the strongest ties to the organization. Often when presented with a quandary of this sort, a donor who cares about the organization is likely to be thrilled that another donor has made a large gift and be perfectly willing to select an alternate space.
- On rare occasions, both donors may have strong reasons for selecting the library. Perhaps one gift was to be in honor of the donor's librarian mother, for example, and the other arose out of a strong conviction of the need for such a library. If both donors are adamant about naming the library, one might consider naming different aspects of the library. Perhaps the collections might be named for one donor and the reading area for another. Or, one might suggest naming the library after both donors—The Smithson-Kirk Library.
- The key to resolving all of these cases is to communicate fully and openly with the donors, involving them in the process of determining a solution that they are both happy (or at least willing) to live with.
- Covering up or obscuring the problem and/or delaying contacting the donors is likely only to create more difficulties. Clarity, honesty, and immediacy are the best approaches to this issue—as they are to many others as well.

Story #6. The Gift That Might Have Been Tied to a Contract

We knew that one of our lead gifts might come from an area company that was one of several bidders on a major contract that our organization had put out for bids just as the campaign was progressing. Because of the timing of the campaign, we asked for the gift well before our organization had to make the contract decision, but the corporation delayed their response to our request. We suspected that they were waiting to see if they received the contract. We were fortunate that the company, though not the low bidder, provided services that most closely fit what we were looking for and our committee decided to award it the contract. Approximately one month later, we received the signed pledge form for the amount we had requested. We were uncomfortable about the potential conflicts (both actual and perceived) in that process. Were there specific steps we might have taken to lessen the potential for the appearance of unethical behavior?

- These issues arise in one form or another in many campaigns. In fact, many companies in that situation would not make a campaign gift if they were not awarded the contract. This behavior often makes good sense and represents no conflict of interest at all. Consider that the business may have had no contact with the organization prior to submitting the proposal, and would probably have no ongoing relationship were it not to get the contract and therefore would not be likely to have the motivation to make the gift. Most organizations, however, consider it sound business practice to support client organizations.
- More troublesome is the possibility that a contract may be awarded by a nonprofit not because of the quality of work or the cost quoted in the proposal but as a way of influencing a gift. This practice is most certainly to be discouraged. During a campaign period, an organization would be well served to use the most rigorous of business practices when requesting proposals from businesses with whom it is considering doing business. Every business that is being considered should be treated in the same way, and the process to review proposals should be conducted by a committee that has been instructed to use objective, written standards to select the firm.
- In a similar situation that the author encountered recently, the delay actually helped the client. Between the time the gift of $75,000 has been asked for and the time the contract was awarded, another major corporate donor had increased its campaign gift from $75,000 to $125,000. This gave the author a wonderful opportunity to go back to the company that had kept her waiting and ask it to match the larger gift, which it did.

PUBLIC-RELATIONS NIGHTMARES

"Don't agonize. Organize."
—Florynce Kennedy

Scandals that surface within an organization in the middle of a campaign definitely cause trouble. One needn't look very far to find scandals: murder, rape, allegations of sexual harassment, internal schisms, and labor disputes are just a few of the things that happen to organizations and are particularly challenging if they happen in the middle of a capital campaign.

Story #1. The Symphony Campaign and the Musicians' Strike

There I was, scheduled to have lunch with my friend to ask him for a large campaign gift to build a new symphony hall, and the headlines of the morning paper are about the musicians' strike. What timing!

- What timing, indeed. But canceling the lunch is quite certainly not the appropriate response. In fact, over drinks or lunch, the solicitor may agree with the prospect to discuss the labor situation at the symphony but to postpone their discussion of a gift to the campaign until the labor issues are resolved.
- However, because the strike presumably has to do with the operating budget and short-term issues and the construction of a new symphony hall has longer consequences, the prospect may not be put off at all.
- The solicitor should be sensitive to the mood and reaction of the prospect before determining the best strategy.

Story #2. National Fund-Raising Scandals

Within a couple of short years, the misuse of money at the United Way and the exposure of the fraud at the New Era Foundation seemed to undermine donors' faith in the nonprofit community. Our organization was a United Way member and had both given to and received money from the New Era Foundation. We are planning a campaign and wonder how these facts will affect our prospects.

- Both the United Way and the New Era scandals did undermine people's belief and trust in the nonprofit world at a national level. Local nonprofits that have built strong relationships with people in their community are often unaffected by such erosions of confidence.
- Some organizations that lost money in the New Era debacle actually garnered positive public relations by making full and complete disclosures about what happened and by inviting local donors to make contributions to make up for the funding deficits caused by the default of New Era funds. Because the New Era story was of such interest to the press, organizations that managed the press coverage well actually attracted a great number of new donors.
- National scandals encourage local giving. In fact, local, community-based nonprofits may benefit as more donors decide to increase their support to local organizations and decrease their gifts to larger national causes.

Story #3. Potential Public-Relations Problems

Our campaign was in full swing when one of our former patients decided to sue us for malpractice. Although from our perspective the staff had behaved conscientiously and professionally, the patient had encountered medical complications weeks after leaving our care and was turning over every stone to assign blame. We had accurate and careful documentation that we thought would clear us should the case come to trial, but nonetheless we were concerned that the story might be covered badly in the paper just before our campaign kickoff.

- Preparation and planning in case of a public-relations disaster can go a long way toward preventing or at least minimizing the damage. When a potential problem like this one is in the wind, an organization should develop a strategy for dealing with the press. Draft a press release stating the situation in a clear, honest, unemotional way.
- Assign one person to be the spokesperson for the organization should the problem become a target for the press. Inform everyone else who is closely associated with the organization and the campaign about the situation and the strategy for handling it. Provide key volunteers (board members and campaign leaders) with specific written instructions about what to say should they be called by the local newspaper, radio, or television media.
- Should the media become involved, early and full disclosure is almost always the best strategy. Openness defuses the media; defensiveness and covert behavior only whet the appetite of most journalists.
- Make sure that key campaign volunteers are thoroughly informed early, so they don't get caught short

hearing about the potential problem from someone outside the organization. It is truly embarrassing to learn about a brewing scandal while one is soliciting a prospect.

Story #4. The Board Chair Who Was Accused of Shoplifting

We were just beginning to talk about a capital campaign when the chairman of our board was arrested for shoplifting! He maintained that he had been exchanging shirts that he had purchased at the store earlier but that as he went to pick up the new sizes, the floorwalker accused him of trying to steal the two shirts. Our chairman couldn't produce his receipt for the original purchase and the store detectives turned him over to the local law-enforcement officials. The local newspaper photographed him being led away by the police in handcuffs and the next day they ran the photo in the paper. How, if at all, should this affect our campaign planning?

- Whether or not the chairman is actually guilty of shoplifting, the image of him in handcuffs will undoubtedly undermine his credibility in the community and his tarnished image may well affect the reputation of the organization while he is chairman of the board.
- Conversely, however, an organization should stand up for what it believes to be right, and steady support for the chairman through his problems may be the right thing to do even if it is not the short-term best public-relations stance.
- Most certainly the chairman should be involved and not excluded from discussions about how, if at all, the organization should react. Although it might be tempting to exclude the chairman from discussions of his situation, this would only further complicate the situation.

ERRORS AND MISTAKES

"If I had my life to live over again, I'd dare to make more mistakes next time."
—*Nadine Stair*

Like it or not, errors do occur. The most common campaign errors occur around counting gifts and pledges. This seemingly simple task is actually quite complex, and many campaigns find themselves at some time or another during the course of the campaign having counted one gift twice or having not counted a gift because it wasn't entered properly in the system or even having lost a pledge. There are, of course, other errors as well, such

as leaving out people's names, misspelling names, or including the names of people who wished to be anonymous. It is also common, even in the era of computer spell-check programs, to send out major-gift proposals with spelling or grammatical errors. Most of these errors are small and do not warrant specific stories. A few reminders and suggestions may put them in their proper perspective.

Story #1. We Thought We Had . . . But We Hadn't

We got to the end of our campaign, sneaking over our goal by just a few hundred dollars. Even though it was by inches and not miles that we succeeded, succeed we did! And in our jubilation at completing what had been a very challenging campaign, we called all of our leaders, primary campaign workers, major donors, and a good number of other people who in one way or another had made the campaign a success. We were thrilled. They were thrilled.

The day after all of our calls were made and my feet once again were nearing the ground, the development assistant, who also logged gifts and kept track of campaign counting, crept into my office, her head low, to tell me that she had found an error. She had recorded one $15,000 gift twice and had, therefore, credited the campaign with $15,000 more than it had raised. We were not $436 dollars over goal. Rather we were $14,564 short! My feet landed back on the ground with a harsh thump!

- This issue raises three related topics: how to correct the error and ensure that there are no more like it in the system; how to make up the shortfall as quickly as possible; and who to tell and who not to tell.
- Although confessing one's errors is often an impressive and effective way to begin correcting the problem, there are times when one should do so broadly and times when only a few people need know. In this case, one might inform the campaign chair and board chair and involve them in developing and carrying out a strategy to close the gap quickly. If this can be done, there is no reason to interrupt the celebratory mood among the organization's constituents.
- It is sometimes difficult to know when to communicate about one's errors broadly and when to keep them in the family. These are important issues of judgment, and if the error is large, these judgments should be determined in collaboration with the campaign leadership.

Story #2. Sometimes Careless Errors Help

We worked like mad to meet the deadline of a major foundation that we were asking for a challenge grant.

We prepared what we thought was a good proposal and sent it off thinking that we had asked for a challenge grant that had to be met by June of 2000. We were most surprised, therefore, when we got notice that our proposal had been accepted and we had until June of 2001 to meet their challenge. When we went back to check our proposal, we realized that we had made an error. In one place we had put the earlier date and in another we had mistakenly put the later date. Our reviewer had looked at the later date and did not comment on our inconsistency.

- Often people read what we send them quickly and do not notice small errors or inconsistencies. As a general rule of thumb, therefore, it is not wise to point out or correct small errors in written material after it has been sent. With larger errors or misspelled names, however, one would be wise to send a corrected version of the material.

Story #3. The Editing Prospect

We sent a leadership-gift package to a major donor in our area whom we knew quite well. Within three days we had the package on our desk with several corrections and suggestions about how we might make it more succinct. There was no comment or letter about our request, just his suggestions for how it might be better. What should we have done?

- Most written material can be made better, and a sharp pencil and an astute editing eye is something most organizations could well use. How fortunate this organization is to have a donor prospect with those skills. If that were the author's prospect, she would not hesitate to incorporate the prospect's suggestions, checking carefully for typos and the like and send it back to him as soon as possible with a note of thanks for his part in improving the solicitation material that will be used as a model for many other requests. The author bets that the exchange will help solidify the prospect's gift.
- Of course, to err is human. In fact, when most of us find an error in someone else's work, if he or she is genuinely pleased to have it pointed out so he or she can correct it, we, the error finders, feel as though we have made a positive contribution to the process.
- The difficult part of foolish errors is that once we learn that we have made them we indeed do feel foolish. And foolish is not what we think we are hired to be, so we get defensive and behave in ways that are often counterproductive.
- The ability to embrace one's errors, communicate clearly about them, and correct them with pride is a wonderful strength to be recognized and applauded.

Of all of the strengths one could list, this is one of the most difficult and least common.
- Open, nondefensive responses usually save the day.

ORGANIZATIONAL AND PROJECT PROBLEMS

"Heaven sends us misfortunes as a moral tonic."
—*Lady Marguerite Blessington*

Because capital campaigns and the projects they fund take many months to complete, many unforeseen events occur during those periods. Most of those occurrences are minor, but occasionally minor problems mushroom into full-blown disasters; and because capital campaigns and organizations need the confidence of their donors and constituents to thrive, these disasters often have important consequences.

Story #1. The Bottom Fell Out of Our Market in the Middle of the Campaign

Our organization had been financially strong for several years. Our market boomed and money flowed. As a consequence, we began a capital campaign so that we could renovate a new larger site to accommodate our rapid growth. But as the campaign began, our market collapsed for reasons that had little or nothing to do with how we were conducting our business. We went from having a profit of nearly $500,000 in one year to losing $700,000 the next. Our campaign leadership and committee members had all joined us in part because of our financial strength and we were afraid to tell them what was going on.

- Most campaign leaders are savvy business leaders who are willing to call on their experience to help solve problems. Leaving them out of the loop is a dangerous and potentially damaging strategy.
- Fear has stopped many people from doing what they should.
- As long as the organization can develop a convincing and careful plan to show how the short-term difficulties can be overcome and that the organization has the funds to cover the immediate future, the problem may be quite acceptable to the leadership.
- Be sure that it is wise to continue. Sometimes organizations in a campaign mode blindly continue for fear of losing face. If the project itself no longer makes sense for the organization, stop to reevaluate rather than letting momentum carry you along.

- Everyone working on the campaign should be thoroughly briefed on the situation. Everyone should have a chance to discuss it with the organization's leadership and understand how the situation will affect both the campaign and the organization. That way, everyone will be able to respond appropriately to questions as they arise.

Story #2. The Zoning Board Turned Us Down

We live in a small town and have lots of good will in the community, so when we decided to expand our center we assumed that we could get it through the zoning board without any problem. Unfortunately, at the zoning hearing one of our neighbors decided that she didn't want us to expand and she organized forces against us. To our horror they turned us down flat. The project for which we had already raised half the money couldn't be built!

- This is a time for planning and communications. Presumably the center must still expand. Perhaps it will build a satellite site elsewhere; perhaps it will redesign the expansion to make it more acceptable. Maybe the entire center will move to a new building. While the organization regroups and explores other alternatives, donors must be informed.
- In general, when people are well informed, they are quite reasonable. Most donors to the campaign will be willing to wait until the goals of the campaign are met as long as they know what is going on. But the organization must bend over backward to keep them informed month by month or even weekly as the planning progresses. No one who has made a gift should have to wonder what has or will become of his or her money.
- Building bridges is especially important in a small community. One might invite the person who led the charge against the zoning change to be part of the discussions to figure out how to provide a bigger center to serve the community.

Story #3. It Cost More Than We Anticipated

We set out to raise $750,000 and we did. Then we built our building. When it came to furnishing the building, I just couldn't keep the costs down. In fact, I knew that if I didn't do it right this time, I'd probably never

get the chance again. When the project was completed I had spent nearly $250,000 more than we had planned for, but the building was just right.

- Don't let the cost overruns spoil the success of the campaign. This organization was very successful, but if one is not careful, it would be easy to have the organization feel that it has failed. The energy that comes from a successful campaign is one of its most important aspects. Don't lose it.
- Unless the ways to raise that money are apparent, consider taking out a mortgage on the building rather than beating the donors to extend the campaign. Then let a few years go by and launch a new campaign that incorporates paying off the mortgage as one of its goals.
- Plan better. Boards tend to get a bit testy when they feel that their arms have been twisted. Involving them in the decision process up front usually leads to better long-term results. If you don't trust their judgments and decisions, either work with them, give in to them, or resign.

NATIONAL DISASTERS OR ACTS OF GOD

"The only people who never fail are those who never try."

—Ilka Chase

We all like to think of ourselves as being more or less in control of our lives and the destinies of our organizations. But as recent events have remined us, awful things way beyond our power to control do occur, and when they do, they have a profound effect on our ability to raise funds.

Extraordinary events like terrorist attacks, wars, bombs, earthquakes, floods, and famines require extraordinary reactions on the part of our volunteers and our donors. These disasters don't consider the timetables of our capital campaigns, and when they occur, they may well disrupt and even ruin what we have spent years building.

Although we would choose not to have to accommodate them, accommodate them we must, and the more generously we are able to put our own self-interests and those of our organizations aside and lend our support to the larger community good, the stronger we are likely to emerge when life returns to normal.

Appendix B
Glossary of Common Campaign Terms

Ad hoc committee: *Ad hoc* literally translates from Latin to mean "to this." An ad hoc committee is a group of people who come together around a specific task. While ad hoc committees have neither permanent standing nor the ability to determine an organization's direction, they can be powerful in making recommendations to a standing committee or a board of directors. An ad hoc committee can be an excellent way to temporarily involve people in an organization.

Advance gifts: All gifts raised during the quiet phase of the campaign are often referred to as advance gifts. These gifts are raised "in advance of" the campaign kickoff.

Annual fund: The term annual fund refers to all funds raised for an organization with the expectation that they are renewable every year. These funds generally go to support the overall annual operating budget. This term is often used in a more limited context to refer to the results of a specific annual direct mail appeal.

Board-restricted endowment: Money that has been set aside by the board of directors to serve as a long-term cash reserve is referred to as board-restricted endowment. Often, a designated percentage of these funds (usually 4–6%) is transferred every year for the organization's operating budget. These funds are sometimes referred to as "quasi-endowment."

Campaign cabinet: This is one of the names for the ad hoc committee that oversees the campaign. This committee is sometimes referred to as the campaign steering committee.

Campaign chair: The campaign chair is the volunteer who is the public representative of the campaign. Chairpersons generally solicit or assist with the solicitation of lead gifts. They also serve as the primary volunteer spokespersons for the campaign. Some campaigns have two or more co-chairs who share the position.

Campaign kickoff: The campaign kickoff is the event that punctuates the shift from the quiet or nucleus-fund phase of the campaign to the public phase. The event is generally a celebration of the success of the leadership-gift phase and announces the public campaign goal. It also recognizes the donors who have given in the early phase and involves the volunteers who will help solicit the gifts during the public phase.

Campaign plan: A campaign plan is a written document that spells out the salient characteristics of the campaign. A plan generally includes the following: the case for support, a working goal and gift range chart, a donor recognition plan, a statement of campaign policies, a timetable, and a description of the campaign structure.

Campaign planning committee: A campaign planning committee is an ad hoc committee that meets several times specifically to develop the various aspects of the campaign plan. This committee always includes some board members and may also include key members of the broader community.

Campaign planning study: Sometimes called a feasibility study, this study is a process conducted by consultants that tests the organization's external readiness for a campaign and evaluates the potential for giving.

Capital campaign: The term capital campaign is often used to refer to a fund-raising campaign undertaken to help an organization with expenses for brick-and-mortar projects. This term is often used loosely to refer to several types of campaigns that are occasional occurrences in the life of an organization and that generally help an organization move to a new level of size and/or accomplishment.

Case for support: This phrase is often used to refer to the case statement. See below.

Case statement: The case statement is a written document that describes the project for which money is to be raised that sets forth the reasons donors may wish to make gifts to support the proposed project. The case generally begins as a brief written document. The language of the case is then adapted throughout the campaign in solicitations, proposals, public-relations campaigns, and other communications vehicles.

Challenge grant: A gift that is made strategically to inspire other donors to make gifts to the campaign is called a challenge grant. Challenge gifts can be designed to serve the needs of the organization. They generally require a campaign to raise some sort of matching gifts and have a predetermined deadline. They can be used to generate gifts of specific sizes or from defined groups of constituents.

Combined campaign: A combined campaign raises funds for both bricks-and-mortar projects and for the endowment.

Comprehensive campaign: A comprehensive campaign raises funds for capital projects, special projects, endowment, and operating. These campaigns generally count annual giving as a part of the campaign goal. They are common in fund raising for colleges and universities.

Donor-restricted endowment: Donor-restricted endowments are segregated endowment funds that were given by a donor with restrictions about the funds use. These funds are sometimes referred to as a true endowment and are distinct from a board-restricted or quasi-endowment.

Donor wall: A wall or display that recognizes the gifts of donors to a fund-raising campaign is often referred to as a donor wall.

Endowment: Endowments are restricted funds that are invested by the organization, yielding income that might be made available to the organization for its operations. Endowments fall into two categories: board-restricted and donor-restricted.

Feasibility study: Sometimes referred to as campaign planning studies, these studies are conducted by consultants to help an organization evaluate how much money it will be able to raise and test the strength of the case and the readiness of the organization to undertake a campaign.

General gifts: Sometimes called "stewardship" gifts or "special" gifts, this term refers to the lowest third of the gift levels on the gift range chart.

Gift range chart: A gift range chart is a table that shows a rational pattern of gifts required to raise a particular amount of money. The chart, sometimes referred to as a table of gifts, is used as the basic planning tool for every campaign.

Honorary chairperson: Honorary chairperson is the title sometimes given to someone who has agreed to serve in a visible position in a campaign but who is not willing or able to carry out the functions of the campaign chairperson. Usually people who are invited to be honorary chairpersons are well known in their community and their affiliation with a campaign gives other people a sense of confidence in the campaign's prospects for success.

Lead gifts: Lead gifts are the largest gifts made to a campaign. Together, they usually make up more than 50 percent of the campaign goal. In a small campaign, they may be gifts of $10,000 or more. In a large campaign, they may be defined as gifts of $250,000 or $1,000,000 or more. But whatever their size, these gifts are the gifts without which the campaign will not reach its goal.

Letter of intent: Although many organizations finalize most gifts by having the donor fill out and sign a pledge form, some organizations use letters of intent as the conveyance for the gift. Technically speaking, the letter of intent does not imply a contractual obligation in as rigorous a manner as a contract or a pledge form. In practice, however, letters of intent are often used to tie down the terms and conditions of large gifts. As with a pledge form, a letter of intent is signed by the donor. In some cases, the receiving organization countersigns the letter to indicate that the contract has been accepted.

Major gift: This term has come to refer to the mid-level gifts in a campaign, between the lead gifts and the general or stewardship gifts.

Naming opportunities: Donors to a campaign are often recognized for their generosity by permanently associating their names with a room or a special fund. These naming opportunities both motivate donors and reward them for their gifts.

Nucleus fund: The nucleus fund refers to money raised during the quiet phase of the campaign through lead gifts and gifts from the board and other organizational insiders.

Pace-setting gifts: A generous gift that sets the giving standard in any aspect of the campaign might be referred to as a pace-setting gift. More commonly, however, this term is used to refer to the high range of the major-gift category. Some campaigns create a pace-setter division that solicits the gifts just under the lead gifts.

Planned gifts: Although when considered literally, this term refers to any gift made after some consideration, the term is usually used to refer to deferred gifts or estate gifts.

Pledge form: This form is the standard response form for a campaign gift. These forms, when signed by the donor, constitute contracts between the donor and the organization. The form must state the amount of the gift, the pledge period, the date on which the gift is pledged, and the anticipated payment schedule. Some pledge forms also include other information, such as a brief description of the campaign goal, a sample payment schedule, and a summary of the donor recognition plan.

Public goal: Once an organization has raised a significant amount of funds needed to reach its campaign goal, it announces the campaign and its dollar goal. Prior to the announcement, the campaign leadership will review the progress of the campaign and revise the goal accordingly so that it is low enough to be feasible but high enough to challenge the broad base of donors who have not yet been solicited.

Public phase: The public phase of the campaign begins at the campaign kickoff when the public goal is announced and extends to the completion of the campaign.

Quasi-endowment: Funds that are not restricted by the donor but are designated by the staff or board to function as endowment are referred to as "quasi-" or "pseudo-endowment."

Quiet phase: The quiet phase of a campaign is that portion prior to the campaign kickoff during which the lead gifts and "family" gifts are raised. This is referred to as the quiet phase because it precedes any public announcement of the campaign or campaign goal.

Steering committee: The steering committee is an ad hoc committee that oversees the ongoing effort of the campaign. This committee is usually composed of the campaign chairs and the heads of the various other solicitation divisions and committees. This committee meets periodically during the campaign to assess its progress.

Stewardship gifts: In an effort to make the lower level gifts of a campaign seem just as important as the lead gifts, people sometimes refer to these as stewardship gifts.

Table of gifts: Sometimes referred to as a gift range chart, the table of gifts shows the abstract pattern in which gifts should come in to achieve a specific campaign goal for a specific organization. The patterns outlined in these tables always show fewer high level gifts, more gifts at the midlevel, and the greatest number of gifts at the low level. This pattern, however, should reflect the general characteristics of the organization conducting the campaign. Although tables of gifts are most often used in campaign fund raising, they are also very useful tools for planning an annual giving program.

Wasting endowment: A wasting endowment is a fund that has been established with the anticipation that it will be spent over predetermined number of years. Foundations sometimes make gifts specifically for this purpose to help an organization grow to a new level, providing capital for a period of years but forcing the organization to develop alternative funding streams that will replace it when it has wasted away.

Working goal: The working goal is the campaign goal used during the quiet phase of the campaign. The working goal is reconsidered prior to the campaign kickoff and is often raised or lowered before the public goal is announced.

Appendix C
Bibliography

Alexander, G. Douglass. "Setting Campaign Goals: A Tricky Business," *NSFRE Journal* (Summer 1991): 16–18.

American Association of Fund Raising Counsel Trust for Philanthropy. *Giving USA: The Annual Report on Philanthropy for the Year 1994.* New York: American Association of Fund Raising Counsel, 1995.

Ashton, Debra. *The Complete Guide to Planned Giving: Everything You Need to Know to Compete Successfully for Major Gifts.* 2d ed. Boston: JLA Publications, 1991.

Bailey, Trevor. "How Visions Take Shape." *Hoke Communications 18*, no. 4 (1987): 52.

Bancel, Marilyn. "Preparing Your Capital Campaign." In *Excellence in Fund Raising Workbook Series,* Timothy L. Seiler, editor. San Francisco: Jossey-Bass Publishers, 2000.

Barrett, Richard D., and Molly E. Ware. 2002. *Planned giving essentials: A step by step guide to success.* Gaithersburg, MD: Aspen Publishers, Inc.

Bayley, Ted. *The Fundraiser's Guide to Successful Campaigns.* New York: McGraw-Hill, 1988.

Blanton, Carol. "The Pitfalls and the Promise of Telephone Fundraising." *Grassroots Fundraising Journal* 13 (December 1994): 3–6.

Broce, Thomas. *The Guide to Raising Money from Private Sources.* Norman, OK: University of Oklahoma Press, 1979.

Cheney, Carol. "Designing the Campaign." Currents (November/December 1995): 34–38.

Ciconte, Barbara Kushner, and Jeanne Jacob. *Fund Raising Basics: A Complete Guide.* Gaithersburg, MD: Aspen Publishers, Inc., 1997.

Council for Advancement and Support of Education. *Management Reporting Standards for Educational Institutions.* Revised February 1996. Available from CASE by calling 1–800–554–8536 or through their Web site at www.case.org.

Craig, Donald. "The Askable Moment." *CASE Currents* (December 1991): 30–33.

Crawford, Jean, and Judith Potts. "How to Survive a Capital Campaign." *Fund Raising Management* (July 1986): 39–46.

Dailey, B. "From Zero to Millions, The Anatomy of a Major Gift Solicitation, from Identification to Follow-Up." *CASE Currents* (November/December 1990).

The text of the Declaration of Independence is available on the World Wide Web at http://www.nara.gov/exhall/charters/declaration/decmain.html.

DePree, Max. *Leadership Jazz.* New York: Currency Doubleday, 1992.

Dove, Kent E. *Conducting a Successful Capital Campaign.* San Francisco, CA: Jossey-Bass Publishers, 2000.

Fredricks, Laura. *Developing Major Gifts: Turning Small Donors into Big Contributors.* Gaithersburg, MD: Aspen Publishers, Inc., 2001.

Geever, Jane C. "How to Select and Use Fund Raising Consultants." In *Achieving Excellence in Fund Raising,* edited by H. A. Rosso and Associates. San Francisco: Jossey-Bass Publishers, 1991.

Giese, T. Robert, and J. Richard Murray. "Planned Giving in a Capital Campaign." *Hoke Communications 18,* no. 12 (1988).

Gough, Samuel N., Jr. *Major Gift Programs: Practical Implementation.* Gaithersburg, MD: Aspen Publishers, Inc., 1997.

Grace, Kay Sprinkel. "Managing for Results." In *Achieving Excellence in Fund Raising,* edited by H. A. Rosso and Associates. San Francisco: Jossey-Bass Publishers, 1991.

Gurin, Maurice G. *What Volunteers Should Know for Successful Fund-Raising.* New York: Stein and Day, 1982.

Hall, Holly. "Raising More Money by Doing Research on Contributors." *The Chronicle of Philanthropy* (12 January 1993): 32–34.

——. "The Long and Short of Writing Letters to Raise Money." *The Chronicle of Philanthropy* (9 February 1993).

——. "Direct-Mail Fund Raising Bounces Back." *The Chronicle of Philanthropy* (23 February 1993): 30–34.

——. "What Fund Raisers Do When Donors Object to Making a Gift." *The Chronicle of Philanthropy* (10 August 1993): 36–38.

——. "How Small Charities Can Borrow Big Ideas for Capital Campaigns." *The Chronicle of Philanthropy* (21 September 1993): 39–40.

——. "How to Avoid Pitfalls in Picking the Chair of a Capital Campaign." *The Chronicle of Philanthropy* (8 March 1994): 40–42.

Hall, Johanne. "Intuition or Intellect: How to Recognize the Askable Moment." *CASE Currents* (December 1991): 34–36.

Hartsook, Robert F. "What To Do When the Campaign Is Over." *Fund Raising Management* (November 1995): 32–33.

Hauman, David J. *The Capital Campaign Handbook.* Washington, DC: The Taft Group, 1987.

Joyaux, Simone P. *Strategic Fund Development: Building Profitable Relationships that Last*, 2nd edition. Gaithersburg, MD: Aspen Publishers, 2001.

Kihlstedt, Andrea, and Robert Pierpont, editors. *Capital Campaigns, Realizing Their Power and Potential.* New Directions for Philanthropic Fundraising #21. San Francisco, Jossey-Bass Publishers, 2000.

Klein, Kim. *Fundraising for Social Change.* Inverness, CA: Chardon Press, 1988.

——. Grassroots Fundraising Series (videocassette). The Headwater Fund, 1995. 612-879-0602.

——. "Setting Up the Major Gift Meeting. *Grass Roots Fund-raising Journal* 9 (June 1990): 1–6.

Lange, Scott, and Charles Hunsaker. "Information Systems: Managing the Database." In *Capital Campaigns, Realizing Their Power and Potential*, edited by Andrea Kihlstedt and Robert Pierpont. San Francisco: Jossey-Bass Publishers, 1998.

Levy, Barbara R., and Barbara Marion. *Successful Special Events: Planning, Hosting, and Evaluating.* Gaithersburg, MD: Aspen Publishers, Inc., 1997.

Management Reporting Standards for Educational Institutions. Revised February 1996. Council for Advancement and Support of Education. Available from CASE by calling 1–800–554–8536 or through their Web site at www.case.org.

Marshall, John E. III, and Eugene R. Tempel. "Dynamics of the Challenge Grant." In *Capital Campaigns, Realizing Their Power and Potential*, edited by Andrea Kihlstedt and Robert Pierpont. San Francisco: Jossey-Bass Publishers, 1998.

Marx, Karl. 1875. "The Critique of the Gotha Program." In *The Marx-Engels Reader.* Edited by Robert C. Tucker. New York: W.W. Norton and Co., 1972.

McGrath, Kevin. "Cultivating the Long-Term Donor." *NonProfit Times* (21 October 1993).

Mead, Margaret. *The Last Word: A Treasury of Women's Quotes.* Edited by Carolyn Warner. Englewood Cliffs, NJ: Prentice Hall, 1992.

Moore, Jennifer. "Donor Details on the Net." *The Chronicle of Philanthropy* (10 August 1995): 29–32.

——. "Fund Raisers Debate Where to Draw the Line in Digging Up Personal Data on Potential Donors." *The Chronicle of Philanthropy* (8 September 1992): 23.

O'Brien, Carol. "Thinking beyond the dollar goal." In *Capital Campaigns: Realizing Their Power and Potential. New Directions for Philanthropic Fundraising #21*, edited by Andrea Kihlstedt and Robert Pierpont. San Francisco: Jossey-Bass Publishers, 1998.

Prince, Russ Alan, and Karen Maru File. *The Seven Faces of Philanthropy.* San Francisco: Jossey-Bass Publishers, 1994.

Quigg, H. Gerald. *The Successful Capital Campaign from Planning to Victory Celebration.* Washington, DC: Council for the Advancement and Support of Education, 1986.

Reid, Russ. "Why Do People Give?" *Reid Report* (occasional undated newsletter): 1.

Rosso, Henry A. "Asset Building Through Capital Fund Raising." In *Achieving Excellence in Fund Raising*, edited by H. A. Rosso and Associates. San Francisco: Jossey-Bass Publishers, 1991.

——. "Preparing a Case that Empowers Fund Raising." In *Achieving Excellence in Fund Raising*, edited by H. A. Rosso and Associates. San Francisco: Jossey-Bass Publishers, 1991.

Scanlan, Eugene A. *Corporate and Foundation Fund Raising: A Complete Guide from the Inside.* Gaithersburg, MD: Aspen Publishers, Inc., 1997.

Schneiter, Paul H. *The Art of Asking: How to Solicit Philanthropic Gifts.* Ambler, PA: Fund Raising Institute, 1985.

Schumacher, Edward C. *The Capital Campaign Survival Guide.* Seattle, WA: Elton-Worf Publishing, 2000.

Scott, Miranda D. "Using Online Databases for Prospect Research." *Fund Raising Management* 28, no. 8 (1993): 44–49.

Sheldon, K. Scott. "Foundations as a Source of Support." In *Achieving Excellence in Fund Raising*, edited by H. A. Rosso and Associates. San Francisco: Jossey-Bass Publishers, 1991.

Thompson Letter, The. The Thompson Group, Nashua, NH, 1989.

Warwick, Mal. "How to Raise $1,000 Gifts by Mail." *NonProfit Times* (February 1993): 41–43.

Whitley, Frank V. "The 15 Worst Errors in Community Capital Campaigns." *Fund Raising Management* (September 1992): 43–46.

Williams, Karla A. *1997. Donor focused strategies for annual giving.* Gaithersburg, MD: Aspen Publishers, Inc.

Williams, M. Jane. *Capital Ideas: Step by Step: How to Solicit Major Gifts from Private Sources.* Ambler, PA: Fund Raising Institute, 1979.

———. *Big Gifts.* Rockville, MD: Fund Raising Institute, 1991.

Wyman, Ken. *Face to Face: How to Get Bigger Donations from Very Generous People.* 1993. Written for the Canadian federal government's Voluntary Action Program, available through Ken Wyman & Associates, 64B Shuter Street, Suite 200, Toronto, ON, Canada, M5B 1B1, 416–363–2926.

Index

A

Active listening, 148
Ad hoc committee, defined, 239
Administration, development office, 17
Advance gift
  defined, 239
  solicitation, 8–9
American Association of Fund-Raising
  Counsel, 71–72, 73
Annual fund, defined, 239
Annual giving
  capital campaign
    folding annual into capital
      campaign, 105
    maintaining both, 105
    relationship, 105
  development office, 17
  redesigning, 223
Annual report, 221
Appointment, 146–147
Appraisal, 104
Archives, 221–222
Asking for specific amount, 70
Association of Fundraising
  Professionals, 73
Association of Professional Researchers
  for Advancement, 123

B

Bequest, 104–105
Board, 12, 20, 83–84. *See also* Working
  board
  board chair, 3
  board member rebels, 229–230
  board member roles, 84
  campaign consultant, 70
  campaign steering committee,
    conflict, 231
  chain of command, 84
  commitment, 10, 83
  educating about campaign, 84
  embarrassment by member, 236

feasibility study report, 55
involving, 83–84
nucleus fund, 129
organizational readiness, 15
potential for conflict, 83
Board giving
  board's financial role, 130–131
  developing goals, 129–131
  proposal letters, 133–135
  self rating, 132–133
  small-group rating session, 131–132
  soliciting board gifts, 133–135
  soliciting committee members, 135
  statements of intent, 133, 134
  working board, 129–130
Board-restricted endowment, defined,
  239
Bricks and mortar campaign, 5
Broad base solicitation, 169–180
Budget
  campaign consultant fees, 77–79
  capital campaign, 106–107
  special events, 158
Business planning, organizational
  readiness, 16–17

C

Call report form, 146, 149
Campaign consultant
  benefits, 68–71
  board, issue of board giving, 70
  campaign planning, 81
  campaign planning committee, 91
  campaign responsibilities, 62
  case for support, 81
  characterized, 68–71
  churches and, 71
  development director, 72
  emotional support, 71
  evaluation form, 74
  experience, 68–69
  feasibility study, 49–51, 79, 80
    committee, 53

consultant reporting schedule, 50
drafting case for support, 50
expectations, 49–51
information gathering, 50
questions, 50–51
report contents, 51
report distribution, 51
study cost, 51
timetable, 51
who will work with consultant, 50
feedback, 77
fees, 77–79
fund raiser, differentiated, 71
hiring, 77
  contract or letter of agreement, 77
impossible expectations, 71
learning from mistakes, 81
motivation, 70
occasional guidance, 81
organizational culture, 71
organizational fit, 72
organizational workload, 71
outsider's viewpoint, 69
professional standards, 71–72
putting problems in perspective, 69
recruitment, 71–73
references, 77
resident consultant, 79–80
scope of services, 79
selection, 72, 73–77
  committee, 74–75
  interviewing, 75–76
  preparing material for, 74
  rating form, 75
  reviewing printed material from,
    75–76
service provider, 26–27
as skilled writer and editor, 70
small campaigns, 80
software, 23
soliciting consultants' proposals, 76
state registration, 71, 72, 77
taboo subjects, 70
taking tough stands, 70

using strategically, 80–81
Capital campaign
  annual giving
    folding annual campaign into
      capital campaign, 105
    maintaining both, 105
    relationship, 105
  board, full and early commitment, 10
  broad benefits, 1–2
  budget, 106–107
  case for support, 10
  celebration, 9, 30, 100, 217
    celebrating end, 217
    celebrating success, 225
  changes brought about by, 222–223
  characteristics, 1, 6–7
  clear organization, 11
  clear policies, 11
  collecting pledges, 216–217
  compelling need, 9–10
    community vs. organizational, 9
  cost-effectiveness, 1
  creating positive atmosphere, 85
  credible plan, 10
  defined, 239
  defining key campaign positions,
    58–60
  doing the right thing, 225
  elements critical to success, 9–11
  evaluation, 218–220
  final campaign period, 215–216
  finishing, 215–217
  follow-up, 9
  general solicitation, 9
  gifts and pledges keep coming, 216
  going public, 154
  gratitude, 225
  institutionalizing power of, 222–224
  involving other people, 224–225
  lead-gift solicitation, 7, 8
  lessons, 224–225
  long-range planning, 6
  looking ahead, 224, 225
  major gift, 2
    early solicitation, 11
    importance, 11
    prospect identification, 11
  most funds raised before campaign
    announcement, 7
  number of qualified prospects, 10
  organization
    goals and values, 6
    moves to higher level, 6
    visibility and stature, 2
  other types of fund raising compared,
    1
  personal solicitation, 11
  phases, 7–9, 99–100, 154, 155
    campaign planning process,
      99–100

  celebration, 100
  duration, 9
  kickoff, 100
  pre-campaign preparation, 7, 8
  preparing for, 31–85
  previous fund-raising success, 10
  as rare occurrences, 6
  recognizing your own power, 225
  resources, 10
  self-education, 80
  sharing ownership, 225
  staff, 10
  strategic planning, 6
  structure, 96–99
    non-solicitation committees, 97–98
    principles, 96–97
  success factors, 13–30
  survival tips, 30
  timetable, 11
  top-down, inside-out order of
    solicitation, 11
  transformative power of, 1–2
  troubleshooting, 226–238
  types of campaigns, 4–6
  volunteer, 2, 25–26
    effective volunteer leadership,
      10–11
    opportunities for involvement, 2
  written proposal, 11
    lead-gift proposal, 11
Capital campaign announcement,
  183–186
Capital campaign brochure, 194–196
Capital campaign cabinet, defined,
  239
Capital campaign chair, 63–68
  campaign credibility, 63
  campaign planning committee, 68
  characteristics, 63–65
  communication, 66
  defined, 239
  job description, 67, 68
  lead gift, 64, 66, 138
  meeting, 67
  motivating other volunteers, 65
  public visibility, 66
  recruitment, 230
    discussion questions, 67–68
  responsibilities, 66–67
  small gift from, 232–233
  soliciting gifts, 66–67, 228–229
  team approach to campaign
    leadership, 65
  time and energy, 64, 66
  when to enlist, 68
Capital campaign communications
  plan, 181–183
Capital campaign consultant. See
  Campaign consultant
Capital campaign director, 10

Capital campaign event, evaluation,
  220
Capital campaign goals, 6, 7, 40, 156
  challenges, 226–228
  development, 31–32
    non-monetary goals, 93
  exceeding, 228
  failing to meet, 227–228
  realistic, 10
  refining, 92–93
Capital campaign kickoff, 154–156
  benefits, 154–156
  defined, 239
Capital campaign letterhead, 190–192
  listing names, 190–191
Capital campaign materials, 190–198
  editing prospect, 237
  evaluation, 219–220
  preparing, 156
Capital campaign newsletter, 197–198
Capital campaign plan, defined, 239
Capital campaign planning, 7, 8, 86–
  107
  campaign consultant, 81
  development director, 24
  first stage, 31–32
  importance, 86
  process, 86–92
Capital campaign planning committee,
  82, 86–91
  campaign chair, 68
  campaign consultant, 91
  defined, 239
  meetings, 89–91
  membership, 87–88
  planning document, 89
  recruitment, 88–89
    invited co-conspirators, 88
    worksheet, 89
  responsibilities, 89
  size, 87
  structure, 82
  tasks, 87
  written materials, 91
Capital campaign planning study,
  defined, 239
Capital campaign readiness,
  development office, 19–20
  test for, 19
Capital campaign report, 221
Capital campaign steering committee,
  82–83, 98–99
  board, conflict, 231
Capital campaign team, 58
  expanding, 81–83
Capital campaign theme, 188–190
Capital campaign video, 196–197
Case discussion, index-card technique,
  92
Case for support, 32–39

answers basic questions about organization, 35
both rational and emotional, 35
brief, 35
broad implications for community, 35
building ownership by gathering opinions, 38–39
campaign consultant, 81
checklist, 39
content, 33
Declaration of Independence as, 33–34
defined, 32
development, 32
direct mail, refocusing, 178–179
draft, 33–36
easy to remember, 35–36
feasibility study committee, 52
framework for comments, 38, 39
gathering and processing information, 36
guidelines for effective layout, 38
interview, 37
as investment prospectus, 35
involving insiders, 36–37
moving people to action, 36
optimistic, 35
points, 35
process, 33
refining, 91–92
segments, 34–35
statements supportable and defensible, 35
uses, 32
using committee to develop, 37
volunteer, 36
who should write, 36–37
writing process, 37–38
Case statement, defined, 240
Certified Fund-Raising Executive, 71–72
Challenge grant, 151–153
advantages, 151–152
defined, 240
Kresge Foundation, 152–153
types, 152
Charitable lead trust, 104
Charitable remainder trust, 104
Check, gift processing, 20–21
Chronicle of Philanthropy, 72
Church, fund raiser/campaign consultant, 71
Co-conspirators' meeting, 88
Combined campaign, 5
defined, 240
Communications, 60, 62, 181–183, 181–198, 228–233
campaign chair, 66
developing communications plan, 181–183

elements, 182–183
who develops, 182
development office, 18–19
e-communications, 185–186
informing staff about campaign, 26–27
insider communications, 184–185
planning chart, 183
power of materials in positioning campaign, 186
Communications firm
clarifying responsibilities and schedules, 187–188
selecting, 187–188
Communications professional, 186–188
Community leadership
feasibility study, 117
prospect screening, 117–118
Comprehensive campaign, 5–6
defined, 240
Computer, 22
Confidentiality, feasibility study, 56
Constituency, 19
Coordination, 60, 62
Core committee, 82
Corporate Foundation Profiles, 126
Corporate profile, 121
Corporate relations, development office, 17
Corporation
giving guidelines, 125
lead gift
proposal, 150
soliciting, 150–151
Courthouse records, 125
Cultivation committee, 98
Culture of philanthropy, 2–4
creation of, 3
donor, 2
testing for, 3–4

D

Deadline, 29
Deferred gift, 104
Delegation, 29
Designer, 186–187
Desktop publishing, 187
Development assistant
campaign activity levels, 61, 63
campaign responsibilities, 62
defining staff roles, 60
Development cycle, 4
Development director, 59–60
campaign activity levels, 61, 63
campaign consultant, 72
campaign planning, 24
defining staff roles, 60
managing from middle, 59–60
responsibilities, 62

staff campaign, 136
Development office
administration, 17
annual giving, 17
campaign readiness, 19–20
communications, 18–19
corporate relations, 17
culture, 18
development program, 17
donor relations, 18
endowment program, 18
evaluating development systems, 20–23
foundation relations, 17
gift accounting and acknowledgment, 18
information systems, 18
major-gift program, 17
planned-giving program, 18
preparing, 20–30
prospect research, 18
public relations, 18–19
readiness, 17–20
software, 22–24
staff, 24–27
leadership, 17
structure, 17
volunteer, 18
Development software. *See* Software
Development team, 24–25
creative, flexible, and visionary, 24–25
details, 24
Direct mail, 176–180
advantages, 177–178
brochure, 196
case for support refocusing, 178–179
celebrating success with last-chance appeal, 180
conclusion, 180
mailing list segmentation, 179–180
reaching closure, 178
special characteristics for capital campaign, 179
Division chair, job description, 166, 168
Donor
being asked to give, 14–15
culture of philanthropy, 2
death of major donor, 230
default, 216–217, 233–234
development office, 18
donor information, 22
donor readiness, 13–15
evaluation, 15
kinship with others in organization, 14
long-term relationship, 2–3
mission, 14
motivation, 13

organizational effectiveness, 14
organizational involvement, 14
patients as prospective donors, 27
prospect numbers, 10
rating of organization's donor lists, 43
treatment, 2
Donor-centered philanthropy, 3–4
Donor-focused development, 127–128
Donor recognition, 93–96, 207–210
  ceremonies, 209–210
  commitment, 209
  desire for anonymity, 209
  donor listing practice, 94
  giving categories, 93–94
  motives, 207–208
  naming opportunities, 94–96
  planning guidelines, 93
  plaque, 3, 94
Donor-restricted endowment, defined, 240
Donor wall, defined, 240
Dun & Bradstreet Corporate Reporting Services, 125–126

E

E-communications, 185–186
Electronic screening, 117
Endowment, defined, 240
Endowment campaign, 5, 224
  development office, 18
Envelope, 192–194
Errors totaling pledges, 236–237
Evaluation report, 220–221
Executive director, 3, 24, 25, 58–59
  campaign activity levels, 61, 63
  campaign responsibilities, 62
  defining staff roles, 60
  internal issues, 26–27
  leading from behind, 59
  leading from front, 59
  organizational readiness, 15
  performance inadequacies, 229
  personal giving, 136
Expert appraiser, 104

F

Feasibility study, 43–57, 91
  benefits, 46
  campaign consultant, 49–51, 79, 80
    consultant reporting schedule, 50
    drafting preliminary case for support, 50
    expectations, 49–51
    information gathering, 50
    questions, 50–51
    report contents, 51

    report distribution, 51
    study cost, 51
    timetable, 51
    who will work with consultant, 50
  characterized, 43–44
  checklist, 56
  common objections, 45–46
  community leadership, 117
  confidentiality, 56
  defined, 240
  focus, 47–48
  fund raising vs. general, 43–44
  gathering information, 48–49
  gift range chart, 48
  interview, 54
    thanking participants, 54
  need for, 45–46
  preliminary case for support, 48
  process, 48–49
  recommendations, 56
  relationship building, 45
  timing, 46–47
  who conducts, 48
Feasibility study committee, 52–54
  campaign consultant, 53
  case for support, 52
  developing list of people to be interviewed, 52
  drafting letters for interview prospects, 53
  members, 52
  reviewing questions, 53
  reviewing report draft, 53–54
Feasibility study report, 55–57
  board, 55
  contents, 51, 55
  distribution, 51
  drafts, 55
  feasibility study committee, 55
  reporting schedule, 50
Feedback, campaign consultant, 77
Filing system, 28
Financial audit, 106
Follow-up, 9
  evaluation, 220
Foundation
  development office, 17
  giving guidelines, 127
  lead gift
    proposal, 150
    soliciting, 149–151
  researching, 126–127
Foundation Center, 126
Foundation profile, 120
Fund raiser, campaign consultant, differentiated, 71
Fund raising
  fear of, 168–169
  market downturn, 237–238

power of personal relationships, 11
previous success, 10
scandals, 235
terminology, 3, 4
types of campaigns, 4–6

G

General gift, 96, 97
  defined, 240
  gift range chart, 169, 171
  solicitation, 9
Gift acknowledgment, 21
  development office, 18
Gift annuity, 104
Gift-counting period, 102
Gift in kind, 104
Gift of life insurance, 104
Gift processing, 20–21, 21–22, 105–106
  accounting
    how to value gifts, 103–105
    what to count, 103
    when to start counting, 103
  check, 20–21
  development office, 18
  donor information, 22
  pledge, 21
  securities, 21
Gift range chart, 93
  campaign road map, 40–42
  defined, 240
  developing, 40–42
  feasibility study, 48
  general gift, 169, 171
  just 10 Rule, 40
  major gift, 160
  naming opportunities, 95
    low-level gifts, 95–96
  90/10 Rule, 40
  pattern of giving, 40, 41
  prospect planning, 42–43
  prospects required, 43, 44
Gift reporting, 105–106
Gift support history, 19
Gift, tied to contract, 234
Giving levels, naming opportunities, 94–96
Graphic designer, 186–187
Grassroots Fundraising Series, 114
Gratitude, 199–214, 213–214, 225. *See also* Thank you

H

Historical record, organizational fundraising, 221–222
Honorary chairperson, defined, 240
Humor, 30

I

Immediacy, 29
Index-card technique, case discussion, 92
Information systems, development office, 18
In-kind gift, 104
Inside-out soliciting, 97
Interview
  case for support, 37
  confidentiality, 56
  feasibility study, 54
    thanking participants, 54

J

Job description
  campaign chair, 67, 68
  division chair, 166, 168
  special events committee chairperson, 68
Just 10 Rule, 40

K

Kresge Foundation, challenge grant, 152–153

L

Lead gift, 40, 96–97
  campaign chair, 64, 66, 138
    soliciting, 138
  corporation
    proposal, 150
    soliciting, 150–151
  cover letter, 143
  defined, 240
  donor default, 233–234
  foundation
    proposal, 150
    soliciting, 149–151
  power, 153
  progress report, 144, 145
  proposal, 11, 141–142
  setting up appointment, 146–147
  solicitation, 7, 8, 137–149
    ask for gift, 148
    ask questions and listen, 148
    follow up, 149
    make case, 148
    personal commitment, 147
    practice, 147
    preparation, 147
    process, 146–149
    right order, 139, 140
    solicitation meeting, 147–148
    team approach, 149
  solicitation material, 139–144
  solicitor training, 144–145
Leadership, 63

needs, 64
Letter of intent, defined, 240
Logo, 188–190
Long-range planning, capital campaign, 6

M

Mail merging, 24
Mailing label, 192–194
Major gift, 2, 20, 96, 97
  defined, 240
  development office, 17
  early solicitation, 11
  gift range chart, 160
  importance, 11
  proposal letter, 163–165
  prospect identification, 11
  retracted, 232
  solicitation, 160–169
    acknowledging donors, 166
    adapting to specific constituencies, 169
    completing unfinished solicitation, 166
    division leaders, 166
    job descriptions, 166
    maintaining contact during solicitation period, 165–166
    matching prospects, 162–163
    meetings, 166, 167
    process, 160–166
    reporting success, 166
    solicitation division, 97, 98
    soliciting solicitors, 161
    tasks, 166, 167, 168
    team captains, 166
    thanking solicitors, 166
    training, 165, 166–167
  volunteer, enlisting, 161
Media, campaign message, 157
Meeting
  campaign chair, 67
  prospect screening, 115–117
  scheduling, 29
Memento, 206–207
Mission
  donor, 14
  receptionist, 3
Motivation, 13–14
  campaign chair motivating other volunteers, 65
  campaign consultant, 70
  categories, 14
  donor, 13

N

Naming opportunities, 94–96

defined, 240
  gift range chart, 95
  giving levels, 94–96
  two gifts to name one, 234
National Center for Non-Profit Boards, 73
Newsletter, 197–198
90/10 Rule, 40
Note card, 192–194
Notebook, 28
Nucleus fund, 129–137
  board, 129
  defined, 129, 240

O

Organizational culture, 210–211
Organizational cycle, 4
  strategic planning, 4
Organizational readiness, 15–17
  board, 15
  business planning, 16–17
  community, 15–16
  evaluation, 15
  executive director, 15
  project planning, 16
  strategic planning, 16

P

Pace-setting gift, defined, 241
Paper management, 27–29
People skills, 25
Personal property, 104
Personal relationship, 14
Personal solicitation, 102
  capital campaign, 11
  volunteer, 11
Phonathon. *See also* Telephone solicitation
  determining whom to call, 172
  duration, 173–174
  following through, 175–176
  location, 174
  motivating volunteers, 175
  organizing volunteer, 172–176
  pledge form, 175
  preparing supporting materials, 174–175
  pre-phonathon mail appeal, 174
  prospect information form, 175
  recruiting volunteers, 172–173
  report form, 176
  reporting results, 176
  scripts, 175
  setting dates and times, 174
  solicitor training, 175
  volunteers vs. paid solicitors, 172
Planned giving, 224

defined, 241
development office, 18
Plaque, 3, 94
    approval from donors, 213
    design, 211–212
    location, 211–212
    organizational culture, 210–211
    selling tool vs. recognition device,
        210
    timing, 213
    wording, 212–213
Pledge
    collection, 216–217
    errors totaling, 236–237
    gift processing, 21
    pledge form, 192–194
        defined, 241
    pledge period, 102
Pooled income fund, 104
Preliminary dollar goal, development,
    31–32
Pre-phonathon mail appeal, 174
Printer, 22
Prioritizing, 29
Progress thermometer, 198
Proposal letter
    major gift, 163–165
    method, 133–135
Prospect
    categories, 43
    gift range chart, 42–43
        estimating number of prospects
            required for each gift, 42–43
    identifying qualified prospects, 160
    individual prospect information
        sheet, 119
    patients as prospective donors, 27
    prospect development plan, 19
    prospect-to-gift ratio, 42–43
Prospect information system, 118–123
    corporations, 121
    foundations, 120
    information relevance, 122
    simple data-capture systems, 122
    strategic data capture, 122–123
Prospect research, 109–127
    annual reports of organizations with
        similar mission, 114
    close to home, 111
    commitment continuum, 112–113
    defined, 109
    development office, 18
    discretion, 124
    donor-focused development, 127–128
    financial capacity, 124–125
    giving patterns, 110
    judgment, 127
    online research tools, 123
    philanthropic interests, 124–125
    plaque walk, 114

previous donors, 112
process management, 128
relationship with organization, 111
repeated gifts, 113
researching corporations, 125–126
researching foundations, 126–127
    990-PF forms, 126
researching individuals, 124–125
search for commitment, 110–111
search for insiders, 111–112
search for money, 109–110
search for power, 110
secondary sources, 123–127
trust and security, 127
types of donors, 113
where not to look, 111
Prospect screening, 114
    ability to give, 115, 116
    community leadership, 117–118
    electronic screening, 117
    inclination to give, 115, 116
    levels, 114
    meeting, 115–117
    one-on-one conversations, 114
    ratings, 117
    small groups of high-level donors,
        114–115
prspct-1, 123
Public goal, defined, 241
Public phase, defined, 241
Public recognition
    ceremonies, 209–210
    commitment, 209
    desire for anonymity, 209
    donor, 207–210
    motives, 207–208
    volunteer, 207–210
Public relations, 235–236
    development office, 18–19
    evaluation, 219–220
Public relations committee, 97–98

Q

Quasi-endowment, defined, 241
Quiet phase, 97, 98
    defined, 241

R

Real estate information, 125
Real property, 104
Receptionist, 3
Recognition ceremony, 209–210
Recordkeeping system, 19
Resident consultant, 79–80

S

Securities, 103–104

gift processing, 21
Sense of duty, 14
Service provider
    vs. administrators, 26–27
    campaign consultant, 26–27
Software, 22–24
    campaign consultant, 23
    computer-development consultant, 23
    selection, 23–24
Solicitation, 149
    advance gift, 8–9
    board gifts, 133–135
    general gift, 9
    general solicitation, 9
    lead gift, 7, 8, 147–148
    location, 149
    major gift, 11
    period, 102
    process, 102–103
    volunteer recruiting, 230–231
Solicitor
    call report form, 146
    major gift
        acknowledging donors, 166
        adapting to specific constituencies,
            169
        completing unfinished solicitation,
            166
        division leaders, 166
        job descriptions, 166
        maintaining contact during
            solicitation period, 165–166
        matching prospects, 162–163
        meetings, 166, 167
        recruiting, 161
        reporting success, 166
        tasks, 166, 167, 168
        team captains, 166
        thanking solicitors, 166
    training, 165, 166–167
        evaluation, 220
        workshop, 169, 170
Special events
    budget, 158
    disadvantages, 156
    event-planning considerations,
        158–160
    staff campaign, 137
Special events committee, 97, 98,
    157–158
    chairperson job description, 68
    guidelines, 158
Special gift, 206–207
Special project campaign, 5
Specific amount request, 70
Staff, 10, 59–60
    anticipating campaign workloads, 61,
        63
    development office, 24–27
        leadership, 17

structure, 17
shifting roles, 60
support, 60, 62
tasks handled by, 60–61, 62
Staff campaign, 136–137
    development director, 136
    dual goal, 136
    importance, 136
    sensitivity, 136
    solicitation, 136–137
    special events, 137
State registration, campaign consultant,
    77
Status, 66
Steering committee, defined, 241
Stewardship, 221
Stewardship gift, defined, 241
Strategic gift, 151–153
Strategic planning, 3
    capital campaign, 6
    organizational cycle, 4
    organizational readiness, 16

T

Table of gifts. *See* Gift range chart
Team captain, responsibilities, 171
Team spirit, 30
Telephone solicitation, 170–176, 177.
    See also Phonathon
    volunteers vs. paid solicitors, 172
Thank you
    acknowledging non-donors, 207,
        208

donor-oriented thank-you letter, 201,
    202
letter/note, 149, 201, 202–205
    to stranger, 204, 205
need for honesty and authenticity,
    200
number, 206
organizational-oriented thank-you
    letter, 201, 202
personal gesture, 201
thanking donors personally, 200–201
    donors one doesn't know,
        201–206
Timetable, 99–102
    alternatives, 101–102
    considerations, 102
    gift-counting period, 102
    month-by-month schedule, 100–101
    pledge period, 102
    presenting, 100
    solicitation period, 102
    timeline, 100–101
Token of appreciation, 206–207
Tombstone graphics, 187
Top-down soliciting, 96–97
Training
    lead-gift solicitor, 144–145
    phonathon, 175
    solicitor, 165, 166–167
        evaluation, 220

V

Valuation, 103–105

Verbal pledge, 216
Visibility, 66
Volunteer
    capital campaign, 2, 25–26
        effective volunteer leadership,
            10–11
        opportunities for involvement, 2
    case for support, 36
    clear organization, 11
    as development director, 25–26
    development office, 18
    enlisting, 83, 156
    information on, 22
    major gift, 161
    management, 52
    personal solicitation, 11
    phonathon, 172–176, 177
    public recognition, 207–210
        commitment, 209
        desire for anonymity, 209
        motives, 207–208
    solicitation recruiting, 230–231

W

Wasting endowment, defined, 241
Web site, 198
Working board, 10, 83
    board giving, 129–130
Working goal, defined, 241
Written proposal, capital campaign, 11
    lead-gift proposal, 11
Written statement of case, needs, and
    goals, 19

About the Author

Andrea Kihlstedt has earned her reputation as a capital campaign consultant by guiding one campaign after another to a successful conclusion. She is known for her creative and participatory approach to planning and fund raising. She counsels social service, educational, and cultural institutions, both assisting with campaigns and providing short-term consultancies, training, and assessments.

Ms. Kihlstedt helped develop a three-day capital campaign course for The Fundraising School in Indianapolis. She teaches that course periodically in Indianapolis and elsewhere. In 1998, she co-edited *Capital Campaigns:* *Realizing Their Power and Potential,* published by Jossey-Bass.

Ms. Kihlstedt holds a bachelor's degree from the University of Pennsylvania and a master's in Philosophy from Brown University. She is a Johns Hopkins Fellow in Change Management and a graduate of the Small Group Facilitators Intensive Program.

An active volunteer in the arts, Ms. Kihlstedt works with organizations that support the work of developing artists and that realize and encourage the power of the creative arts in bridging cultural gaps. Ms. Kihlstedt splits her time between Lancaster, Pennsylvania, and New York City.